Follower-Centered Perspectives on Leadership

A Tribute to the Memory of James R. Meindl

A volume in
Leadership Horizons, The Series
Series Editor: Mary Uhl-Bien

Leadership Horizon, The Series

Mary Uhl-Bien, *Series Editor*
James R. Meindl, *Founding Editor*

Grounding Leadership Theory and Research: Issues and Perspectives (2002)
edited by Ken Parry and James R. Meindl

Teaching Leadership: Innovative Approaches for the 21st Century (2003)
edited by Raj Pillai and Susan Stites-Doe

Implicit Leadership Theories: Essays and Explorations (2005)
edited by Birgit Schyns and James R. Meindl

Follower-Centered Perspectives on Leadership

A Tribute to the Memory of James R. Meindl

Edited by

Boas Shamir
The Hebrew University of Jerusalem

Rajnandini Pillai
California State University San Marcos

Michelle C. Bligh
Claremont Graduate University

Mary Uhl-Bien
University of Central Florida

INFORMATION AGE
PUBLISHING

Greenwich, Connecticut 06830 • www.infoagepub.com

Library of Congress Cataloging-in-Publication Data

Follower-centered perspectives on leadership : a tribute to the memory of
James R. Meindl / edited by Boas Shamir ... [et al.].
     p. cm. – (Leadership horizons)
  Includes bibliographical references.
  ISBN-13: 978-1-59311-547-0 (pbk.)
  ISBN-13: 978-1-59311-548-7 (hardcover)
  1. Leadership. 2. Social groups. 3. Group identity. 4. Social
psychology. 5. Meindl, James R. I. Meindl, James R. II. Shamir, Boas.
  HM1261.F65 2007
  303.3'4–dc22

                                                                    2006032369

CONTENTS

SERIES EDITOR'S NOTE

With the passing of Jim Meindl in 2004, we lost a scholar of international standing who was respected and admired for his work on the romance of leadership and follower-centered perspectives. In this volume of the *Leadership Horizons* series, it is only fitting that we pause to think of the many tremendous influences that Jim's work and thought leadership had on the fields of management and organizational behavior.

Jim started the *Leadership Horizons* series in 2001 to explore new developments and fresh perspectives in theory and research on leadership. He was seeking to promote work that "aggressively pushes beyond current leadership orthodoxy" and that "critically examines conventional thinking and practices" (from the Series' description). In the current volume, we explore how Jim's own work accomplished just this, by challenging traditional thinking and opening up new avenues for thinking about leadership and followership. As demonstrated in this volume, his ideas have inspired many to consider leadership and followership in new ways, leaving a lasting legacy on the field and on the individuals who were inspired by his work. To honor Jim's impact on the leadership field, Information Age has decided to dedicate an award to honor the contribution to the *Leadership Horizons* series that best reflects the spirit and intellectual ingenuity that Jim brought to his work. Beginning with this volume, a panel of scholars will evaluate the chapters to identify the article that best meets the mission of the series as identified by Jim—that offers new developments and fresh perspectives, aggressively pushes beyond current leadership orthodoxy and critically examines conventional thinking and practices, and advances an applied scholarship model, wherein sound academic work is connected, either directly or more speculatively, to real-world problems and controversies. The winners will be announced in future volumes, and awards will be distributed at Academy of Management national meetings.

Follower-Centered Perspectives on Leadership, pages vii–viii
Copyright © 2007 by Information Age Publishing

On a more personal note, Jim was highly beloved by many students and colleagues around the world. His students had a tremendous respect for him as a scholar, professor, coauthor, mentor, and also as a friend. As remarked by Pillai, Kohles, and Bligh (Chapter 7, this volume), Jim had a quick wit, great sense of humor, and a real "zest for life." However, he was also a tremendously humble person who never bragged about himself, belittled others, or even mentioned his accomplishments. In this way, he served not only as an intellectual leader, but also a role model and an inspiration for those around him.

This volume is a tribute to Jim and his legacy.

—Mary Uhl-Bien
University of Central Florida

INTRODUCTION

FROM PASSIVE RECIPIENTS TO ACTIVE CO-PRODUCERS

Followers' Roles in the Leadership Process

Boas Shamir
The Hebrew University of Jerusalem

ABSTRACT

In this introductory chapter I try to set the framework for the book. The chapter has three parts. In the first part, I review the roles that followers have occupied in leadership theories. Five such roles are identified: (1) followers as recipients of the leader's influence; (2) followers as moderators of the leader's influence; (3) followers as subsitutes for leadership; (4) followers as constructors of leadership; and (5) Followers as leaders (self-leadership and shared leadership). The contribution of James R. Meindl to the development of follower-centered prespectives on leadership is highlighted. In the second part, I argue that an understanding of leadership requires viewing both leaders and followers as co-producers of leadership relationships. I further argue we should "reverse the lenses" and, in addition to focusing on leaders and their impact on followers, we should focus on followers' impact on leaders and the leadership process. I provide some examples of the implications of such reversal of the lenses for theory and research. In the third part, I introduce the other chapters included in the book.

Follower-Centered Perspectives on Leadership, pages ix–xxxix
Copyright © 2007 by Information Age Publishing

We must know much more about the hitherto nameless persons who comprise the followers of leaders if we are to develop adequate understanding of the reciprocal relationship. (Burns, 1978, p. 61)

The majority of leadership theories and studies have tended to emphasize the personal background, personality traits, perceptions, and actions of leaders. From this perspective, the followers have been viewed as recipients or moderators of the leader's influence, and as vehicles for the actualization of the leader's vision, mission or goals. As Yukl and Van Fleet concluded, after reviewing the literature, "Most of the prevailing leadership theories have been simple, unidirectional models of what a leader does to subordinates" (1992, p. 186). In a similar vein, Northhouse characterized this dominant perspective as treating leadership as "a one-way event—the leader affects the subordinates" (2004, p. 113), and Goffee and Jones criticize it for portraying followers as "an empty vessel waiting to be led, or even transformed, by the leader" (2001, p. 148). In view of this state of affairs, Lord, Brown, and Freiberg asserted, "The follower remains an underexplored source of variance in understanding leadership processes" (1999, p. 167), and Graen and Uhl-Bien suggested that "Clearly, more research is needed on followers and the leadership relationship" (1995, p. 222).

James R. Meindl (1995) referred to the dominant perspective of leadership studies as *leader-centered*. From this perspective, leader characteristics and actions determine the emergence of leadership and its consequences. Therefore, theory development and research on leadership from this perspective focus mainly on the impact of leader characteristics and behaviors on the followers, the group, and the organization. Organizations, many of which also adopt the leader-centered perspective, focus mainly on selecting leaders with required characteristics and developing their leadership skills and capabilities. Leadership development is viewed as synonymous with leader development. Furthermore, both the positive and negative consequences of leadership are attributed mainly to the leader's personality or behavior.

This dominant leader-centered perspective has come under criticism in recent years because it exaggerates the impact of leaders on followers and organizations. As Meindl, Ehrlich, and Dukerich wrote over 20 years ago, "It appears that as observers of and as participants in organizations, we may have developed highly romanticized, heroic views of leadership—what leaders do, what they are able to accomplish, and the general effects they have on our lives" (1985, p. 79). According to such views, the leader is single-handedly capable of determining the fate and fortunes of groups and organizations. Critics (e.g., Bennis, 1999; Gronn, 2004) have argued that these views are unrealistic because every significant achievement is a result of collective effort, to which many people contribute. They further argued that the leader-centered perspective has potentially negative implications.

For instance, exaggerated perceptions of the role of leaders and their impact may contribute to an overdependence of followers on leaders. They may also serve to legitimize unjustified and inflated status and power and earning differentials among members of groups and organizations.

While criticisms of overly leader-centered views of leadership are quite wide-spread now (see, in addition to above-cited authors, Beyer, 1999; Collinson, 2005; Lord & Brown, 2004; Pearce & Conger, 2003; Yukl, 1998), James R. Meindl, together with his students and colleagues, went beyond criticism to explain theoretically and demonstrate empirically why the leader-centered view is so dominant and to offer a follower-centered perspective on leadership as an alternative to the dominant approach. Meindl (1990, 1995; Meindl et al., 1985) argued that it is the followers rather than the leaders who construct both the phenomenon of leadership and the images of specific leaders and hence both the emergence of leadership and its consequences are largely influenced by followers' cognitive processes and interfollower social influence processes. His contributions are described in more detail later in this chapter and in other chapters of this book.

This book is a tribute to Meindl, his work, and his legacy. Following Meindl, we believe the leader-centered perspective on leadership relies too heavily on the role of leader characteristics and behaviors in producing leadership and its consequences. In this book, we attempt to correct and complement the leader-centered perspective by showing that the roles of followers in leadership processes are broader and more consequential than the roles that have been given to them in traditional, leader-centered theories. To this end, we invited a group of authors to contribute theoretical and empirical chapters on various leadership issues as they are viewed from a follower-centered perspective. Some of the chapters were written by Meindl's former colleagues and students and extend his theories. Others were written from different theoretical perspectives. Together, they demonstrate the importance and value of focusing on followers in our attempts to understand the leadership process.

In this introduction, I try to set the stage for the following chapters. First, I briefly review the roles that followers have occupied in various leadership theories. In many theories, even those that have been called the "new leadership theories" (Bryman, 1992), followers occupy the traditional role of recipients of influence. At best, their characteristics are viewed as moderators of the impact of leaders' traits and behaviors on other variables. There are, however, theoretical perspectives in which followers occupy more central and active roles as potential substitutes for leadership, constructors of leadership, or co-leaders. These theories are also reviewed. Following this review, I argue for a balanced perspective on leadership, one that is neither entirely leader-centered nor entirely follower-centered, but views both leaders and followers as co-producers of the leadership relationship and its consequences. I submit that at this point in time, since the dominant view is still leader-centered, we need to balance our knowledge and understanding of leadership by "reversing our lenses" and paying more attention to the active roles of followers in the leadership process. I provide some examples and tentative research questions to illustrate the implications of such an approach. Finally, I briefly introduce the chapters included in this book.

ROLES OF FOLLOWERS IN LEADERSHIP THEORIES

The Traditional View: Followers as Recipients of Leader Influence

As argued above, the traditional theoretical perspective views the leader as the causal agent. Thus traditional leadership theories posit the leader's traits and behaviors as the independent variables and followers' perceptions, attitudes, and behaviors as the dependent variables. This traditional view characterizes not only early theories (e.g., Fleishman, Harris, & Burtt, 1955; Lewin & Lippit, 1938; Stogdill & Coons, 1957) but also more recent theories, including theories of transformational and charismatic leadership (e.g., Bass, 1985; Conger & Kanungo, 1998; Shamir, House, & Arthur, 1993). These theories are behavioral theories. Their arguments have the following structure: A leader behavior (e.g., articulating a vision, setting a personal example, intellectual stimulation) affects followers' attitudes and behaviors (e.g., commitment to the organization, exerting extra effort at work). According to this view, which is illustrated in Figure I.1, followers do not play an active role in the leadership process.

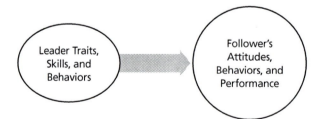

Figure I.1.   The traditional view: Followers as recipients of influence.

Followers as Moderators of Leader Impact

Many other influential theories still posit followers as passive recipients of influence but acknowledge that the leader's influence may be moderated by the characteristics of the followers. According to these theories, known as contingency theories, the leader's influence on followers' attitudes and performance depends on followers' characteristics. Thus, according to Hersey and Blanchard (1977), the effectiveness of the leader's behavioral style (whether he or she is primarily task-oriented, primarily people-oriented, high on both dimensions, or low on both dimensions) depends on followers' level of maturity—their abilities and motivation. According to Fiedler (1967), the effectiveness of task-oriented versus people-oriented leaders depends, among other things, on followers' initial attitude toward the leader and acceptance of the leader. In House's (1971) path–goal theory of leadership, the effectiveness of leader behaviors depends on followers' needs. For instance, in some situations followers may need more structure and guidance in order to achieve their goals, and therefore a structuring leadership style would be effective. In other situations they may primarily need support from the leader and in such situations, a more supportive, people-oriented leadership style is likely to be effective. For Vroom and Yetton (1973), the appropriateness and effectiveness of a participative leadership style depends, among other things, on whether the followers are knowledgeable about the decision issue and whether they share the values of the leader. This view of followers as both recipients of influence and moderators of the impact of leader behaviors is illustrated in Figure I.2. Like the previously discussed traditional view, it "prioritizes leaders, addressing followers only in relation to their susceptibility to certain leader behaviors or styles" (Collinson, 2005, p. 1424).

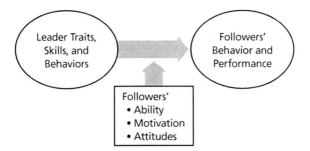

Figure I.2.   Followers as moderators of leader influence.

Followers as Substitutes for Leadership

The substitutes for leadership theory (Kerr & Jermier, 1978), while not a follower-centered theory, assigns the followers a potentially more dominant role than the previously outlined theories. According to this theory, there are conditions that can neutralize or negate the need for leadership. Among these conditions are certain followers' characteristics. The theory emphasizes followers' training, experience, and job-related knowledge. It implies that when followers are highly able, highly motivated, and have internalized norms that support task performance, these follower characteristics may substitute for leadership in the sense of providing all the needed guidance, support, and motivation. When followers are endowed with those characteristics, the behavioral style of the leader may not matter and leader behavior does not have a significant effect on such outcomes as followers' performance and satisfaction. This theory represents a radical deviation from the traditional view by giving the leader a much more modest role in the leadership process and implying that followers can lead themselves. However, it has not focused explicitly on the role of followers and their behaviors. The active role of followers in substituting for leadership is not developed in this theory. Because it does not go much further beyond claiming that certain follower characteristics may neutralize the effects of leader behavior, the substitutes for leadership theory can be viewed as an extreme version of the previously discussed theories that posit followers' characteristics as moderators of the leader's influence.

Leadership as a Follower-Driven Phenomenon: Followers as Constructors of Leadership

A much more central and explicit role is given to followers in theories that present leadership as cognitively or socially constructed by followers. A version of this idea can be found in several theories. According to some *psychoanalytic theories* (Hill, 1984; Kets de Vries, 1988; Lindholm, 1988; see also Shamir, 1991), leadership is largely the product of projection and transference processes of the followers. Projection is the process of attributing to another person our ideals, wishes, desires, and fantasies. Transference is the process of responding to another person as if that person was one's mother, father, or another significant person from early childhood. Psychoanalytic theories suggest that, especially in times of crisis or threat, when they are confused, unsafe, or helpless, followers regress to early childhood patterns of perception and behavior. They become attached to leaders and idealize them and obey them not because of the leaders' characteristics or behaviors, but because the leader symbolizes a father, a mother, or some other omnipotent figure, which is able to reduce anxiety and provide psychological safety to the followers. Thus according to these psychoanalytical theories, it is largely the followers who produce their leadership.

The idea that followers play an active role in the construction of leadership can also be found in Lord's *leadership categorization theory* (Lord, 1985; Lord, Foti, & De Vader, 1984), which is based on general cognitive categorization principles. This theory proposes and demonstrates that people have culturally learned leadership cognitive schema, called leadership prototypes, which they use to identify and assess leaders. The schema includes many characteristics of a prototypical leader. However, people do not have to perceive all the components of the schema to attribute leadership to a person. Once they identify a small number of prototypical characteristics or behaviors in a person, they complete the picture and attribute the entire prototype to that person and designate him or her a "leader." Hence, at least partially, the way followers perceive their leader, and consequently their responses to the leader, are not determined only by the leader's characteristics and behavior but to a large extent also by followers' cognitive schema and social perception processes.

A different cognitive explanation for the construction of leadership by followers was offered by Meindl. According to his "romance of leadership" thesis (Meindl et al., 1985), leadership is a perception that results from organization members' biased preference to understand important but ambiguous and causally indeterminate events in terms of salient individuals that can be plausibly linked to these events. Leadership is a conveniently available explanation category. By attributing power and causality to leaders, organization members achieve a sense of understanding and control over their environment. Meindl and colleagues (1985) have further argued that observers of organizational outcomes have a biased inclination to attribute causality erroneously to leaders ("the fundamental attribution error"). According to this explanation, leaders' behavior or personality has very little to do with the construction of a leadership relationship. Rather, the effect depends primarily on the nature of the circumstances, the need to explain organizational outcomes, and the organizational salience of certain figures. The source of the phenomenon is in the followers, not in the leaders.

A second major thesis advanced by Meindl (1990), *social contagion*, concerns interfollower processes that result in common attributions to the leader. According to this argument, interfollower influence processes are instigated by stress or excitement-arousing situations. Under such circumstances, there is a high level of free-floating, unlabeled arousal, in search of expression channels. With the help of certain members of the group (not the leader), who by exhibiting charismatic effects become social models, desires for the expression of the arousal or stress are channeled and

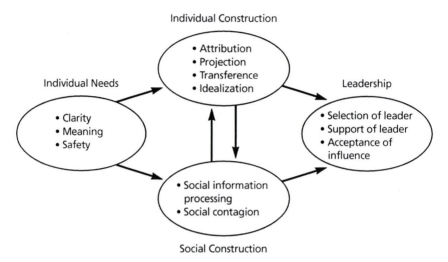

Figure I.3.   Leadership as a follower-driven phenomenon: The social construction of leadership.

defined in terms of leadership and charisma. Thus a "social contagion" process is set in motion. The attribution of leadership and charisma to a certain individual and the affective and behavioral consequences of this attribution originate from the group, and not from the leader. In fact, it does not matter who occupies the leadership position. Therefore, according to this rather radical perspective, leaders are irrelevant and interchangeable, and leader behavior and leader traits should be taken out of the explanation of leadership. (In a later article, Meindl [1995] has offered a less radical version of these arguments where the social construction approach is offered as a complementary approach from which to study and understand leadership processes, not necessarily the only "correct" one.)

In a related study, Pastor, Meindl, and Mayo (2002) predicted and demonstrated that, in line with the social contagion proposition, the social construction of leadership also depends on the structure of social networks. Specifically, the more individuals are proximal to each other within a social network the more likely they are to share leadership perceptions.

The social construction of leadership is also emphasized by the more recent *social identity theory of leadership* (van Knippenberg & Hogg, 2003), which proposes that leader emergence and acceptance depend on the extent to which the leader is prototypical of the group, namely represents and embodies the central group characteristics and its aspirations, values, and norms. This theory posits the group before the leader. When followers are part of a group (which is the typical situation) and identify with the group, they accept as leader a person who embodies the central characteristics of the group. In one version of the theory (Hogg, 2001), the social construction of leadership by the group has three aspects. First, due to the prototypicality of a group member, this member appears to exercise influence over other members. Second, the most prototypical member is consensually liked by group members. Being socially attractive empowers that person, enables him or her to influence other members, and eventually imbues him or her with prestige and status. The final phase of this process is an attribution one, in which members misattribute the leader's behavior and influence to personality rather than to his or her prototypical position in the group, thus constructing a charismatic personality for the leader.

The general outline of construction of leadership perspective is illustrated in Figure I.3.

Followers as Leaders: Shared Leadership

While the construction of leaders and leadership by followers represents a follower-centric approach, it still maintains the distinction between leaders and followers. An even more radical perspective regarding the roles of leaders and followers is offered by theories of shared, distributed, or dispersed leadership (Gronn, 2004; Pearce & Conger, 2003, Ray, Clegg, & Gordon, 2004), which doubt the usefulness of the distinction between leaders and followers. Having their roots in the substitutes for leadership theory, the self-leadership approach (Manz & Sims, 1980), and the literature on self-managing work teams (Manz & Sims, 1987), these theories suggest that leadership is not a role but a function or an activity that can be shared among members of a group or organization. According to these normative theories, there should be no fixed roles of leaders and followers. Everyone should be regarded as both a leader and a follower. Milder versions of this approach suggest that the guidance of the group can rotate among its members, depending on the demands of the moment and the particular skills and resources required at that moment. Any member can lead the group for a certain period, for instance, during a phase of a project, and then step back to allow others to lead when the demands of the task change.

Stronger versions of this approach imply that the team can lead its work collectively by creating norms of behavior, contribution, and performance, and by supporting each other and maintaining the morale of the group. According to these ideas, team processes take care of leadership functions and substitute for individual leadership.

Strictly speaking, the shared leadership approach is neither leader-centered nor follower-centered because it rejects the distinction between leaders and followers. However, because of its critical stance toward traditional leadership concepts and the central and active role it assigns to team members, it is closer in spirit to a follower-centered perspective than to the dominant leader-centered perspective.

TOWARD A BALANCED MODEL

Shared Leadership is an Oxymoron and There Can Be No Substitutes for Leadership

The phenomenon of leadership appears to be a universal phenomenon evident in all human societies and some nonhuman societies as well. Myths of leadership appear to be rather similar in different societies. Furthermore, cross-cultural studies of leadership reveal differences, but also considerable similarities. For instance, while the GLOBE project (House, Hanges, Javidan, & Dorfman, 2004) was designed to reveal cross-cultural differences in implicit theories of leadership, when reading the GLOBE results one is struck by the many similarities and commonalities found across the 62 cultures studied. These commonalities suggest that the phenomenon of leadership is a basic feature of human (and some nonhuman) groups. Leadership tends to emerge even among preschool children who do not have a collective purpose and even when groups try hard to prevent its emergence, like in the traditional Israeli Kibbutz. While collective action can sometimes happen and be effective without a leader, this is rather uncommon, especially for collectives that exist for a considerable period of time.

More importantly, notions of shared leadership and leadership substitutes are based on conceptualizing leadership as a function or an activity. If one views leadership as a function or an activity it can indeed be shared by group members or substituted for by members' skills, experience, knowledge, motivation, and norms and by other organizational arrangements. However, for me, leadership is not a function that can be shared or substituted for but rather a social relationship, which is characterized by disproportionate social influence. By my definition, leadership exists only when an individual (sometimes a pair or a small group) exerts disproportionate noncoercive influence on others, that is, his or her influence on the group or organization is greater than that of the other members. Viewed in this way, leadership can never be fully shared and cannot be substituted for. There is no leadership without leaders and followers because without leaders and followers a leadership relationship does not exist. In other words, leadership can never be fully shared, equally distributed among members of a group, or substituted for because such a distribution or substitution annuls the meaning of the term "leadership." Leaderless collective action, while possible under certain circumstances, should not be called shared leadership, for this is an oxymoron.

My rejection of the terms "shared leadership" and "substitutes for leadership" does not imply a heroic or romanticized view of leadership that exaggerates the role played by a single individual in collective endeavors and achievements. Other members of a group or organization play a crucial role in every such achievement. Followers also play a crucial, sometimes a dominant, role in the construction of a leadership relationship. My point is only that there is no need to dismiss the leaders to make room for followers in trying to understand the phenomenon of leadership.

Followers as Co-Producers of Leadership and Its Consequences

If we view leadership as a social relationship, it follows that as in any other relationship, both sides contribute to its formation, nature, and consequences. Leadership emerges in the interaction between leaders and followers. Indeed, many writers (e.g., Graen & Uhl-Bien, 1995; Grint, 2000; Hollander, 1993; Jermier, 1993; Klein & House, 1995; Yukl & Van Fleet, 1992) agree that leadership is a relationship that is jointly produced by leaders and followers. Graen and Uhl-Bien (1995), for instance, suggested that a comprehensive representation of the leadership process requires that attention be given simultaneously to three domains: the leader, the follower, and the relationship. In support, they cite three unpublished doctoral dissertations that examined leadership from this multiple domain perspective as well as several studies that examined characteristics of followers that contribute to the development of a high leader–member–exchange (LMX) relationship between leaders and followers.

However, outside the LMX perspective, beyond paying lip service to the importance of followers, few attempts have been made to theoretically specify and empirically assess the joint roles of leaders and followers in the leadership process. Indeed, even theoretical frameworks that conceive of leadership as a relationship often do not assign followers an active role in the development of this relationship. An example is Klein and House's (1995) conceptualization of charisma using the fire metaphor. According to Klein and House, charisma is a relationship between a leader who has charismatic qualities (the spark), followers who are open to charisma (flammable material), and a charisma-conducive environment (oxygen). However, by viewing followers as "flammable material" waiting to be ignited by the leader, Klein and House have portrayed them in a limited and passive role. In this respect, their model is not very different from the view of followers' characteristics as moderators of the leader's influence, which was described earlier in this chapter.

Therefore, to explain the phenomenon of leadership in a comprehensive manner, we need a balanced model of leadership that includes both leaders and followers as causal agents. On the one hand, such a model needs to correct the overemphasis on leaders in many current theories of leadership and include the many ways by which followers influence the leadership process. On the other hand, such a model cannot ignore the leader and be totally follower-centered, as thousands of studies (Bass, 1990) have demonstrated the impact of leader characteristics and behaviors on followers' motivation, attitudes, and performance.

The general outline of such a model is presented in Figure I.4 (see Uhl-Bien, Graen, & Scandura, 2000, p. 147, for a very similar model). The figure indicates that leadership is a relationship. The consequences of leadership are attributed in this model to the nature of the relationship. The nature of the relationship in turn is jointly influenced by leaders' characteristics and behaviors and followers' characteristics and behaviors. Thus both leaders and followers are viewed as co-producers of leadership. In addition, the model indicates that each side of the relationship is influenced by the other side: Followers' characteristics and behaviors are influenced by the leader, and the leader's characteristics and behaviors are influenced by the followers. While the influence of the leader on followers' characteristics and behaviors has been extensively studied, the influence of followers on the leader's characteristics and behaviors has been largely neglected.

The skeletal model illustrated in Figure I.4 is just a general outline presenting relationships among broad categories of variables. It does not specify in detail the relationships between the variables implied in the model and does not constitute a theory. Its purpose is to present a general framework for understanding and studying leadership. As suggested by Graen

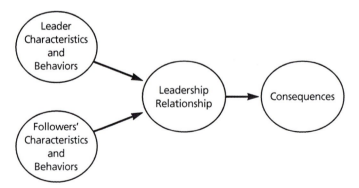

Figure I.4.   A leadership co-production model.

and Uhl-Bien (1995), a comprehensive understanding of the leadership process requires simultaneous attention to all categories of variables and relationships indicated in this framework. However, since much more attention has been given to the influence of leaders on followers and the consequences of leadership, at this stage of the development of leadership studies, the dominant approach to leadership should be corrected by paying more attention to the influence of followers on leaders, the leadership process, and its consequences.

In other words, while ultimately our approach to the study of leadership should be neither leader-centered nor follower-centered, at this stage, the study of leadership would benefit from a more follower-centered perspective. Important advances in this direction have been made in the last 20 years by James Meindl and his associates and by other contributors to the construction of leadership approach discussed earlier in this chapter. However, there are many more possibilities to examine the role of followers in the leadership process both theoretically and empirically. It is important to examine not only how followers contribute to the construction of a leadership relationship but also how they empower the leader and influence his or her behavior and what is their contribution to determining the consequences of the leadership relationship. Some of these possibilities are illustrated in the next section.

REVERSAL OF THE LENSES: SOME EXAMPLES

A follower-centered perspective to leadership entails a "reversal of the lenses." As a first stage toward a more balanced understanding of leadership, it requires that instead of focusing on leaders as causal agents and followers as recipients of leader influence, as we do in most of our studies, we view the followers as the causal agents and examine their impact on the leaders and the leadership relationship. In other words, it requires that we view followers' characteristics and behaviors as the "independent variables" and leader characteristics and behaviors as the "dependent variables." Following are some examples of such reversal of the lenses.

An Empirical Example: Followers' Impact on Transformational Leadership

Several early studies (e.g., Crowe, Bochner, & Clark, 1972; Farris & Lim, 1969; Lowin & Craig, 1968; McFillen, 1978; Sims & Manz, 1984) have demonstrated that supervisors' leadership style is influenced by subordinates' level of performance. Despite these studies, which advocated a "reciprocal determinism" approach to leadership, namely viewing leader behavior as both a cause and an effect of follower behavior, the topic of followers' influence on leader behavior has been largely abandoned in the leadership literature. Recently, Dvir and Shamir (2003) have revisited this approach, focusing on followers' level of development rather than their performance and on transformational leadership behavior rather than on the more traditional leadership styles examined in the early studies.

The originator of transformational leadership theory, James McGregor Burns, conceived of such leadership as a mutual influence process between leaders and followers. "Transforming leadership is a dynamic, reciprocal process in which both leaders and followers are being transformed by each other" (Burns, 1978, p. 61). In contrast with this statement, practically the entire vast body of research on transformational leadership has ignored the role of followers in this process. It has conceived of transformational leadership as a leadership style, a certain combination of leader behaviors, and has studied the effects of this style on followers' attitudes and on individual and collective performance (e.g., Lowe, Kroeck, & Sivasubramaniam, 1996). An example of this line of research is illustrated in Figure I.5.

Dvir and Shamir (2003) decided to reverse the lenses. Whereas the primary focus of transformational leadership theory is on how such leadership contributes to the development of followers, Dvir and Shamir hypothesized that followers' level of development may influence the level of transformational leadership exhibited by the leader. They conceived of follower level of development as including three facets: (1) motivation (self-actualization needs), (2) level of empowerment (self-efficacy, a critical-independent approach, and active engagement in the task), and (3) morality (a collectivistic orientation and internalization of organizational values). They reasoned that followers' level of development affects transformational leader behavior because leaders are more likely to delegate responsibilities to "mature" and independent followers, more likely to appeal to intrinsic motivation of followers who have higher order needs and an expressive orientation, more likely to direct intellectual stimulation to followers with critical-independent thinking, and are more likely to direct value-laden messages to followers with a "principled" or moral orientation. These predictions are consistent with Burns's assertion that "leaders may modify their leadership in recognition of followers' preferences, or in

Figure I.5.   Traditional prediction of transformational leadership theory.

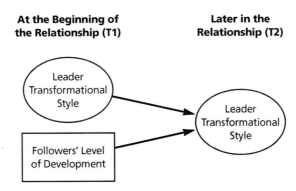

Figure I.6.   Hypothesized effect of followers' development level on leader behavior (Dvir & Shamir, 2003).

order to anticipate followers' responses, or in order to harmonize the actions of both leader and follower with their common motives, values and goals" (1978, p. 426).

Dvir and Shamir (2003) carried out their investigation in a military situation, specifically the basic training of new recruits to the army. Their main focus was on 729 recruits who were led by 54 platoon leaders. The design of their study was longitudinal. At Time 1, during the first weeks of basic training, they measured the leaders' transformational leadership behavior. They also measured followers' level of development (a combination of six variables). At Time 2, toward the end of basic training, $3\frac{1}{2}$–4 months later, they again measured the transformational leadership behavior of the platoon leaders. As illustrated in Figure I.6, they expected transformational leadership behavior at T2 to be predicted not only by transformational leadership behavior at T1 but also by followers' level of development at T1.

When transformational leadership behavior at T2 was regressed on the two predictors, it was found that transformational leadership behavior at T1 accounted for 21% of the variance, but an additional 8% of the variance was accounted for by followers' initial level of development. Dvir and Shamir concluded that followers' initial level of development predicts subsequent transformational leadership after controlling for initial level of transformational leadership and that a balanced approach to the study of transformational leadership needs to incorporate the characteristics of followers and their effects on the leader, not only the effects of leader behaviors on the followers.

A Theoretical Example

In a recent paper, Howell and Shamir (2005) attempted to correct the leader-centered view of charismatic leadership. They started from a leader-centered distinction between two types of charismatic leadership proposed by Howell (1988). Howell suggested a distinction between *personalized* and *socialized* charismatic leaders. Her distinction was based on the power motivation of the leaders and the way they use their power. Personalized charismatic leaders, she argued, seek power to advance themselves and their self-interests. They employ their power in an unrestrained manner. Such leaders tend to demand blind obedience by their followers, restrict followers' access to information, discourage dissenting views, and create overdependence of followers on them. Their leadership often has destructive consequences for both individuals and the organization or group they lead. Socialized charismatic leaders, in contrast, seek power to advance collective aims and interests and employ their power in a restrained manner. They do not restrict dissenting views or followers' access to information, do not expect or demand blind obedience by followers, and do not create overdependence on them. Consequently, their leadership is less likely to lead to destructive consequences and more likely to have positive effects on individuals and groups.

In contrast with this leader-centered perspective on personalized and socialized charismatic leadership, Howell and Shamir (2005) suggested, following Weierter (1997), that the two types of leadership should be viewed as two types of relationships rather than as two types of leaders. Viewing them as types of relationships immediately suggests that the followers, not only the leader, contribute to the emergence and nature of the type of charismatic relationship between leaders and followers. Following the work of Lord and colleagues (1999) and Kark and Shamir (2002), Howell and Shamir proposed that the type of charismatic relationship that develops between leaders and followers depends to a large extent on followers' self-concepts and the nature of their identification with the leader.

Specifically, followers with low self-concept clarity and those whose self-construal is at the relational level (define themselves in terms of relationship with significant others) are likely to form a personalized charismatic relationship with the leader, which is based on personal identification. Followers with high self-concept clarity and those whose self-construal is at the collective level (define themselves primarily on the basis of belonging to groups and collectives) are likely to form a socialized identification with the leader, which is based on their identification with a group or an organization and the extent to which the leader embodies, represents, and advances collective identities and values. In other words, Howell and Shamir (2005) reversed the lenses and argued that the nature of charismatic leadership depends primarily on the followers, not the leaders.

This argument has far-reaching implications. Followers who form a socialized charismatic relationship with the leader place constraints on the leader's influence, play an active role in determining the values expressed by the leader, are less dependent on the leader, and are less open to manipulation by the leader. In contrast, followers who form a personalized charismatic relationship with the leader are not only more dependent on the leader and more vulnerable to the leader. Their unquestioning admiration and obedience of the leader may affect the leader's self-concept, increase his or her self-efficacy, and influence his or her behavior. In the case of a leader who seeks power for personal purposes, followers' support and admiration may feed the leader's desire for absolute personal power and delusions of omnipotence. But even if the leader initially does not seek self-aggrandizement or personal power, personalized charismatic relationships may "overempower" the leader because such relationships include adoration, idolization, and unquestioning obedience of the leader. The leader may internalize the exaggerated reflected appraisals of followers and eventually develop an illusion of omnipotence. This, in turn, may lead to the abandonment of ethical restraints and other restraints on the use of power.

Thus a major implication of Howell and Shamir's (2005) analysis is that the followers may be responsible no less than the leader for the consequences of charismatic leadership. Previous writings about the "dark side" of charisma (Conger, 1990; House & Howell, 1992; Howell & Avolio, 1992; Sankowsky, 1995) tended to attribute the negative consequences mainly to the traits and behaviors of the leader. Howell and Shamir's analysis suggests that the "blame" for such consequences may be with the followers as well.

Howell and Shamir's (2005) theoretical analysis has attempted to correct the heroic bias in current charismatic leadership theories by focusing on the followers' role in the charismatic leadership process. They have rejected unidirectional explanations of charismatic leadership, which view charisma as either totally leader-produced or totally follower-produced. Rather, they have defined charisma as a relationship that is jointly produced by leaders and followers. At the same time, their theoretical analysis gives followers a much more central role than they have had traditionally in theory and research on organizational leadership in general and charismatic leadership in particular. Previous writings have placed the responsibility for the development and outcomes of charismatic relationships squarely on the shoulders of the leader. Howell and Shamir have argued that the nature of these relationships and their impact rest on the follower as well.

A Historical Example: Hitler

Examples of followers' influence on the leader's self-concept and behavior can be drawn even from the most archetypical case of dictatorial leadership—the case of Adolf Hitler. The majority of writings on Hitler is leader-centered and focuses on his personality and actions. Ian Kershaw's (1999, 2001) recent biography of Hitler reveals two surprising findings in this regard. First, contrary to common belief, Hitler did not view himself as a great leader from the beginning. Well into his 30s, he viewed himself only as the drummer who gathers the troops or the masses (*trommler und sammler*) for the great leader to arrive and lead them to victory. It is only later that he started to see himself as that great leader, and it is likely that this perception changed in part as a result of feedback from followers. In other words, followers' attitudes and behavior probably empowered Hitler and affected his self-concept.

Second, contrary to the common view of Hitler as the initiator of all the important moves against the Jews, and as an absolute dictator whose followers' actions stemmed from his orders, in many instances, starting from the boycott on Jewish businesses in 1933, through the Nuremberg laws of racial discrimination in 1935 and the crystal night in 1938 to the final approach to the solution of the Jewish problem, formulated some time in 1941, Hitler followed his followers in some respects. For various reasons, some of them tactical, Hitler was less radical then some of his followers and in some of his decisions and actions reacted to pressures from below. Kershaw (2001) also writes that in many cases the followers anticipated Hitler's wishes as they perceived them, and took actions that, in their opinion, would please the Führer. In some cases he legalized their actions a posteriori, and in other cases, like the Nuremberg laws, the result was a compromise between followers' pressures and Hitler's opinions or instincts. Hitler initially advocated transportation to Palestine as the solution to the Jewish problem and his view of the final solution in the extermination camps evolved gradually through several years, partly as a result of followers' influence. An even more extreme view of followers' influence on Hitler's leadership was expressed by Albert Speer, who wrote, "Certainly the masses roared to the beat set by Hitler and Gobbles' baton; yet they were not the true conductors. The mob determined the theme" (1970, pp. 19–20).

A Hypothetical Example: The "Reverse" Pygmalion Effect

Howell and Shamir's (2005) analysis and Hitler's historical example suggest that one important way in which followers play an active role in the leadership process is by empowering the leader and increasing his or her self-efficacy perceptions. Self-efficacy perceptions are influenced, among other things, by others' expectations. Many studies of the Pygmalion effect (Eden, 1990) have shown that significant others' positive expectations increase the self-efficacy of people and ultimately their performance. All Pygmalion studies, however, have focused on superiors' expectations of their subordinates. They demonstrated that leader's expectations of followers act as self-fulfilling prophecies and increase followers' motivation and performance. Reversing the lenses would lead us to hypothesize that similar Pygmalion effects will be found in the other direction as well. Followers' positive expectations of their leader can be expected to increase the leader's self-efficacy and confidence and consequently his or her ability to display charismatic behaviors such as developing an even more challenging vision of the future. A similar hypothesis can be developed with respect to what Eden (1990) calls the Galatea effect, namely the effects of negative superiors' expectations on followers' self-efficacy and performance. Reversing the lenses would lead us to hypothesize that followers' negative expectations would "disempower" the leader, decrease his or her self-efficacy, and consequently inhibit certain actions and decrease his or her performance.

Such positive or negative expectations may exist prior to followers' exposure to leader behaviors and be based on the leader's reputation, or they may develop out of first impressions of the leader and the degree to which these impressions fit followers' leadership prototypes. The point is that reversing the lenses and adopting a follower-centered perspective would lead us to study how followers' expectations (natural or experimentally manipulated) affect leaders' self-efficacy and behavior.

Another Hypothetical Example: Leaders' Resistance to Change

According to the literature, many organizational changes are delayed, slowed down, or even fail due to employees' psychological difficulty to accept the change and adjust to it. For instance, a recent study (Bovey & Hede, 2001) cites a survey among 500 large Australian organizations, which found that employee resistance was cited as the most frequent problem encountered by management when implementing change. The literature on leadership and change portrays the leaders as change agents and the subordinates as either recipients or resistors of the change. The phenomenon of resistance to change is placed squarely on subordinates' shoulders. The literature therefore focuses on the reasons for subordinates' resistance to change and various ways to overcome this resistance.

However, anyone who has worked in organizations knows there are many instances where changes are suggested or initiated by followers and the leaders resist them. They may do so because the suggested change does not fit their vision or plans, because they cannot or do not want to allocate required resources, or for psychological reasons such as inertia, conservativeness, or fear. Therefore, in order to fully understand change or lack of change in organizations, we need to reverse the lenses and, in addition to focusing on leaders as change agents and followers as recipients of change, focus on followers as change agents and leaders as supporters or resistors of change. This is important especially if we accept the view (Beer, Eisenstadt, & Spector, 1999) that most significant changes in organizations do not start at the top of the organization. Rather, they originate from problem-solving attempts throughout the organization. The role of leaders according to this view is not to initiate change and implement it from above, but rather to support, encourage, and nurture change efforts that often start by individuals and groups in various parts of the organization. This implies a shift in the study of leadership and change. Rather than focusing solely on leaders as agents of change and followers as recipients or resistors of change, we should also look for and study instances where the followers initiate or advocate changes and the leaders resist them as well as instances where the followers initiate changes and the leaders support and encourage them.

SUMMARY: FOLLOWERS' ROLES IN THE CO-PRODUCTION OF LEADERSHIP

In this introduction, I reviewed the roles that followers occupy in various leadership theories. I argued that most theories are still leader-centered and view followers as recipients or moderators of leaders' influence, but there are also theories that are more follower-centered in the sense of positing followers in more active roles as substitutes for leadership, constructors of leadership, or co-leaders. I suggested that an understanding of leadership processes requires a balanced approach that views both leaders and followers as co-producers of leadership relationships and their consequences. Ultimately, leadership has to be understood as a reciprocal and dynamic interaction process between leaders and followers, taking into consideration the characteristics, actions, and reactions of both sides (Collinson, 2005). However, I submitted that, at this time, in order to balance the dominant leader-centered approach, our lenses should be reversed and more research attention should be given to followers' impact on the leadership relationship and on leaders' behavior. I gave some theoretical, empirical, and hypothetical examples to illustrate the implications of such a reversal of the lenses. To summarize, here is a list of some of the ways by which followers affect the leadership process, which should be further studied:

- Followers' needs, identities, and cognitive schema affect leader selection and emergence as well as leader endorsement and acceptance.

- Interfollower structures and processes such as social networks and social contagion influence the emergence of leadership and affect its consequences.
- Followers' expectations, values, and attitudes determine the latitude of leader behavior.
- Followers' expectations of the leader act as self-fulfilling prophecies and affect the leader's motivation and performance.
- Followers' acceptance of the leader and their support of the leader affect the leader's self-confidence, self-efficacy, and behavior.
- Followers' characteristics (e.g., self-concept clarity) determine the nature of the leadership relationship formed with the leader.
- Followers' attitudes and characteristics (e.g., level of development) affect leader behavior (e.g., transformational leadership).

Understanding leadership from a perspective that acknowledges the many active roles that followers play in the leadership process has some practical implications as well. For instance, acknowledging that the leader is only one element in the leadership relationship, and followers play a major, sometimes dominant, role in the development of leadership relationships, immediately leads to the conclusion, emphasized by Day (2000), that leadership development is not synonymous with leader development. Perhaps, unfortunately for those of us who are involved in leader selection and training or consultation to leaders, developing leaders may sometimes have only a limited effect on leadership development since such development depends also on the followers, and their contributions to the process are not always under the leader's influence or control.

Another example concerns leadership evaluation. Much of leader evaluation is conducted from a leader-centered view that romanticizes the leader. It focuses on the leader's characteristics and behaviors. However, to the extent that followers play an active role in the leadership process, they are also responsible for the consequences of leadership. A leadership evaluation that focuses only on the leader is likely to attribute too much credit or blame to the leader, as clearly suggested by the work of Meindl and his associates (1985). A fuller development of the practical implications of a more balanced approach to leadership evaluation is beyond the scope of this chapter. Clearly, however, leadership evaluation cannot rely only on evaluation of the leader.

INTRODUCTION TO THE BOOK CHAPTERS

The chapters included in this book are not intended to romanticize the image of Meindl as a scholar and an intellectual leader but rather to further exemplify and extend the implications of trying to understand leadership from perspectives that acknowledge the active roles of followers in the leadership process.

The first four chapters represent some of the follower-centered perspectives reviewed earlier in this introduction: the psychoanalytical perspective, leadership categorization theory, the social identity theory of leadership, and the shared leadership approach.

Largely influenced by psychoanalytic perspectives, Jean Lipman-Blumen argues in Chapter 1 that follower fears, needs, and expectations render them dangerously susceptible to the illusions spun by "toxic leaders" who inflict serious and enduring harm on others. Followers' perceptions of leaders arise from a complex set of human needs and fears that impel them not only to tolerate, but often to prefer, and sometimes even create, toxic leaders. She suggests, for instance, that the need to be "chosen," the need for membership in a human community, the certainty of death, and the quest for safety and certitude often send followers into the arms of such leaders. Similarly, the search for meaning and opportunities for heroism make followers easy prey for leaders who project a larger-than-life image and provide extravagant, simplistic answers to their existential concerns. In line with psychoanalytic theories, Lipman-Blumen finds the roots of this phenomenon in infancy and early childhood because individuals are born into dependency, and are therefore imprinted with the propensity for reliance on those they perceive as stronger and more knowledgeable than they are. Despite that, Lipman-Blumen does not accept a fatalistic view of followers' subordination to toxic leaders. We are not powerless against toxic leaders, she argues, unless we define ourselves as such and by so doing create a self-fulfilling prophecy.

Chapter 2, in sharp contrast, is written from a cognitive psychology viewpoint. In this chapter, Megan Medvedeff and Robert Lord offer a further development of Lord's leadership categorization theory (Lord & Maher, 1991), which specifies the content of cognitive categories that define leadership and explains leadership perceptions in terms of the match of perceived characteristics to leadership prototypes held by perceivers. In combination with causal attribution processes, leadership categorization theory was also used to explain the inference processes by which performance knowledge is used by followers to infer that leadership has occurred, a topic also addressed by Meindl's romance of leadership theory. Medvedeff and Lord note two limitations of categorization theory: First, it is overly cognitive and tends to ignore emotional components that are important in leadership. Second, it does not have dynamic qualities that explain how leadership perceptions can change over time or across situations. They describe recent developments in cognitive science that enable an extension of leadership categorization theory to acknowledge that leadership is not only in the eye of the beholder but also in the body and emotions of the beholder. They also offer a more dynamic perspective that shows how leadership schema can be flexible across situations and how leadership perceptions can change.

In Chapter 3, written from a more social psychological perspective, Daan van Knippenberg, Barbara van Knippenberg, and Steffen Giessner outline how the social identity perspective on leadership complements and extends Meindl's social contagion model. Specifically, they discuss how a shared social identity among group members sets the stage for the social sharedness of leadership perceptions, including leadership endorsement and perceptions of leadership effectiveness. They argue that the social contagion and social identity perspectives complement each other by identifying various followers' reference points for constructing leadership and responding to leadership. Although the social construction perspective and the social identity perspective do not identify the same determinants of leadership perceptions, they seem to be in agreement about the process through which perceptions are socially shared. Van Knippenberg and colleagues also identify some of the moderators of followers' tendency to romanticize leaders on the basis of information about performance and describe studies that show the effect of leader performance on leader endorsement is stronger for nonprototypical leaders than for prototypical leaders. To balance the follower-centered perspective, they also address the leaders' active role in trying to influence the social construction of their leadership.

In Chapter 4, Lynn Offermann and Noelle Scuderi review relevant work published under the labels of shared leadership, distributed leadership, collective leadership, team leadership, co-leadership, emergent leadership, and self-managed teams to examine broader participation in leadership roles. They discuss the theoretical and operational similarities and differences of these constructs and propose a framework for conceptualizing the sharing of leadership. They also discuss possible antecedents and outcomes, and conclude that the studies they review show considerable evidence of the potential value of sharing leadership. Offermann and Scuderi expect that interest in various forms of shared leadership will continue to grow as organizations show increased awareness of the virtues of self-managed teams. To promote further research on this topic, Offermann and Scuderi discuss measurement issues and provide suggestions for future work on follower engagement in leadership, including further examination of the potential liabilities of a "company of leaders" when too many cooks may spoil the broth and where a single leader or a couple of co-leaders may be more effective options.

The next three chapters offer follower-centered perspectives on followers' attribution of charisma to the leader. The impact of social networks on attributions of charisma to the leader is the topic of Chapter 5 by Margarita Mayo and Juan Carlos Pastor. Mayo and Pastor use the social contagion model as their point of departure to describe a social network model of charismatic leadership using social network concepts and techniques. Following their earlier work with Meindl (Pastor et al., 2002), they emphasize that followers are not just connected to their leaders, they are also connected to other followers and therefore followers' attributions of leadership are, to a great extent, the result of individuals interacting with one another, sharing information about the leader, and comparing each others' views. It follows that attribution of charisma travels through the social paths that connect people with one another. Mayo and Pastor suggest that proximity in the network and the intensity of the relationships between group members are the basic mechanisms of social contagion. Frequent and emphatic interpersonal communication produces similarity of attributions of charisma among group members because it provides proximate others with more opportunities to compare and test their ideas about the leader. Mayo and Pastor offer a research agenda to further examine these processes.

In Chapter 6, Chao Chen, Liuba Belkin, and Terri Kurtzberg also focus on followers' attribution of charisma to a leader. They situate their theoretical model in the context of organizational change and place organizational members' emotions at the center of their proposed research model. They suggest that charisma attributions depend on the change strategy adopted by the organization: A growth strategy is more likely to increase attributions of charisma to a change leader than a retrenchment strategy. They further suggest that this happens because a growth strategy arouses optimistic emotions and creates emotional convergence among organizational members whereas a retrenchment strategy arouses pessimistic emotions and creates emotional divergence. Chen and colleagues also suggest certain moderators of this general effect. Relying on the romance of leadership notion, they suggest that attribution of charisma would be moderated by members' optimistic disposition and the tendency to romanticize leaders. Relying on the social contagion notion and the work of Pastor and colleagues (2002) described in Chapter 5, they suggest that such attributions will also be moderated by the organizational network's density—the frequency of contact and communication among organizational members.

Perceptions of charisma are also at the center of Chapter 7 by Raj Pillai, Jeffrey Kohles, and Michelle Bligh. In an attempt to explain how and why presidential approval ratings in national polls change over time, Pillai and colleagues present a study that examined how followers' perceptions of crises and effectiveness influenced their evaluations of President George W. Bush's transformational and charismatic leadership over a period of 5 years. Like Chen and colleagues in Chapter 6 and following earlier work by Pillai and Meindl (1991, 1998) and Bligh, Kohles, and Meindl (2004), they too emphasize the role of crisis in affecting perceptions of leadership. They argue that changes in leadership perceptions may depend on the type of crisis faced by the leader and his or her effectiveness in dealing with the crisis. Based on data collected over eight time periods, they distinguish differential effects for two types of crises—terrorism crisis, which is perceived to be not under the leader's control, and economic crisis, which is perceived to be under the leader's control such that he or she can be blamed for its consequences. They show that crisis can decrease approval of a leader when the leader can be blamed for the crisis. In contrast, when the crisis is not under the leader's control, it can present him or her with opportunities to take bold and decisive actions, which may have a positive effect on followers' attributions of charismatic and transformational leadership.

Another extension of Meindl's earlier work is offered in Chapter 8, by Brad Jackson and Eric Guthey, who build on Chen and Meindl's (1991) work on the role of the media in constructing images of leaders. Chen and Meindl described, on the basis of analysis of printed articles, how the business press, in conjunction with their reading publics, construct a leader's image over time in line of radical changes in the fortunes of the leader's firm. Instead of focusing on printed articles, Jackson and Guthey focus on the visual construction of leader images in photographs and portraits. They argue that CEO images and portraits do not merely reflect the views of the business community, the commercial and organizational imperatives of the media, or the collective conceptions of organization and leadership dominant in the national culture at large. Such images also function very actively as rhetorical tools in ongoing symbolic struggles over the legitimacy of individual business leaders, and over the social legitimacy of corporate organization. They illustrate their arguments with an examination of the media images of former Hewlett-Packard CEO Carly Fiorina.

A more radical extension, but fully consistent with Meindl's romance of leadership notion and the social construction perspective on leadership, is offered in Chapter 9, by Mary Uhl-Bien and Raj Pillai. Instead of focusing on the social construction of leadership, they focus on the social construction of followership. They suggest that just as leadership is in the eye of the beholder, so is followership. Therefore, they focus on how views of followership are constructed and represented in the thought systems and meanings the followers construct for themselves and one another. They suggest that, like leadership schema, followership schema are also developed through socialization and past experience with leaders and other followers, stored in memory, and activated when followers begin to see another person as more capable and competent than themselves. More specifically, Uhl-Bien and Pillai suggest that a corollary to the romance of leadership is the "subordination of followership." Leadership is enacted when followers begin seeing themselves (and acting) as followers. In organizations, that means seeing themselves as subordinates. When people construct themselves as followers they often lower their expectations and their behaviors to meet the label. Many detrimental consequences could be attributed to followers' behaviors, such as lack of initiative and denial of responsibility, that emanate from the way they construct their own roles. Thus, like Lipman-Blumen in Chapter 1, Uhl-Bien and Pillai address followers' responsibility for the detrimental effects of leadership. However, they do it from a social construction rather than a psychoanalytic perspective.

Another angle from which the followers' role in the leadership process can be examined is the study of what happens when the leader departs. In Chapter 10, Melissa Carsten and Michelle Bligh present an exploratory study of followers' perceptions of the leader's vision and its implementation both prior to and after the announcement of a leader departure. They present a follower-centered perspective on vision implementation, arguing that followers construct different understandings of the leader's vision and their role with respect to that vision. Hence, followers can play an important role in enhancing or resisting the vision. Using interviews with faculty and staff members conducted before and after the departure of a university president, they found, interestingly, that followers perceived the vision as more closely associated with the leader after his departure but, as could be expected, they were less concerned with achieving the vision after the leader's departure. Carsten and Bligh also demonstrate that followers can simultaneously show commitment to the abstract vision and cynicism for the method of implementation. This study raises several other possibilities regarding followers' role in the implementation of a vision after the leader's departure. For instance, when followers continue to embrace the vision after the leader's departure, this may influence their acceptance of a new leader, which is likely to depend on the extent to which the new leader is committed to the old leader's vision or attempts to bring a new vision to the organization.

In Chapter 11, Dian Marie Hosking takes the social construction of leadership perspective even further than the other chapters by offering a postmodern approach to the study of leadership. She challenges taken-for-granted knowledge and assumptions about leadership and calls for work that problematizes the nature of leadership. In contrast with modernist approaches that take individuals as given, having certain enduring qualities such as personality and motivation, Hosking focuses on what she calls "relational realities," which include constructions of self in reaction to other, as well as constructions of leadership, and of leaders and followers. Her approach starts with processes, not persons, and views persons, such a leader and follower, as relational realities that are made in processes. The interesting questions for Hosking are how is someone constructed as a leader and how are leadership realities made, sustained, and changed? Her emphasis is on multiple ways of constructing realities and on local-cultural and local-historical processes rather than on general principles or propositions. To demonstrate the implications of this approach, she discusses its implications for leadership training and development focusing on three aspects: who participates, who defines program content, and the content itself. She advocates inclusive participation rather than participation only by appointed leaders, blurring leader–nonleader divides, theorizing leadership as a collective activity or process, not imposing predefined notions and contents but rather generating locally grown content, and a more dialogical or even multi-logical approach to leadership training and development.

In Chapter 12, Michelle Bligh, Raj Pillai, and Mary Uhl-Bien attempt to integrate the previous chapters by focusing on several overarching themes and ideas that seem to weave across and through the various contributions to this volume. They show how the chapters enact and extend different aspects of Meindl's emphasis on perceptions of leadership, their construction, and their effects on leadership relations and processes. They exemplify this theme by focusing more specifically on how various chapters treat the construction of charismatic leadership. Another theme they stress is the importance of context in leadership processes and how different aspects of the context enter the analysis offered by various chapters. On the basis of the chapters and the potential connections among them, Bligh and colleagues suggest many questions and possible directions for future research. In closing, they emphasize an important point, namely that Miendl's ideas and other follower-centered perspectives are not "anti-leadership." They do not aim to exclude the leader's contributions to the leadership process or to replace the leader-centered approach but rather to correct some biases inherent in this approach and complement it in order to achieve a deeper and fuller understanding of leadership.

In the final chapter, Karl Weick offers a retrospective evaluation of James Meindl's contribution both to leadership studies and to organization science more broadly. Weick was the editor of *Administrative Science Quarterly*, that published Meindl's original work on the romance of leadership (Meindl et al., 1985). He is in a good position to discuss the implication of Meindl's work for organization studies because his own work on sensemaking in organizations fits well with Meindl's ideas. Following Meindl and others, Weick questions the validity of the leader–follower separation, especially in the traditional stimulus–response form, where the leader is the stimulus and the followers respond. He shows how the meaning of stimuli (the leader) unfolds in more complex ways, often after the "response" has been made, and how followers construct the leader and their own following not only in response to their images but also in response to their actions. His chapter also implies several directions for future research. He notes that the original formulation of the romance of leadership was too individualistic and failed to sufficiently consider interactions, conversations, social influence, networks, and other interfollower relations that are key sources of conceptions. (This issue has been addressed in Meindl's later work on social contagion and his work with Mayo and Pastor on networks.) He also questions Meindl's assumption that the romance of leadership is always functional for followers and suggests that people may not always prefer clarity and rather prefer ambiguity and a blurred conception of their leader. Finally, he emphasizes that followers have a choice in matters of leadership construction and suggests there are instances of "negative romance" when followers choose not to idealize the leader but to belittle or even ignore him or her. This chapter clearly demonstrates the rich potential of follower-centered perspectives on leadership to advance our understanding of leadership and organizations.

REFERENCES

Bass, B. M. (1985). *Leadership and performance beyond expectations*. New York: Free Press.

Bass, B. M. (1990). *Bass and Stogdill's handbook of leadership*. New York: Free Press.

Beer, M., Eisenstadt, R. A., & Spector, B. A. (1990). Why change programs don't produce change. *Harvard Business Review, 68*, 158–166.

Bennis, W. (1999). The end of leadership: Exemplary leadership is impossible without the full inclusion, cooperation, and initiatives of followers. *Organizational Dynamics, 28*, 71–79.

Beyer, J. M. (1999). Taming and promoting charisma to change organizations. *Leadership Quarterly, 10*, 307–330.

Bligh, M. C., Kohles, J. C., & Meindl, J. R. (2004). Charisma under crisis: Presidential leadership, rhetoric, and media responses before and after the September 11th terrorist attacks. *Leadership Quarterly, 15*, 211–239.

Bovey, W. H., & Hede, A. (2001). Resistance to organizational change: The role of cognitive and affective processes. *Leadership and Organizational Development Journal, 22*, 372–381.

Bryman, A. (1992). *Charisma and leadership in organizations*. London: Sage.

Burns, J. M. (1978). *Leadership*. New York: Harper & Row.

Chen, C., & Meindl, J. R.(1991). The construction of leadership images in the popular press: The case of Donald Burr and People Express. *Administrative Science Quarterly, 36*, 521–551.

Collinson, D. (2005). Dialectics of leadership. *Human Relations*, 58, 1419–1442.

Conger, J. A. (1990). The dark side of leadership. *Organizational Dynamics*, 19, 44–55.

Conger, J. A., & Kanungo, R. N. (1998). *Charismatic leadership in organizations*. Thousand Oaks, CA: Sage.

Crowe, B. J., Bochner, S., & Clark, A. (1972). The effects of subordinates' behaviour on managerial style. *Human Relations, 25*(3), 215–237.

Day, D. V. (2000). Leadership development: A review in context. *Leadership Quarterly, 11,* 581–614.

Dvir, T., & Shamir, B. (2003). Follower developmental characteristics as predictors of transformational leadership: A longitudinal field study. *Leadership Quarterly, 14,* 327–344.

Eden, D. (1990). *Pygmalian in management.* Lexington, MA: Heath.

Farris, G. F., & Lim, F. G. (1969). Effects of performance on leadership, cohesiveness, influence, satisfaction, and subsequent performance. *Journal of Applied Psychology, 53,* 490–497.

Fiedler, F.E. (1967). *A theory of leadership effectiveness.* New York: McGraw-Hill.

Flieshman, E. A., Harris, E. F., & Burtt, H. E. (1955). *Leadership and suprevision in industry.* Columbus, OH: Bureau of Educational Research, Ohio State University.

Goffee, R., & Jones, G. (2001). Followers: It's personal too. *Harvard Business Review, 79,* 148.

Graen, G. B., & Uhl-Bien, M. (1995). Relationship-based approach to leadership: Development of leader–member–exchange (LMX) theory over 25 years: Applying a multi-level multi-domain perspective. *Leadership Quarterly, 6,* 219–247.

Grint, K. (2000). *The arts of leadership.* Oxford, UK: Oxford University Press,

Gronn, P. (2002). Distributed leadership as a unit of analysis. *Leadership Quarterly, 13,* 423–451.

Hersey, P., & Blanchard, K. (1977). *The management of organizatinal behavior.* Englewood Cliffs, NJ: Prentice-Hall.

Hill, M. A. (1984). The law of the father: Leadership and symbolic authority in psychonalysis. In B. Kellerman (Ed.), *Leadership: Multidisciplinary perspectives.* Englewood Cliffs, NJ: Prentice-Hall.

Hogg, M. A. (2001). A social identity theory of leadership. *Personality and Social Psychology Review, 5,* 184–200.

Hollander, E. P. (1992). Leadership, followership, self, and others. *Leadership Quarterly, 3,* 43–54.

House, R. J. (1971). A path–goal theory of leader effectiveness. *Administrative Science Quarterly, 16,* 321–339.

House, R .J., & Howell, J.M. (1992). Personality and charismatic leadership. *Leadership Quarterly, 3,* 81–108.

House, R. J., Hanges, P. J., Javidan, M., & Dorfman, P. W. (Eds.) (2004). *Leadership, culture, and organizations: The GLOBE study of 62 societies.* Thousand Oaks, CA: Sage.

Howell, J. M. (1988). Two faces of charisma: Socialized and personalized leadership in organizations. In J. A. Conger, R. N. Kanungo, & Associates (Eds.), *Charismatic leadership: The elusive factor in organizational effectiveness* (pp. 213–236). San Francisco: Jossey-Bass.

Howell, J. M., & Avolio, B. J. (1992). The ethics of charismatic leadership: Submission or liberation? *Academy of Management Executive, 6,* 43–54.

Howell, J., & Shamir, B. (2005). The role of followers in the charismatic leadership process: Relationships and their consequences. *Academy of Management Review, 30,* 96–112.

Jermier, J. M. (1993). Introduction: Charismatic leadership: Neo-Weberian perspectives. *Leadership Quarterly, 4*, 217–233.

Kark, R., & Shamir, B. (2002). The dual effect of transformational leadership: Priming relational and collective selves and further effects on followers. In B. J. Avolio & F. J. Yammarino (Eds.), *Transformational and charismatic leadership: The road ahead* (pp. 67–91). Oxford, UK: Elsevier Science.

Kerr, S., & Jermier, J. M. (1978). Substitutes for leadership: Their meaning and measurement. *Organizational Behavior and Human Performance, 22*, 375–403.

Kershaw, I. (1999). *Hitler: 1889–1936 Hubris.* New York: Norton.

Kershaw, I. (2001). *Hitler: 1836–1945 Nemesis.* New York: Norton.

Kets de Vries, M. F. R. (1988). Prisoners of leadership. *Human Relations, 41*, 261–280.

Klein, K. J., & House, R. J. (1995). On fire: Charismatic leadership and levels of analysis. *Leadership Quarterly, 6*, 183–198.

Lewin, K., & Lippit, R., (1938). An experimental approach to the study of autocracy and democracy. *Sociometry, 1*, 292–300.

Lindholm, C. (1988). Lovers and leaders: Comparative models of romance and charisma. *Social Science Inforamtion, 27*, 3–45.

Lord, R. G., & Brown, D. J. (2004). *Leadership processes and follower self-identity.* Mahwah, NJ: Erlbaum.

Lord, R. G., Brown, D. J., & Freiberg, S. J. (1999). Understanding the dynamics of leadership: The role of follower self-concepts in the leader/follower relationship. *Organizational Behavior and Human Decision Processes, 78*, 167–203.

Lord, R. G., Foti, R. J., & De Vader, D. L. (1984). A test of cognitive categorization theory: Internal structure, information processing and leadership perceptions. *Organizational Behavior and Human Performance, 34*, 343–378.

Lord, R. G., & Maher, K. J. (1991). *Leadership and information processing.* Boston: Routledge.

Lowe, K. B., Kroeck, K. J., & Sivasubramaniam, N. (1996). Effectiveness correlates of transformational and transactional leadership: A meta analytic review of the MLQ literature. *Leadership Quarterly, 7*, 385–425.

Lowin, A., & Craig, J. R. (1968). The influence of level of performance on managerial style: An experimental object-lesson in the ambiguity of correlational data. *Organizational Behavior & Human Performance, 3*, 440–458.

Manz, C. C., & Sims, H. P. (1980). Self-management as a substitute for leadership: A social learning perspective. *Academy of Management Review, 5*, 361–367.

Manz, C. C., & Sims, H. P. (1987). Leading workers to lead themselves: The external leadership of self-managing work teams. *Administrative Science Quaretly, 32*, 106–128.

McFillen, J. M. (1978). Supervisory power as an influence in supervisor–subordinate relations. *Academy of Management Journal, 21*(3), 419–433.

Meindl, J. R. (1990). On leadership: An alternative to the conventional wisdom. In B. M. Staw & L. L. Cummings (Eds.), *Research in organizational behavior* (pp. 159–203). Greenwich, CT: JAI Press.

Meindl, J. R. (1995). The romance of leadership as a follower-centric theory: A social constructionist approach. *Leadership Quarterly, 6*, 329–341.

Meindl, J. R., Ehrlich, S. B., & Dukerich, J. M. (1985). The romance of leadership. *Administrative Science Quarterly, 30*, 78–102.

Northouse, P. G. (2004). *Leadership theory and practice.* London: Sage.

Pastor, J. C., Meindl, J. R., & Mayo, M. (2002). Network effects model of attributions of charismatic leadership. *Academy of Management Journal, 45*(2), 410–420.

Pearce, C. L., & Conger, J. A. (2003). *Shared leadership: Reframing the hows and whys of leadership.* Thousand Oaks, CA: Sage.

Pillai, R., & Meindl, J.R. (1991).The impact of a performance crisis on attributions of charismatic leadership: A preliminary study. *Proceedings of the 1991 Eastern Academy of Management Meetings,* Hartford, CT.

Pillai, R., & Meindl, J. R. (1998). Context and charisma: A "meso" level exmination of the relationship of organic structure, collectivism, and crisis to charismatic leadership. *Journal of Management, 24,* 643–671.

Ray, T., Clegg, S., & Gordon, R. A. (2004). A new look at dispersed leadership: Power, knowledge and context. In J. Storey (Ed.), *Leadership in organizations.* London: Routledge.

Sankowsky, D. (1995). The charismatic leader as narcissist: Understanding the abuse of power. *Organizational Dynamics, 23,* 57–71.

Shamir, B. (1991). The charismatic relationship: Alternative explanations and predictions. *Leadership Quarterly, 2,* 81–104.

Shamir, B., House, R. J., & Arthur, M. B. (1993). The motivational effects of charismatic leadership: A self-concept based theory. *Organization Science, 4,* 577–594.

Sims, H. P., & Manz, C. C. (1984). Observing leader behavior: toward reciprocal determinism in leadership theory. *Journal of Applied Psychology, 69,* 222–232.

Speer, A. (1970). *Inside the Third Reich.* New York: Macmillan.

Stogdill, R. M., & Coons, A. E. (1957). *Leader behavior: Its desription and measurement.* Columbus: Bureau of Educational Research. Ohio State University.

Uhl-Bien, M., Graen, G. B., & Scandura, T. (2000). Implications of leader–member exchange (LMX) for strategic human resource management systems: relationships as social capital for competitive advantage. In G. Ferris (Ed.), *Research in personnel and human resource management* (Vol. 18, pp. 137–185). Stamford, CT: JAI Press.

Van Knippenberg, D., & Hogg, M. A. (2003). A social identity model of leadership effectiveness in organizations. In B. M. Staw & R. M. Kramer (Eds), *Research in organizational behavior* (Vol. 25, pp. 243–295). New York: Elsevier.

Vroom, V. H., & Yetton, P. W. (1973). *Leadership and decision making.* Pittsburgh, PA: University of Pittsburgh Press.

Weierter, S. J. M. (1997). Who wants to play "follow the leader"?: A theory of charismatic relationships based on routinized charisma and follower characteristics. *Leadership Quarterly, 8,* 171–194.

Yukl, G. (1998). *Leadership in organizations* (4th ed.). Upper Saddle River, NJ: Prentice-Hall.

Yukl, G., & Van Fleet, D.D. (1992). Theory and research on leadership in organizations. In M.D. Dunnette & L.M. Hough (Eds.), *Handbook of industrial and organizational psychology* (2nd ed., pp. 147–197). Palo Alto, CA: Consulting Psychologists Press.

CHAPTER 1

TOXIC LEADERS AND THE FUNDAMENTAL VULNERABILITY OF BEING ALIVE

Jean Lipman-Blumen
Claremont Graduate University

ABSTRACT

This chapter explores the paradoxical phenomenon of followers who knowingly tolerate, sometimes prefer, and even create toxic leaders. Sharing Meindl's follower-centric perspective, it focuses primarily upon followers' perceptions of leaders, which arise from a complex set of existential and psychological needs and fears, leaving followers exquisitely vulnerable to toxic leaders. First, the chapter examines four psychological concerns: (1) the need for authority figures to keep us safe and provide key resources; (2) the need to feel we are the "chosen"; (3) the need for membership in the human community; and (4) the fear of personal impotence to challenge a bad leader. Then, the analysis shifts to three existential dimensions that contribute to followers' susceptibility to toxic leaders: (1) the certainty of death, coupled with the uncertainty of its circumstances; (2) the yearning, as well as the opportunities, for heroism in an unfinished world; and (3) our need to resolve the tensions between exhilaration and desolation, coupled with our

Follower-Centered Perspectives on Leadership, pages 1–17
Copyright © 2007 by Information Age Publishing
All rights of reproduction in any form reserved.

search for meaning. The final section of the chapter considers both individual options and organizational policies designed to prevent and combat toxic leadership.

TOXIC LEADERS AND THE FUNDAMENTAL VULNERABILITY OF BEING ALIVE

Buffeted by the uncertainty of life and the certainty of death, followers seek out leaders who promise to keep them safe, instill meaning into their lives, and create opportunities for immortality. If that were all that followers sought from leaders, it would, indeed, constitute a very tall order; however, they want much more.

Followers' very human needs and expectations render them dangerously susceptible to the illusions spun by toxic leaders. Toxic leaders, who inflict serious and enduring harm on others, nonetheless attract and seduce followers, who remain in their thrall for surprisingly long periods of time. The purpose of this chapter is to explore several critical underpinnings of this Faustian connection.

James Meindl's "romance of leadership" perspective underscored the importance of perceptions that followers construct about leaders (Meindl, 1995). These perceptions, Meindl argued, can be "divided...into those that are associated with individual followers and those that emanate from the social-organizational contexts in which followers are embedded". This chapter focuses on individual followers' perceptions of leaders that arise from a complex set of human needs and fears, although elsewhere I have addressed the social-organizational context as well (Lipman-Blumen, 2005a).

THREE COMPLEX WEBS

The "toxic leadership" conceptual framework, on which this chapter draws, shares Meindl's follower-centric perspective. It identifies three intersecting webs of factors that, in combination, create followers' exquisite susceptibility to the illusions offered by toxic leaders.

The first web encompasses followers' individual *internal* needs and anxieties, both psychological and existential. The second web draws on factors in the *external social* context. This second web includes the certainties of culture, its institutions, traditions, and norms, as well as the *un*certainties that arise from the unique historical moment, punctuated by change, natural disasters, and war, along with sociopolitical, economic, and technological crises. The third web links the *psychosocial* factors, such as the need for self-esteem, the achievement ethic, and the call to heroism. These psychosocial forces arise from the friction generated by the rub of individuals' specific needs, abilities, and experiences against the challenges they face in an unfinished and unfinishable world.

The combined strands of these intersecting webs entangle followers in ways that impel them not only to tolerate, but often to prefer, and sometimes even to create, toxic leaders. For toxic leaders manipulate their followers' ordinary human needs and exploit their existential circumstances. They do so by creating illusions designed to allay the fears and address the human condition to which we all are heir.

In this chapter, as previously indicated, I limit my discussion to the first web of *individual* factors. First, I address followers' psychological needs and, then, their existential anxieties that render them so receptive to toxic leaders.

INDIVIDUAL PSYCHOLOGICAL NEEDS AND FEARS

At least four psychological factors structure followers' openness to leaders, in general, and their special and perilous predilection for toxic leaders, in particular.

The Need for Authority Figures to Keep Us Safe and Provide What We Want

Young children are raised and socialized by seemingly omniscient and omnipotent parents and other caretakers who provide security, love, and other life-enhancing resources. In return, those who raise us expect obedience, presumably because their altruistic and affectionate demands are based on their greater knowledge of how to keep us safe.

These early authority figures loom large in our lives, deeply branding our psyches with the importance of pleasing and obeying them. As children, we realize we cannot get along without them, since these larger-than-life figures provide us with the basics of food, shelter, clothing, care, safety, and love that we cannot provide for ourselves. We see the artistic reflection of this magnification of leaders' stature in Michelangelo's awe-inspiring 17-foot marble sculpture of the young David, who would come to be King of the Israelites.[1]

Choice and freedom initially exceed the reach of young humans, born into dependency. The possibility of autonomy and free choice becomes feasible only as we grow and begin to function on our own. Yet, by that time, we have already learned to rely on those we perceive as stronger and more knowledgeable than we are.

Over time, our parents and other caretakers, too, teach us the norms and expectations of society and the socially appropriate means to meet them. They guide us in the attitudes and skills that will enable us to succeed in this fearsome world. They expose us to social networks that help us navigate in our environment. We gradually recognize that these authority figures actually do have valuable knowledge and power, at least until adolescent hubris prompts us to question their authority and brilliance.

Shaped by this potent amalgam of dependence, love, and sometimes intimidation, we learn—but not without ambivalence—to obey the parents and others who care for us. Fired in the kiln of our childhood, this ambivalence toward authority figures remains with most of us throughout our lives.

In developed societies, adolescence is commonly marked by a notorious struggle to reject the yoke of parental control and stand tall as self-reliant, responsible adults. As grown-ups, we want to dance to our own tune. When our parents and other caretakers recede into the shadows, we think we are on our own, composing our own music.

Nonetheless, the melody of parental care and control is profoundly embedded in our psyches. Despite our yearning for autonomy, when we hear those familiar strains, we begin to tap our toes. Before long, we find ourselves dancing mindlessly to that nostalgic tune, ignoring its dark undertones. This time, however, the conductors are likely to be other authority figures—bosses, pastors, professors, presidents, or any other would-be leaders—who, unlike our parents, may not know, much less cherish, our best interests.

When life and well-being are threatened, we easily fall back into our earlier patterns, readily exchanging our freedom for the leader's illusory promise of safety. Erich Fromm's classic treatise, *Escape from Freedom* (1941), described how that phenomenon has reasserted itself throughout history, repeatedly resulting in our abject submission even to the most toxic leaders.

A clear example of adults' willingness to exchange their freedom for safety comes from the post-9/11 American political scene. Since the 2001 terrorist attacks on the United States, a surprising number of Americans have indicated their willingness to trade off certain civil liberties in exchange for the promise—one might argue "the illusion"—of safety.

For example, a national poll conducted by the *Los Angeles Times* in January 2006 revealed that 51% of those polled agreed that "Americans should give up civil liberties for safety from terrorism," compared to 40% who felt that "Americans should protect civil liberties." In that same poll, while 62% of the participants felt "the country needs to move in a new direction," only 46% indicated they intended to vote for the opposition party in the next congressional election (Brownstein, 2006). These figures suggest that even when adults disagree with the direction in which their president is leading, if they believe their safety is threatened, a substantial percent still cling to that leader. Thus, as adults, our willing deference to authority reemerges in the face of threats to our safety.

Eventually, even absent potential danger to ourselves, we tend to submit to authority figures simply because they press those unconscious buttons that open the door to an earlier, less autonomous time in our lives. The well-known experiments conducted by Stanley Milgram demonstrated that our deeply ingrained respect for authority makes it disturbingly easy for an authority figure to command our acquiescence (Milgram, 1974). The simple words, "The experiment must continue," intoned by a lab-coated authority figure, were enough to induce an impressively large percentage of adults to give what they thought were painful, possibly lethal, electric shocks to another adult.

Fortunately, our knee-jerk compliance with the demands of authority figures is not the whole story. And, of course, for some adults, authority figures evoke just the opposite effect: a knee-jerk resistance and hostility.

As children, we also gradually learn to exert our own countervailing power, first by crying, and eventually by far more beguiling and sophisticated stratagems. Early on, we learn to read the faces of the powerful, to interpret their moods, and—by micromanipulation and various other countervailing ploys—offset their wrath and other negative consequences (see Lipman-Blumen, 1984, 1992).[2] We carry these skills into our adult encounters with those more powerful than ourselves, particularly leaders who lay claim to our allegiance and tractability. So, we retain some capacity to withstand toxic leaders, if only we choose to call upon it.

The Need to be the "Chosen"

The second psychological need relevant to our susceptibility to toxic leaders stems from our desire to be selected as the "chosen."[3] We yearn to be the "chosen," the most loved, the first in the eyes of others. Within the family, we struggle to be first in our parents' eyes. Small wonder that sibling rivalry is more often the case than the exception.

Historically, we can trace this longing at least as far back as the Old Testament, wherein the Israelites perceived themselves to be God's "Chosen People." They held a sacred status, in contrast to the Canaanites and Moabites, who were seen as the "Other." During the Reformation, both the Lutherans and Calvinists believed, with certain subtle distinctions, in predestination. This doctrine held that God had irrevocably chosen some individuals, before their birth, for salvation and others for damnation (Fromm, 1941).[4] This immutable religious predestination led to a profound sense of powerlessness. The inevitable uncertainty about one's "chosenness" predisposed the less secure to cower before any strong, authoritarian leader who held out the balm of safety and assured selection.

The notion of the "chosen" need not be restricted to religious groups. Language, nationality, ethnicity, intelligence, educational and socioeconomic level, or, in some instances, even body type can serve as a rationale for "chosenness." Thus, various secular groups—Harvard graduates, Navy Seals, Nobel Prize laureates, Enron employees in their heyday, blond and blue-eyed "Aryans"—may perceive themselves (and be perceived by others) as the "chosen."

Yet, someone or something must designate that group as the "chosen." When the designator is a leader who recruits other followers to join his or her "chosen" group, the result is not difficult to imagine. Followers who resonate to such an invitation are likely to fall into step willingly behind that leader.

The notion of the "chosen" axiomatically calls up its counterpart: the "nonchosen" or simply the "Other." Small group research teaches us that one reliable method for creating cohesive bonds within a group is the presence of an external enemy. That "Other," different from and reviled by the internal members, often serves as the scapegoat for the group's ills.

The "Other" is the unchosen, the despised, the impure, and so on. In fact, the "Other's" presence represents a decidedly contaminating threat to the community of the "chosen." The leader's exhortations to cleanse the community of the "Other" often galvanize that part of the toxic leader's program designed to enhance the purity of the "chosen." Certainly, the Nazi ideology that Germany would become a purified "Aryan" nation had such roots. Stalin, too, called for purifying the Socialist state of "vermin," using language that ominously echoed Hitler's rallying cry against "undesirable" groups.

Both the "chosen" and the "Other" are commonly designated on the basis of a single identity, focused on to the exclusion of their multiple identities. Amartya Sen has described the "illusion of destiny" based on the single identity (e.g., Jew, female, Asian, American, homosexual, etc.) selected to the exclusion of the many identities to which we all may lay claim. This chosen identity is then perceived as the *only* one, the destined basis for interaction with that individual or group (Sen, 2005). And women, as Simone de Beauvoir (1953) so eloquently explained, were the quintessential "Other," perceived solely on the basis of their gender identity, while their other diverse identities were completely ignored.

The strength of our desire to be selected as one of the "chosen"—and conversely to avoid being categorized as the "Other"—makes us vulnerable to the leader who promises to anoint us as the elect. Clearly, this desire to be among the ranks of the "chosen" has psychological and sociological correlates whose delineation exceeds the scope of this chapter. Yet, our perception of the distinction between ourselves and the "Other" can predispose us to engage in negative enterprises to demonstrate our superiority. Leaders who play on this very human predisposition often mislead us into toxic action.

The Need for Membership in the Human Community

Those who do not manage to enter the elite ranks of the "chosen" nonetheless feel the need for membership in the larger human community. Plato understood that humans were "social animals," who learn to be human through their interactions with others. Those rare individuals who grow up beyond the boundaries of society, like the Wild Boy of Avignon, never quite become fully human.

Social belonging is a deep and pervasive need for which we humans willingly sacrifice much. And even when the group demands an expensive and problematic ticket of admission, our need for belonging too often overrides our reservations.

Thus, for many of us, the leader who offers us membership in some subculture of the human community—even a countercultural community—may appear to have an important gift to bestow upon us. To maintain their membership, the Cult Davidians, under the leadership of David Koresh, and the members of the People's Temple, who followed Jim Jones to Guyana, willingly sacrificed not only material and social goods, but even their lives. In recent decades, membership in inner-city gangs has grown astronomically, even though the expected lifespan of gang members rarely stretches beyond adolescence (see Howell, 1998).[5]

A brief caveat is relevant here: In an effort to call attention to these previously ignored forces, let us not fall victim to the "romance of leadership." More specifically, by highlighting the leader's manipulation of our human need for membership in some community larger than ourselves, I do not mean to reduce other causative forces to an oversimplified attribution to the leader's behaviors and qualities. So let us not forget that peer pressures, the perceived absence of options, and previous experiences of failure and exclusion, as well as numerous other factors, may contribute to the followers' capitulation.

Admittedly, we have chosen extreme examples to emphasize our point. But in these and less toxic groups, the leader must somehow convince us that this community has its own inherent worth, despite its adherence to norms and values that fly in the face of society's accepted conventions.

Sanity, security, identity, and meaning all flow from our membership in the human community. Moreover, the community protects us not only from our inner fears, but also from threats that lie beyond the community's gates. To remain part of the human community, we are willing to curtail our freedom and tolerate distortions of our natures, our values, and sometimes our very lives, often at the behest of a toxic leader. Short of physical death, the most severe punishment society can inflict upon its members is exile—social death. Ostracism, isolation, and marginalization fall just shy of that drastic measure.

Both exile and disparagement by the group are serious penalties that arouse our anxiety and dread. For without the company and high regard of those we love and value, our lives lose their meaning. The Hitler Youth Movement offers a sad example. Historians have noted that, in addition to the ardent young followers who constituted its core, the Movement included many youngsters who privately eschewed the values of the group but feared ostracism by their peers. Thus, leaders who offer us—even the most deviant among us—the chance for membership in the human community, no matter how marginal that part of the human community may be, readily win our allegiance and compliance.

The Fear of Personal Inability to Challenge a Bad Leader

A fourth psychological driver completes this set: the fear that, as individuals, we lack the power to challenge most leaders, especially toxic, seemingly omnipotent leaders. While we may feel thoroughly competent in our jobs, our families, and our personal circle of colleagues and friends, we often believe ourselves to be powerless to confront leaders. Our tendency to attribute to them greater intelligence, wit, strength, and resources makes us reluctant to stand up to any leader. Toxic leaders, who deftly use illusions to project a larger-than-life image, intimidate us even more.

Chilled by the long shadow of a toxic leader, individual followers may not realize that others share their concerns and, with sufficient reassurance and protection, would willingly join forces to challenge the leader (Asch, 1956). As considerable experimental research on consensus suggests, the belief that no other group members share one's opinion easily silences most potential dissenters (Asch, 1972; Sherif, 1972). More encouragingly, when even one ally appears, the dissenter is much more likely to take heart and speak out.

Sometimes, the paranoid atmosphere generated by the toxic leader proves so menacing that individual followers shrink from asking others' opinions of the leader. After all, such inquiries might inadvertently reveal a lack of allegiance and expose these followers not only to their peers' rejection, but also to the leader's wrath.

When we observe that even those members of the group whom we deem more senior, more powerful, and more knowledgeable than ourselves are reluctant to take on the leader, any confidence we might have been mustering quickly evaporates. With our confidence thus undermined, we tend to keep our own counsel and hope—often vainly—for the more experienced group members, particularly opinion leaders, to act on our behalf.

Worse yet, when we find ourselves immersed in a large group, we may abrogate completely our personal responsibility for action. Le Bon's

(1895/2002) classic analysis of the behavior of individuals in crowds suggests that people in such circumstances often act in ways that would violate their consciences if they were by themselves.

Moreover, when we perceive ourselves to be one small entity in a swarm of millions, such as voters often do on Election Day, we may discount the value of our personal action and lapse into inaction. The subsequent revelation that a very small number of votes would have changed the outcome of the election may energize us belatedly, but usually not sufficiently to change our behavior in the next election.

One last consideration: The negative model revealed by the fate of individual whistleblowers frequently dampens our enthusiasm for single-handedly taking on toxic leaders. C. Fred Alford (2001) has documented the adverse consequences suffered by individual whistleblowers who insisted upon individually challenging toxic leaders and their organizations. And although we applaud the integrity and fortitude of the quixotic, solo whistleblowers, we rarely offer them jobs in our own organizations.

These four powerful and complex psychological forces are not the only barriers to confronting toxic leaders. In fact, several deep-seated existential concerns, to which we now turn, add their strength to the powerful forces that induce us not only to tolerate, but often to adulate, toxic leaders.

THE EXISTENTIAL DIMENSION

At least three existential forces combine with our psychological yearnings and perceptions to heighten our responsiveness to leaders. They speak to the fundamental existential question: What is the meaning of our "basic vulnerability of being alive?" (Marcus, 2006). This triad of existential forces intersects in ways that almost always increase our special susceptibility to toxic leaders.

The Certainty of Death, the Uncertainty of Its Circumstances

First, as humans, each of us lives in that unstable space between the certainty of our physical death and the *un*certainty of the specific conditions under which it will occur. The realization that we are powerless to predict or prevent our death understandably fosters both dread and anxiety. Our efforts to deal with those discomforting emotions often provoke still other problems.

First, we seek to escape the pain of our existential dread by repressing it into the depths of our unconscious (Becker, 1973). There our anxiety operates out of sight, quietly and firmly seizing control of many actions we have ostensibly taken for other, more conscious reasons. Even in the darkness of our unconscious, however, our dread also plays a constructive role. It enables us to escape the paranoia and paralysis that perseverating on our cruel fate could create.

Next, we embark on an endless search for the chimera of security and certainty that would lay our anxiety to permanent rest. That trek can take us to the health food counter, the gym, the fortuneteller, or the psychiatrist, or sometimes to charlatans who promise us the key to eternal life.

Our quest for safety and certitude frequently also sends us into the arms of toxic leaders, who promise to keep us safe as long as we enlist in their crusade. All they require is dutiful compliance with their dictates, even when they cross the ethical line or push us into immoral or illegal jeopardy.

Driven by existential anxiety, we find leaders garbed as omnipotent saviors quite irresistible. When such leaders temporarily fulfill our needs, we easily succumb, as Meindl (1995) noted, to the "romance of leadership." Oblivious to more complex and subtle contributing forces, we tend to attribute the outcome solely to the leader.

Toxic leaders speak with reassuring certainty, be it of the enemy's (i.e., the "Other's") hidden weapons of mass destruction or the culpability of parties whose guilt remains unproven. Only later—often when it is too late—do we realize we've been deluded, though, perhaps, we wouldn't have rejected that leader even if we had known in time.

With existential anxiety ticking at our core, the illusion of certainty helps us forget our appointment in Samarra.[6] The leader, we tell ourselves, knows things that we don't know. We can count on our great leader—even when we can't count on ourselves—to deal with the uncertainties of human existence.

Opportunities for Heroism in an Unfinished World

Second, unlike most species, we humans are acutely aware of the immense heroic challenges that beckon us in this unfinished world. Out there, we see diseases to conquer, planets to explore, artistic heights to climb, and countless other challenges calling us to glory.

The illusions toxic leaders feed us promise that we can transcend death through dazzling achievements. The goals such leaders set for us are a vital part of their own august illusions. Toxic leaders are commonly in search of some unrealistic nirvana, an unattainable holy grail. Most often, their vision is designed to enhance the leader's "chosen" group and eliminate the "Other," the "evil ones," the "infidels," or simply the "competition." Too often their grandiose illusions entail harming others, rather than bringing out the best in their followers and/or improving the lot of some deprived or diminished group. Their invitation to immortality is often too tempting for followers to resist.

Tied to our yearning for immortality, these tantalizing opportunities prompt us to strive for superhuman accomplishments. Those heroic deeds, we hope, will leave our image stamped indelibly on the minds of generations yet unborn. For, as Napoleon understood, "There is no immortality except the memories left in the minds of men." By creating a heroic after-image, we manage to cheat death, if only symbolically.

Thus, leaders who identify enterprises aglitter with glorious—sometimes vainglorious—possibilities have great appeal. There are many leaders, toxic and otherwise, who offer such enticements. So, how are followers to recognize when a toxic leader's grandiose illusions are simply masquerading as noble visions? Distinguishing between the difficult, but achievable, noble dreams of positive leaders (like those of civil rights leader Martin Luther King, Jr.), dreams that can enhance the world without hurting others, and the formidable, unattainable, destructive illusions of toxic leaders is a serious and subtle task (Lipman-Blumen, 2005a).[7]

Constructive visions can make us aspire to previously unimaginable heights, from outstanding feats of athletic prowess, creativity, intelligence, and altruism to military brilliance and bravery. And although many of those efforts may represent our unconscious strivings to control our world and thwart death, great good to humankind frequently derives from such endeavors. By contrast, the overblown visions of toxic leaders promise us greatness at an immense cost to others and often to ourselves as well. They characteristically lead to harm and destruction—often in the name of some higher force (see Lipman-Blumen, 2005b).

Exhilaration, Desolation, and Meaning

Heroic success exhilarates us. In the name of a glorious cause, even near misses can be elating. Perhaps it is the very process of responding to a heroic challenge that provokes our exhilaration. Yet, the joy of our triumphs cannot stifle the desolation unleashed by our awareness of inescapable death. The need to reconcile these antithetical forces evokes enormous tension. It is from this wellspring of tension that our expectations for ourselves, as well as for our leaders, flow. In fact, the urgency to resolve these existential contradictions molds followers' behavior, particularly their willingness to put themselves at the mercy of a toxic leader's flamboyant illusions.

The existential riddle bedevils us: How are we to make sense of this mind and body that grow from dependent infancy to powerful, independent adulthood, capable of extraordinary accomplishments, only to be reduced ultimately to dust? That is exactly where leaders can make a difference.

Constructive leaders ask us to engage in the Herculean work of decoding the complex purposes of life writ large. They also urge us to ponder the meaning of our own existence, our successes and failures, our triumphs and tragedies. Some constructive leaders labor alongside us, helping to decipher and integrate contradictory meanings, meanings that grow even more complex as the challenges of one era recede and those of a new historical moment emerge. Others leave the task of adapting to new challenges to us, while they simply provide a safe "holding environment" for our work (Heifetz, 1994). In so doing, constructive leaders help us to bear the unbearable, but the burden remains our own.

Toxic leaders, on the other hand, make it easy for us, providing extravagant, simplistic, answers, like the glory of a Thousand Year Reich or the purification of the world contaminated by the evil "Other." They goad us to strive for unattainable grails, like Mao Tse Tung's elusive Seven-Year Plans and his death-dealing Cultural Revolution.

On a far different scale, the leaders of Enron Corporation promoted their own alluring vision. They assured their employees that Enron's unique "new business model," secretly bolstered by complex and fraudulent financial practices, would change the world. According to the Enron vision, only the weak-kneed "losers," who were "downsized" each quarter, were not up for the glorious competitive battle. The illusion was intoxicating.[8]

The meanings toxic leaders put forward are laced too often with misperceptions and misdiagnoses. They tend to mistake evil acts for glorious enterprises achieved through moral virtue. They may even portray their immoral, destructive, or downright evil enterprise as a gallant, self-sacrificial act on their own and their followers' part.

Moreover, toxic leaders commonly misconstrue moral virtue for human weakness. Those who protest their destructive schemes they denigrate as "cowards." A case in point: SS leader Heinrich Himmler's speech to his troops, thanking them for "shouldering the terrible but unavoidable task of exterminating millions of people" (Hankiss, 2001; Mitscherlich & Mitscherlich, 1975). Himmler assured his troops,

> Most of you will know what it means to have 100 or 500 or 1000 corpses lie before you. That we have endured this has hardened us, and—with a few exceptions of human frailty—we remained decent. It is a victorious page in our history that has never been and never will be written.

The meaning of life and of our own lives, in particular, is usually complex and most often unclear. Sometimes, the real meaning is too painful to confront. So, leaders of any stripe who offer to help us discern the significance of our existential journey are welcome. The problem, however, remains: how to recognize and avoid those toxic leaders who seize upon our search for meaning as an opportunity to ensnare us in their destructive undertakings.

ORGANIZATIONAL AND INDIVIDUAL OPTIONS

We are not powerless against toxic leaders unless we define ourselves as such and by so doing create a self-fulfilling prophecy. There are both organizational and individual strategies and solutions that we can devise to protect ourselves and the institutions we value against toxic leadership.

Organizational Policies

On the group and organizational level, we can create various bulwarks against installing and sustaining toxic leaders. Revising and creating new organizational policies to safeguard us against the inclusion and tolerance of toxic leaders begins with a strong screening and selection process. "Outing" a toxic leader before that individual enters the organization—through serious and widespread due diligence—is far easier than ousting that individual after he or she has gained an official, inside foothold. Checking with the widest network of the candidate's former associates and colleagues is a *sine qua non* for selecting a nontoxic leader. During the selection process, exposing that individual to members at every level of the organization, from vice presidents to support staff, and giving serious consideration to all interviewers' concerns are steps in the right direction.

Once on board, the leader must be held to account. This requires an organization whose culture demands transparency and accountability. The Sarbanes-Oxley Act of 2002 is a welcome beginning, but it is not the whole answer.

Infringements on accountability should be curtailed when they first appear. Various accountability mechanisms, such as regular "town meetings," in which the leader holds periodic open forums for the most diverse internal audience, promote openness, integrity, and responsibility. A formal annual review by the board, which considers the results of a written, anonymous survey of both internal members of the organization and a sample of various external constituencies, will provide an early detection system for symptoms of developing toxicity.

Reasonable term limits and respectable departure options, such as a transition year as organizational historian before returning to the ranks or permanently leaving the organization, can help to prevent leaders, even the good ones, from digging in for the permanent haul. Open channels of communication between organizational members and oversight groups, including the board, can keep a leader from straying down the toxic road. Whistleblower protections need to be strengthened and implemented.

These and many other organizational policies and mechanisms, beyond the scope of this chapter, represent insurance against many toxic maladies, from creeping cronyism and corruption to flagrant fraud. They can help to identify and curtail toxic leadership in the making and toxic leaders on the make.

Individual Strategies

On an individual level, we can call upon our enduring ambivalence to authority figures and other strengthening aspects from our personal upbringing and education to move us to action. Doing our homework by testing our own perceptions of the leader's toxicity against the view of other, more experienced, and widely respected colleagues is essential. If we find that others share our concerns, we can seek out compatriots and form coalitions to set limits on toxic leaders. Opinion leaders, along with a small set of respected supporters, can bring their concerns to the leader and propose a plan for addressing nascent problems that stem from incipient or later-stage toxic leadership.

Many toxic leaders, however, do not recognize their own toxicity. Thus, they are not particularly amenable to being counseled, particularly by people they perceive to be their followers. Attempts to confront or counsel a toxic leader are best undertaken with knowledgeable others. Working with like-minded colleagues is a stronger and safer way to approach toxic leaders, who often are quite adept at picking off "lone rangers," who challenge them single-handedly.

If the toxic leader resists complaints and rejects offers of coaching, then taking the message to higher levels within the organization may be the next step. The board may be the only group with sufficient clout to demand the leader undertake professional coaching or counseling. Clearly, when the leader's behavior breaches legal barriers, reporting illegal activities to appropriate authorities is mandatory.

One last-ditch measure to rid an organization of a toxic leader, whose egregious ineptitude, unethical behavior, and/or illegal acts are undermining the organization, involves enlisting the media. This is a difficult and potentially dangerous alternative, since the media often have their own agendas, which may not coincide with the protestors' or the organization's. Still, media attention has helped to unseat seemingly unassailable CEOs and leaders in diverse organizations, in various arenas. Witness the role of the media in toppling unethical and criminal leaders at Enron, as well as the inept and heavy-handed president at Harvard.

But there is still more difficult and preventive work that each and every one of us who follows a leader must shoulder. Taken together, our very human psychological needs and existential anxiety expose our Achilles' heel to toxic leaders. Meindl's (1995) basic insight about the "romance of leadership" is a powerful key for unlocking the mystery surrounding this fatal attraction. It serves as a serious warning for followers to look more deeply into their own suppressed fears and longings.

As followers or constituents, we must not fail to address at least two critical personal tasks. First, we need to search within ourselves, not look to leaders and others, for the meaning of our lives. That meaning develops through the choices that we make and the behaviors that we enact. Taking responsibility for our decisions and actions is the most direct route for establishing and savoring the meaning of our personal journey.

Second, as Søren Kirkegaard (1843/1985) reminded us, to deal with our existential fears and dread, as well as our profound psychological needs, we must raise them to a level of consciousness where we can confront and work to understand them. Once we confront those buried concerns, we can see them for what they are and deprive them of their hidden hold on us. Then, perhaps, we may engage them as midwife to our creativity. Finally, we may learn to use our anxieties and human needs as a "call to being," even as a way of dealing with the fundamental vulnerability of being alive (Delumeau, 1990).

NOTES

1.   The marble sculpture, carved 1501–1504, stands in the Galleria dell'Accademia, Florence, Italy.

2.   Micromanipulation is "the art of influence at the interpersonal level. From necessity, the powerless use micromanipulation, while the powerful engage in macromanipulation, the process of influence at the societal or social policy level."

3.   The notion of the "chosen" versus the "Other " described in this chapter, while bearing superficial similarity to leader–member–exchange (LMX) theory, departs from this "mainstream" leadership conception in certain critical ways. For example, in the "chosen versus 'Other'" paradigm, one is selected on the categorical basis of a single dimension of one's identity, rather than on the basis of an individual assessment of the "chosen" in terms of multiple dimensions, such as his or her personal abilities, talents, and usefulness to the leader. Second, in the "chosen versus 'Other'" framework, there is no necessary personal or individual relationship between the members of these groups and the leader. Third, there is no negotiation for selection. Nor is there an interactive process of role taking, role making, or routinization of the relationship between individual members of the "chosen" and the leader. While admission into the "in-group" may, indeed, operate in terms of the LMX theory, the "chosen versus 'Other'" theoretical perspective refers to a more truncated, impersonal process, a process by which whole groups of individuals—not specific individuals—are categorized as acceptable or unacceptable, sacred or defiling.

4. Nonetheless, there could be no absolute certainty as to which fate any particular individual had been assigned. Consequently, the need for certainty that one had been chosen for salvation led to various efforts to quell the doubt (that) *"remained in the background and had to be silenced again and again by an ever-growing fanatic belief that the religious community to which one belonged represented that part of mankind which had been chosen by God"* (Fromm, 1941, p. 108). One's actions could not influence one's fate. Nonetheless, according to Calvinist teaching, tireless and successful moral and secular action was interpreted as a sign that one was, indeed, among the "chosen."

5. By 1996, there were 31,000 gangs and 846,000 members in the United States, according to the U.S. Department of Juvenile Justice and Delinquency Prevention.

6. W. Somerset Maugham, in 1933, retold the fable about the servant who sought to elude Death, whom he had glimpsed in a Baghdad marketplace, by borrowing his master's horse to ride to Samarra. What the servant did not understand, however, was that Death planned to meet him later that evening at an "appointment in Samarra."

7. And, of course, we must realize that, because each historical era is bound by its own limitations—technological, scientific, physical, and artistic—even the most truly noble visions may be unimplementable at a given moment in time—like human flight in the era of Icarus.

8. The medieval Latin derivation suggests that "intoxicating" stems from the same root as "toxic," meaning "to smear with poison."

REFERENCES

Alford, C. F. (2001). *Whistleblowers: Broken lives and organizational power.* Ithaca, NY: Cornell University Press.

Asch, S. E. (1956). Studies on independence and conformity: A minority of one against a unanimous majority. *Psychological Monographs, 70*(9).

Asch, S. E. (1972). Group forces in the modification and distortion of judgments. In E. P. Hollander & R. G. Hunt (Eds.), *Classic contributions to social psychology* (pp. 330–39). New York: Oxford University Press.

Becker, E. (1973). *The denial of death.* New York: Basic Books.

Brownstein, R. (2006, January 27). Bush's ratings sink, but trust remains. *Los Angeles Times,* pp. 26–27.

de Beauvoir, S. (1953). *The second sex.* New York: Knopf.

Delumeau, J. (1990). *Sin and fear: The emergence of a Western guilt culture, 13th–18th centuries.* New York: St. Martin's Press.

Fromm, E. (1941). *Escape from freedom.* New York: Avon Books.

Heifetz, R. A. (1994). *Leadership without easy answers.* Cambridge, MA: Belknap.

Hankiss, E. (2001). *Fears and symbols: An introduction to the study of Western civilization.* Budapest: Central European University Press.

Howell, J. C. (1998, August). Youth gangs: An overview. *Juvenile Justice Bulletin.* Washington, DC: U.S. Department of Justice, Office of Justice Programs, Office of Juvenile Justice and Delinquency Prevention.

Kierkegaard, S. (1985). *Fear and trembling: Dialectical lyric by Johannes de Silentio.* London: Penguin. (Original work published 1843)

Le Bon, G. (2002). *The crowd: A study of the popular mind.* Mineola, NY: Dover Publications. (Original work published 1895)

Lipman-Blumen, J. (1984). *Gender roles and power.* Englewood Cliffs, NY: Prentice-Hall.

Lipman-Blumen, J. (1992). Connective leadership: Female leadership styles in the 21st-century workplace. *Sociological Perspectives, 35*(1), 183–203.

Lipman-Blumen, J. (2005a). *The allure of toxic leaders: Why we follow destructive bosses and corrupt politicians—and how we can survive them.* New York: Oxford University Press.

Lipman-Blumen, J. (2005b, Spring). Toxic leadership: When grand illusions masquerade as noble visions. *Leader to Leader, 36,* 29–36.

Marcus, B. (2006, February 12). Enigma machines. *New York Times Book Review,* p. 10.

Meindl, J. R. (1995). The romance of leadership as a follower-centric theory: A social constructionist approach. *Leadership Quarterly, 6*(3), 329–341.

Milgram, S. (1974). *Obedience to authority: An experimental view.* New York: Harper & Row.

Mitscherlich, A., & Mitscherlich, M. (1975). *The inability to mourn* (Beverley R. Placzek, Trans.). New York: Grove.

Sen, A. (2005, April 16). *Identity and violence: The illusion of destiny.* Keynote address, Harvard Alumni Day, Cambridge, MA.

Sherif, M. (1972). Experiments on norm formation. In E. P. Hollander & R. G. Hunt (Eds.), *Classic contributions to social psychology* (pp. 320–329). New York: Oxford University Press.

CHAPTER 2

IMPLICIT LEADERSHIP THEORIES AS DYNAMIC PROCESSING STRUCTURES

Megan E. Medvedeff and Robert G. Lord
University of Akron

ABSTRACT

Research on implicit leadership theories developed from Rosch's (1978) ideas on the function and structure of cognitive categories and has been very successful in specifying the content of categories that define leadership. It has also explained leadership perceptions in terms of the match of perceived characteristics to category prototypes held by perceivers and identified the consequences of categorization for understanding leadership perceptions. Although this line of research has been very successful, there are important developments in the field of cognitive science that can be used to better understand why the use of cognitive categories is necessary for perceivers to interpret sensory input. This chapter describes these developments in cognitive science and shows their relevance to understanding the processes involved in the development and use of leadership schema. This approach will allow the development of a more dynamic perspective, including the role of affect and an understanding of how leadership schemas can be both stable over time and flexible across situations.

Follower-Centered Perspectives on Leadership, pages 19–50

It is widely recognized that schemas have a pervasive effect on social perceptions such as leadership (Fiske & Taylor, 1991; Kunda, 1999; Lord &
Maher, 1991) as well as on other types of organizational sensemaking
(Gioia & Poole, 1984; Weick, 1995). Such thinking has emphasized the role
of perceivers in social perception processes. For example, Meindl (1995)
maintains that leadership is a follower-centered process such that leadership is in the eye of the beholder as well as reflecting patterns of leader
trait and characteristics (Judge, Bono, Ilies, & Gerhardt, 2002; Lord,
DeVader, & Alliger, 1986). The importance of these follower-centered view-
points has recently been noted by Epitropaki and Martin (2004, 2005) who
found that cognitive schemas pertaining to leadership are relatively stable
and have important consequences for understanding the development of
dyadic-level processes related to the quality of leader–member exchanges
and broader attitudes toward organizations. As their work illustrates, schemas are important cognitive structures that guide social perceptions, social
behavior, and the development of social relationships, often operating
implicitly outside of a perceiver's awareness.

The focus of this chapter is on schema related to leadership, which have
been examined relatively extensively over the last 25 years by research
focusing on implicit leadership theories (e.g., Engle & Lord, 1997; Epitropaki & Martin, 2004, 2005; Lord & Maher, 1991; Offermann, Kennedy,
&Wirtz, 1994). This research developed from Rosch's (1978) ideas on the
function and structure of cognitive categories, suggesting that implicit
leadership theories reflect the normal use of cognitive categories to assimi-
late leadership information. Such research has been very successful in
specifying the content of categories that define leadership, explaining
leadership perceptions in terms of the match of perceived characteristics
to category prototypes held by perceivers, and showing the consequences
of categorization for understanding leadership perceptions and the assimi-
lation of information related to leadership. This approach is consistent
with Meindl's (1995) emphasis on follower's social-cognitive processes as
providing a crucial component in understanding leadership perceptions.
Although this line of research has been very productive, we believe that
there are important developments in the field of cognitive science that can
be used to better understand why the use of cognitive categories is necessary for perceivers to interpret sensory input.

The goal of this chapter is to describe these developments in cognitive
science and show their relevance to understanding the processes involved
in the development and use of leadership schema. Prior research has
focused largely on the content of leadership schema; however, this chapter
focuses on more general processes related to categorization and perception. This approach facilitates the development of a more dynamic perspective, which allows us to see how leadership schemas can be both stable

over time and flexible across situations. It also allows us to include the role of affect as an important component of dynamic processes.

This chapter is organized in the following manner: We first begin with a general overview of categorization theory and the role of categorization in organizational sensemaking. Next, we introduce implicit leadership theories (ILTs) and highlight the strengths and weaknesses of taking a categorical approach to conceptualizing ILTs. Then, we discuss dynamic aspects of ILTs, specifically addressing affective influences and the implications of recent advances in cognitive science. Finally, we show how these fresh perspectives can be incorporated into our understanding of leadership perceptions.

COGNITIVE CATEGORIES

Categorization is vital to human thought and behavior. Applying categories to the world, as we experience it, allows us to determine the meaning that we ultimately extract from it. Everything we experience is at least partially colored by our mental representations and expectations (Johnson-Laird, 1989; Meindl, 1995). This coloring of perceptions through categorization simplifies information processing by allowing us to treat many categorized stimuli as equivalent. It also helps us link perceptual stimuli, such as a current leader, with information about category members assimilated from prior experience with many leaders. Such simplification allows us to easily make attributions, facilitates appropriate responses and behaviors, promotes effective communication, and provides organization to memory, but it can also misrepresent some information (Kunda, 1999; Moskowitz, 2005). Categorization processes are needed because we cannot encode and store all aspects of incoming stimuli that we experience in our environments. Human information processing, including memory and attentional resources, are limited. Thus, stimuli and experiences are encoded with the help of cognitive simplifying mechanisms such as categories (Lord & Maher, 1991; Macrae, Milne, & Bodenhausen, 1994).

Categories are cognitive structures that represent knowledge about a stimulus (e.g., automobiles, leadership) and its attributes (Fiske, 1995). Cognitive categories have been referred to by many names, including schema, stereotypes, concepts, and scripts, although some of these labels are based on specific assumptions about the content or structure of that category. Regardless of the label, these mental representations serve as classification tools that guide perceivers' subsequent interpretations and allow them to extract meaning from the surrounding world (Kunda, 1999; Moskowitz, 2005; Rosch, 1978). To better understand how categories affect social information processing, it is helpful to examine how categories are structured.

Category Structure

Categories are organized into hierarchical networks, with the most specific members at the bottom, and the broader, more abstract members at higher levels (Lord & Maher, 1991). Rosch (1978) organizes categories into a three-level hierarchy of superordinate, basic, and subordinate categories that vary in abstractness, inclusiveness, and number of features. For example, in discussing leadership, the most abstract, *superordinate level* categorization would differentiate between leaders and nonleaders. According to Rosch, *basic level* categorization is the most inclusive level at which objects share many common attributes that are distinct from the attributes of other basic level categories. This is also the highest level in which one can create an image that would represent the entire category (Kunda, 1999). According to Lord, Foti, and De Vader (1984), basic level leadership categories include leaders in specific contexts (e.g., political leader, business leader, etc.). At the lowest, *subordinate level* categorization, we break specific contexts down even further. For example, we may categorize a political leader as either liberal or conservative or we may distinguish among hierarchical level (e.g., national presidents, state governors, city mayors).

Perceivers categorize social stimuli to simplify information processing and conserve cognitive resources (Macrae et al., 1994). That is, members of a category are treated as being equivalent for encoding and retrieval purposes. For example, when we classify a person as a leader, we assume they have the characteristics that are typical of leaders (Lord, Foti, & Phillips, 1982). Cantor and Mischel (1979) demonstrated that social categories and concepts could also be organized along a hierarchy with differing levels of abstraction. As we move into social contexts, we need to examine not only independent hierarchies, but also how independent hierarchies work together because social hierarchies often have fuzzy boundaries and do not fit neatly into mutually exclusive hierarchies (Rosch, 1978). A key insight provided by Rosch's theory was that although fuzzy at their boundaries, cognitive categories were well defined in their most typical instances by common prototypes of category members. *Prototypes* are abstract sets of features that are widely shared by category members. They serve as proxies for more detailed information when new stimuli are categorized.

Category-Based Information Processing

Gilbert, Pelham, and Krull (1988) suggested that the processes underlying the perception of others and their behavior, which is of importance for understanding leadership perceptions, involve three stages: *categorization* of the behavior, *characterization* of the person, and *correction* of the character-ization by accounting for situational constraints. It was assumed that cate-gorization and characterization were relatively automatic processes that allow the perceiver to make inferences of other's dispositions based on the observed behavior. Correction is more controlled, requiring attention and cognitive resources to make allowances for the situation. Thus, people make dispositional attributions and characterize others in a relatively auto-matic manner. Such reasoning is very consistent with Meindl's (1990) argu-ment that perceivers have romanticized views of leadership that overemphasize the causal role of leaders. Furthermore, they rely on these romanticized views rather than carefully analyzing causality in inferring leadership. Gilbert, however, recognizes that more careful causal reasoning may be involved in social perceptions. Specifically, he maintains that under certain circumstances (e.g., low cognitive load) people are able to correct those characterizations based on situational constraints (for a review, see Gilbert, 1989). The ability to correct is an important function in the need for category flexibility. That is, categorization and causal attributions may undergo dynamic changes based on situational constraints while maintain-ing a stable structure.

Smith and Miller (1983) provided support for a two-stage model of causal attributions, where input is processed by making use of previous schema and tentative, schema-based judgments regarding causality. The causal information is thus stored in memory along with a representation of the input pattern. This material is then readily available for retrieval if asked or if needed to mediate additional inferences. Thus, Smith and Miller dem-onstrated that previously experienced behavior and schema are used as interpretive cues to make inferences regarding future behavior. In line with our argument in respect to leadership perceptions, stored leadership schema plus causal attributions contribute to perceptions of leadership.

Lord, Brown, Harvey, and Hall (2001) argue that category, or schema, activation can be understood in terms of neural networks. These networks allow us to define leadership (or any other category) as a whole, based on a pattern of characteristics, and they can account for the processes outlined by Gilbert (1989) and Smith and Miller (1983). Following this argument, a *schema* is composed of a large number of interconnected traits that form a mutually activating (recurrent) network (Smith, 1996). These intercon-nected units receive information not only from behavioral input and per-son perceptions, but also from higher order contextual constraints, such as values and affect. In terms of leadership perceptions, culture, the leader, and the follower serve to constrain the activation of a leadership schema in a particular context.

An input pattern causes activation in the interconnected units which continue to activate each other. The amount of activation (or inhibition) flowing between various constraints and units is determined by weights connecting units. Weights are critical features of the network as they allow information to be recreated in a context-sensitive way based on differing patterns of input. That is, stability in categories comes from the weights, which are slowly learned through experience and thus are resistant to change, and flexibility comes from the situational sensitivity of different input patterns or behaviors. Flexibility occurs because as networks become activated, stable levels of activation develop that optimize the fit between behavioral inputs, higher-order constraints, and unit connections. This dynamic, settling-in process creates a stable state that is called an *attractor*, which also corresponds to a mental unit such as a prototype. (Attractors will be discussed in greater depth in a later section of this chapter.) Through such dynamics, leader behavior is inherently linked to perceiver's schema, values, and self-concept (Lord & Brown, 2004).

This brief introduction to neural networks helps us to understand spontaneous trait inferences. Spontaneous trait inferences occur when we infer the dispositional characteristics of others by observing their behavior, without any awareness or intention to make such inferences (for a review, see Uleman, Newman, & Moskowitz, 1996). In such cases, the inferred traits may or may not be true descriptions of others' dispositions, but they serve as an interpretive guide for the others' behavior (Van Overwalle, Drenth, & Marsman, 1999). In terms of the connectionist process, spontaneous trait inferences allow us to fill in the gaps in our perceptions with related information. When a specific pattern of input is activated in a recurrent network, all interrelated units are activated as well. This leads to the activation of multiple traits, some of which were not present in the initial behavioral input. Thus, related traits are inferred based on the pattern of activation across the network. Based on our previous overview of categories, we now move into the specific category of interest: implicit leadership theories.

CATEGORIES AND LEADERSHIP: IMPLICIT LEADERSHIP THEORIES

As already mentioned, categories can be applied to a multiplicity of objects and social processes, which includes leadership. Based on the work of Lord and colleagues (Lord et al., 1982, 1984; Lord & Maher, 1991), a *recognition-based theory* of leadership perceptions developed, which maintained that leaders were recognized as leaders in the same manner that we recognize a bird as a bird or a table as a table. Thus, leadership perception is a perceptual process whereby stimuli can be mapped into classifications (e.g., leader vs. nonleader) that can be treated equivalently. Leadership classification is often based on the degree of match of a target stimulus to a previously learned prototype that defines a particular leadership category. This matching process involves processing an entire set of features or a Gestalt, rather than independently evaluating individual features (Smith & Foti, 1998). When a match occurs, the leadership prototype is activated (Fischbein, 2005). For example, Phillips and Lord (1982) argued that once someone has been characterized as a leader, the activated leader prototype causes followers to selectively attend to, encode, and retrieve information consistent with this categorization, and to provide consistent information when such information is not available. This type of leadership recognition process tends to be automatic, depends on exposure to the behaviors of others and on preexisting knowledge about leadership, and it closely reflects Rosch's (1978) original ideas about categorization.

According to Lord and Maher (1991), leadership perceptions can also be based on an *inference process*, in which perceivers reverse their functional understanding of leadership (i.e., leadership causes good performance) to work backward from performance knowledge to infer whether leadership has occurred. A critical aspect of this inferential process is the assessment that leaders had a causal impact on performance (Murphy & Jones, 1993). Furthermore, inferential processes also require that perceivers generalize from their causal analysis of a specific outcome to infer that it was produced by dispositional aspects of the leader (Ensari & Murphy, 2003). Thus, leadership inferences may often reflect fundamental attribution errors (Ross, 1977), which involve the general tendency to make dispositional inferences from very limited information. Such attributional reasoning, while technically an error, allows perceivers to make sense of outcomes or behaviors by classifying the social actor as being a particular type of person who has a known pattern of traits and can produce specific types of outcomes. Thus, such inferential categorization allows for the application of general knowledge about leadership to understand specific outcomes, and it is consistent with romanticized views of leaders (Meindl, 1995), which overemphasize a leader's causal impact. Early research on leadership inferences maintained that such reasoning was guided by perceiver's implicit leadership theories.

Implicit leadership theories (ILTs) involve both knowledge of leadership categories and the functional relation of category attributes to outcomes such as good performance. Thus, they pertain to both recognition and inferential leadership perceptions. Rosch (1978) recognized that categories had both sets of defining attributes and functions associated with them (e.g., chairs have legs and seats, and we can sit on them.) Thus, ILTs are knowledge structures that guide sensemaking as well as form a basis for leadership perceptions (Engle & Lord, 1997; Epitropaki & Martin, 2004). Studies of ILTs have examined both how perceivers make inferences from outcomes and the underlying structure of leadership categories. Meindl

(1995; Meindl, Ehrlich, & Dukerich, 1985) made a particularly important contribution by emphasizing that perceivers actively construct these explanations and that there are individual differences in the tendency to see leaders as a potent causal explanation for organizational outcomes. Although ILTs help us to make inferences and judgments, they also impose constraints on one's ability to correct or modify these inferences. This is because sensemaking is often based on automatic processes that occur outside of awareness, and thus they cannot be directly reversed. In addition, once perceivers classify a social actor as being a leader, either through inferential or recognition-based processes, they have activated a category structure and associated knowledge that automatically guides subsequent thinking.

Structure of Implicit Leadership Theories

We argue that leadership is a cognitive category that is hierarchically organized and contains trait-based prototypes used in comparison of observed behavior to ILTs. At the superordinate, or most abstract, level of categorization, leaders and nonleaders are differentiated based on a general prototype. Lord and his colleagues proposed 11 different contexts, or basic level categories, to further distinguish leaders. These contexts include military, education, business, religious, minority, finance, labor, media, national politics, world politics, and sports and consist of many traits (subordinate categorization) unique to each context. Although each of the 11 contexts share general aspects of leadership (e.g., intelligence; Lord et al., 1984), many of the traits required to be perceived as a religious leader differ from the traits perceived for a leader in the military. Offermann and colleagues (1994) conducted an extensive investigation of how undergraduate subjects and full-time workers described leaders in an attempt to get at the underlying dimensionality of ILTs. Their results were generally consistent with the findings of Lord and colleagues (1984), suggesting a general stability in content imposed on ILTs. Offermann and colleagues identified eight underlying dimensions of ILTs, which include sensitivity, dedication, tyranny, charisma, attractiveness, masculinity, intelligence, and strength.

Epitropaki and Martin (2004) sought to explain whether ILTs remain stable or change over time. By examining the content of ILTs from the same sample measured at two separate time periods, they found support for their schema stability hypothesis, as ILTs remained stable for up to 1 year. This result is consistent with prior research that found that schemas are resistant to change unless the environment is dramatically altered.

Epitropaki and Martin's research reflects a concern with more dynamic processes associated with ILTs. We have addressed this issue as well, revising our notion of what categories are to reflect recent thinking, which represents category prototypes (and stereotypes) in terms of a stable pattern created by the interaction of units in neural networks (Kunda & Thagard, 1996; Smith, 1996).

However, connectionist models (for a review, see Bechtel & Abrahamsen, 2002) argue that change can occur when the context changes. Using a connectionist model, Lord and colleagues (2001) argued that leadership prototypes are actually recreated each time they are used, rather than stored and retrieved intact from long-term memory. Thus, not only is leadership a social construction of perceivers (Meindl, 1995), the actual prototypes used to guide leadership perceptions are also constructed by perceivers at the time of use. This recreation of schemas allows these cognitive structures to be situationally sensitive. Different patterns of stimuli or observed behavior activate different aspects of ILTs (seen in different patterns of activation across the network). Following from Epitropaki and Martin's (2004, 2005) argument, the content or defining traits of ILTs may remain stable, but the structure activated when ILTs are used, as suggested by connectionist models, allows for flexibility in the application of ILTs to various person stimuli. It is obvious that ILTs are more dynamic than suggested by categorization theory and in the next section we suggest how emotions can influence these dynamics.

EMOTIONS AND DYNAMIC PROCESSES

Two weaknesses of categorization theory are that (1) it is overly cognitive and tends to ignore emotional components that are important in leadership, and (2) it does not have dynamic qualities that explain how leadership perceptions can change over time or across situations. Both of these concerns are addressed in this section.

The Role of Emotions in Leadership Perceptions

Although emotions have been recognized as being an important part of reactions to leaders and an integral part of leadership and leadership processes (Brown & Keeping, 2005; Cherulnick, Donley, Wiewel, & Miller, 2001; Kellett, Humphrey, & Sleeth, 2002; Lord & Brown, 2004; Meindl, 1995), emotions have not been fully integrated into the conceptual basis of categorization theory. This is largely because theories in cognitive science ignore the role of emotions, and the leadership perception processes have been seen as primarily cognitive. However, this situation is changing in a fundamental way as social cognitive theory has begun to recognize that social cognitions are highly dependent on many aspects of perceivers such as sensory, emotional, and motor reactions to social stimuli.

Recent research (Barrett, Niedenthal, & Winkielman, 2005; Niedenthal, Barsalou, Winkielman, Karuth-Gruber, & Ric, 2005) maintains that rather than being stored as highly abstract, amodal constructs, most knowledge is represented in a manner that is highly dependent on modality-specific systems in perceivers. Modality-specific systems are heavily interconnected regions of the brain that coordinate to create a specific experience (e.g., perception, introspection, motor movements). Not only is such sensory information closely related to reactions triggered by the encoding context, these modality-specific reactions are stored and later are partially simulated when the construct is accessed. For example, when thinking about an individual who previously made one angry, physiological and emotional reactions that occurred in response to that individual are partially reactivated, comprising a fundamental aspect of the meaning that we have constructed. Thus, cognitions are generally embodied in that they reflect the modality-specific systems of perceivers.

Furthermore, these embodiments occur "online" as the social stimulus is initially perceived, and "offline" as one later recreates perceptions as part of a reflective process. The importance of sensory processes associated with visual perceptions to constructs such as leadership perceptions, is nicely illustrated by a study conducted by Phillips and Lord (1982). This study concerned causal attributions and their effect on leadership processes, finding that group performance information had a greater effect on leadership perceptions when the potential leader was seen as being causally responsible. Causal attributions were manipulated by changing the camera angle used to videotape the stimulus material so as to make the potential leader either more or less central in the visual field, and consequently more or less salient as a social stimulus. Although the same information was available in high and low salience conditions, its effect on perceiver's leadership and causal attribution ratings differed dramatically. Both causal attributions and leadership ratings were substantially higher in the high versus low salience condition. In addition to its effect through causal attributions, perceptual salience had a strong direct effect on leadership perceptions, a result implying that visually based sensory perceptions were an important component of the leadership perception process. These results are not explainable without recognizing the role of perceptual salience because the same verbal and expressive behavior was clearly visible and audible in both the high and low salience conditions, which were actually taped concurrently.

The results of Phillips and Lord (1982) might be thought of as being online because ratings of leadership and causal attribution ratings were made immediately after viewing the stimuli. The potential for offline embodiment effects are shown in a series of studies (Naidoo, Walters, Lord, & Dubois, 2005) that looked at the role of visualization processes on emotional reactions and leadership perceptions. In these studies, we argued that typical questionnaire measures of leadership often underestimated the importance of emotions in leadership processes because they provide very abstract, verbally based questionnaire items as rating prompts. In contrast, most actual leadership situations involve real leaders that provide much richer stimuli for perceivers. Real leaders provide dynamic visual and auditory stimuli, as well as internal stimuli including perceivers' hopes and fears that are elicited by the leader.

In an attempt to provide a richer source of stimuli associated with offline embodiment when previous leaders were rated, the Naidoo and colleagues (2005) study had subjects in an experimental condition perform a visualization exercise before they made leadership ratings. Specifically, they asked subjects to imagine that their leader was in the room with them, and they asked them to think of how the leader looked, what the leader sounded like, and how the subjects would actually feel in the presence of their leader. They also measured subjects' current emotional state using the Positive and Negative Affect Schedule (PANAS; Watson, Clark, & Tellegen, 1988). Using this procedure, the first study of Naidoo and colleagues had subjects rate their actual work supervisor, and found that emotions were a much more central component of ratings when they first visualized their leader.

Their second study had subjects view a 13-minute, professionally developed videotape of a military event or read a transcript of that event. Subjects then made leadership and PANAS ratings immediately after watching this video, and again after a 3-week delay. Prior to making the delayed ratings, half of the subjects performed the visualization exercise previously described.

Visualization had three important effects. First, ratings of current positive and negative affect at the second rating period were more strongly related to the original leadership ratings in the leader visualization condition. Second, emotions measured at the second session were more highly related to original emotions in the visualization condition. Third, leadership ratings in the second session were more highly related to original leadership ratings in the leader visualization conditions. In short, as embodiment theories would predict, subjects were capable of reactivating their initial sensory and emotional reactions when asked to, and these reactivated effects not only affect emotions and leadership ratings, they increased the accuracy of memory for prior leadership ratings.

These findings suggest that not only is leadership "in the eye of the beholder" (Meindl, 1995), it is in the body and emotions of the beholder. Moreover, these follower-centered effects are not merely an online reaction to a leader as they are experienced in real time, but they can also be reactivated at a later point in time, providing an important offline component of the leadership process. We should also note that because there are chronic individual differences in affective orientation, the Naidoo and colleagues (2005) study first controlled for these individual differences, and it was affective reactions compared to these baseline differences that were associated with experimental effects. The point in raising this issue is that in any leadership situation, differences in follower reactions that reflect their own chronic emotional tendencies will affect leadership perceptions through such embodied effects. Such differences help explain why the same objective leadership event will have different meanings to different perceivers. It also helps us understand why the same leader may be perceived differently by different subordinates. Specifically, some subordinates like their leader more than other subordinates, and liking has a profound effect on perceptions of leadership (Brown & Keeping, 2005).

Although individual differences in perceiver emotions are an important part of leadership processes, emotions may also reflect reactions to specific events (Weiss & Cropanzano, 1996). Lord and Brown (2004, Chap. 6) proposed that many leadership events are interpreted affectively, and Naidoo and Lord (2004) found that even subliminal affective stimuli presented for very brief periods (30 ms) can influence affect and associated ratings of charismatic leadership. Thus, moment-to-moment dynamics in appraising both situations and leaders may reflect affective reactions, not just as they are processed in abstract, verbal terms, but also in terms of more comprehensive embodied reactions.

ADAPTIVE RESONANCE THEORY AND DYNAMIC PROCESSES

An Introduction to Adaptive Resonance Theory

Grossberg (e.g., 1976, 1999; see also Carpenter & Grossberg, 1985) developed *adaptive resonance theory* (ART) to explain the interaction of top-down and bottom-up processes in processing and perceiving stimuli. ART emphasizes that context is important in perceptual processes, which suggests that leadership perceptions may be explained by this theory. As such, ART can be an important extension for understanding ILTs for many reasons. First, ART offers an explanation as to why categories are necessary to explain leadership. Second, ART suggests that prototypes are learned as a whole, which is consistent with ILT reasoning. Third, ART suggests a specific parameter that helps to explain Rosch's (1978) conceptualization of category hierarchies. Finally, using ART we can explain the stability–plasticity dilemma; that is, why the structure of ILTs stays the same while still allowing for flexibility in application. Before we address each of these issues, let us introduce ART and apply it, albeit generically, to leadership perceptions.

The ART paradigm is consistent with cognitive and behavioral models and uses a combination of feedback and higher-level control to engage in a matching comparison of external stimuli to internal memories or stored representation. ART proposes that all conscious states of the brain are *resonant states* that trigger the learning of cognitive and sensory representations. In its most fundamental form, resonance means causing to be reinforced. Thus, resonant states represent a sustainment of a given stimuli in consciousness. These resonant states of the brain are the results of matching processes that involve mental representations, or top-down inputs, and external stimuli, or bottom-up inputs. The brain matches incoming patterns of context-specific, external stimuli with previously experienced patterns held in long-term memory. When a match exists, relevant information is selectively augmented and brought into working memory, leading to a resonant, activation-sustaining state. In contrast, the activation of irrelevant information that does not match internal schema naturally dissipates or is actively suppressed. According to ART, bidirectional feedback loops create resonant states from congruent top-down and bottom-up information; resonant states last longer, long enough to permit learning, and are more active than states based on either top-down or bottom-up input alone. Figure 2.1 provides a schematic of the dynamic resonant process in ART.

Need for Categories

Taking this first principle of ART and applying it to leadership perceptions, we can begin to understand the dynamic processing aspects of ILTs at a deeper level and why we need categories to guide perception. Individuals hold implicit theories, or assumptions, about how leaders are supposed to behave and these assumptions allow us to experience others' behavior in the moment and retrieve information about that person from past encounters. The implicit theories influence one's perception of, and subsequent behavior toward, potential leaders. In terms of ART, the content and structure of ILT categories and prototypes are mental representations that create top-down expectations. When one encounters a potential leader or is witness to potential leader-like behavior, that external input is encoded as a representation at a preconscious level and combined with previous trait knowledge (e.g., the person was intelligent, decisive, confident). Thus, initial interpretation occurs outside of con-

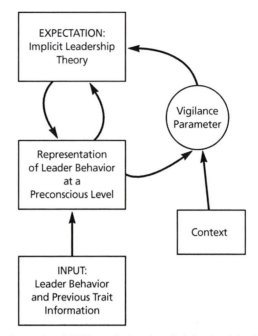

Figure 2.1.   A schematic of ART applied to implicit leadership theories. Modeled after Grossberg (1999, p. 25). As we observe and perceive leader behavior, it is encoded and integrated with any other information we hold about that particular leader as a preconscious level representation. This behavioral representation is matched to our expectations, or ILT. When the representation of behavior matches our ILT, a resonant state occurs, sustaining the representation in memory and allowing us to classify the leader as a leader. The vigilance parameter monitors the matching processes, regulating the stringency of the matching process. The rigidness of the vigilance parameter is influenced by the context and behavioral representation, with a more relaxed vigilance parameter leading to more flexibility in matching behavior and thus, more opportunities for resonance. If the behavioral representation fails to match to our ILT, the entire system resets to either (1) search for another, more suitable expectation or (2) learn a new prototype.

sciousness (Graf & Schacter, 1985). The brain then attempts to match the behavior to previously experienced patterns that are held in long-term memory; these patterns are one's ILTs (see Figure 2.1). If this search ends with a match, the stored representation can incorporate the matched portions of the new stimuli. Thus, snippets of other's behavior that we encounter are automatically compared to our expectations (ILTs) about leader behavior. If there is a match, we can consciously classify that person as a leader based on a global pattern of trait interpretations that resonate with ILTs and use that category accordingly. In other words, the resonance process, which requires that an ILT exist in memory, leads to leadership interpretations.

If, on the other hand, the observed behavior does not match with our ILT, the search results in mismatch. However, this is not the end of the road. According to ART, when a mismatch occurs, the process resets to search for another memory representation or expectation that may fit the observed behavior. In this way, behavior could be categorized into another implicit theory that has nothing to do with leadership. For example, leadership attempts by females are often encoded into gender-based categories rather than leadership categories. This is because of a closer match of the entire stimulus pattern to typical female rather than typical leader characteristics (Heilman, Block, Martell, & Simon, 1989). If subsequent searches fail to result in a match, we may create a new mental representation to incorporate the observed behavior by combining the two initial categories (e.g., we create a female leader subtype). These leadership subtypes are more of an exemplar and can be represented as shallower attractor basins in a neural network sense. We will return to this idea at the end of this chapter. Over time, this new representation may come to resonate with a previously held ILT, thus expanding the range of leadership behaviors we perceive and moving away from an exemplar-based ILT (Fiske & Neuberg, 1990).

Aggregate Patterns and Learning

Mismatches help to explain how new prototypes are learned and why they are learned as a whole. When a mismatch occurs (and no other search results in a match), the behaviors or knowledge are not merely discarded as unusable or inapplicable. Instead, new representations are created and prototypes are born. The match-based learning utilized by ART networks allow schema to change only when incoming stimuli are close enough to our previously held expectations. Thus, when something completely new occurs, we must accommodate the new information. Because this "mismatch leading to new a category" process operates similarly to an all-or-none rule, prototypes are learned as a whole. All the novel information or contextually relevant behaviors are linked together not only during the encoding process where we create a representation in working memory, but also during the interpretation process, where we devise a new category or prototype.

A system operating according to ART has two subcomponents: an attentional system and an orienting system. The attentional subsystem matches the bottom-up input with top-down activations to stabilize learning and create resonant states. If a mismatch occurs between the input and expectations, the orienting subsystem takes control to detect novelties. In short, new stimuli patterns are judged to be either new examples of concepts that were previously stored or new concepts. In order for a stimulus, such as speech perception or behavior classification to become conscious, a resonant state must take hold, whereby the match allows conscious recognition or the creation of a new representation.

Origin of Hierarchical Structure

This matching process is monitored by what Grossberg and colleagues refer to as a vigilance parameter. The vigilance parameter controls the tolerance for matching (see Figure 2.1). That is, a more relaxed vigilance parameter allows more variations of an external stimulus to be matched with an existing expectation. In terms of leadership behavior, with a relaxed vigilance parameter we would categorize more individuals as leaders according to our ILTs. This is because fewer aspects of behavior must match the ILT, allowing for more flexibility in our perceptions of leadership. For example, people with romanticized beliefs about leadership may have particularly abstract and flexible ILTs. On the other hand, a stringent vigilance parameter would define a narrower match to one's ILT. Thus, in order for one to be perceived as a leader, he or she would have to virtually fit all the aspects of our ILT. Effectively, the vigilance parameter creates a dynamic continuum with a general leadership prototype on one pole and a specific leadership exemplar at the other.

The vigilance parameter can easily be meshed with Rosch's (1978) category hierarchy. A relaxed vigilance parameter signals a more abstract, or superordinate, representation of the category, thus allowing more matches. As the vigilance parameter becomes more rigid, we move down the hierarchy toward more concrete, or subordinate, categories and exemplars. This also corresponds to the application of more constraints (e.g., context) in a connectionist network, which would produce a more specific prototype. Referring back to our original example of category levels, we can now explain the difference between a leader and nonleader or between a political and managerial leader in terms of ART's vigilance parameter.

Stability–Plasticity

ART models can self-organize in real time, which produces stable recognition while receiving new external stimuli input beyond what was originally stored. ART models have direct access to categories and are able to self-adjust during memory searches. Applied to leadership perceptions, we are able to encode and process new behaviors that we have not previously witnessed. This process is flexible enough to accommodate the new knowledge, without risking the loss of older knowledge structures, thus "solving" the stability–plasticity dilemma. That is, witnessing new leader-like behaviors does not override and erase any previously held expectation regarding leadership. Thus, although the structure of ILTs remains stable over time (Epitropaki & Martin, 2004), there is flexibility in their applications. The important thing to remember is that we rarely encounter the exact same situation twice; as the context of leadership changes, so do the behaviors we perceive. To the extent that we have flexible vigilance parameters monitoring the matching processes, there is variability in the behaviors that match our ILTs. For example, in one situation we may have a match to an abstract prototype that would result from a loose vigilance parameter. But in another situation, we may have a stringent vigilance parameter that provides a more concrete expectation and the need for an exemplar to match.

The match-based learning utilized by ART networks allow memories and schema to change only when incoming environmental stimuli is close enough to stored internal patterns or expectations or when something completely new occurs. We can incorporate these new leader-like behaviors into our existing ILTs or create a fundamentally different ILT. For example, if we witness strong religious leadership, we may match this behavior with a different ILT category than what we would match to managerial leadership. This feature makes ART systems well suited to situations that require the online learning of evolving databases, such as leadership behaviors. This is similar to the memory retrieval processes distinguishing exemplars and prototypes as suggested by Martell and Evans (2005). At this point, we are unable to conclude whether the resonance process allows for prototype morphing (Lord et al., 2001). It is plausible that resonance changes the structure of higher-level expectations but also that the instantiation process changes the higher level structure.

Grossberg (1999) presents extensive research supporting ART in basic sensory and perceptual mechanisms, which include, for example, sound and speech categorization. He argues that ART demystifies the processes involved in the following example of phonemic restoration (developed by Warren & Sherman, 1974):

> Suppose that a listener hears a noise followed immediately by the words "eel is on the…" If this string of words is followed by the word "orange," then "noise-eel" sounds like "peel." If the word "wagon" completes the sentence, then "noise-eel" sounds like "wheel." If the final word is "shoe," then "noise-eel" sounds like "heel." (p. 9)

Warren (1984) argued that the bottom-up occurrence of noise ("eel") is not enough for us to consciously hear it. In fact, we expect to hear a sound based on previous language experience, and the expectation influences what we actually hear. ART suggests this is because individual words are stored as memory traces (bottom-up input) that activate stored word and sound traces from long-term memory (Grossberg, 1999). The incoming sounds are categorized and activate expectations (top-down priming).

These expectations selectively amplify some features of the sound, while suppressing others in order to focus attention to the matching information. As the incoming sound is matched to our expectation, a resonant state begins to take hold as a continual feedback loop eventually locks in the sound, achieving conscious, auditory perception. Thus, meaning and phonetics are linked together through the resonant feedback just discussed.

This example is important for understanding leadership perceptions as it suggests that a stimulus or behavior is just not enough. It is the context that guides our expectations and subsequent interpretation of leader behaviors. As we move from objective experiences, such as identifying a word, to more subjective experiences, such as identifying leadership, context has even more of an impact. Our previous example illustrated the role of momentary contextual emphasis, but when external contexts do not provide enough cues to resolve ambiguity, perceivers may be forced to rely on their own biases and implicit theories (Meindl et al., 1985). This process also emphasizes that both immediate and cumulative histories are important in dynamic systems. Immediate histories create the momentary context for perceiving, and cumulative histories create the categorical structures used to supplement the momentary interpretations.

In the following section we examine such dynamic effects in leadership perceptions. But first we comment on whether Grossberg's theory is actually appropriate for processing at a level higher than visual or auditory perception. Shimamura (2000) argued for the extension of ART applications to higher-level processing. He suggested that the top-down filtering system that facilitates relevant information in working memory while inhibiting irrelevant information is analogous to a center-on, surround-off receptive field. That is,

> cortical processing is sharpened by both the enhancement of relevant activity (center-on) and by the inhibition of irrelevant activity (surround-off). Although this mechanism may be viewed as a ubiquitous operation that controls many aspects of neuronal processing, on a larger scale the prefrontal cortex may implement such a dynamic filtering mechanism more globally to control task-relevant information processing. (p. 319)

Thus, while ART is applicable to sensory and perceptual mechanisms, extending this view we can see how the same mechanisms may operate in more complex, dynamic processing systems (e.g., ILTs). In fact, in a recent meta-analysis, Johnson, Chang, and Lord (2006) argued that ART processes likely control mechanisms with respect to goal striving. In particular, it may be beneficial to apply ART as the mechanism for activating goal-relevant information and inhibiting goal-irrelevant information.

In summary, we have argued that ART has much appeal to furthering our understanding of leadership perceptions. Not only does this model fit with connectionist networks, but it also offers explanations for several current issues in the ILT literature. ART maintains that prototypes are learned as a whole and explains why categories are necessary to understand leadership. ART also identifies the vigilance parameter that is crucial in understanding category hierarchies. Finally, building on connectionist networks, ART helps to settle the stability–plasticity dilemma. We continue with this line of thought by introducing more advances in dynamic models of leadership next.

Our argument, developed in the following section, is that similar processes apply to leadership, in that when ART activates one potential leadership category, it also inhibits competing categories. Thus, when social systems change patterns over time, there will be a stickiness or cognitive inertia that tends to retard the shifting of cognitive categories that guide leadership perceptions. As explained in the following section, cognitive inertia, which may reflect the effects of top-down resonance on the interpretation of new stimulus patterns, tends to produce discontinuous, nonlinear rather than linear changes in perceptions.

Dynamic Models of Leadership Perceptions

Researchers interested in modeling dynamic processes such as changes in leadership perceptions often represent the behavior of a perceptual system as a flow through a multidimensional "phase" space. Trajectories representing system states over time in this phase space often converge in regions that are called attractors. As noted by Hopfield (1982), attractor regions are points of minimal energy of a system and they are points of stability. Attractors are often represented as basins or wells in a phase–space landscape, with deeper basins associated with more stable attractors that are harder to escape. In other words, strong interpretations of a stimulus are hard to override with new information. Hopfield also proposed that interactive neural networks can create attractor regions as they settle into an interpretation of a stimulus, and that attractors also correspond to prototypical interpretations of stimuli. We would add that when perceivers create a resonant state in terms of ART, they would also be creating an attractor. Thus, Grossberg's vigilance parameter may have important implications for the dynamics of attractor creation and modification. In this case, abstract categories are evidenced by a more flexible vigilance parameter and have deeper basins that are harder to escape. A stringent vigilance parameter is indicative of an expectation that more closely resembles an exemplar, and thus has a shallower basins that does not readily prevent escape.

Hanges, Lord, Godfrey, and Raver (2002) addressed the relation of category prototypes to attractors created by neural networks. They reasoned that changes in social categories were analogous to shifts from one attractor to another. A specific mathematical model, called a cusp catastrophe, represents such change processes. In the *cusp catastrophe model* a dependent variable (y) is predicted from two parameters, an *asymmetry parameter* (a) that separates the two competing attractors, and a *bifurcation parameter* (b) that affects the nature of change as the system switches from one attractor to another. Grossberg's notion of differences in vigilance would then likely map onto the bifurcation parameter in a cusp catastrophe model.

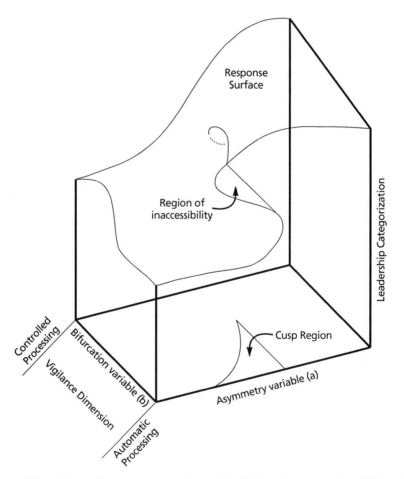

Figure 2.2.   A dynamic, cusp catastrophe model of changing perceptions. High values of asymmetry variable (a) represent classifying the target as a leader and low values reflect classifying an alternative person as the leader. Values of bifurcating variable (b) influence the form and process related to changes in leadership ratings.

Figure 2.2 shows a cusp catastrophe model. The folded plane that defines the upper surface represents behavior, in this case leadership perceptions, which varies as a function of the asymmetry and bifurcating variables. There are smooth gradual changes on the back surface that Lord and Maher (1991) proposed were associated with careful, controlled processing of social information. The front surface, in contrast, shows a discontinuous change pattern as a social stimulus gradually varies from being consistent with one attractor to being more consistent with a competing attractor. Lord and Maher proposed that changes on this front surface reflected the consequences of more automatic processing of changing social stimuli. They noted that automatic processing is dependent on the use of social categories and reliance on the ILTs that we have been discussing in this chapter. In terms of Grossberg's ART, this would correspond to having a less stringent vigilance parameter, and using more abstract, inclusive categories that are more difficult to change.

ART emphasizes that perception involves the interaction of stimulus characteristics and the cognitive structures of perceivers. Thus, a reluctance to use different categories to describe a changing social stimulus may reflect less careful processing of the stimuli, as suggested by Lord and Maher's reference to more automatic processing, or it may reflect the use of more inclusive categories, as suggested by a liberal vigilance parameter in Grossberg's terms. In either case, we would expect deeper attractor basins and a great reluctance to recategorize a stimulus. For dynamic stimuli, this means that prior categorizations would be retained longer than they should when a stimulus changes. It is for this reason that the front surface in Figure 2.2 actually folds over itself, creating a region (the cusp region), where the same combination of parameters (a) and (b) would predict two distinct values (one on the upper and one on the lower surface) depending on the category that had been active in prior categorization. In other words, in this region resonance from prior perceptions would distort the perception of new incoming stimuli to conform to the pattern of the category defining the attractor region, and this distortion would make it difficult for perceivers to notice small shifts in a category member's behavior. Because one's immediate perceptual history affects stimulus perception, the direction of change is crucially important for predicting perceptions on the front surface of Figure 2.2. Specifically, for regions in the middle of the asymmetry variable, whether you are on the lower or upper surface depends on whether you began on the left or the right of the figure. This dependence on direction and history is called *hysteresis* in catastrophe theory terms.

Several studies of leadership perceptions show that dynamic leadership perceptions fit a catastrophe model, demonstrating both hysteresis and bimodality in the cusp region. Specifically, we have found that emergent leadership processes in groups follow a catastrophe model in that once one person emerges as a leader they tend to retain that leadership position, even when competing group members are exhibiting a behavioral pattern that is more consistent with leadership prototypes. Three separate studies using a similar paradigm provide support for this model (Brown, Lord, Hanges, Marchioro, & Tan, 2005; Hanges et al., 2005).

Because these studies all use the same paradigm for measuring and modeling dynamic leadership ratings, we will describe the procedure in some detail. These perceivers viewed a series of nine videotaped group interactions of the same four-person group (two males and two females). These videotapes were created so that they could be viewed in two alternative orders—going from vignette 1 to 9 or from 9 to 1. In vignette 1, one of the males exhibited a disproportionate amount of leadership; in vignette 9, one of the females exhibited most of the leadership behavior; and in vignette 5, these two individuals exhibited equal amounts of leadership. Thus, a hysteresis effect in a catastrophe model would predict that the leadership ratings of the male or female leader in vignette 5 would vary depending on the order of stimulus presentation, with the female being rated higher in the $9 \rightarrow 1$ order and the male higher in the $1 \rightarrow 9$ order. Importantly, the Hanges procedure uses continuous ratings of leadership for all four videotaped individuals. This rating was collected by having subjects move a computer mouse on a diamond-shaped grid as they watched the videotaped segments. Each corner of the diamond was associated with a specific group member, and raters were instructed to move the curser closer to the person exhibiting the most leadership.

Hanges and colleagues (2005) conducted two separate studies using this procedure. The first study used a catastrophe flags approach (Gilmore, 1981) to illustrate the discontinuous change of the nature predicted by catastrophe theory. Specifically, they showed that responses were bimodal (with each mode corresponding to high ratings for one of the competing leaders), that shifts from one leader to another were discontinuous (there was an abrupt and dramatic shift in ratings as the attractor switched from the male to the female leader or vice versa), and hysteresis occurred in that the ratings of vignette 5 depended on raters' immediate experience. Vignette 5 showed equal amounts of leadership behavior for both the male and female leaders; but ratings of this vignette were higher for the female leader in the $9 \rightarrow 1$ order and higher for the male when vignettes were seen in the $1 \rightarrow 9$ order. The second study used a different analytic technique that actually modeled the response surface shown in Figure 2.2 as a function of two latent variables (the asymmetry and bifurcating variables) using a maximum likelihood procedure developed by Cobb (1981). This procedure, which models the nonlinear change, explained 54% of the variance in ratings, whereas a linear model only explained 37% of the variance.

Because this procedure also estimates the bifurcation variable as a function of individual differences, we can learn what types of people tend to produce discontinuous compared to continuous changes in leadership perceptions. Loadings on the bifurcation variables that were indicative of discontinuous change occurred for three individual differences. First, individuals high on Need for Closure, who tend to be uncomfortable with ambiguity and are close-minded, showed a more discontinuous change pattern. Second, individuals with more biased gender attitudes showed a more discontinuous change pattern. Third, individuals who tended to make internal causal attributions also showed discontinuous change patterns. Although not investigated in this study, there could be other individual differences that would foster a discontinuous change pattern such as commitment to one's hierarchical leader or romanticized beliefs regarding leadership in general (Meindl, 1995).

Brown and colleagues (2005) used a very similar methodology in an additional study, again finding that a nonlinear, cusp catastrophe model explained more variance in dynamic leadership ratings (59%) than a linear model (40%). Furthermore, using Cobb's maximum likelihood procedure, they found several individual difference variables that loaded on the bifurcating parameter, indicating more discontinuous change. First, individuals who were self-schematic in terms of leadership were predicted to have stronger leadership schema that would be harder to change once activated. Consistent with this prediction, self-schema strength loaded on the bifurcating parameter in the appropriate direction. Similarly, as predicted, individuals who endorsed equal sex roles (King & King, 1993) exhibited a more linear change from one leader to another, whereas individuals with more stereotypic sex role beliefs showed a discontinuous pattern of change. In contrast to the Hanges and colleagues (2005) study, they did not find Need for Closure to load significantly on the bifurcating parameter.

These three studies of dynamic changes in leadership ratings all show nonlinear change patterns that were more pronounced when individuals thought gender was an important component of leadership processes and when perceivers were themselves self-schematic in leadership or when they made internal causal attributions. Thus, factors that could be thought of as creating deeper attractor basins by reinforcing the use of ILTs all produced more discontinuous change. In other words, such perceivers stuck with prior categorization too long when new leadership interpretations were more appropriate. This is akin to using a less stringent vigilance parameter in ART or using more automatic perceptual processes as suggested by Lord and Maher (1991). However, rather than being less concerned with accuracy, raters showing discontinuous change patterns seemed to be overrelying on schematic interpretations of stimuli and paying less attention to actual behavior.

Emotions and Dynamic Processes

We have suggested that there are important micro-level dynamics that pertain to both emotions and to the way that we use ILTs to guide leadership perceptions. In this section, we briefly address the idea that emotions may alter the dynamics underlying leadership perceptions. The idea that emotions can serve as a reorienting mechanism has been recognized for many years (Simon, 1967). Certainly, unexpected events can attract attention and elicit more careful information processing, particularly if they result in negative outcomes (Bless, 2001).

We see two potential types of effects that should be considered in conjunction with work on ILTs and information processing. First, emotional reactions may precede changes in the way an individual is categorized. That is, feelings with respect to a leader may change before actual leadership ratings change. Perceivers often experience strong affective reactions to leadership that demonstrates courage (Worline, Wrzesniewski, & Rafaeli, 2002), and they also can react very negatively to unjust leadership acts (Bies, 2001; Fitness, 2000). We suspect that when strong reactions are also coupled with internal attributions to the leader, leadership categorization will also change. In such cases, emotional reactions may actually cause changes in leadership perceptions.

Another, more subtle role for emotions is that they may increase or decrease the vigilance with which we process social information. Thus, they may change the location of a perceiver on the attractor landscape shown in Figure 2.2. For example, raters in a positive mood may tend to use broader categories and more heuristic judgment processes (Isen & Daubman, 1984), while raters in negative moods may process information at a more detailed level (Bless, 2001). Such effects imply changes in the vigilance of ART processes or they may shift raters from more automatic to more controlled processing. Thus, positive affect should be associated with discontinuous change, and negative affect with more gradual changes in leadership ratings. None of the catastrophe analyses described previously included affect-related individual differences or dynamic measures of affect, so we have no data on this expectation. Future research following this paradigm should measure dynamic changes in affect, and they should also measure individual differences related to affective orientation (Watson, Wiese, Vaidya, & Tellegen, 1999) or the tendency to react intensely to affective events (Larsen & Diener, 1987).

CONCLUSIONS

Our purpose has been to consider the implications of cognitive processes for understanding the role of ILTs and leadership perceptions. This research developed from a social-cognitive tradition, and has always had a strong grounding in both cognitive and social science, yet we thought that there were recent developments in both cognitive science and in the integration of emotions and cognitions that warranted consideration. This work extends the important insights of Meindl, which emphasized (1) the follower's role in constructing leadership perceptions and (2) the general importance of perceivers' romanticized beliefs regarding leadership for resolving causal ambiguity for performance outcomes.

Table 2.1 highlights some of these more recent developments, summarizing their implications for understanding the cognitive processes that underlie leadership perceptions. We believe that these developments in

Table 2.1.   Comparison of Traditional and Current Perspectives on Cognitive Processes Related to Categorization

Topic	Traditional Perspective	New Perspective
Nature of categories	Perceiver's internal representations using symbol structures of external patterns	Emergence of patterns in connectionist networks; symbolic representation not required
Role of affect	Affect largely ignored or treated as an abstract cognitive variable	Affect is incorporated in embodied cognitions and is also viewed as modulating changes in categories
Need for categories	Cognitive simplifications needed because of perceiver's limited processing capacity	Bottom-up/top-down resonance required for conscious perceptions
Aggregate learning patterns	Prototype and exemplar models were competing theories; prototypes abstracted from repeated exposure to category exemplars	Bottom-up/top-down mismatches create new exemplar-based categories based on complete stimulus pattern; prototypes formed by loosening vigilance parameter
Origin of hierarchical structure	Not explained	Explained by vigilance parameter in ART
Stability–plasticity	Minor inconsistencies are ignored; large inconsistencies in content are noticed and verbally encoded through conscious, controlled processing	Category content is maintained because conflicting stimuli (mismatches) result in new categories; plasticity occurs through modulation by vigilance parameter
Changing categories	Categories changed incrementally by conscious elaboration and additional experience	Nonlinear change patterns depicted as shifts between attractors (category prototypes)

cognitive science offer a fresh perspective in understanding the use of ILTs to interpret and perceive leadership. This perspective has important scientific and practical implications. In this concluding section, we mention several specific scientific implications and provide one integrative example showing the practical value of this perspective.

Scientific Implications

Emergence and ILT Measurement

From a methodological perspective the possibility that categories reflect emergent processes may mean that we cannot capture the full effects of cognitive categories in artificial settings or with abstract, symbolic measures. By asking perceivers about their implicit theories, which is a common practice in research on ILTs, we may not be able to capture the aspects of ILTs that emerge in specific situations. There are two possible implications of this point. First, some leader-relevant characteristics may have effects that are outside of awareness and thus cannot be captured with explicit measures. Second, the effects of certain characteristics may be quite different when examined in isolation compared to their effects in combination with many other leader-relevant characteristics. These implications highlight the need for implicit measures to fully tap into ILTs.

Vigilance and Affect

Another interesting research avenue is to investigate the nature of the vigilance parameter introduced in the ART model (e.g., Carpenter & Grossberg, 1985; Grossberg, 1999). Specifically, are there individual differences or situational factors that could influence the stringency of the vigilance parameter? We see many potential individual differences, but will only comment on one here: affect. There is a lot of support for the notion that affect biases the way people interpret various stimuli (Bless, 2001; Isen & Daubman, 1984). In general, positive affect induces a reliance more on heuristics and preexisting scripts and schemas. This effect may be caused by a more relaxed vigilant parameter, which allows for more matches. Thus, individuals with high levels of positive affect may see more potential leader behaviors as indicative of leadership. On the other hand, negative affect is associated with more caution during processing and a tendency to delay initial categorization. Thus, individuals with elevated levels of negative affect may have more stringent vigilant parameters, which narrow the range of potential leader behaviors that will result in a match.

There could be both negative and positive consequences of the effect of negative affect. An immediate result of negative affect and more stringent vigilance parameters is the search for more appropriate category matches.

Thus, leader-like behaviors could be classified into nonleader behavior categories. For example, a directive behavior may be seen as "pushy" rather than as leadership. However, on the positive side, new leader categories may be more readily created as the result of multiple mismatches. This creates a richer categorical structure for understanding leadership for individuals who may be high on negative affect. Although we have illustrated such effects of vigilance in terms of affect, many other individual difference variables such as need for cognition, cognitive complexity, or being self-schematic in terms of leadership may also increase vigilance and produce similar effects in the development and use of ILTs.

Implications for Practice

Implications for understanding practical problems can best be seen by considering how the principles identified in Table 2.1 combine to affect specific leadership issues. An important practical issue is why potential leaders are perceived differently if they are female as compared to being male. This gender bias can be understood in terms of the persistence of ILTs that differentiate males and females despite changing workforce demographics and also in terms of the dynamic processes associated with creating resonance between potential female leaders and perceiver's ILTs.

Schein (2001) reviewed several studies that indicated that ILTs that are more consistent with typical male than typical female characteristics have not changed dramatically, at least for male perceivers, since her initial research in the early 1970s. These disappointing findings can be explained by applying Grossberg's ART, as noted in the stability–plasticity row in Table 2.1. Stable category content is maintained in the face of inconsistencies because mismatches result in a search for a new category rather than a broadening of the initial category. Thus, potential female leaders provoke a search for a better-fitting cognitive category, perhaps one that is gender based, rather than an adaptation of traditional ILT content. As a consequence, the abstract definition of leadership does not change.

However, as just noted, focusing on explicit content does not allow a full understanding of the range of ILTs or the dynamics associated with resonant processes in leadership perceptions. One must also consider the role of vigilance. Flexibility in ILT application (e.g., plasticity in ART terms) can occur when vigilance parameters change, permitting perceivers to automatically apply a more abstract (or more specific) category as a guide to the matching process. Depending on the level of the vigilance parameter, perceivers may be more or less likely to accept potential female leader behaviors as matching an abstract leadership prototype. Thus, a unique insight offered by ART is that *it may be much more effective to address factors that modulate vigilance (e.g., affect, need for cognition, being self-schematic in leadership) in reducing gender bias than to focus on changing category structure.* For example, if organizations fostered positive affect or a more liberal approach to leadership perceptions, the perception of female leaders using abstract-level prototypes could change immediately because they would only have to match a few rather than many leadership characteristics to create resonance. As noted by Hogue and Lord (2006), constraints from many other aspects of an organizational context may also affect the emergence of leadership prototypes. Thus, positive affect or other factors that affect the vigilance parameter could eliminate operating biases in leadership perceptions without first having to change category content. Over time, however, we would expect additional qualities or behaviors associated with being a female leader to eventually come to resonate with existing ILTs. In fact, as Schein's (2001) research shows, this change may have already occurred for many female perceivers.

REFERENCES

Barrett, L. F., Neidenthal, P. M., & Winkielman, P. (2005). *Emotion and consciousness.* New York: Guilford Press.

Bechtel, W., & Abrahamsen, A. (2002). *Connectionism and the mind.* Malden, MA: Blackwell.

Bies, R. J. (2001). Interactional (in)justice: The sacred and the profane. In J. Greenberg & R. Cropanzano (Eds.), *Advances in organization justice* (pp. 89–118). Stanford, CA: Stanford University Press.

Bless, H. (2001). The consequences of mood on the processing of social information. In A. Tesser & N. Schwartz (Eds.), *Blackwell handbook of social psychology* (pp. 391–412). Oxford, UK: Blackwell.

Brown, D. J., Lord, R. G., Hanges, P. J., Marchioro, C., & Tan, J. A. (2005). *Leadership perceptions: A dynamic perspective.* Working paper.

Brown, D. J., & Keeping, L. M. (2005). Elaborating the construct of transformational leadership: The role of affect. *Leadership Quarterly, 16,* 245–272.

Cantor, N., & Mischel, W. (1979). Prototypes in person perception. In L. Berkowitz (Ed.), *Advances in experimental social psychology* (pp. 3–52). New York: Academic Press.

Carpenter, G. A., & Grossberg, S. (1985). Category learning and adaptive pattern recognition: A neural network model. *Proceedings of the Third Army Conference on Applied Mathematics and Computing, ARO-86-1,* 37–56.

Cherulnik, P. D., Donley, K. A., Wiewel, T. S., & Miller, S. R. (2001). Charisma is contagious: The effects of leader's charisma on observers' affect. *Journal of Applied Social Psychology, 31,* 2149–2159.

Cobb, L. (1981). Parameter estimation for the cusp catastrophe model. *Behavioral Science, 26,* 75–78.

Engle, E. M., & Lord, R.G. (1997). Implicit theories, self-schemas, and leader–member exchange. *Academy of Management Journal, 40,* 988–1010.

Ensari, N., & Murphy, S. E. (2003). Cross-cultural variations in leadership perceptions and attribution of charisma to the leader. *Organizational Behavior and Human Decision Processes, 92,* 52–66.

Epitropaki, O., & Martin, R. (2004). Implicit leadership theories in applied settings: Factor structure, generalizability, and stability over time. *Journal of Applied Psychology, 89,* 293–310.

Epitropaki, O., & Martin, R. (2005). From ideal to real: A longitudinal study of implicit leadership theories on leader–member exchanges and employee outcomes. *Journal of Applied Psychology, 90,* 659–676.

Fischbein, R. L. (2005). *Spreading activation in connectionist leader prototypes: The impact of crisis.* Unpublished doctoral dissertation, University of Akron.

Fiske, S. T. (1995). Controlling other people: The impact of power on stereotyping. In N. R. Goldberger & J. B. Veroff (Eds.), *The culture and psychology reader* (pp. 438–456). New York: New York University Press.

Fiske, S. T., & Neuberg, S. L. (1990). A continuum of impression formation, from category-based to individuating processes: Influences of information and motivation on attention and interpretation. In M. P. Zanna (Ed.), *Advances in experimental social psychology* (Vol. 23, pp. 1–74). San Diego, CA: Academic Press.

Fiske, S. T., & Taylor, S. E. (1991). *Social cognition* (2nd ed.). New York: McGraw-Hill.

Fitness, J. (2000). Anger in the workplace: an emotion script approach to anger episodes between workers and their superiors, co-workers and subordinates. *Journal of Organization Behavior, 21,* 147–162.

Gilbert, D. T. (1989). Thinking lightly about others: Automatic components of the social inference process. In J. S. Uleman & J. A. Bargh (Eds.), *Unintended thought* (pp. 189–211). New York: Guilford Press.

Gilbert, D. T., Pelham, B. W., & Krull, D. S. (1988). On cognitive busyness: When person perceivers meet persons perceived. *Journal of Personality and Social Psychology, 59,* 601–613.

Gilmore, R. (1981). *Catastrophe theory for scientists and engineers.* New York: Dover Publications.

Gioia, D. A., & Poole, P. P. (1984). Scripts in organizational behavior. *Academy of Management Review, 9,* 449–559.

Graf, P., & Schacter, D. L. (1985). Implicit and explicit memory for new associations in normal and amnesiac subjects. *Journal of Experimental Psychology: Learning, Memory, and Cognition, 11,* 501–518.

Grossberg, S. (1976). Adaptive classification and universal recoding, I: Parallel development and coding of neural feature detectors. *Biological Cybernetics, 23,* 121–134.

Grossberg, S. (1999). The link between brain learning, attention, and consciousness. *Consciousness and Cognition, 8,* 1–44.

Hanges, P. J., Lord, R. G., Day, D. V., Sipe, W. P., Grandwohl-Smith, W. C., & Brown, D. J. (2005). *Leadership and gender bias: Dynamic measures and nonlinear modeling.* Manuscript submitted for publication.

Hanges, P. J., Lord, R. G., Godfrey, E. G., & Raver, J. L. (2002). Modeling nonlinear relationships: Neural networks and catastrophe analysis. In S. Rogelberg (Ed.), *Handbook of research methods in Industrial/Organizational psychology* (pp. 431–455). Oxford, UK: Blackwell.

Heilman, M. E., Block, C. J., Martell, R. F., & Simon, M. C. (1989). Has anything changed? Current characterizations of men, women, and managers. *Journal of Applied Psychology, 74,* 935–942.

Hogue, M., & Lord, R.G. (2006). *A multilevel, complexity theory approach to understanding gender bias in leadership.* Manuscript submitted for publication.

Hopfield, J. (1982). Neural networks and physical systems with emergent collective computational abilities. *Proceedings of the National Academy of Science USA, 79,* 2254–2258.

Isen, A. M., & Daubman, K. A. (1984). The influence of affect on categorization. *Journal of Personality and Social Psychology, 47,* 1206–1217.

Johnson, R. E., Chang, C.-H., & Lord, R. G. (2006). Moving from cognition to behavior: What the research says. *Psychological Bulletin, 90,* 381–415.

Johnson-Laird, P. N. (1989). Mental models. In M. I. Posner (Ed.), *Foundations of cognitive science* (pp. 469–499). Cambridge, MA: MIT Press.

Judge, T. A., Bono, J. E., Ilies, R., & Gerhardt, M. W. (2002). Personality and leadership: A qualitative and quantitative review. *Journal of Applied Psychology, 87,* 765–780.

Kellett, J. B., Humphrey, R. H., & Sleeth, R. G. (2002). Empathy and complex task performance: Two routes to leadership. *Leadership Quarterly, 13,* 523–544.

King, L. A., & King, D. W. (1993). *Sex role egalitarianism scale manual.* Port Huron, MI: Sigma Assessment Systems, Inc.

Kunda, Z. (1999). *Social cognition.* Cambridge, MA: MIT Press.

Kunda, Z., & Thagard, P. (1996). Forming impressions from stereotypes, traits and behaviors: A parallel–constraint–satisfaction theory. *Psychological Review, 103,* 284–308.

Larsen, R. J., & Diener, E. (1987). Affect intensity as an individual difference characteristic: A review. *Journal of Research in Personality, 21,* 1–39.

Lord, R. G., & Brown, D. J. (2004). *Leadership processes and follower self-identity.* Mahwah, NJ: Erlbaum.

Lord, R. G., Brown, D. J., Harvey, J. L., & Hall, R. J. (2001). Contextual constraints on prototype generation and their multilevel consequences for leadership perceptions. *Leadership Quarterly, 12,* 311–338.

Lord, R. G., De Vader, C. L., & Alliger, G. M. (1986). A meta-analysis of the relation between personality traits and leadership perceptions: An application of validity generalization procedures. *Journal of Applied Psychology, 71,* 402–410.

Lord, R. G., Foti, R. J., & DeVader, C. L. (1984). A test of leadership categorization theory: Internal structure, information processing, and leadership perceptions. *Organizational Behavior and Human Performance, 34,* 343–378.

Lord, R.G., Foti, R.J., & Philips, J.S. (1982). A theory of leadership categorization. In J.G. Hunt, U. Sekaran, & C. Schriesheim (Eds.), *Leadership: Beyond establishment views* (pp. 104–121). Carbondale: Southern Illinois University Press.

Lord, R. G., & Maher, K. J. (1991). *Leadership and information processing: Linking perceptions and performance.* Boston: Unwin Hyman.

Macrae, C. N., Milne, A. B., & Bodenhausen, G. V. (1994). Stereotypes as energy-saving devices: A peek inside the cognitive toolbox. *Journal of Personality and Social Psychology, 66,* 37–47.

Martell, R. F., & Evans, D. P. (2005). Reducing the effect of performance expectations on work behavior rating. *Journal of Applied Psychology, 90,* 956–963.

Meindl, J. R. (1995). The romance of leadership as a follower-centric theory: A social constructionist approach. *Leadership Quarterly, 6,* 329–341.

Meindl, J. R., Ehrlich, S. B., & Dukerich, J. M. (1985). The romance of leadership. *Administrative Science Quarterly, 30,* 78–102.

Moskowitz, G. B. (2005). *Social cognition: Understanding the self and others.* New York: Guilford Press.

Murphy, M. R., & Jones, A. P. (1993). The influence of performance cues and observational focus on performance rating accuracy. *Journal of Applied Social Psychology, 23,* 229–258.

Naidoo, L. J., & Lord, R. G. (2004, June). *Leadership during affective events.* Paper presented at the first Gallup Leadership Institute conference, Omaha, NE.

Naidoo, L. J., Walters, N. E., Lord, R. G., & Dubois, D. A. (2005, April). *Seeing is retrieving: Recovering emotional content in leadership perceptions.* Paper presented at the annual convention of the Society for Industrial and Organization Psychology, Los Angeles.

Neidenthal, P. M., Barsalou, L. W., Winkielman, P., Karuth-Gruber, S., & Ric, F. (2005). Embodiment in attitudes, social perception, and emotion. *Personality and Social Psychology Review, 9,* 184–211.

Phillips, J. S., & Lord, R. G. (1982). Causal attribution and perceptions of leadership. *Organizational Behavior and Human Performance, 33,* 125–138.

Offermann, L. R., Kennedy, J. K., & Wirtz, P. W. (1994). Implicit leadership theories: Content, structure, and generalizability. *Leadership Quarterly, 5,* 43–58.

Rosch, E. (1978). Principles of categorization. In E. Rosch & B. B. Lloyd (Eds.), *Cognition and categorization* (pp. 28–48). Hillsdale, NJ: Erlbaum.

Ross, L. (1977). The intuitive psychologist and his shortcomings: Distortions in the attributional process. In L. Berkowitz (Ed.), *Advances in experimental social psychology* (pp. 174–221). New York: Academic Press.

Schein, V. E. (2001). A global look at psychological barriers to women's progress in management. *Journal of Social Issues, 57,* 675–688.

Shimamura, A. P. (2000). Toward a cognitive neuroscience of metacognition. *Consciousness and Cognition, 9,* 313–323.

Simon, H. (1967). Motivational and emotional controls of cognition. *Psychological Review, 74,* 29–39.

Smith, E. R. (1996). What do connectionism and social psychology offer each other? *Journal of Personality and Social Psychology, 70,* 893–912.

Smith, J. A., & Foti, R. J. (1998). A pattern approach to the study of leadership emergence. *Leadership Quarterly, 9,* 47–160.

Smith, E. R., & Miller, F. D. (1983). Mediation among attributional inferences and comprehension processes: Initial findings and a general method. *Journal of Personality and Social Psychology, 44,* 492–505.

Uleman, J. S., Newman, L. S., & Moskowitz, G. B. (1996). People as flexible interpreters: Evidence and issues from spontaneous trait inferences. In P. Zanna

(Ed.), *Advances in experimental social psychology* (Vol. 29, pp. 211–279). San Diego, CA: Academic Press.

Van Overwalle, F., Drenth, T., & Marsman, G. (1999). Spontaneous trait inferences: Are they linked to the actor or to the action? *Personality and Social Psychology Bulletin, 25,* 450–462

Warren, R. M. (1984). Perceptual restoration of obliterated sounds. *Psychological Bulletin, 96,* 371–383.

Warren, R. M., & Sherman, G. L. (1974). Phonemic restorations based on subsequent context. *Perception and Psychophysics, 9,* 150–156.

Watson, D., Clark, L., & Tellegen, A. (1988). Development and validation of brief measures of positive affectivity and negative affectivity: The PANAS scales. *Journal of Personality and Social Psychology, 54,* 1063 –1070.

Watson, D., Wiese, D., Vaidya, J., & Tellegen, A. (1999). The two general activation systems of affect: Structural findings, evolutionary considerations, and psychobiological evidence. *Journal of Personality and Social Psychology, 76,* 820–838.

Weick, K. E. (1995). *Sensemaking in organizations.* Thousand Oaks, CA: Sage.

Weiss, H. M., & Cropanzano, R. (1996). Affective events theory: A theoretical discussion of the structure, causes, and consequences of affective experiences at work. In B. M. Staw & L. L. Cummings (Eds.), *Research in organizational behavior: An annual series of analytical essays and critical reviews* (Vol. 18, pp. 1–74). Stamford, CT: JAI Press.

Worline, M. C., Wrzesniewski, A., & Rafaeli, A. (2002). Courage and work: Breaking routines to improve performance. In R. G. Lord, R. J. Klimoski, & R. Kanfer (Eds.), *Emotions in the workplace: Understanding the role and structure of emotions in organizational behavior* (pp. 295–330). San Francisco: Jossey-Bass.

CHAPTER 3

EXTENDING THE FOLLOWER-CENTERED PERSPECTIVE

Leadership as an Outcome of Shared Social Identity

Daan van Knippenberg
Erasmus University Rotterdam

Barbara van Knippenberg
Free University Amsterdam

Steffen R. Giessner
Erasmus University Rotterdam

ABSTRACT

We outline a social identity analysis of leadership effectiveness that extends some of the core propositions of Jim Meindl's follower-centered perspective on leadership. We propose that the shared social identity of leader and followers provides a basis for responses to leadership, rendering leaders that are seen as group prototypical (representative of the shared social identity) and pursuing the group's best interest more likely to be seen as effective leaders.

Follower-Centered Perspectives on Leadership, pages 51–70
Copyright © 2007 by Information Age Publishing

Moreover, contingent on goal definition, leader group prototypicality is argued to moderate responses to leader performance (cf. the "romance of leadership" identified by Meindl). As a counterpoint to this follower-centered analysis, we also discuss leaders' active role in this process of follower social construction of leadership, and advocate analyses of leadership effectiveness that integrate both perspectives.

There is no leadership without followership. In a sense, leadership is defined by people following. Not surprisingly, then, the core question in leadership research has always been what makes leaders effective in influencing and mobilizing followers. Despite impressive efforts invested in answering this question (e.g., Bass, 1990; Chemers, 2001; Yukl, 2002), however, leadership research can be criticized for overly focusing on leader characteristics and behavior, and paying less attention to the role of followers than probably it should have. As one of the important exceptions to this general rule, the follower-centered perspective on leadership championed by Jim Meindl (1990, 1993, 1995) outlines how followers play a critical role in leadership effectiveness, not just because there is no leadership without people following but because leadership effectiveness is contingent on followers' social construction of leadership.

This emphasis on the role of followers in leadership effectiveness resonates well with a social identity perspective on leadership effectiveness (Hogg, 2001; Hogg & van Knippenberg, 2003; van Knippenberg & Hogg, 2003b). The social identity analysis of leadership emphasizes the fact that leadership processes are enacted in the context of a shared group membership, where followers respond to leaders in part on the basis of the leader's characteristics and behavior as a group member. In this chapter, we outline how this social identity analysis complements and extends Meindl's groundbreaking work. In line with Meindl's analysis of contagion processes underlying leadership endorsement, we discuss how a shared social identity among group members sets the stage for the social sharedness of leadership perceptions, and how leaders' representativeness of this shared social identity (i.e., leader group prototypicality) is part of this socially shared reality that feeds into perceptions of leadership effectiveness and leadership endorsement. We also discuss how social identity affects the contagion processes discussed by Meindl, and thus the strength of the socially shared reality that feeds into leadership perceptions. Finally, we discuss a series of experiments that connect with Meindl's analysis of the "romance of leadership" (Meindl, Ehrlich, & Dukerich, 1985) and identify some of the moderators of this tendency for performance information to feed into leadership perceptions.

LEADERSHIP IS IN THE EYE OF THE BEHOLDER:
A FOLLOWER-CENTRIC PERSPECTIVE ON LEADERSHIP

Whereas many theories of leadership seem to take leaders' characteristics and behaviors as more or less an objective given (cf. Bass, 1990; Chemers, 2001; Yukl, 2002), there is a strong case to be made for the proposition that part of what we identify as leadership—or as effective leadership—is in the eye of the beholder. People's perceptions of leaders may be guided by their preconceptions of what constitutes good leadership. Relatively irrespective of the validity of these preconceptions, people may be more likely to perceive a leader as a good leader if the leader's characteristics and behaviors match people's implicit theories of effective leadership (Lord, 1977; Lord, Foti, & DeVader, 1984; Lord & Maher, 1991; Meindl, 1995; Meindl et al., 1985). If one's implicit leadership theories for instance suggest that men are better leaders than women, a male leader's characteristics and achievements are more likely to be perceived in a favorable light than a female leader's characteristics and achievements (Eagly, 2003; Eagly & Karau, 2002; Ridgeway, 2003). Because the favorability of leadership perceptions may set the stage for leader influence over followers, effective leadership thus arguably flows in part from follower conceptions of leadership rather than from leadership per se. Or put differently, to a certain extent effective leadership may entail matching followers' scripts of effective leadership (Meindl, 1995).

Meindl highlighted two aspects of this follower-centric approach to leadership effectiveness in particular. First, following from the notion that effective leadership to a certain extent is a social construction, leadership perceptions may be socially shared among followers, and through contagion processes, such shared perceptions may emerge through a network of followers (Meindl, 1990, 1993, 1995). Applying principles of social network theory, Pastor, Meindl, and Mayo (2002) for instance predicted and found that individuals who were more proximal within the social network were more likely to share (charismatic) leadership perceptions. Moreover, consistent with a social contagion model of leadership perceptions, the sharedness of charismatic leadership perceptions increased over time. The social construction of leadership may thus not only occur at the level of the individual, but may also be a socially shared phenomenon. This social contagion process among followers may contribute to leaders' rise and ability to mobilize whole groups of followers as well as to leaders' downfall and losing the favor of their subordinates or constituents.

Second, Meindl highlighted the fact that group or organizational performance outcomes (e.g., growing profits, a failure to land a deal) in particular may be subject to this social construction process, where especially performance changes are attributed to leadership. Meindl coined the term "romance of leadership" to refer to this tendency to overattribute events, and especially performance-related events, to leadership (Meindl & Ehrlich, 1987; Meindl et al., 1985). Indeed, there is quite consistent evidence that even in the face of essentially the same information about leadership, stronger attributions to leadership are made when group or organizational performance changes, and leaders that are associated with group or organizational success are more positively evaluated than leaders who are associated with failure (Haslam et al., 2001; Lord, Binning, Rush, & Thomas, 1978; Meindl & Ehrlich, 1987; Meindl, Ehrlich, & Dukerich, 1985; Phillips & Lord, 1981).

In combination, then, these insights suggest that leaders' (presumed) effectiveness in part flows from followers' conceptions of leadership and attributions to leadership, and that this is a process that may occur at the level of the individual follower but also at the level of a group of followers when people create a shared social reality defining effective leadership and making sense of the actual leadership (cf. Weick, 1995). Although not inspired by work by Meindl, Lord, or others within this leadership tradition but by social psychological analyses of social influence (e.g., Turner, 1985; Turner, Hogg, Oakes, Reicher, & Wetherell, 1987), a social identity analysis of leadership (Hogg, 2001; Hogg & van Knippenberg, 2003; van Knippenberg & Hogg, 2003b) connects quite well with the perspective championed by Meindl, and may complement and extend work by Meindl and others in a number of ways.

A SOCIAL IDENTITY ANALYSIS OF LEADERSHIP EFFECTIVENESS

Theories of self-categorization and social identity describe how the self is not only defined in individual terms (i.e., characteristics that identify the self as a unique individual, the individual self, or "I"), but also in terms of group or organizational memberships (i.e., characteristics that identify the self as a group member, the collective self, or "we"; Sedikides & Brewer, 2001; Tajfel & Turner, 1986; Turner et al., 1987). Self-categorization theory (Turner, 1985; Turner et al., 1987) describes how group members' cognitive representation of their group is reflected in group prototypes that capture group-defining characteristics (cf. Rosch, 1978). When the self is defined in terms of a group membership, people tend to perceive the self in terms of these group prototypical attributes, and as a consequence group-defining features tend to guide individuals' perceptions, attitudes, and behavior. This self-definition in collective terms is reflected in the concept of social (or organizational) identification, the perception of oneness of self and group. Accordingly, group identification may be seen as an important predictor of the extent to which attitudes and behavior are informed by group membership.

Over the last 15 years or so, the social identity approach to self-definition and social behavior has increasingly been applied to understand group processes relevant to organizational behavior (e.g., Ashforth & Mael, 1989; Dutton, Dukerich, & Harquail, 1994; Haslam, 2001; Haslam, van Knippenberg, Platow, & Ellemers, 2003; Hogg & Terry, 2000; van Knippenberg, 2003). The study of leadership has been one of the key areas for the development of this analysis (Haslam & Platow, 2001; Hogg, 2001; Hogg & van Knippenberg, 2003; Platow, Haslam, Foddy, & Grace, 2003; van Knippenberg & Hogg, 2003a, 2003b; van Knippenberg, van Knippenberg, De Cremer, & Hogg, 2004). Van Knippenberg and Hogg (2003b) propose that identification with a collective has at least two consequences that are important to our understanding of leadership effectiveness. First, people typically (also) rely on others to make sense of novel or ambiguous situations and events, or determine their position on issues where no "objective" reference point exists such as for norms and values (Festinger, 1954), and groups with which people identify are a key source of information about social reality (Abrams & Hogg, 1990; Turner, 1985; Turner et al., 1987; van Knippenberg, 2000a). Group prototypes reflect the social reality shared by the group (and thus in a sense group consensus). As a result, group members may be particularly influenced by information that is seen to reflect group prototypical values, norms, attitudes, or behaviors.

Group members' tendencies to use group prototypes as sources of information about social reality may also help predict and explain differences in leadership effectiveness. Because leaders not only lead groups but also are a member of the group they lead, group members' responses to leadership also tend to be informed by the leader's characteristics as a group member. As a function of the match between personal characteristics and group prototypical characteristics, some leaders are more prototypical than others. That is, some leaders are seen to represent the shared social identity and to embody what group members have in common—differentiating the group from other groups—more so than other leaders. Because identification leads group members to rely on group prototypes, group prototypical leaders tend to be more influential and effective than less prototypical leaders (Hogg, 2001; Hogg & van Knippenberg, 2003; van Knippenberg & Hogg, 2003b).[1]

Second, identification with a group elicits group-oriented motivation (e.g., Dutton et al., 1994; Haslam, 2001; Lord & Brown, 2004; Shamir, 1990; Tyler & Blader, 2000; van Knippenberg, 2000b). Through self-definition in collective terms, the collective interest is experienced as the self-interest (i.e., the collective self-interest), and group members are motivated to pursue, represent, and defend the group or organizational interest. The key issue here for our understanding of leadership effectiveness is that group members may thus also be expected to desire others, and especially the leader of the group or organization, to take the collective interest to heart and to actively contribute to the pursuit of the collective interest. Leaders that are seen to be more committed to the group and to engage more in group-oriented behavior (i.e., behavior that is seen to serve the group's interest) may thus be more effective than leaders that are less seen to be group-oriented (Haslam & Platow, 2001; Hogg & van Knippenberg, 2003; Platow, Hoar, Reid, Harley, & Morrison, 1997; van Knippenberg & Hogg, 2003b; van Knippenberg & van Knippenberg, 2005; cf. Conger & Kanungo, 1987; Shamir, House, & Arthur, 1993).

Group prototypical leaders are not only seen as representing shared social reality. Because they represent the collective identity they are also more trusted to be group-oriented than less prototypical leaders (Giessner, van Knippenberg, & Sleebos, 2005; Platow, Haslam, Foddy, & Grace, 2003; Platow & van Knippenberg, 2001; van Knippenberg & Hogg, 2003b; van Knippenberg & van Knippenberg, 2005). As a consequence of this greater trust in leader group-orientedness, endorsement of group prototypical leaders is less contingent on their actual engagement in group-oriented acts than endorsement of less group prototypical leaders. This interactive effect of leader group prototypicality and leader group-oriented behavior has been demonstrated for leader acts of self-sacrifice on behalf of the collective (van Knippenberg & van Knippenberg, 2005), the extent to which leaders' distributive decisions were group-favoring (Platow & van Knippenberg, 2001), and the extent to which leaders invoke the collective interest rather than individual self-interest (Platow, van Knippenberg, Haslam, Spears, & van Knippenberg, 2006).

The influence of leader group prototypicality and leader group-orientedness is contingent on follower self-definition in terms of the collective. In other words, identification with the group, and contextual salience of this identification, moderates the extent to which leader group prototypicality (e.g., Hains, Hogg, & Duck, 1997; Hogg, Hains, & Mason, 1998) and leader group-orientedness (e.g., Platow et al., 1997; Platow & van Knippenberg, 2001) affect leadership effectiveness. Leader group prototypicality and leader group-orientedness are more predictive of leadership effectiveness the more people identify with the group and social identity is salient. Greater ambiguity of and uncertainty about (self-relevant) social reality may also inspire a greater reliance on group memberships and group prototypes (Hogg, 2000). Accordingly, a desire to reduce uncertainty—either situationally or dispositionally determined—also moderates the relationship between leader group prototypicality and leadership effectiveness. Leader group prototypicality is more predictive of leadership effectiveness when follower desire to reduce uncertainty is stronger (Pierro, Cicero,

Bonaiuto, van Knippenberg, & Kruglanski, 2005a, 2005b; cf. van Knippenberg, van Knippenberg, & van Dijk, 2000).

Although neither the leadership categorization perspective (Lord & Maher, 1991) nor the social construction perspective (Meindl, 1995) explicitly point to leader group prototypicality and leader group-orientedness as determinants of leadership perceptions, there seem to be clear parallels with the social identity analysis of leadership (cf. Lord & Hall, 2003; van Knippenberg & Hogg, 2003b). All these perspectives identify followers' reference points for leadership as informing responses to leadership, and accordingly we may advance the follower-centered perspective on leadership by exploring possibilities to integrate these different perspectives. In the following, we address this issue by zooming in on the two issues highlighted in Meindl's analysis of leadership—social contagion processes and the romance of leadership.

SOCIAL IDENTITY AND SOCIAL CONTAGION OF LEADERSHIP PERCEPTIONS

Meindl (1990, 1993, 1995) proposed that followers' leadership perception may be formed and spread in a process of social contagion. In a process of collective sense making (Weick, 1995), group members may affect each others' leadership perceptions in social interaction, in effect creating a shared social reality defining their response to the collective's leadership. Meindl argued that insights from social network analysis could be used to predict the spread of leadership perceptions as social constructions. This proposition was corroborated by Pastor and colleagues (2002), who showed that proximity in the social network and the progress of time predicted sharedness of leadership perceptions (i.e., sharedness of perceptions arguably is a proxy for social contagion). The notion of social contagion and sharedness of perceptions is well aligned with a social identity analysis of social influence.

In the social identity analysis, social perceptions, beliefs, and attitudes are proposed to be formed (in part) by reference to fellow group members' perceptions, beliefs, and attitudes. Group-normative (i.e., group prototypical) perceptions, beliefs, and attitudes thus may emerge and be established as the product of the social influence processes through which groups create a shared social reality (Turner, 1985, 1991; Turner et al., 1987). These shared prototypic representations of the group may then form a basis for subsequent shared responses to leadership based on leader group prototypicality. Indeed, just as Pastor and colleagues (2002; Meindl, 1995) argued that perceptions of leader charisma may flow from contagion processes, Platow and colleagues proposed in reference to leader group prototypicality's effect on perceptions of charisma that charisma is "a special gift we bestow on you for being a representative of us" (Platow et al., 2006, p. 303; see also van Knippenberg & Hogg, 2003b; van Knippenberg & van Knippenberg, 2005). Thus, although the social construction perspective and the social identity analysis do not necessarily identify the same determinants of leadership perceptions, they seem to be in agreement over the process through which leadership perceptions become socially shared.

This is also evident in the similarity between on the one hand the moderators of group members' tendency to rely on group memberships and group prototypicality identified in the social identity analysis, and on the other hand the factors that are proposed to be conducive to perceptions of charisma in the social construction perspective. Whereas the social identity analysis points to identification and social identity salience as the key moderator of the influence of leader group prototypicality, Pillai and Meindl (1998) proposed that collectivistic orientations (i.e., emphasizing the collective identity) are conducive to perceptions of charismatic leadership. In a related vein, both analyses point to the role of crisis and uncertainty (Meindl, 1995; Pierro et al., 2005a, 2005b; Pillai & Meindl, 1998; van Knippenberg & Hogg, 2003b; van Knippenberg, van Knippenberg, & Bobbio, in press) in determining responses to leadership.

Interestingly, the social identity perspectives would also argue that social sharedness of leadership perceptions becomes more likely with higher follower identification with the collective and greater uncertainty and crisis. Research on the determinants of social identification may thus be fruitfully applied to identify the determinants of social contagion processes in leadership perceptions. This would for instance point to group or organizational status and prestige (Ashforth & Mael, 1989; Dutton et al., 1994; Tajfel & Turner, 1986) and group or organizational distinctiveness (Brewer, 1991; Dutton et al., 1994) as determinants of social contagion processes. This analysis of the determinants of social sharedness also provides an interesting link with the perspective on followers' conception of leadership as a determinant of leadership perceptions provided by leadership categorization theory (Lord & Hall, 2003; Lord & Maher, 1991).

Hogg and colleagues propose that not only does leader group prototypicality increasingly become a basis for responses to leadership as followers identify more with the group and social identity is more salient, but also that with higher identification the extent to which leader characteristics match the standards for effective leadership described in leadership categorization theory and reflected in implicit leadership theories becomes a smaller influence on leadership perceptions (Fielding & Hogg, 1997; Hains et al., 1997; Hogg et al., 1998; see also Platow & van Knippenberg, 2001). Thus, leadership categorization theory may be seen as capturing responses to leadership under low identification conditions, while the social identity analysis of leadership may more accurately describe responses to leadership under conditions of high follower identification with the group (Lord & Hall, 2003; van Knippenberg & Hogg, 2003b). Because conditions of higher group identification are also likely to be conditions of greater social sharedness of leadership perceptions, greater sharedness of responses to leadership is likely to go hand-in-hand with greater reliance on group prototypes (vs. implicit leadership theories). Because socially shared cognition typically has a greater influence on group functioning than cognition that is less shared (Tindale & Kameda, 2000), the more impactful social constructions of leadership may be the ones more heavily influenced by leader group prototypicality and leader group-orientedness.

The social identity analysis and the social contagion analysis thus are well aligned. The social identity analysis also complements and extends the social contagion analysis proposed by Meindl and colleagues by (1) identifying leader group prototypicality and leader group-orientedness as factors feeding into responses to leadership, and identifying the conditions under which prototypicality and group-orientedness versus implicit leadership theories are more likely to influence (perceived) leadership effectiveness; (2) identifying a class of factors that render social sharedness of leadership perceptions more likely (i.e., factors that feed into group identification); and (3) proposing that leader group prototypicality and group-orientedness are likely to be more influential under conditions of greater social sharedness. In addition, the social identity analysis may also be applied to extend the specific case of follower construction of leadership emphasized by Meindl—the "romance of leadership"—in responses to leaders associated with success or failure in achieving group or organizational goals.

SOCIAL IDENTITY AND THE ROMANCE OF LEADERSHIP

The follower-centered perspective on leadership proposed by Meindl not only maintains that leadership is to a substantial extent socially constructed, it also emphasizes the fact that leadership is often invoked as an explanatory mechanism. Attributions to leadership help make sense of events, and indeed Meindl argued that people overattribute events—especially (changes in) organizational performance—to leadership (Meindl et al., 1985). Meindl and colleagues (1985) proposed the term "romance of leadership" to capture this tendency to overattribute group and organizational events to leadership. While the romance of leadership as it may be observed in the tendency for performance information to feed into leadership perceptions is well documented (e.g., Awamleh & Gardner, 1999; Haslam et al., 2001; Lord et al., 1978; Meindl & Ehrlich, 1987; Meindl et al., 1985; Phillips & Lord, 1981), little is yet known about factors influencing the extent to which information about organizational, group, or leader performance feeds into leadership perceptions, leader endorsement, and thus ultimately the basis for leadership effectiveness.

Leaders almost inevitably sooner or later find themselves in a situation where they are associated with failure to achieve group or organizational goals. Leaders' ability to maintain follower endorsement—and thus their basis for leadership effectiveness—despite such associations with failure would thus seem crucial to their continued effectiveness as a leader. Accordingly, identifying the factors that may help leaders overcome or deflect associations with failure would seem important for our understanding of leadership effectiveness. Recent research by Giessner and colleagues (Giessner & van Knippenberg, 2005; Giessner et al., 2005) inspired by the social identity analysis of leadership addressed this issue.

Building on the notion that leader group prototypicality inspires trust in the leader and thus gives prototypical leaders more leeway in their behavior than nonprototypical leaders (Platow & van Knippenberg, 2001; van Knippenberg et al., 2000), Giessner and colleagues (2005) proposed that group prototypicality would to a certain extent buy a leader a "license to fail." Whereas endorsement of nonprototypical leaders was expected to be markedly stronger when they were associated with success in achieving group or organizational goals rather than with failure to do so, endorsement of group prototypical leaders was expected to be relatively strong even after a failure to realize group or organizational goals as a consequence of the greater trust in prototypical leaders.

Giessner and colleagues (2005) put this prediction to the test in a scenario experiment among supporters of the German Green Party in which leader prototypicality and leader success versus failure in achieving group goals were manipulated. The supporters received a short vignette describing a prototypical or nonprototypical leader that was developed in consultation with Green Party supporters and partly based on the election program of the Green Party. The prototypical leader was described as having studied political science and emphasizing core issues of the Green Party (e.g., exit from the use of nuclear power industry). In contrast, the non-prototypical leader was described as having studied engineering and emphasizing less central political issues of the Green Party (e.g., maintenance of the employees' wage in the case of illness). Next, the supporters were informed that this leader either experienced success or failure in a negotiation which was described as being important for the Green Party. Afterward, the supporters had to evaluate the leader's effectiveness. As displayed in Figure 3.1, the study significantly supported the predictions. Furthermore, the stronger evaluations of leadership effectiveness of prototypical leaders as compared with nonprototypical leaders after failure were mediated by trust.

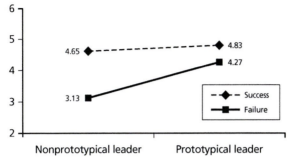

Figure 3.1.   Perceptions of leadership effectiveness as a function of leader group prototypicality and leader performance, adapted from Giessner et al. (2005), Experiment 1.

A second study by Giessner and colleagues (2005) aimed to replicate these findings in a controlled laboratory study. Using such a laboratory setting made it possible to actually immerse participants in the leadership situation. All participants were placed in separate cubicles and were led to believe that they would work together, through a computer network, in a four-person team with one leader and three followers. In reality, all participants worked individually and were placed in a follower role, and the presence and performance of the leaders was simulated through computerized feedback. Leader prototypicality was manipulated by bogus personality test feedback indicating that the leader was either very typical or very atypical for the team (cf. van Knippenberg & van Knippenberg, 2005). Leader performance was manipulated through feedback regarding a negotiation task in which the leader secured (success) or failed to secure (failure) points for the team. Finally, participants evaluated leadership effectiveness. The results replicated the findings of the scenario study and again indicated that trust in leadership was a mediating mechanism by which prototypical leaders compared with nonprototypical leaders received stronger evaluations of leadership effectiveness after failure.

In a follow-up study, Giessner and van Knippenberg (2005) developed the notion that the moderating effect of leader group prototypicality on responses to leader performance was contingent on the degrees of freedom for social construction. Following Brendl and Higgins (1996), Giessner and van Knippenberg distinguished between minimal versus maximal goal definitions. Minimal goals define end states that should minimally be achieved. If, for instance, a certain minimal level of profit is not secured, bankruptcy is inevitable; therefore, any performance below the minimal level results in a negative outcome. Not achieving a minimal goal thus is negative regardless of how close one comes to achieving the goal (Neumann, Mummendey, Kessler, Schubert, & Waldzus, 2005). Maximal goals, in contrast, define end states that ideally would be achieved. If, for example, realizing a certain amount of profit would move the organization up from fourth place to market leader, realizing enough profit to make it to second place, but not to first, does not need to be a negative event. Not achieving a maximal goal thus is not necessarily evaluated negatively (although it may be), and the closer one comes to achieving the goal, the more positive the evaluation of one's performance (Neumann et al., 2005). Maximal goals thus leave more degrees of freedom for responses to failure to achieve the goal than minimal goals.

Accordingly, Giessner and van Knippenberg (2005) argued that the moderating effect of leader group prototypicality on responses to leader failure would primarily be evident for failure to achieving maximal goals, where there is leeway for interpretation of—especially—leader failure to achieve the goal. For minimal goals, responses to prototypical leaders failing to achieve the goal were not expected to be more positive than to nonprototypical leaders that failed to achieve the goal. As in the previous study, this hypothesis was put to the test in a lab experiment as well as a scenario experiment. The lab experiment was mainly based on the lab experiment conducted by Giessner and colleagues (2005). However, participants received only leader failure feedback. Furthermore, besides manipulating leader prototypicality, goal definition was manipulated. In the maximal goal condition, the leader's goal was framed as an ideal goal that should be achieved. In the minimal goal condition, the goal was framed as an ought goal that must be achieved. After the failure feedback, participants indicated their evaluation of leadership effectiveness. Results confirmed predictions. Only when performance goals were defined as goals that should ideally be realized did prototypical leaders receive more favorable responses than nonprototypical leaders (see Figure 3.2).

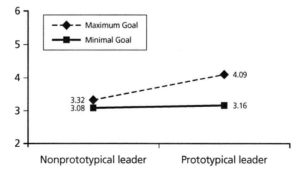

Figure 3.2.   Perceptions of leadership effectiveness after failure as a function of leader group prototypicality and minimal versus maximal goal definition, adapted from Giessner and van Knippenberg (2005), Experiment 1.

The aim of the scenario experiment was threefold. First, the results should be replicated with more mundane realism. Second, the experimental design was extended by adding a success condition to show that the interactive effects of leader prototypicality and goal definition are mainly evident after leader failure. Third, trust in leadership was tested again as the mediating mechanism of the leader prototypicality effect within the maximal goal/leader failure condition. The scenario described a leader of an internationally oriented consulting agency team. The nonprototypical leader was described as atypical of the team; that is, different from the team members with little in common with the team members. The prototypical leader was described as very typical of the team, similar to the team members with a lot in common with the team members (adapted from van Knippenberg & van Knippenberg, 2005). Next, it was explained that a core responsibility of the leader was to acquire new business value for the team. In the maximal goal condition, this goal was framed as an ideal goal that the leader should reach. In the minimal goal condition it was said that this ought goal must be reached. Afterward, participants received information that the leader reached the goal (success) or failed to reach the goal (failure). Perceptions of leadership effectiveness and leader trust were measured. As predicted, a three-way interaction was observed. After successful achievement of group goals, leader prototypicality and goal definition did not interact to affect perceptions of leadership. However, after failure to achieve the group goal, the interaction of leader prototypicality and goal definition from the laboratory study was replicated. Furthermore, the study confirmed again the mediating role of trust in the leader for the relationship between leader prototypicality and leadership effectiveness within the maximal goal/leader failure condition.

These studies show that while leader characteristics such as leader group prototypicality may moderate the tendency to hold leaders accountable for failures to achieve group or organizational goals, the extent to which they do so is contingent on the room for the subjective interpretation of failure to achieve the performance goal. They also point to an asymmetry in responses to leaders associated with success versus failure. Whereas responses to leaders associated with success were favorable even for non-prototypical leaders, after failure, prototypical leaders could enjoy markedly more favorable responses. All in all, the findings from the studies by Giessner and colleagues further substantiate the notion that leadership perceptions are in part a product of social construction processes. They also show that the social identity perspective provides a viable framework to explore the romance of leadership identified by Meindl (1995; Meindl et al., 1985) in more depth (cf. Haslam et al., 2001).

Whereas the discussion so far has, for obvious reasons, largely emphasized the follower side in the follower-centered perspective, this is not to say that leaders cannot play an active role in influencing follower social construction of leadership. Leaders may actively seek to convey certain images that match followers' conceptions of effective leadership (cf. Meindl, 1995) and thus build and secure a basis of endorsement and effectiveness among their followers. In the following, we address this issue from the perspective of the social identity analysis of leadership.

SOCIAL IDENTITY AND LEADERS' ACTIVE ROLE IN FOLLOWER SOCIAL CONSTRUCTION

Two thousand years ago the proudest boast was civis Romanus sum. *Today, in the world of freedom, the proudest boast is* Ich bin ein Berliner. *All free men, wherever they may live, are citizens of Berlin, and, therefore, as a free man, I take pride in the words* Ich bin ein Berliner.

—John F. Kennedy

U.S. president John F. Kennedy was not born in Berlin. He was not even German. When he claimed to be from Berlin—*Ich bin ein Berliner*—in a speech for a Berlin audience in response to the East-German resurrection of the Berlin Wall in the heydays of the Cold War, he clearly was making a symbolic statement. In effect, he was defining a group (*all free men*) that allowed him to claim to his Berlin audience that he and they were members of the same group. Kennedy suggested that he was not just an outsider talking to them, but in fact a representative of their group. By proudly claiming to be *ein Berliner*, Kennedy conveyed an image that may have fed straight into his audience's perception of Kennedy as a leader, and not just as "a" leader, but as a leader of their group—*their* leader.

Whether the issue of follower construction of leadership is approached from the romance of leadership perspective, from the perspective of leadership categorization and implicit leadership theories, or from the perspective of the social identity analysis of leadership, the implication is that leaders with an intuitive or more conscious grasp of these processes may build and sustain their basis for leadership by conveying an image that provides a favorable match with followers' implicit or explicit standards of high-quality leadership (Meindl, 1995; Reicher & Hopkins, 2001, 2003; van Knippenberg & Hogg, 2003b; van Knippenberg et al., in press). In the social identity analysis of leadership, this notion is most explicitly captured by Reicher and Hopkins's (2001, 2003) argument that effective leaders are "entrepreneurs of identity."

Reicher and Hopkins suggest that effective leadership involves the active management of followers' definition of the shared social identity and followers' perceptions of leader's group prototypicality and the group-normativeness of the leader's vision and proposed course of action. To illustrate this point, Reicher and Hopkins (2003), for instance, cite political leaders in the Scottish elections that attributed different characteristics to the Scottish national identity to fit the claim that their party represented Scottish national identity. In a similar vein, van Knippenberg and colleagues (2004) cite examples of leaders of political parties with names that invoke the national identity, just like, for instance, Benito Mussolini in Italy invoked the Roman empire, presumably not only to flag the national identity but also to provide a link with the nation's glorious history (cf. Reicher & Hopkins, 2003; Shamir et al., 1993). As the quote from Kennedy's speech in Berlin illustrates, leaders may even define a new social identity (i.e., all free men) to suggest a shared group membership to their audience. In a similar vein, van Knippenberg and Hogg (2003b) discuss how leaders may deliberately display—or suggest—group-oriented behavior to influence followers' openness to their influence. In these ways, leaders may construe an image of themselves as a representative of, or even the embodiment of, the collective identity and thus increase their effectiveness in mobilizing followers for their cause.

An important thing to note here, however, is that the evidence for leaders' engagement in these processes is more or less exclusively anecdotal. Further development of the analysis of leaders' active role in follower construction of leadership thus would clearly benefit from more systematic, quantitative research into these processes. Ultimately, this may yield a perspective on leadership that is neither follower-centered nor leader-centered, but that truly captures the interplay between leaders and followers in defining leadership and creating a basis for leadership effectiveness.

TO CONCLUDE

In the present chapter, we aimed to explore the implications of the social identity analysis of leadership for the follower-centered perspective of leadership championed by Jim Meindl. As we hope to have illustrated in this chapter, the social identity analysis corroborates key points raised by Meindl and develops and extends the follower-centered perspective on leadership in a number of ways. Perhaps most importantly, it also hints at ways to integrate an active role for leadership into an account of leadership that is more attuned to the pivotal role followers play in the leadership processes. In this respect, it seems that the bulk of the work still needs to be done, but the clear promise also seems to be that there is a lot to be gained by developing this interactive leader–follower perspective further. In this sense indeed, Jim Meindl's heritage is alive and well, and stimulating the development of leadership research.

NOTE

1. Sometimes groups are defined by little more than their followership of a leader. As a strong case in point, take assassinated Dutch politician Pim Fortuyn. New on the political scene, only months before the election Fortuyn founded a political party with a name that left little to guess about what defined the party, and Fortuyn's prototypicality of that party: Lijst Pim Fortuyn. His party attracted a somewhat unlikely group of electable people who seemed to be united mainly, if not only, by their admiration of and identification with Fortuyn and his ideas. Shortly before the election, Fortuyn was shot dead. While his party still won a landslide victory, it fell to pieces within a year and is now reduced to almost nothing.

    Cases like these raise the question of how group prototypicality can play a role when the group is still in the process of being defined by its leadership. In Fortuyn's case, and potentially in many others, at least a partial answer to that question seems to be that Fortuyn represented a large group of people with a strong dislike for "traditional" politics and politicians. His effectiveness as a leader seemed to derive in part from his ability to define a group with which people could identify and of which he would be seen as representative (i.e., not so much his political party as the electorate supporting this party). The fact that his party fell apart after Fortuyn's demise suggests that in the end the party was defined too much by the person rather than by characteristics more generally shared amongst his followers.

REFERENCES

Abrams, D., & Hogg, M. A. (1990). Social identification, self-categorization and social influence. *European Review of Social Psychology, 1,* 195–228.

Ashforth, B. E., & Mael, F. (1989). Social identity theory and the organization. *Academy of Management Review, 14,* 20–39.

Awamleh, R., & Gardner, W. L. (1999). Perceptions of leader charisma and effectiveness: The effects of vision content, delivery, and organizational performance. *Leadership Quarterly, 10,* 345–373.

Bass, B. M. (1985). *Leadership and performance beyond expectations.* New York: Free Press.

Bass, B. M. (1990). *Bass and Stogdill's handbook of leadership: Theory, research and managerial applications.* New York: Free Press.

Brendl, C. M., & Higgins, E. T. (1996). Principles of judging valence: What makes events positive or negative? In M. P. Zanna (Ed.), *Advances in experimental social psychology* (Vol. 28, pp. 95–160). San Diego, CA: Academic Press.

Brewer, M. B. (1991). The social self: On being the same and different at the same time. *Personality and Social Psychology Bulletin, 17,* 475–482.

Chemers, M. M. (2001). Leadership effectiveness: An integrative review. In M. A. Hogg & R. S. Tindale (Eds.), *Blackwell handbook of social psychology: Group processes* (pp. 376–399). Oxford, UK: Blackwell.

Conger, J. A., & Kanungo, R. N. (1987). Towards a behavioral theory of charismatic leadership in organizational settings. *Academy of Management Review, 12,* 637–647.

Dutton, J. E., Dukerich, J. M., & Harquail, C. V. (1994). Organizational images and member identification. *Administrative Science Quarterly, 39,* 239–263.

Eagly, A. H. (2003). Few women at the top: How role incongruity produces prejudice and the glass ceiling. In D. van Knippenberg & M. A. Hogg (Eds.) *Leadership and power: Identity processes in groups and organizations* (pp. 79–93). London: Sage.

Eagly, A. H., & Karau, S. J. (2002). Role congruity theory of prejudice toward female leaders. *Psychological Review, 109,* 573–598.

Festinger, L. (1954). A theory of social comparison processes. *Human Relations, 7,* 117–140.

Fielding, K. S., & Hogg, M. A. (1997). Social identity, self-categorization, and leadership: A field study of small interactive groups. *Group Dynamics, 1,* 39–51.

Giessner, S. R., & van Knippenberg, D. (2005). *"License to fail": Influence of goal definition, leader group prototypicality, and leader performance on perceptions of leadership effectiveness.* Manuscript submitted for publication.

Giessner, S. R., van Knippenberg, D., & Sleebos, E. (2005). *License to fail?: Leader prototypicality, leader performance, and leadership endorsement.* Manuscript submitted for publication.

Hains, S. C., Hogg, M. A., & Duck, J. M. (1997). Self-categorization and leadership: Effects of group prototypicality and leader stereotypicality. *Personality and Social Psychology Bulletin, 23,* 1087–1100.

Haslam, S. A. (2001). *Psychology in organisations: The social identity approach.* London: Sage.

Haslam, S. A., Platow, M. J., Turner, J. C., Reynolds, K. J., McGarty, C., Oakes, P. J., et al. (2001). Social identity and the romance of leadership: The importance of being seen to be 'doing it for us'. *Group Processes and Intergroup Relations, 4,* 191–205.

Haslam, S. A., & Platow, M. J. (2001). Your wish is our command: The role of shared social identity in translating a leader's vision into followers' action. In M. A. Hogg & D. J. Terry (Eds.), *Social identity processes in organizational contexts* (pp. 213–228). Philadelphia: Psychology Press.

Haslam, S. A., van Knippenberg, D., Platow, M., & Ellemers, N. (Eds.) (2003). *Social identity at work: Developing theory for organizational practice.* Philadelphia: Psychology Press.

Hogg, M. A. (2000). Subjective uncertainty reduction through self-categorization: A motivational theory of social identity processes. *European Review of Social Psychology, 11,* 223–255.

Hogg, M. A. (2001). A social identity theory of leadership. *Personality and Social Psychology Review, 5,* 184–200.

Hogg, M. A., Hains, S. C., & Mason, I. (1998). Identification and leadership in small groups: Salience, frame of reference, and leader stereotypicality effects on leader evaluations. *Journal of Personality and Social Psychology, 75,* 1248–1263.

Hogg, M. A., & Terry, D. J. (2000). Social identity and self-categorization processes in organizational contexts. *Academy of Management Review, 25,* 121–140.

Hogg, M. A., & van Knippenberg, D. (2003). Social identity and leadership processes in groups. *Advances in Experimental Social Psychology, 35*, 1–52.

Lord, R. G. (1977). Functional leadership behavior: Measurement and relation to social power and leadership perceptions. *Administrative Science Quarterly, 22*, 114–133.

Lord, R. G., Binning, J. F., Rush, M. C., & Thomas, J. C. (1978). The effect of performance cues and leader behavior on questionnaire ratings of leadership behavior. *Organizational Behavior and Human Performance, 21*, 27–39.

Lord, R. G., & Brown, D. J. (2004). *Leadership processes and follower identity.* Mahwah, NJ: Erlbaum.

Lord, R. G., Brown, D. J., & Freiberg, S. J. (1999). Understanding the dynamics of leadership: The role of follower self-concepts in the leader/follower relationship. *Organizational Behavior and Human Decision Processes, 78*, 1–37.

Lord, R. G., Foti, R. J., & DeVader, C. L. (1984). A test of leadership categorization theory: Internal structure, information processing, and leadership perceptions. *Organizational Behavior and Human Performance, 34*, 343–378.

Lord, R., & Hall, R. (2003). Identity, leadership categorization, and leadership schema. In D. van Knippenberg & M. A. Hogg (Eds.) *Leadership and power: Identity processes in groups and organizations* (pp. 48–64). London: Sage.

Lord, R. G., & Maher, K. J. (1991). *Leadership and information processing: Linking perceptions and performance.* Boston: Unwin Hyman.

Meindl, J. R. (1990). On leadership: An alternative to the conventional wisdom. In B. M. Staw & L. L. Cummings (Eds.), *Research in organizational behavior* (Vol. 12, pp. 159–203). Greenwich, CT: JAI Press.

Meindl, J. R. (1993). Reinventing leadership: A radical, social psychological approach. In J. K. Murnighan (Ed.), *Social psychology in organizations* (pp. 89–118). Englewood Cliffs, NJ: Prentice-Hall.

Meindl, J. R. (1995). The romance of leadership as a follower-centric theory: A social constructionist approach. *Leadership Quarterly, 6*, 329–341.

Meindl, J. R., & Ehrlich, S. B. (1987). The romance of leadership and the evaluation of organizational performance. *Academy of Management Journal, 30*, 91–109.

Meindl, J. R., Ehrlich, S. B., & Dukerich, J. M. (1985). The romance of leadership. *Administrative Science Quarterly, 30*, 78–102.

Neumann, J., Mummendey, A., Kessler, T., Schubert, T., & Waldzus, S. (2005). *Minimum goal representation as determinant of explicit rejection and exclusion of deviants.* Manuscript submitted for publication.

Pastor, J.-C., Meindl, J. R., & Mayo, M. C. (2002). A network effects model of charisma attributions. *Academy of Management Journal, 45*, 410–420.

Phillips, J. S., & Lord, R. G. (1981). Causal attributions and perceptions of leadership. *Organizational Behavior and Human Behavior, 28*, 143–163.

Pierro, A., Cicero, L., Bonaiuto, M., van Knippenberg, D., & Kruglanski, A. W. (2005a). Leader group prototypicality and leadership effectiveness: The moderating role of need for cognitive closure. *Leadership Quarterly, 16*, 503–516.

Pierro, A., Cicero, L., Bonaiuto, M., van Knippenberg, D., & Kruglanski, A. W. (2005b). *Leader group prototypicality and resistance to organizational change: The moderating role of need for closure and team identification.* Manuscript submitted for publication.

Pillai, R., & Meindl, J. R. (1998). Context and charisma: A "meso" level examination of the relationship of organic structure, collectivism, and crisis to charismatic leadership. *Journal of Management, 24,* 643–671.

Platow, M. J., Haslam, S. A., Foddy, M., & Grace, D. M. (2003). Leadership as the outcome of self-categorization processes. In D. van Knippenberg & M. A. Hogg (Eds.), *Leadership and power: Identity processes in groups and organizations* (pp. 34–47). London: Sage.

Platow, M. J., Hoar, S., Reid, S. A., Harley, K., & Morrison, D. (1997). Endorsement of distributively fair and unfair leaders in interpersonal and intergroup situations. *European Journal of Social Psychology, 27,* 465–494.

Platow, M. J., & van Knippenberg, D. (2001). A social identity analysis of leadership endorsement: The effects of leader ingroup prototypicality and distributive intergroup fairness. *Personality and Social Psychology Bulletin, 27,* 1508–1519.

Platow, M. J., van Knippenberg, D., Haslam, S. A., van Knippenberg, B., & Spears, R. (2006). A special gift we bestow on you for being representative of us: Considering leader charisma from a self-categorization perspective. *British Journal of Social Psychology, 45,* 303–320.

Reicher, S. D., & Hopkins, N. (2001). *Self and nation.* London: Sage.

Reicher, S., & Hopkins, N. (2003). On the science of the art of leadership. In D. van Knippenberg & M. A. Hogg (Eds.), *Leadership and power: Identity processes in groups and organizations* (pp. 197–209). London: Sage.

Ridgeway, C. L. (2003). Status characteristics and leadership. In D. van Knippenberg & M. A. Hogg (Eds.), *Leadership and power: Identity processes in groups and organizations* (pp. 65–78). London: Sage.

Rosch, E. (1978). Principles of categorization. In E. Rosch & B. B. Lloyd (Eds.), *Cognition and categorization* (pp. 27–48). Hillsdale, NJ: Erlbaum.

Sedikides, C., & Brewer, M. B. (2001). *Individual self, relational self, collective self.* Philadelphia: Psychology Press.

Shamir, B. (1990). Calculations, values, and identities: The source of collectivistic work motivation. *Human Relations, 43,* 313–332.

Shamir, B., House, R., & Arthur, M. B. (1993). The motivational effects of charismatic leadership: A self-concept based theory. *Organization Science, 4,* 577–594.

Tajfel, H., & Turner, J. C. (1986). The social identity theory of intergroup behavior. In S. Worchel & W. Austin (Eds.), *Psychology of intergroup relations* (pp. 7–24). Chicago: Nelson-Hall.

Tindale, R. S., & Kameda, T. (2000). Social sharedness' as a unifying theme for information processing in groups. *Group Processes and Intergroup Relations, 3,* 123–140.

Turner, J. C. (1985). Social categorization and the self-concept: A social cognitive theory of group behaviour. In E. J. Lawler (Ed.), *Advances in group processes* (Vol. 2, pp. 77–122). Greenwich, CT: JAI Press.

Turner, J. C. (1991). *Social influence.* Buckingham, UK: Open University Press.

Turner, J. C., Hogg, M. A., Oakes, P. J., Reicher, S. D., & Wetherell, M. S. (1987). *Rediscovering the social group: A self-categorization theory.* Oxford, UK: Blackwell.

Tyler, T. R., & Blader, S. L. (2000). *Cooperation in groups. Procedural justice, social identity, and behavioral engagement.* Philadelphia: Psychology Press.

van Knippenberg, B., & van Knippenberg, D. (2005). Leader self-sacrifice and leadership effectiveness: The moderating role of leader prototypicality. *Journal of Applied Psychology, 90,* 25–37.

van Knippenberg, D. (2000a). Group norms, prototypicality, and persuasion. In D. J. Terry & M. A. Hogg (Eds.), *Attitudes, behavior, and social context: The role of norms and group membership* (pp. 157–170). Mahwah, NJ: Erlbaum.

van Knippenberg, D. (2000b). Work motivation and performance: A social identity perspective. *Applied Psychology: An International Review, 49,* 357–371.

van Knippenberg, D. (2003). Intergroup relations in organizations. In M. West, D. Tjosvold, & K. G. Smith (Eds.), *International handbook of organizational teamwork and cooperative working* (pp. 381–399). Chichester, UK: Wiley.

van Knippenberg, D., & Hogg, M. A. (2003a). *Leadership and power: Identity processes in groups and organizations.* London: Sage.

van Knippenberg, D., & Hogg, M. A. (2003b). A social identity model of leadership effectiveness in organizations. In R. M. Kramer & B. M. Staw (Eds.), *Research in organizational behavior* (Vol. 25, pp. 243–295). Amsterdam: Elsevier.

van Knippenberg, D, van Knippenberg, B., De Cremer, D., & Hogg, M. A. (2004). Leadership, self, and identity: A review and research agenda. *Leadership Quarterly, 15,* 825–856.

van Knippenberg, D., van Knippenberg, B., & van Dijk, E. (2000). Who takes the lead in risky decision making? Effects of group members' individual riskiness and prototypicality. *Organizational Behavior and Human Decision Processes, 83,* 213–234.

Weick, K. E. (1995). *Sense-making in organizations.* Thousand Oaks, CA: Sage.

Yukl, G. (2002). *Leadership in organizations* (5th ed.). New York: Prentice-Hall.

CHAPTER 4

SHARING LEADERSHIP

Who, What, When, and Why

Lynn R. Offermann and Noelle F. Scuderi
George Washington University

ABSTRACT

The extensive literature in leadership becomes even more complex when we consider situations in which multiple individuals, at least some of whom are in hierarchically subordinate positions, perform the functions that encompass what we know of as leadership. What do we call this form of leadership in which one or more "followers" lead, and what do we know about these situations in terms of organizational outcomes such as unit performance and member satisfaction? The present chapter reviews work published under the labels of collective leadership, shared leadership, distributed leadership, team leadership, co-leadership, emergent leadership, and self-managed teams to examine follower participation in leadership roles. We discuss the theoretical and operational similarities and differences of these constructs and propose a framework for integration that seeks to bring clarity to a literature that often uses terms interchangeably to mean different things. We then review possible antecedents and/or conditions favoring the sharing of leadership and discuss outcomes, concluding with suggestions for future work on follower engagement in leadership.

Follower-Centered Perspectives on Leadership, pages 71–91
Copyright © 2007 by Information Age Publishing
All rights of reproduction in any form reserved.

One of Jim Meindl's major contributions to the field of leadership has been his assertion that many people view leaders as heroic figures and overattribute desirable performance effects to them rather than to other sources (i.e., Meindl, Erlich, & Dukerich, 1985). One of those other, ignored sources of influence is, of course, the leader's "followers." In truth, followers have long shared leadership with those who have "lead" them, whether they have received credit for it or not—often, not. The more recent awareness of tendencies to overattribute leadership and desirable outcomes to leaders has led scholars to broaden their focus to examine how so-called followers can and do share in leadership.

Yet as complex as the literature in leadership can be, the waters become even muddier when we consider situations in which multiple individuals, at least some of whom are in hierarchically subordinate positions, perform the functions and exert the influence that encompass what we know of as leadership. However, if we view leadership as a "process of influence toward the accomplishment of objectives" (Houghton, Neck, & Manz, 2003, p. 124), rather than just a vertical position within the hierarchy of the organization, then the roles or functions that make up leadership may be distributed throughout an organization and/or shared broadly within teams or with specific followers. Similar to the systems approach to under-standing organizations, recognizing the importance of many interacting parts to the overall functioning of the organization within its environment, this "new" view of leadership allows for collective implementation of influ-ence and leadership roles within groups for both maximal group and orga-nizational effectiveness.

Despite the increasing importance of this broader view of leadership, the literature uses a variety of terms, often interchangeably, to mean a host of differing situations in which leadership functions are performed, not by or through a single person, but by more than one person in a group, often without any formal designation or hierarchical title. Yet what do we call this form of leadership in which one or more persons traditionally seen as "fol-lowers" engage in leadership? How do we measure it, and what do we know about these situations in terms of organizational outcomes such as unit performance and member satisfaction?

The present chapter reviews relevant work published under the labels of shared leadership, distributed leadership, collective leadership, team lead-ership, co-leadership, emergent leadership, and self-managed teams to examine broader participation in leadership roles. Our domain consists of any leadership process that involves more than one person assuming lead-ership responsibilities, simultaneously and/or in succession, where one or more of these individuals are not in a position of titular leadership (i.e., are "followers"), and where the presence of more than one person engag-ing in leadership activities is acknowledged either formally or informally by the group or organization. We discuss the theoretical and operational similarities and differences of these constructs and propose a framework for conceptualizing the sharing of leadership. We also discuss possible antecedents and outcomes, including suggestions for future work on follower engagement in leadership.

WHAT'S IN A NAME?

Pearce and Conger (2003) have discussed the historical and conceptual foundations for shared or collective leadership. A variety of management and leadership theories in use over the last several decades are relevant, including leader–member exchange (Graen & Scandura, 1987), substitutes for leadership (Kerr & Jermier, 1978), self-leadership (Manz, 1980; Manz & Sims, 2001), self-managing teams and emergent leadership (Hollander, 1961; Manz & Sims, 1993), active followership (Hollander, 1997), and empowerment (Conger & Kanungo, 1988), among others. For additional discussion on models of shared leadership, see Pearce and Sims (2000), Cox, Pearce, and Perry (2003), and Conger and Pearce (2003).

As the name suggests, sharing leadership implies the involvement of multiple persons in the acts of leadership, including individuals in various levels of the organizational system. Within the context of teams,[1] shared leadership, as opposed to so-called "vertical" leadership, suggests that multiple team members are participating in leadership by moving the team toward goal-accomplishment as opposed to having team members subject themselves to the leadership of a single individual. Burke, Fiore, and Salas (2003) describe shared team leadership as the "leadership function dynamically transferred within the team" (p. 104). As such, shared leadership may be viewed as a mutual influence process (Ensley, Pearson, & Pearce, 2003), a "dynamic, interactive influence process" (Conger & Pearce, 2003, p. 1), or a "collaborative team process in which team members share key leadership roles" (Perry, Pearce, & Sims, 1999, p. 125). This is instead of the traditional downward influence process where leader functions are performed by a single hierarchical or vertical leader (Cox et al., 2003; Houghton et al., 2003). Even well-known champions of leadership such as James MacGregor Burns discuss the presence of this type of empowerment in groups in recent writings. For example, Burns (1998, p. 3) cites collective leadership as an emerging property of groups where "crucial leadership acts" occur in a collective process, shared among empowered team members, as opposed to being initiated by a single, dominating leader.

Unfortunately, as the concept of leadership has broadened to include situations where leadership is seen as involving multiple individuals within a given group, the terms used to describe these situations have also multiplied. Often the same term, when used by different authors, means different things. Existing research highlighting situations with more than one leader in a group most commonly refers to this leadership structure as either shared or collective leadership. Shared leadership has been described as a phenomenon whereby "all members of the team collectively influence each other toward accomplishing its goals" (Avolio, Sivasubramaniam, Murry, Jung, & Garger, 2003, p. 145) or "when all members of a team are fully engaged in the leadership of the team" (Pearce, 2004, p. 48). Raelin (2004, p. 133) describes this form of leadership, whereby "everyone in the group can serve as a leader," as collective leadership.

These definitions of shared leadership reflect situations in which it is the whole collective that shares in leadership. In contrast, other scholars have suggested that it is "the aggregated leadership behavior of some, many or all of the members" of a team (Gronn, 2002, p. 3). Yet the dynamics of a team where leadership is shared by all are likely to be quite different from a team where only some people take on this role. For one thing, in the extreme situation described above where all are participating in leadership, if everyone is involved as a leader, who follows? Or is everyone both leader and follower? How does group performance and viability differ in groups where everyone leads in some form from groups where some people never assume leadership? To be able to answer these and other relevant questions, we need to be able to differentiate subsets of shared leadership.

One such subset of shared leadership is distributed leadership. As implied by the name, the use of this term portrays leadership in organizations as a division of labor among team members of the necessary leadership roles (Barry, 1991; Gronn, 2002). As noted by Hill (2004, p. 4) "responsibility for leadership activity is distributed between group members." These leader roles include functions typically associated with goal accomplishment for effective solo leaders, such as visioning, organizing, and boundary-spanning, and functions associated with team cohesiveness and effectiveness, such as facilitating, coaching, and relationship management (Barry, 1991; Burke et al., 2003). Distributing leadership can be a valuable strategy for maximally using the strengths of various team members when there may not be one single team member who can effectively satisfy the leadership needs of the group as an individual (Burke et al., 2003). To accommodate this reality, roles may be divided among team members, shared by multiple team members simultaneously, or rotated within the team—whatever is necessary for effective goal accomplishment. Thus, the distributed leadership conceptualization implies the prospect of unequal shares of leadership across members as well as the possibility that some members may not lead at all. Yet in examining the terminology surrounding the concept of shared leadership, some studies seem to use the terms shared and distributed leadership interchangeably (i.e., Day, Gronn, & Salas, 2004). Still other studies use similar terms, such as "dispersion" (Neubert & Taggar, 2004) or "team leadership" (Avolio et al., 2003), rather than the word "distributed," to indicate a situation where multiple team members influence one another and the rest of the team.

Another related term is "co-leadership," which may be seen as the most limited case of distributed leadership but which is often identified separately in the literature. As described by Sally (2002), "co-leaders are a uniquely structured team of two people, and co-leadership is a much shorter and more natural step away from shared (but usually unequal) team leadership than it is from a hierarchical single commander" (p. 85). Typically, co-leadership appears in the literature in discussions of leadership at senior levels, where discrete leadership role functions are enacted by two coordinated individuals (e.g., Heenan & Bennis, 1999). For example, in educational settings, often it is the vice principal who deals with student behavioral problems (management-by-exception) while the principal has greater interaction with the community and students at large, ideally providing inspiration and vision. The classic "good cop–bad cop" teaming is another similar model, distributing roles across two individuals whose long-term goals are in agreement, but whose functions and behavior are clearly delineated.

A Proposed Continuum

For a research area trying to expand and develop, varied terminology generates confusion rather than clarity. Chosen definitions can affect how the construct gets operationalized for measurement and can make it difficult both to compare outcomes of individual studies and to build a more comprehensive understanding of the phenomena across studies. As a guide for future research, it would be helpful to have a framework to capture the varying ways in which leadership can be shared and categories into which studies could be placed, as well as a consistent terminology to discriminate across forms of nonvertical leadership.

In that spirit, we propose a continuum of situations where multiple leaders are present within groups that appears diagrammatically in Figure 4.1 and is described in Table 4.1. At the leftmost extreme is the traditional conception of leadership as embodied in a single leader. Although some studies from this perspective have included discussion of the importance of followership and mutual influence processes between leaders and followers, they still maintain some differentiation in status between leaders and followers. Some so-called "followers" have always exerted what we would consider leadership behaviors, albeit without much formal recognition or

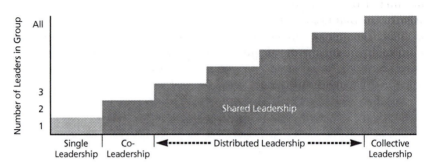

Figure 4.1.   Continuum of single and shared leadership.

Table 4.1.   Characteristics of Alternative Forms of Leadership

General Leadership Model	Traditional "Vertical" Leadership	Shared Leadership		
Specific model	Single leadership	Co-leadership	Distributed leadership	Collective leadership
Nature of leadership	Leadership is associated with one individual only	Leadership is divided between two people	Leadership is distributed broadly, but some members of the group follow rather than lead	Leadership is shared by all in the group
Number of leaders in group	One leader	Two leaders	More than two but less than the number of people in the group	Equal to the number of people in the group

title. Nonetheless, many situations still acknowledge the leadership of only one person in a group.

To the right of single-leader leadership are variants of what we propose falls under the conceptual umbrella of "shared leadership." Co-leadership is the first step away from single leadership, providing roles for two and only two leaders. We suggest that this term be used in situations where there are two leaders and at least one other group member who follows, that is, when the group size is greater than two. Many of these situations still retain verticality, with two people, rather than one, seen as authority figures with greater influence than others in the group. Co-leaders may choose to clearly separate leadership role expectations or enact a flexible job-sharing approach. Although in practice it seems that many such cases are those in which parts of leadership are clearly separate for the two individuals (e.g., one person focusing on task performance, the other on maintaining positive socioemotional relationships and harmony), this conceptualization would allow for undifferentiated roles as well.

Further to the right on our continuum of shared leadership is what we label distributed leadership, referring to situations where there are more than two leaders but where the number of leaders is less than the total number in the group. That is, distribution is not complete, and some members follow rather than exercising leadership responsibilities or influence. Under this scheme, distributed leadership is not full and equal participation in leadership, but rather permits the unequal distribution that is probably a more frequent occurrence in most group situations. Operationally, this can be conceptualized as a proportion of members involved in leadership compared to the number of members of the group, with movement away from co-leadership strongest in those groups with higher proportions of members enacting leadership functions.

At the rightmost extreme is where we propose using the term collective leadership, in situations where there is an expectation and realization of full participation in leadership among the members of a group. This may occur with dyads, where two people share leadership, or in larger groups where the number engaging in leadership is equal to the number of members of the group. In cases where groups function truly interdependently on shared tasks this may be appropriately referred to as "team leadership." Full member participation in leadership is often discussed and highly desired. Nonetheless, we suspect that this state is a rare accomplishment of only the most highly functioning task teams and that most situations of shared leadership fall somewhere along the distributed leadership portion of the continuum.

MEASURING SHARED LEADERSHIP

With a relatively new leadership construct such as shared leadership, it is especially important to ensure that the measure of the construct coincides appropriately with its operational definition. In addition, this measure should occur at an appropriate level of analysis for the construct of interest. In the case of shared leadership, what is more appropriate for examining situations with presumed multiple leaders, the combination of individuals or the group level of analysis? Group-level measures are most certainly appropriate for capturing information about group characteristics, but the question remains as to whether shared leadership is most appropriately examined at the group level without also examining what is happening at the individual level within the group. If we conceptualize shared leadership in terms of degrees ranging from co-leadership to collective leadership, limiting our analysis to group-level measures lumps all forms of shared leadership into one general category. In doing so, we lose potentially valuable information for understanding the true operation of shared leadership. At the same time, aggregation of individual-level measures to a group level of analysis requires both conceptual meaningfulness of the construct at the group level (Kenny & La Voie, 1985), which is most certainly present for shared leadership, and an appropriate agreement among individuals on their evaluations of fellow team members and/or the properties of the group (Klein, Dansereau, & Hall, 1994).

Researchers in the area of emergent leadership have used a number of simple and direct measurement approaches that are relevant in the study of shared leadership in groups. For example, DeSouza and Klein (1995) asked group members specifically to identify whether one or two emergent leaders arose within their groups. Fifty-five groups identified a single emergent leader, 13 groups identified two emergent leaders, and 49 groups identified no emergent leader. However, because their research focus was on more traditional leadership conceptions, when asked to identify emerging leaders, members were not given an option to name more than two leaders, nor was the possibility of shared leadership, as opposed to no leadership, considered for the 49 groups who identified no emergent leader among them. In applying this approach to the study of shared leadership, groups could simply be asked to identify the leader(s) that emerged among the group, defining what is meant by leadership and noting the acceptability of naming multiple individuals as leaders, if appropriate.

Neubert (1999; Neubert & Taggar, 2004) approached measurement of emergent leadership in a similar fashion. Team members were asked to name any person or persons who emerged as a leader during team interactions. A metric termed "informal leadership dispersion" was developed as a ratio of the number of perceived or identified informal leaders in a team divided by the team's size. The resulting value, which incorporates a control for team size, is larger as the number of leaders identified within a team increases, and thus shared leadership, as perceived by multiple team members, increases. Using this metric in a study of 21 manufacturing teams, more than half of the teams (n = 10) nominated more than one informal leader, with four teams nominating two leaders, three nominating three leaders, and three nominating four leaders. Of the remaining teams, two did not nominate any informal leaders, and nine nominated a single person as leader (Neubert, 1999). This provides "real-world" evidence that shared leadership is a naturally occurring phenomena and that leadership often varies in how widely it is distributed in teams.

Taggar, Hackett, and Saha (1999) gathered individual member evaluations of who and how many leaders emerged within a team setting. Each team member then rated every other member on a scale of 1 to 5 as to whether they (1) exemplified strong leadership and/or (2) assumed leadership within the team setting. These two items were averaged to create a leadership score for each team member, with the person obtaining the highest leadership score being assigned emergent leader status by the researchers. In applying this methodology to the study of shared leadership, a leadership cut score could be set to determine the number of "leaders" sharing influence or leadership roles within a group. Alternatively, individual leadership scores could be aggregated within teams and comparisons made across teams based on the degree of shared leadership found through the team's aggregated leadership scores. These aggregate team leadership scores could then be examined in relation to team performance.

Representative of researchers specifically measuring shared leadership, as opposed to emergent leadership, Pearce has measured shared leadership by collecting team member ratings of both the group itself and the formal team leader on five types of leadership behaviors, including aversive, directive, transactional, transformational, and empowering leadership (Pearce & Sims, 2002). Shared leadership is quantified by the ratings team members assign to their group on items reflecting each type of leadership behavior, with some behaviors contributing negatively and others contributing positively to team outcomes. The relative magnitude of the team members' group ratings as compared to the ratings assigned to their leader on the same measure are then compared in order to evaluate the effectiveness of shared leadership as opposed to vertical leadership. This questionnaire methodology successfully taps into the forms of influence exerted and experienced within the groups under study. However, group members are not explicitly asked *whether* leadership is exhibited, nor is the degree of member involvement in leadership roles or responsibilities examined. Rather, team members are asked to rate the leadership exhibited by both the team as a whole and the team leader, providing a baseline assumption that shared leadership is both present within the groups and equally distributed among the team members as a collective whole. In addition, because all team members rate both the team leader and the team members on the same leadership questionnaire, inflation of shared leadership ratings in teams may occur due to the priming of leader-type thinking and associations of leadership to the team that might not have been explicitly recognized or experienced by team members otherwise.

Taking a similar approach, Avolio and colleagues (2003) advocate the use of an adapted version of the individually based Multifactor Leadership Questionnaire (MLQ) to measure shared leadership in team settings. The key consideration for the design of their Team MLQ is the measurement of shared leadership as a group-level construct, where members assess the team as a whole as opposed to assessing team members individually. Like the Pearce and Sims (2002) questionnaire noted above, this method also creates an assumption that shared leadership among the team as a collective whole is exhibited. Team members are not asked specifically whether leadership was in fact shared within their group, nor whether multiple leaders emerged within the team process, leaving a question as to the degree of leadership distribution exhibited in the teams under study. This makes it impossible to discern whether leadership is fully collective (shared by all) or distributed among some unknown subset of members.

While not incorporated into either Pearce and Sims's (2002) or Avolio and colleagues' (2003) research, individual-level team member leadership ratings can be an informative measure of shared leadership in teams, as shown by Taggar and colleagues (1999). By asking team members to assign leadership scores to each of their fellow team members first, and then aggregating the individual leadership scores of each team member into a team leadership score, teams can be compared on the degree to which leadership emerges across team members. Assuming a sufficient level of agreement among team members on leadership scores (Klein et al., 1994), teams with higher scores due to higher team member ratings of leadership might be considered higher in shared leadership.

Mayo, Meindl, and Pastor (2003) also recognized this potential use of individual member ratings in their treatment of shared leadership from a social networks perspective. They present a prototypical questionnaire methodology where individuals rate each of their fellow group members on leadership questions. Their sample questions were derived from trans-actional and transformational leadership approaches, although the authors note that they could be drawn from other leadership approaches as well. This method allows for an assessment of the total amount of influence exerted within a group, as measured by the sum of all individual member ratings as well as each individual's relative contribution to the team's leadership or influence process, representing their prominence or centrality in the social system. Individual prominence is measured by the sum of an individual's ratings from fellow members across all the leadership items. A group-level measure of centrality for use in team or group-level comparisons can then be obtained by calculating the variance of centrality among group members.

Mayo and colleagues (2003) suggest that the highest degree of shared leadership exists when members are both linked to each other and where they attribute influence to each other in an egalitarian way. In the terms proposed in Figure 4.1, this would represent what we call collective leadership, where all members are influential and where differences in leadership participation are minimized among the members of a group. In our view, social networks analysis adds a promising perspective to studying shared leadership that we hope will generate future research. Additional empirical work is needed to fully develop this approach and methodology in order to determine its utility to the study of shared leadership in teams.

ANTECEDENTS AND OUTCOMES OF SHARED LEADERSHIP

With any conceptualization of leadership, it is important to understand the antecedents and required conditions for successful emergence and implementation as well as the outcomes or benefits for groups and organizations. While some findings on shared forms of leadership have been empirically tested, much of the writing on shared leadership is theoretical in nature and is in need of further examination through research. For example, the theoretical conditions that are required for shared leadership have been identified repeatedly in the writings of Pearce and his colleagues (e.g., Cox et al, 2003; Pearce & Conger, 2003; Perry et al., 1999). These include: (1) an expectation for lateral influence and self-leadership within the group as opposed to just anticipating hierarchical influence, (2) individuals developing their skills as both effective leaders and followers, and (3) individuals accepting and enacting peer influence roles and responsibility. Shared leadership requires group members to be both willing and able to exert and submit to lateral influence in order for effective leadership and group performance (Bennett, Harvey, Wise, & Woods, 2003; Houghton et al., 2003). While these proposed conditions appear to be theoretically relevant, they have not as yet been empirically examined.

Other potential prerequisites for effective implementation of shared leadership parallel the qualities of successful teams, such as shared mental models, shared attitudes, a collective team orientation, and a supportive organizational climate, among others (Burke et al., 2003). Although there is probable overlap between these effective team qualities and those characteristic of shared leadership situations, they are different in that successful teams often work under a traditional leadership model with a single leader. Even self-managed teams may choose to structure themselves by selecting a single leader from amongst themselves rather than assume a shared leadership structure.

As evidenced above, there are many possible antecedents to shared leadership suggested in the literature. In the following sections, we discuss several antecedents of shared leadership that we consider particularly viable that could be profitably examined in greater depth in future empirical research to determine their utility. These promising factors are cognitive ability, emotional competence, shared goals, self-leadership, and group size.

Cognitive Ability

In their review of the literature on leadership emergence and effectiveness, Judge, Colbert, and Ilies (2004) determined that cognitive ability (CA) is positively correlated with both leadership emergence and leadership effectiveness. Thus, one could argue that groups made up of multiple members with higher cognitive ability may be more likely to have more than one individual emerge as leaders in the group. In addition, regarding group-level outcomes, general mental ability has been shown to positively affect both team viability (Barrick, Stewart, Neubert & Mount, 1998) and team performance overall (Devine & Phillips, 2001). However, despite the correlation of $r = .29$ between mean CA and team performance in Devine and Phillips's (2001) meta-analysis, CA explained only 8.6% of the variance in team performance, providing evidence for both moderator variables and other predictors.

The presence of shared leadership may provide additional understanding of this CA–performance relationship. Given that cognitive ability predicts leadership emergence, it follows that cognitive ability should predict the emergence of shared leadership (Cox et al., 2003), as the more members there are with greater cognitive ability and thus a greater leadership capability, the more likely multiple leaders will emerge. Improved performance may occur as a result of the extra effort that is expended by multiple leaders' involvement in team activities (Waldersee & Eagleson, 2002). The collaboration and cooperation that is necessary for the enactment of shared leadership may also explain the connection between higher cognitive ability and greater team viability.

Emotional Competence

In addition to cognitive capabilities, persons who are able to discern and manage a group's emotional responses may be more likely to assume leadership. Recent work supports this contention, in that individuals possessing higher levels of emotional competence are also more likely to be identified as leaders and are given higher leadership effectiveness ratings by fellow team members (Offermann, Bailey, Vasilopoulos, Seal, & Sass, 2004). Accordingly, one could reason that groups with higher overall levels of emotional competence will be more likely to share leadership amongst themselves as more individuals within the group possess leadership characteristics (Cox et al., 2003).

Examination of work in the controversial area of emotional intelligence (EI) leads to similar conclusions. Capabilities often associated with emotional intelligence—empathy and social awareness—may be components of what classic leadership theory would term "socioemotional leadership." For example, in previous research empathy has been specifically demonstrated to predict leadership emergence (Kellet, Humphrey, & Sleeth, 2002; Wolff, Pescosolido, & Druskat, 2002). In addition, Boyatzis and Goleman's (2002) measure of EI, the Emotional Competency Inventory (ECI), includes assessments of self-awareness, self-management, relationship management, and social awareness, characteristics that are each likely to correlate positively with shared leadership in groups. Furthermore, relationship management encompasses many traditional leader-like qualities, including developing others, inspirational leadership, influence, communication, change catalyst, conflict management, building bonds, and teamwork and collaboration. Each of these components reveal potential contributions to leadership emergence. Broadening the discussion of EI to the group level, Druskat and Wolff (2001) suggest the construct of group emotional intelligence (GEI), which they characterize as a collective demonstration of emotional awareness, followed by a group's management of both the interpretation of and response to those emotions via group norms. As more members of a group display high levels of emotional competence, the ability to regulate the group's emotional life and reactions should improve, leading to smoother group functioning and greater potential for shared leadership.

Relatedly, when examining the relative contributions of cognitive ability and emotional competence on performance in student teams, Offermann and colleagues (2004) found that a team's emotional competence was actually a better predictor of the team's performance than the collective cognitive ability of the team. Given that the tasks that facilitate collective leadership are generally thought to be those that require interdependence, creativity, and/or are complex in nature (Pearce, 2004), a higher impact of emotional competence as opposed to cognitive ability for shared leadership also seems appropriate, particularly in situations where there are relatively small differences in cognitive ability among members.

Shared Goals

Leadership is unlikely to be shared with those not perceived as also sharing goals for task accomplishment. For example, talented undergraduates are notoriously shy of group projects due to fear of having to pick up the slack for irresponsible peers, in essence taking on a leadership role while being given only equal credit to those either following or loafing. Desiring an "A" grade while others in your group would be comfortable with a "C" will preclude any willingness to share leadership broadly among the members. By graduate school, wariness may still be there, but the prospect of shared leadership should increase as the range of cognitive ability and motivation narrows within teams and teammates are more likely to share goals to enhance learning and performance.

Similarly, given common levels of cognitive ability and training, we would expect that in the workplace shared goals would lead to greater sharing of leadership, as group members see themselves as all working toward the same desired outcome. Shared goals can provide a sense of confidence that effort will be expended and that trust in teammates is justified (Kozlowski, Gully, Salas, & Cannon-Bowers, 1996), factors that should facilitate more collaborative leadership. Nonetheless, sharing goals is not as simple a process as might be imagined. In fact, it likely requires far deeper conversations among members than most members are used to in order to allow members to share their mental maps, unspoken assumptions, and underlying worldviews (Rawlings, 2000). Although this doubtless takes time, the payoff may be in greater member commitment and superior group outcomes.

Self-Leadership

Self-leadership in teams has also been proposed as an important aspect of shared leadership (Burke et al., 2003). Self-leadership in individuals has been defined as the "process through which people influence themselves to achieve the self-direction and self-motivation needed to perform" (Houghton et al., 2003, p. 126). Self-leadership includes effective self-regulation and self-management, including self-observation and analysis, self-goal setting, self-reward, and self-correcting, and is implemented by influencing one's own behaviors, rewards, and cognitions (Manz & Sims, 2001). Houghton and colleagues (2003) explore the concept of self-leadership in teams, emphasizing its inherent requirement for successful shared leadership. When expanded to the group level of analysis, a collectively led team will display active control over their environment through team self-observation and analysis, team-goal setting, and team reinforcement and punishment as needed to effect goal-oriented behavior toward effective team performance (Neck, Stewart, & Manz, 1996). As a team engages in team self-leadership behavior, Neck and colleagues (1996) describe the cognitive aspects of team self-leadership that take shape and reinforce collective leadership within the team. The team forms integrated beliefs and assumptions, engages in self-talk within the group for reinforcement of behavior, and shares a common vision, reinforcing the effectiveness of the collective leadership within the group.

In particular, self-awareness and self-management have been proposed as important aspects of self-leadership, and, as such, may be relevant to examining shared leadership as well. Self-awareness involves both emotional awareness and self-confidence. Self-management includes emotional self-control, trustworthiness, conscientiousness, adaptability, optimism, achievement orientation, and initiative—all individual characteristics that could be researched separately in regard to the likelihood of shared leadership and its success. For example, projecting self-confidence and being seen as conscientious is likely to engender trust from teammates that one can be relied upon to deliver as promised.

Group Size

Another aspect of group composition that may affect the emergence of shared, and possibly even collective, leadership in teams is the size of the team. In theory, as group size increases, one would expect the emergence of fully shared leadership to decrease as the communication, coordination, and collaboration needed for successful collective leadership would likely be harder to achieve (Cox et al., 2003; Perry et al., 1999). At the same time, groups that are too small may not have the appropriate members with varied knowledge, skills, and abilities (KSAs) in order to effectively use a shared leadership strategy based on role differentiation (Conger & Pearce, 2003). Thus, theoretically, there may be an inverted U-shape curved relationship between group size and shared leadership. At the same time, the likely prospect of process losses with increasing group size would suggest that size be capped at whatever minimum level is necessary to tap into all the KSAs that are required for leadership (Steiner, 1972).

Outcomes of Shared Leadership

Not only are the factors that contribute to shared leadership important to consider, but also the potential effects of shared leadership on organizationally relevant outcomes such as group performance. Numerous studies have identified positive outcomes from the presence of shared leadership in teams. For example, Avolio, Jung, Murry, and Sivasubramaniam (1996) related shared leadership to self-reported ratings of effectiveness. Pearce and Sims (2002) demonstrate a positive relationship between shared leadership and overall team effectiveness using multiple sources of effectiveness ratings, including managers, customers, and the teams themselves. More recently, Pearce, Yoo, and Alavi (2004) identify the positive effects of shared leadership in a nonprofit organization on team potency, social integration, and problem-solving quality. A review by Pearce and Sims (2000) also identifies positive outcomes related to organizational citizenship behaviors (OCBs), networking behavior, and increased revenues. Interestingly, there is a lack of empirical data on the effects of shared leadership structures on one of the most commonly researched organizational variables, namely, member satisfaction. This omission certainly presents a viable area for future research.

Beyond the positive effects that occur as a result of shared leadership in group settings, researchers such as Waldersee and Eagleson (2002) and Pearce (1997) and his colleagues (e.g., Pearce & Sims, 2002; Pearce et al., 2004) argue that a shared leadership structure in teams is actually superior to utilizing only a single leader format. Using multiple leaders in teams avoids the individual role conflict resulting from a single leader having to perform both task and relationship functions and ensures that all the important leadership skills are represented when one person may not have all of the KSAs needed to lead effectively. In addition, increased team effectiveness can result as extra effort is expended by multiple leaders' involvement in the team's work process.

For example, Pearce and Sims (2002) demonstrate that high performing teams not only exhibited "more" leadership as seen in higher leadership ratings within those teams relative to other teams, but also showed at least as much or more influence attributed to shared leadership rather than vertical leadership within teams, when lower performing teams attributed more influence within teams to vertical leadership. While shared leadership does not explicitly call for vertical leadership or oversight, the existence of forms of shared leadership also does not preclude the existence of hierarchical leadership in an organization. Ultimately, both vertical and shared leadership can effectively coexist and work cooperatively within an organization to maximize team and organizational performance (Pearce, 2004).

FUTURE DIRECTIONS

Taken together, the studies summarized above show considerable evidence of the potential value of sharing leadership. In addition, as organizations show increased awareness of the virtues of self-managed teams, we expect that interest in varying forms of shared leadership will continue to grow. Practice is ahead of scholarship in this arena, with organizations delegating leadership responsibilities to teams and teams trying to figure out how to best provide the required leadership capabilities from within themselves. Many of these teams do have an external leader as both a resource and a reporting relationship, providing both vertical and shared leadership. There is a great need for researchers to delve further into the processes and outcomes of shared leadership, examining both antecedents and outcomes.

Based on our review of the literature, we have suggested a number of potential antecedents of shared leadership that we feel are particularly promising for future research, including cognitive ability, emotional competence, shared goals, self-leadership, and group size. There are many other factors that could also prove fruitful. In particular, the nature of the task faced by the group may have a potent effect on the emergence of shared leadership. However, task effects may prove more difficult to discern in that they are likely to interact with other factors. For example, the effects of task difficulty are likely to interact with member cognitive ability, where groups with all highly able members may be able to successfully share leadership even on complex tasks, while groups where ability levels are more heterogeneous may not.

We have also suggested some key outcomes of shared leadership that bear further examination, including team effectiveness, member satisfaction, team potency, social integration, problem-solving quality, OCBs, networking behavior, and increased organizational revenue. Other benefits of shared leadership that require additional empirical research include increased collaboration and coordination among team members (an integral part of collective leadership's success), and potentially more creative and innovative solutions to problems via the promotion of dialogue and increased team interaction (Cox et al., 2003). Furthermore, additional research is needed to differentiate potential outcomes resulting from the various forms of shared leadership such as co-leadership, distributed leadership, and collective leadership. Thus, we hope that future studies will find value in the continuum presented here to structure thinking about forms and levels of shared leadership. Using the continuum will allow us to effectively answer questions such as how group performance, team viability, and other outcomes differ in groups where everyone leads in some form from groups where some people in the group never assume leadership. It is also likely that antecedents may differ for different types of leadership, with traditionally structured organizations perhaps finding it more comfortable to try co-leadership or another more limited form of shared leadership before implementing full collective leadership.

In addition, careful consideration as to appropriate measures and methods of discerning shared leadership in future research endeavors should be undertaken. The continuum presented may also be helpful in developing appropriate measures to assess different levels of shared leadership rather than treating them as equivalent. Measures need to allow for determining just how shared group leadership is in a way that encourages neither over- nor underreporting of leadership roles within a group. In terms of method, the social network analysis approach offers considerable promise as well as approaches that allow for simultaneous group- and individual-level understanding of what is transpiring within groups exhibiting shared leadership.

Although the leadership and teams literatures have not always nourished each other as profitably as might be desired, the area of shared leadership is one that strongly calls for more integrative research between the two. As noted above, many of the proposed antecedents of shared forms of leadership parallel prescribed conditions for optimal team effectiveness. In other words, teams are expected to flourish when as many of their members as possible take leadership activities upon themselves as part of their role as a team member.

At the same time, further examination of the potential liabilities of a "company of leaders" also needs to be undertaken. There may be situations in which too many cooks do spoil the broth and where a single leader or co-leaders with delineated role functions may be a more effective option. For example, true shared leadership may prove to be a time-consuming process in order to provide effective group coordination and effort, and some contexts and tasks might require the faster decision time possible with a single leader. In other cases, the advantages of developing leadership capabilities in a broad cadre of staff may far exceed any potential losses in decision time. Providing guidance on when different forms of follower involvement along the leadership continuum suggested here will have an optimal effect on team performance and viability would be the most welcome of future contributions.

NOTE

1.   Although often used interchangeably, teams are distinguished from other forms of groups as being characterized by undertaking shared interdependent work. The term "group" is more generic, and can refer to a wide variety of social collectives who may have common goals but looser task connections.

REFERENCES

Avolio, B. J., Jung, D. I., Murry, W., & Sivasubramaniam, N. (1996). Building highly developed teams: focusing on shared leadership processes, efficacy, trust and performance. *Advances in Interdisciplinary Studies on Work Teams, 3*, 173–209.

Avolio, B. J., Sivasubramaniam, N., Murry, W. D., Jung, D., & Garger, J. W. (2003). Assessing shared leadership: Development and preliminary validation of a Team Multifactor Leadership Questionnaire. In. C. L. Pearce & J. A. Conger (Eds.), *Shared leadership: Reframing the hows and whys of leadership* (pp. 143–172). Thousand Oaks, CA: Sage.

Barrick, M. R., Stewart, G. L., Neubert, M. L., & Mount, M. K. (1998). Relating member ability and personality to work-team processes and team effectiveness. *Journal of Applied Psychology, 83*, 377–391.

Barry, D. (1991). Managing the bossless team: Lessons in distributed leadership. *Organizational Dynamics, 20*(1), 31–47.

Bennett, N., Harvey, J. A., Wise, C., & Woods, P. A. (2003). *Desk study review of distributed leadership.* Nottingham, UK: National College for School Leadership.

Boyatzis, R. E., & Goleman, D. (2002). *The Emotional Competency Inventory.* Boston: Hay Group.

Burke, C. S., Fiore, S. M., & Salas, E. (2003). The role of shared cognition in enabling shared leadership and team adaptability. In. C. L. Pearce & J. A. Conger (Eds.), *Shared Leadership: Reframing the hows and whys of leadership* (pp. 103–122). Thousand Oaks, CA: Sage.

Burns, J. M. (1998). *Empowerment for change. Rethinking leadership working papers.* College Park, MD: Academy of Leadership Press. Retrieved November 9, 2005, from http://www.academy.umd.edu/publications/klspdocs/jburn_pl.htm

Conger, J. A., & Kanungo, R. N. (1988). The empowerment process: Integrating theory and practice. *Academy of Management Review, 13,* 471–482.

Conger, J. A., & Pearce, C. L. (2003). A landscape of opportunities: Future research on shared leadership. In. C. L. Pearce & J. A. Conger (Eds.), *Shared Leadership: Reframing the hows and whys of leadership* (pp. 285–303). Thousand Oaks, CA: Sage.

Cox, J. F., Pearce, C. L., & Perry, M. L. (2003). Toward a model of shared leadership and distributed influence in the innovation process: How shared leadership can enhance new product development team dynamics and effectiveness. In. C. L. Pearce & J. A. Conger (Eds.), *Shared Leadership: Reframing the hows and whys of leadership* (pp. 48–76). Thousand Oaks, CA: Sage.

Day, D. V., Gronn, P., & Salas, E. (2004). Leadership capacity in teams. *Leadership Quarterly, 15*(6), 857–880.

DeSouza, G., & Klein, H. J. (1995). Emergent leadership in the group goal setting process. *Small Group Research, 26,* 475–496.

Devine, D. J., & Phillips, J. L. (2001). Do smarter teams do better: A meta-analysis of cognitive ability and team performance. *Small Group Research, 32*(5), 507–532.

Druskat, V. U., & Wolff, S. B. (2001). Group Emotional Intelligence and its influence on group effectiveness. In C. Cherniss & D. Goleman (Eds.), *The emotionally intelligent workplace* (pp. 133–155). San Francisco: Jossey-Bass.

Ensley, M. D., Pearson, A., & Pearce, C. L. (2003). Top management team process, shared leadership, and new venture performance: A theoretical model and research agenda. *Human Resource Management Review, 13*(2), 329–346.

Graen, G. B., & Scandura, T. (1987). Toward a psychology of dyadic organizing. In B. Staw & L. L. Cummings (Eds.), *Research in organizational behavior* (Vol. 9, pp. 175–208). Greenwich, CT: JAI Press.

Gronn, P. (2002). Distributed leadership as a unit of analysis. *Leadership Quarterly, 13,* 423–451.

Heenan, D. A., & Bennis, W. (1999). *Co-leaders: The power of great partnerships.* New York: Wiley.

Hill, N. S. (2004). *Leading together, working together: The role of team shared leadership in building collaborative capital in virtual teams.* Paper presented at the annual International Leadership Association Conference, Washington, DC.

Hollander, E. P. (1961). Some effects of perceived status on responses to innovative behavior. *Journal of Abnormal and Social Psychology, 63,* 247–250.

Hollander, E. P. (1997). How and why active followers matter in leadership. In E. P. Hollander & L. R. Offermann (Eds.), *The balance of leadership and followership* (pp. 11–28). College Park: Kellogg Leadership Studies Project, University of Maryland.

Houghton, J. D., Neck, C. P., & Manz, C. C. (2003). Self-leadership and SuperLeadership: The heart and art of creating shared leadership in teams. In. C. L. Pearce & J. A. Conger (Eds.), *Shared Leadership: Reframing the hows and whys of leadership* (pp. 123–140). Thousand Oaks, CA: Sage.

Judge, T. A., Colbert, A. E., & Ilies, R. (2004). Intelligence and leadership: A quantitative review and test of theoretical propositions. *Journal of Applied Psychology, 89*(3), 542–552.

Kellett, J. B., Humphrey, R. H., & Sleeth, R. G. (2002). Empathy and complex task performance: Two routes to leadership. *Leadership Quarterly, 13,* 523–544.

Kenny, D. A., & La Voie, L. (1985). Separating individual and group effects. *Journal of Personality and Social Psychology, 48,* 339–348.

Kerr, S., & Jermier, J. M. (1978). Substitutes for leadership: Their meaning and measurement. *Organizational Behavior and Human Performance, 22,* 375–403.

Klein, K. J., Dansereau, F., & Hall, R. J. (1994). Levels issues in theory development, data collection, and analysis. *Academy of Management Review, 19*(2), 195–229.

Kozlowski, S. W. J., Gully, S. M., Salas, E., & Cannon-Bowers, J. A. (1996). Team leadership and development: Theory, principles, and guidelines for training leaders and teams. *Advances in Interdisciplinary Studies of Work Teams, 3,* 253–291.

Manz, C. C. (1980). Self-leadership: Toward an expanded theory of self-influence processes in organizations. *Academy of Management Review, 11,* 585–600.

Manz, C. C., & Sims, H. P., Jr. (1993). *Business without bosses: How self-managing teams are building high performing companies.* New York: Wiley.

Manz, C. C., & Sims, H. P., Jr. (2001). *The new superleadership: Leading others to lead themselves.* San Francisco: Berrett-Koehler.

Mayo, M., Meindl, J. R., & Pastor, J. (2003). Shared leadership in work teams. In. C. L. Pearce & J. A. Conger (Eds.), *Shared leadership: Reframing the hows and whys of leadership* (pp. 193–214). Thousand Oaks, CA: Sage.

Meindl, J. R., Erlich, S. B., & Dukerich, J. M. (1985). The romance of leadership. *Administrative Science Quarterly, 30,* 78–102.

Neck, C. P., Stewart, G. L., & Manz, C. C. (1996). Self-leaders within self-leading teams: Toward an optimal equilibrium. *Advances in Interdisciplinary Studies on Work Teams, 3,* 43–65.

Neubert, M. (1999). Too much of a good thing or the more the merrier? Exploring the dispersion and gender composition of informal leadership in manufacturing teams. *Small Group Research, 30,* 635–646.

Neubert, M., & Taggar, S. (2004). Pathways to informal leadership: The moderating role of gender on the relationship of individual differences and team member network centrality to informal leadership emergence. *Leadership Quarterly, 15*(2), 175–194.

Offermann, L. R., Bailey, J. R., Vasilopoulos, N. L., Seal, C., & Sass, M. (2004). The relative contribution of emotional competence and cognitive ability to individual and team performance. *Human Performance, 17,* 319–243.

Pearce, C. L. (1997). *The determinants of change management team (CMT) effectiveness: A longitudinal investigation.* Unpublished doctoral dissertation, University of Maryland.

Pearce, C. L. (2004). The future of leadership: Combining vertical and shared leadership to transform knowledge work. *Academy of Management Executive, 28*(1), 47–57.

Pearce, C. L., & Conger, J. A. (2003*). Shared leadership: Reframing the hows and whys of leadership.* Thousand Oaks, CA: Sage.

Pearce, C. L., & Sims, H. P., Jr. (2000). Shared leadership: Toward a multi-level theory of leadership. In M. M. Beyerlein, D. A. Johnson, & S. T. Beyerlein (Eds.), *Advances in interdisciplinary studies of work teams: Volume 7. Team development* (pp. 115–139). New York: JAI Press.

Pearce, C. L., & Sims, H. P. (2002). Vertical versus shared leadership as predictors of the effectiveness of change management teams: An examination of aversive, directive, transactional, transformational, and empowering leader behaviors. *Group Dynamics: Theory, Research, and Practice, 6,* 172–197.

Pearce, C. L., Yoo, Y., & Alavi, M. (2004). Leadership, social work, and virtual teams: The relative influence of vertical versus shared leadership in the nonprofit sector. In R. E. Riggio & S. S. Orr (Eds.), *Improving leadership in nonprofit organizations* (pp. 180–203). San Francisco: Jossey-Bass.

Perry, M. L., Pearce, C. L., & Sims, H. P., Jr. (1999). Empowered selling teams: How shared leadership can contribute to selling team outcomes. *Journal of Personal Selling and Sales Management, 19*(3), 35–51.

Raelin, J. A. (2004). Don't bother putting leadership into people. *Academy of Management Executive, 18*(3), 131–135.

Rawlings, D. (2000). Collaborative leadership teams: Oxymoron or new paradigm? *Consulting Psychology Journal: Practice and Research, 52*(1), 36–48.

Sally, D. (2002). Co-leadership: Lessons from republican Rome. *California Management Review, 44*(4), 84–99.

Steiner, I. D. (1972). *Group process and productivity.* New York: Academic Press.

Taggar, S., Hackett, R., & Saha, S. (1999). Leadership emergence in autonomous work teams: Antecedents and outcomes. *Personnel Psychology, 52,* 899–926.

Waldersee, R., & Eagleson, G. (2002). Shared leadership in the implementation of re-orientations. *Leadership and Organization Development Journal, 23*(7), 400–407.

Wolff, S. B., Pescosolido, A. T. & Druskat, V. U. (2002). Emotional Intelligence as the basis of leadership emergence in self-managing teams. *Leadership Quarterly, 13,* 505–552.

CHAPTER 5

LEADERSHIP EMBEDDED IN SOCIAL NETWORKS

Looking at Inter-Follower Processes[1]

Margarita Mayo
Instituto de Empresa

Juan Carlos Pastor
Instituto de Empresa

ABSTRACT

The romance of leadership theory (ROL) provides the theoretical basis to understand leadership from the perspective of the followers and their context. It emphasizes the wider social environment that embeds leaders and followers. In this chapter, we focus on how leadership is embedded in the social networks created by followers. We begin to describe the social psychological bases underlying the romance of leadership notion and its implications for understanding charismatic leadership. Then, we build on Meindl's social contagion theory of charisma to provide a network-based model of charismatic leadership. This model offers a conceptual and methodological framework to explore interfollower processes and it contributes to provide a much-needed socialized account of the charismatic leadership phenomenon. Finally, we suggest a research agenda to test some aspects of leadership embedded in networks.

Follower-Centered Perspectives on Leadership, pages 93–113
Copyright © 2007 by Information Age Publishing
All rights of reproduction in any form reserved.

In the movie *Forrest Gump*, Tom Hanks's character decides to run across North America for "no particular reason." After crossing the nation from coast to coast, he decides to do it again. He catches the attention of the media, who start following him in this marathon and turn Forrest into a celebrity. After he appears on national television, people greet him at every city he crosses. After a while, a few people start following him. They run alongside Forrest, asking him for ideas to solve their problems and reinterpreting anything that happens to them as being caused by Forrest himself, giving him credit for their own ideas. In a few days, Forrest has gotten a large group of followers who think that he is a wise man who knows the secret to happiness and can lead them in their inner search to find their way in this world. They all leave everything behind to follow him and show willingness to do anything for their leader. When Forrest unexpectedly decides to stop and go back home, they all seem perplexed and bewildered. Suddenly, all the energy and self-confidence that they displayed following their leader turns into chaos and confusion. They end up completely disoriented.

Is this an instance of leadership? If we define leadership by its effects on followers, Forrest Gump's followers display all the effects that are distinctive of charismatic leadership: high motivation, identification with the leader, and self-sacrificial behaviors. All this time, however, Tom Hanks's character has said nothing. He has never directed them to do anything, and, in fact, he barely knows that they are following him. If we use conventional leadership theories, it would be difficult to fully understand the leadership of Forrest Gump and his impact on followers. A better understanding of this instance of leadership and followership requires looking beyond the figure of the leader. It requires looking at the followers: their way of thinking and their social interactions with one another. Many of these followers seem to be searching for meaning in their lives. Forrest Gump just happens to be there, at the right time, doing something out of the ordinary. By joining Forrest in his march across the nation, they hoped to fulfill their needs, to reduce their anxieties and fears, and to find a worthwhile goal in their lives. The ambiguity of Forrest's mission (in fact, there was no mission at all) acted as a blank canvas on which each of them could project anything they wanted.

The romance of leadership (ROL) theory (Meindl, 1990, 1993, 1995; Meindl & Ehrlich, 1987; Meindl, Ehrlich, & Dukerich, 1985) provides a theoretical framework to understand leadership from the perspective of the followers and their context. The ROL theory represents an alternative view to conventional approaches to the study of leadership processes in organizations. The organizational leadership literature has been, for several decades, dominated by a leader-centered paradigm that puts the center of attention in the figure of the leader. The majority of studies in this body of research have followed a similar paradigm that considers the characteristics of leaders and their personality and behaviors as the main determinants of subordinates' outcomes, such as motivation, extra effort, and satisfaction. The basic assumption is that to understand leadership, we have to study leaders. Of course, there have been exceptions to this leader-centric view (e.g., Graen, 1976; Kerr & Jermier, 1978) and followers and context do play a role, although secondary, in several contingency models of leadership (e.g., Fiedler, 1967; House, 1971).

In fact, many leadership researchers agree that leadership occurs at the juncture of leaders, followers, and context, and a few researchers have started to pay some attention to the active role of followers and contexts in the leadership process (e.g., Graen & Uhl-Bien, 1995; Howell & Shamir, 2005; Shamir & Howell, 1999). Yet, both perspectives are not equally represented in the leadership literature, which is still disproportionately favorable to the leader-centered view. Virtually no attention has been paid to aspects of the wider social environment, which embed and potentially influence the development of different kinds of relationships between leaders and followers. The result is an undersocialized account of how followers respond to and define their relationship with their leaders. This account makes it difficult to fully comprehend important aspects of the leadership process, such as the ones described above between Forrest Gump and his followers.

As an alternative to this leader-centric perspective, Meindl and his associates (Meindl, 1990, 1993, 1995; Meindl & Ehrlich, 1987; Meindl et al., 1985) developed the notion of the ROL theory to highlight the active role of followers when trying to understand the leadership phenomenon. Meindl has suggested that the ROL is a strategic context for research similar to Kuhn's (1970) conception of scientific paradigms. Paradigms are important to advance science because they guide the entire research process, from the selection of the relevant variables, to the kind of research designs, and to the interpretation of results. The ROL theory provides a new strategic context for research on leadership because it changes the focus of attention away from the figure of the leader, toward the followers and their social context. Whereas the leader-centric perspective considers leadership aspects as dependent variables causing followers' and organizational results, the ROL perspective reverses the casual direction upside down and considers followers and contextual factors as dependent variables influencing different aspects of the leadership process.

In this chapter, we focus on how leadership is embedded in networks taking the ROL perspective. First, we describe a short historical view of the ROL notion and its social psychological bases. Second, deriving from this social account we describe Meindl's theory of social contagion of charismatic leadership. Third, we depart from the conventional social contagion theory to describe a social network model of charismatic leadership using social network concepts and techniques. Finally, we suggest several research implications of a social network perspective to test other aspects of leadership embedded in networks.

A SOCIAL PSYCHOLOGICAL APPROACH TO LEADERSHIP

In Meindl's early writings on the ROL theory (Meindl et al., 1985; Meindl & Ehrlich, 1987; Pillai & Meindl, 1991), leadership is viewed as a purely psychological phenomenon. Taking an attributional perspective, the ROL theory considers that leadership concepts, such as charisma, are seen as important dimensions in the implicit theories that people have about organizations. Followers and observers use leadership concepts to understand organized activity. For instance, in situations of important successes or critical organizational failures, we tend to think of leaders as playing a significant causal role regardless of the true causes of the outcomes. Some authors understood this bias in individuals' perceptions as the negation of leadership (e.g., Bass, 1990; Yukl, 1989). However, rather than a negation of leadership, the ROL theory places the importance of leaders and leadership on a different level, the level of ideologies and collective thinking. As Meindl (1993) puts it "the romance of leadership studies need not to be taken to mean that leadership is trivial" (p. 97). Instead, the ROL theory broadens the conceptualization of leadership by emphasizing its phenomenological significance to organizational actors. Leaders are important, according to the ROL perspective, not only because of what they are or do, but because of what they represent in our minds. The ROL perspective focuses on the importance and "prominence of leadership concepts in the way social actors address organizational problems" (Meindl, 1993, p. 97). From this perspective, leadership is an ideology that emerges in the minds of followers.

Later on, Meindl and his associates (Chen & Meindl, 1991; Meindl, 1990, 1993, 1995; Meindl, Pastor, & Mayo, 2004; Pastor, Meindl, & Mayo, 2002) further developed the ROL notion into a unique theoretical perspective that provides new insights into the study of leadership phenomena and that is grounded in a social psychological tradition. Meindl's later thinking focused on followers' perceptions within their social context, emphasizing the idea that "followers are not just connected to their leaders, they are also connected to other followers" (Meindl et al., 2004, p. 1349). This idea points toward a social contagion theory of leadership. Particularly, those affect-laden aspects of the leadership process, such as charisma, will be more likely to be affected by the social context. Thus, one of the main implications of the ROL theory is the idea that followers' perceptions of their leaders are embedded in social networks. From this perspective, the ROL takes a social information-processing view (Pfeffer & Salancik, 1978) and considers how followers' attributions of leadership are, to a great extent, the result of individuals interacting with one another, sharing information about the leader, and comparing each others' views.

This emphasis on social interaction among followers represents an attempt to recuperate a social psychological tradition, and, at the same time, to incorporate recent advances in organizational behavior research. Leadership had been traditionally a central topic in social psychology (Bogardus, 1929; Lewin & Lippit, 1938; Tannenbaum & Schmidt, 1958). However, since the 1970s, there has been a steady decline among social psychologists interested in leadership. This is unfortunate because we run the risk of developing a narrow view of the leadership phenomenon by missing an important source of research ideas. A social psychological view emphasizes that, to understand behaviors, we have to understand the context and the situation in which actors operate. Allport (1968) defines social psychology as the understanding of people's thinking and behavior as influenced by the real or implied presence of others. From this perspective, the ROL theory emphasizes the role of followers' cognitions and the social factors in the leadership process. The context in which social actors are embedded becomes important. Taking this social psychological approach, the ROL theory attempts to understand how social psychological variables facilitate or inhibit the emergence of different types of leadership.

In particular, the ROL theory adopts a social constructionist view that considers both the cognitive aspects of how followers construe leadership and the social origins of these constructions. First, the ROL theory takes a "constructionist" view in the sense that leadership is more a subjective than objective phenomenon. Individuals are seen as active enactors of their organizational environments (Weick, 1995). Organizations are complex systems in which there are continuous multiple forces operating at the same time, and people's cognitive capabilities are limited. Individuals take chunks of this organizational reality and construct their own realities in their mind, which are later used in their sense-making processes to understand organizational outcomes. Complex organizational realities are modeled in our minds in terms of implicit theories of the organization that function as sense-making devices. These cognitive structures are a simple and biased representation of reality. The ROL suggests that in these social constructions, leadership concepts occupy a predominant position, and are readily available to be used to explain relevant organizational outcomes. Leadership concepts have a prominent role in the cognitive structures that people hold in their minds. People romanticize the concept of leadership and it becomes a critical element in their way of thinking. That is, people use the concept of leadership to explain organizational events, especially when the events are important and ambiguous.

Second, the ROL theory takes a "social" view because it suggests that followers construe their leaders from information that is available in their social environments. This idea departs from the conventional leader-centric approaches that assume that leaders are embedded with true and objective leadership characteristics that can be observed and measured by averaging followers' perceptions and ignoring individual differences among followers. The ROL instead considers that the dispersion or degree of consensus among followers regarding the charismatic appeal of their leaders become relevant. Such focus may provide potentially great insights into the nature of leadership processes. These individual differences regarding the leader may be interpreted not just as random variance, but the result of group members defining their own organizational reality, and developing different constructions of leadership that can only be understood when we examine the pattern of social ties that link group members to one another. Thus, a key element in this social constructivist view of leadership is the network of contacts that bring organizational actors together. If social interactions play such an important role in the social construction of leadership, then the social contagion among a group of followers becomes an important research endeavor.

A SOCIAL CONTAGION THEORY OF CHARISMA

Although the ROL is a theory of leadership in general, its main focus has been on charismatic leadership. After the dissatisfaction with the leadership studies during the 1970s and 1980s, a new approach emerged within the leader-centric approach that offered novel concepts and theories in leadership studies. These new leadership perspectives emphasized concepts such as charisma, visionary leadership, and transformational leadership (e.g., Bass, 1985; Conger & Kanungo, 1988; Nanus, 1992; Tichy & Devanna, 1986). From the ROL perspective, charismatic leadership is particularly relevant because the charismatic relationship between leaders and followers is highly emotional and it has a great potential for being highly romanticized. The charismatic leadership concepts provided the ROL theory with an excellent opportunity to apply its principles and unique take to examine charisma from a novel perspective. For instance, while most leadership researchers followed the dominant leader-centric tradition and focused on the expressive behaviors and personality of the leaders (e.g, Bass, 1985; Conger, 1989; House, Spangler, & Woyke, 1991), Meindl (1990, 1993) likened charismatic leadership to "catching a cold" (p. 101). The core idea is that rather than being dependent on their interactions with the leader, followers' charismatic experiences are affected, to a great extent, by the experiences of other followers. Thus, attributions of charisma to a leader are not solely grounded in the individual interactions between followers and leaders, but, rather, they are, to a great degree, the result of followers' lateral interactions with their peers.

Meindl (1990, 1993) further suggests that charismatic leadership could be modeled as a social contagion process. In his social contagion theory of charismatic leadership, the focus of research changes from the more typically studied charismatic expressions of the leaders, to the contagious expressions and displays of the followers. In this account, the charismatic appeal of the leader is socially constructed, a matter of intersubjectively shared sense making among a group of followers. The defining characteristics of a leader reflect the workings of the social system, whose output— "charisma"—has the status of a social fact, in the Durkheimian sense, and that the actual conduits of this construction process are the naturally occurring social interactions that occur within groups of followers. It is in this sense that we argue that charismatic leadership is embedded in networks and suggest looking at interfollower processes to get a better understanding of both leadership and followership.

Meindl's (1990) original formulation of a social contagion theory of charisma dealt with situations in which the charismatic appeal of a leader spirals up over time. This assumption goes along with the conventional view of social contagion. Contagion usually refers to the spread over time of a particular practice or idea, such as the adoption of an innovation in a social system (e.g., Burt, 1987; Coleman, Katz, & Menzel, 1957; Davis, 1991; for extensive reviews, see Rogers, 1995; Valente, 1995). The cumulative percentage of members of a social system adopting the new practice over time has been found to follow an S-shaped curve, indicating that the diffusion process begins slowly, then peaks up at some point in the middle, and slows again in the final stages of diffusion (see Rogers, 1995). Then, the underlying assumption here is that the social contagion phenomenon is an ever increasing process of adoption that ends when all or most individuals in the social system display the new practice or attitude.

However, this view of social contagion as a continuous increase of adoption may be too narrow and does not account for the whole phenomenon of social contagion. For example, there also exists the possibility that increases and decreases in the adoption response take place at the same time, keeping the overall number of adoptions in the system stable over time. Indeed, some diffusion researchers have pointed out that diffusion research suffers from what Rogers (1995) calls a "pro-innovation" bias, which is "the implication in diffusion research that an innovation should be diffused and adopted by all members of a social system and that the innovation should be neither re-invented nor rejected" (p. 100). According to this wider view of social contagion, contagion does not imply cumulative increasing adoption, but rather a "cumulative increasing degree of influence upon an individual to adopt or reject an innovation, resulting from the activation of peer networks" (Rogers, 1983, p. 234). Thus, Meindl's (1990) original formulation of a social contagion theory of charisma can be reformulated in terms of social influence among peer networks. This reconceptualization takes us into a social network model of charismatic leadership that assumes that a social system can produce peer network-dependent distributions of leadership perceptions at any level of evaluation, along a charismatic to noncharismatic continuum.

A NETWORK-BASED MODEL OF CHARISMATIC LEADERSHIP

Several authors have suggested that the use of network theory and methods provide the necessary tools for clarifying some of the basic social influence processes (e.g., Ibarra & Andrews, 1993). A social network is a routine pattern of interpersonal contacts that can be identified as organizational members exchanging information, resources, influence, affect, or power. Particularly, network theory serves to specify the content of the network, and to operationalize the concept of proximity as the basic mechanism of contagion.

First, the nature of the network is essential because it defines the kind of relations and links among participants in the social structure. The transactional content of the network is defined by what is exchanged in the relationship. In general, network researchers make a distinction between instrumental and expressive networks (Krackhardt & Porter, 1985; Tichy, Tushman, & Fombrum, 1987). First, instrumental or "job-related communication" develops around work-role performance and is directly associated with the prescribed objectives of the job. Second, the expressive or friendship network is characterized by the exchange of personal information and the development of close friendship relationships. The content of the network is likely to be correlated with the distribution of charisma perceptions. The argument here is that social influence is more effective when the message comes from a credible source. Friendship ties denote relationship based on trust while task-related ties are instrumental relationships based on work roles. Even though a good deal of influence in organizations travels through formal and job-related networks, the information spreading through the grapevine of trusting relationships may be more credible and have a higher impact on individuals' attitudes.

Second, proximity in the network is the basic mechanism of social contagion. The basic building block of a social network is the relationship, or in network terms, the link or tie. One of the characteristics of the link is its intensity. The intensity of the relationship refers to the frequency to which two individuals exchange information. For example, a strong link between person A and person B exists if they talk more than five times a week. However, the definition of a strong link is relative and depends on the average expectation for that particular social system. According to our social network model of charismatic leadership, we suggest that frequent and emphatic interpersonal communication produces similarity of attributions of charisma among group members because it provides proximate others with more opportunities to compare and test their ideas about the leader.

Taking a network approach to social contagion of charismatic leadership implies that evidence of contagion is presented when: (1) Person A displays an attitude or behavior; (2) Person B is exposed to Person A through specific connections, such as task or friendship ties, and (3) subjects change their attitudes and actions in ways that are consistent with those with whom they are connected in the social system. Thus, from a social network perspective, social contagion of charismatic leadership is defined as a change in the attributions of charisma to the leader of peers in a social system that follows the pattern of communication exchange among individuals. In the end, the relative change among individuals will increase their homogeneity with respect to their attributions of charisma to the leader in the entire social system. This social network model of charismatic leadership contemplates situations of both high charisma and situations of low charisma. It is possible for a leader to be perceived as highly charismatic in one department of the organization and not charismatic in another department. Thus, evidence of contagion is the spread of charisma perceptions with significant net gains in the charisma of the leader. But also, evidence of contagion is the "redistribution" of attributions of charisma in a social system without net gains in the attributed charisma to the leader. The key issue becomes how these attributions of charisma are aligned with the pattern of social relationships that connect followers with one another.

Some Theoretical Considerations

The theoretical background for our network-based social contagion model of charismatic leadership derives from the social psychological study of small groups (Back, 1951; Festinger, 1950, 1954; Festinger, Schachter, & Back, 1950; Heider, 1958; Schachter, 1959; Sherif, 1936, 1965), and the social information-processing approach (SIP) (Lord & Smith, 1983; Salancik & Pfeffer, 1978; Thomas & Griffin, 1983). These perspectives assume that, in general, sense making is largely a social process by which individuals learn the meaning of the events by interacting with others. Individuals need to reduce uncertainty by having normative understanding of their surroundings, and their direct interactions with proximate others in the social structure play an important role in this process. As with other social contagion models, the social constructionist view of charismatic leadership that we propose rests on the socialization that occurs between the agent and the target of contagion. Frequent interpersonal communication would produce similarity of attributions of charisma among group members because it provides proximate others with more opportunities to compare and test their ideas about the leader. Attributions of charisma, therefore, will travel through the social paths that connect people with one another.

In particular, social comparison (Festinger, 1954) and balance theory (Heider, 1958) help us understand some of the mechanisms by which network proximity produces homogeneity in leadership perceptions. Social comparison occurs when people are uncertain about the correctness of their perceptions and the leadership qualities of the leader are almost always ambiguous and subject to interpretation. Thus, in order to compare the appropriateness of their perceptions, individuals turn to those proximate in their social networks. Also, according to balance theory, if individuals are connected by a positive relationship, such as friendship ties, they will tend to develop views of third parties that are consistent with this relationship. For example, if two friends have different views of a third person (e.g., the leader), they are in an unbalanced state that creates feelings of uncertainty, instability, and cognitive dissonance (Festinger, 1957). One way for individuals to reduce the psychological discomfort associated with cognitive dissonance and restore balance to their relationships is to change their cognitions (Newcomb, 1961).

Preliminary Empirical Evidence

Based on these ideas, Pastor and colleagues (2002) conducted two studies to examine the distribution and change of charisma attributions to a leader within a group of followers. In the first study, they examined the attributions of charismatic leadership to the director of a police organization. The director had been on the job for the last 17 years and had just retired. The 55 employees, including police officers, lieutenants, investigators, and staff, evaluated the leadership style of the director and provided information about the frequency of their social interactions with one another. Consistent with a social contagion model of charisma, they expected the distribution of the leadership perceptions to the director to correspond with the underlying social network structure of the employees.

Using network analytic techniques, they found that those individuals proximate in the friendship network had similar attributions of leadership.

In order to add some graphic data, a sociogram of the friendship network in the police organization is provided in Figure 5.1. The graph shows each individual indicating their formal position in the organization. The links among the individuals indicate friendship ties: they socialize and talk about things other than work several times a week. As can be seen, the most central individual is Lieutenant 5 who is linked directly or indirectly to all managers, including Manager 1, who was the interim director of the police organization while the board was searching for a new director. After 2 months, no candidate was found and Lieutenant 5 became the new director of the police organization. The friendship network is usually a good proxy for the trust network and those central in the network are individu-

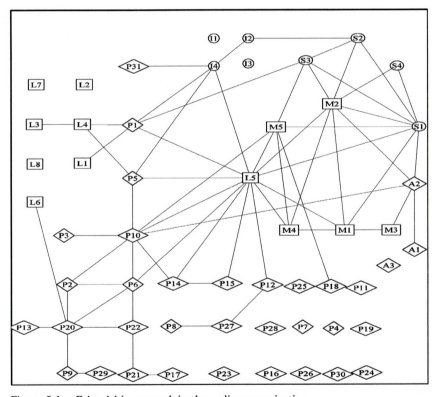

Figure 5.1.   Friendship network in the police organization.
Note: For ease of viewing, only strong links are presented. Strong links are defined as reciprocated links with a frequency of interaction greater than twice per week.
Key: M, managers; P, patrol officers; L, lieutenants; A, assitants; I, investigators.
Figure produced by KracPlot 3.0 (Krackhardt, Blythe, & McGrath, 1995).

als highly trusted by numerous members of the organization. His central position in the network made him an ideal candidate for the top position in the organization.

According to our network model, Lieutenant 5's views about the outgoing director ought to have a great influence over those individuals who are proximate to him. In fact, we found that centrality in the friendship network showed a statistically significant correlation with the average perception of charisma to the leader (measured as the absolute value of the z-scores) ($r = -.27, p < .05$). That is, the attributions of charismatic leadership of those individuals occupying central positions in the friendship network are good estimates of the average perception of charisma in the entire group. In contrast, organizational members in the periphery of the friendship network tend to have more extreme views of the leader as compared with their colleagues. The results of this study provided support for our social contagion model of charisma.

In a second study, Pastor and colleagues (2002) replicated these results in a longitudinal field design with a sample of business students in three business courses. Students were asked about the leadership style of their professor and the frequency of their social interactions with other classmates at three different time periods: time 1 (the 5th week of classes), time 2 (the 10th week), and time 3 (the 15th or last week). They found that, by the end of the semester, proximity in the social network was related to similarity of attributions of charisma. Furthermore, they found that over time people proximate in the social structure tend to converge in their views about the charisma of the leader, especially group members connected by friendship ties. These two studies highlight the importance of understanding the socialized aspects of leadership attributions in general and charismatic leadership attributions in particular. Yet, this work is just a first glimpse of a research agenda looking at interfollower processes. Future research can benefit from this network approach to better understand the complexities of a more socialized account of leadership.

A RESEARCH AGENDA

A social network approach provides a theoretical framework and methodological tools to untangle some of the complexities in the emergence and spread of charismatic experiences among followers. The model outlined here raises a number of intriguing possibilities for research and theory. We suggest some recommendations for a future research agenda applying network theory and methods to understand the intersection between the context, the leaders, and the followers in the social contagion process of charismatic leadership.

The Context: What Role Does the Density of the Network Play in the Diffusion of Charismatic Leadership?

The characteristics of the network as a whole may also play an important role in a social contagion process of leadership as a social context. In particular, a social system with high frequency of communication among its members may be a better conduit of social information about the leader than a social system with low frequency of communication. In network terms, the density of the network may affect the speed of diffusion. One could expect a moderating effect of network density on the relationship between social networks and the distribution of leadership attributions. Indeed, the density of the social network has been found to play a role in the diffusion of innovations. For instance, Valente (1995) analyzed the relationship between network density and the rate of diffusion of innovations in three studies and found that there was a relationship between network density and the speed of diffusion.

To further explore this notion, we conducted a follow-up analysis of our network data with the three classes that we used in our previous study (Pastor et al., 2002). While examining the pattern of social ties within each class, we noticed that the three classes differed significantly in the density of their networks. At time 1, the three classes showed similar degrees of density. However, from time 1 to time 2, Class A increased the density of the task network by 112% (see Figure 5.2), and the friendship network by 81%; whereas Class B increased the number of links by only 6% and 8%, respectively, and Class C experienced a decreased in the number of links, –7% for the task network and –8% in the friendship network. The results of the proximity–similarity effects in the friendship network are strong and statistically significant for class A (QAP $r = .075$, $p < .05$), moderate and marginally significant for Class B (QAP $r = .046$, $p = .07$), and weak and nonsignificant for class C (QAP $r = .026$, ns).[2] These results suggest that the density of the network is necessary for the diffusion of charisma perceptions among members of the group. Of course, these findings are based only on three classes but are consistent with the idea of a moderating effect of network density on the relationship between social structures and the distribution of followers' attributions of charisma. This is an interesting idea for future research, and can be tested on a larger number of networks.

The Leader: How Can Leaders Manage Contexts and Constructions?

Our network-based model of charismatic leadership emphasizes leadership as an emergent phenomenon and considers the active role of followers

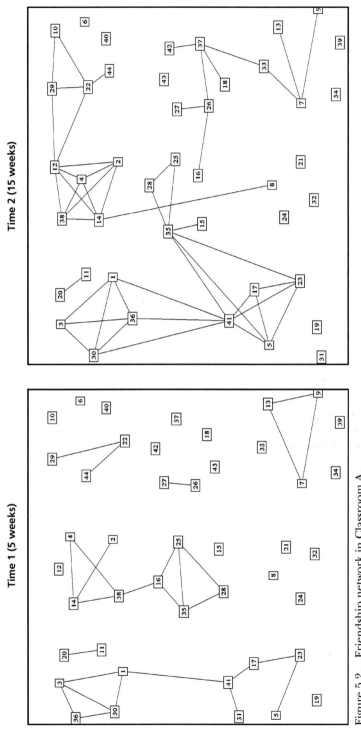

Figure 5.2. Friendship network in Classroom A.

Note: For ease of viewing, only strong links are presented. Strong links are defined as reciprocated links with a frequency of interaction greater than twice per week. Numbers were assigned randomly to the students in the class. Figures produced by KracPlot 3.0 (Krackhardt et al., 1995) in the leadership process. This, however, does not mean that leaders cannot affect the constructions that followers make of a particular leadership image. In particular, leaders can play an important role in modeling the social context and managing their own leadership images. First, leaders' actions can have an important effect on the social network structure of followers. A closer examination of the three classes also suggests the interplay between the leader's actions and the diffusion of followers' attributions of charisma. The high network density of Class A led us to take a closer look at this class. The professor of this section had divided the class into small subgroups that worked throughout the semester on group projects. This factor may have caused individuals to increase their connections with other peers, particularly within their own groups. Participation in these group projects provided students with more chances for interactions, as reflected in the high density of the networks, which in turn facilitated the social contagion process of leadership attributions. That is, each task group designed by the professor may have developed their particular view of him. To examine this idea, we conducted an ANOVA test on attributions of charisma for the eight task groups and found no statistically significant differences at Time 1, but strong and statistically significant differences among these task groups at Time 2 ($F_{7,36} = 3.61$, $p < .01$). These exploratory findings allow us to speculate that modeling some features of the social context is key to facilitating or inhibiting the spread of charisma perceptions.

Second, leaders may also affect the leadership images that followers develop over time. In fact, Pastor, Mayo, and Meindl (2004) argue that "the management of leadership images becomes one of the key challenges of business leaders in this century" (p. 144). They argue that followers develop mental maps of the organization in which the concept of the leader occupies a central position and it is related to other relevant organizational concepts, such as past, future, success, or the concept of my-self. Leaders need to pay attention to these leadership images that emerge in followers' minds, especially during periods of change and crisis in order to reduce the gap between the desired and the actual leadership images. As suggested by Pastor and colleagues, "the analysis of leadership images can be used to develop and present management strategies that leverage the shape and content of the leadership image to change followers' mental maps and facilitate the change process" (p. 152).

The Followers: Who Are the First Followers to Succumb to the Charisma Virus?

Another important question refers to who among the followers is more likely to develop attributions of charisma in the first stages of the social contagion process. Using the "catching a cold" metaphor, the question is, who is more likely to be infected first with the charisma virus? In order to have a complete picture of the social contagion of charisma, we need to consider the origins of the infection. Several personality characteristics may predispose individuals to be likely candidates to develop perceptions of charismatic leadership. Here, we suggest two personality characteristics that may work as precursors of attributions of charisma: agreeableness and affect intensity.

The dimension of agreeableness of the Big 5 personality factors (McCrae & Costa, 1991) refers to a person's propensity to defer to others. Highly agreeable individuals, also called adapters, defer to many others, including spouses, religious leaders, friends, bosses, or pop-culture idols. Adapters prize harmony more than they prize having their say or their way. The adapter profile forms the core of such roles as teaching, social work, and psychology. At the extreme, adapters—also called "tender-minded"—can become dependent personalities who lose their sense of self. In contrast, people with low scores in the agreeableness factor, also called challengers, focus more on their own needs and norms than the needs of others. Business and military leaders tend to be low in agreeableness. Extreme scores reflect tough-minded personalities that can turn into narcissistic and authoritarian personalities with the corresponding loss of their sense of feeling toward others. We suggest that individuals with high agreeableness scores will be more likely to defer to a charismatic leader and merge their self-concept with the mission and vision of the leader, especially in situations of crisis and uncertainty.

Another personality characteristic that can make individuals react early in the diffusion of charisma attributions is affect intensity (see Larsen & Diener, 1987). Individuals differ with respect to their emotional reactions to the context. While some individuals display mild reactions to positive and negative events, others have strong emotional reactions. The concept of affect intensity seems to capture this individual characteristic. Larsen and Diener (1987) point out that "given the same level of emotional stimulation, individuals high on the affect intensity dimension will exhibit stronger emotional responses regardless the specific emotion evoked" (p. 2). Affect intensity is therefore a personal characteristic that amplifies the emotions of an individual, but does not influence the content of emotions that will be experienced. Because a high level of emotional attachment with the leader is a key characteristic of followers' charismatic experiences, one could expect that individuals high on affect intensity will be more likely to be engaged in charismatic relationships with the leader. Along these lines, Pastor, Mayo, and Shamir (2006) found that followers' emotional arousal levels, whether induced in the lab or mood related, facilitate the emergence of charisma attributions to leaders with a certain level of charismatic appeal. Affect intensity might act in a similar way from a trait perspective, amplifying the emotional response of followers to charismatic leaders. Future research should examine how followers' personality characteristics may draw them toward charismatic relationships.

The Diffusion: What Role Do Individuals' Positions in the Social Network Play?

A relevant research question in our network model of charisma is the role of individual actors in the spread of charisma perceptions within the social system. From a social network perspective, individuals differ in their relative position with respect to other members of the social network. Using Meindl's (1990) "catching a cold" metaphor and once the charisma virus reaches one or few individuals in the social system, the question is, are there key individuals who can slow down or accelerate the infection? We suggest that individuals' position in the social network may be related to their contagious power in the social system. In network terms, individuals' position in the social network is usually referred to as centrality. Central individuals who have many links to other members of the social system are key in the diffusion process. Two relevant conceptualizations of centrality for our network-based model of social contagion are *closeness* centrality and *betweenness* centrality.

First, closeness centrality refers to the average distance between one individual and the rest of the members of the network. It captures the potential reach of one individual to influence the other members of the social system. Individuals with a high degree of closeness centrality are in the best position to "infect" the rest of the members of the network very quickly. When high closeness centrality individuals develop perceptions of charismatic leadership, the other members of the network are relatively close to the "infection." In addition, to be able to reach other network members easily, individuals with a high closeness centrality in the friendship network have a high level of credibility and influence in the group (e.g., Brass & Burkhardt, 1993; Krackhardt, 1990). For instance, Krackhardt (1990) found that this type of central individuals in a social system were attributed more power and influence by their peers. Accordingly, high closeness centrality individuals are key in the spread and diffusion of perceptions of leadership. Once they become infected with the charisma "virus" they are potent transmitters of the infection to a high number of organizational members.

Second, *betweenness* centrality refers to the extent to which actors fall between different parts of the social system that would otherwise be disconnected. Freeman (1979) suggests that this measure is an indication of how much power a person has in the communication network. If a person is mediating the relationship among several individuals, he or she may withhold or distort the information that is being transmitted. In network terms, these individuals do not need to have many connections, but they are strategically situated, acting as *gatekeepers* in the diffusion process. If high betweenness centrality individuals fail to perceive the leader as charismatic, they might block the charisma infection to other parts of the organization. Future research should examine how individuals occupying central positions in their groups have more power and are in the best position to influence other members regarding leadership attributions.

CONCLUDING REMARKS

Other authors have already suggested that leadership resides in the intersection of leaders, followers, and context (Hollander, 1978; Klein & House, 1995). Yet, while such views are widely espoused, leaders—rather than followers and their interpersonal context—have dominated the attention of organizational theorists and researchers. In this chapter, we have offered a more socialized account of leadership, highlighting the importance of interfollower processes. Focusing on charismatic leadership, we build on Meindl's (1990, 1993) social contagion theory of charisma to provide a network-based model of charismatic leadership. A social network perspective offers a rich conceptual and methodological framework to explore interfollower processes and it contributes to provide a much-needed socialized account of the charismatic leadership phenomenon that also incorporates the context and the leader.

NOTES

1. The authors would like to acknowledge financial support provided by MCYT SEC2002-02968.
2. These results are based on the Quadratic Assignment Procedure (QAP) with 1,000 random permutations (Krackhardt, 1988).

REFERENCES

Allport, G. W. (1968). *The person in psychology: Selected essays by Gordon W. Allport.* Boston: Beacon Press.
Back, K. (1951). Influence through social communication. *Journal of Abnormal Social Psychology, 46,* 9–23

Bass, B. M. (1985). *Leadership and performance beyond expectations.* New York: Free Press.

Bass, B. M. (1990). *Bass and Stogdill's handbook of leadership.* New York: Free Press.

Bogardus, E. S. (1929). Leadership and attitudes. *Sociologist and Social Research, 13,* 377–387.

Brass, D., & Burkhardt, M.E. (1993). Potential power and power use: An investigation of structure and behavior. *Academy of Management Journal, 36,* 441–470.

Burt, R. S. (1987). Structural contagion and innovation: Cohesion versus structural equivalence. *American Journal of Sociology, 92,* 1287–1335.

Chen, C., & Meindl, J. R. (1991). The construction of leadership images in the popular press: The case of Donald Burr and People Express. *Administrative Science Quarterly, 36,* 521–551.

Coleman, J., Katz, E., & Menzel, H. (1957). The diffusion of an innovation among physicians. *Sociometry, 20,* 253–270

Conger, J. A. (1989). *The charismatic leader.* San Francisco: Jossey-Bass.

Conger, J. A., & Kanungo, R. (1988). *Charismatic leadership.* Thousands Oaks, CA: Sage.

Davis, G. (1991) Agents without principles? The spread of the poison pill through the intercorporate network. *Administrative Science Quarterly, 36,* 583–613.

Festinger, L. (1950). Informal social communication. *Psychological Review, 57,* 157–166.

Festinger, L. (1954). A theory of social comparison processes. *Human Relations, 7,* 117–140.

Festinger, L. (1957). *A theory of cognitive dissonance.* New York: Row Peterson.

Festinger, L., Schacter, S., & Back, K. (1950). *Social pressures in informal groups: A study of human factors in housing.* Palo Alto, CA: Stanford University Press.

Fiedler, F. E. (1967). The effect of inter-group competition on member adjustment. *Personnel Psychology, 20*(1), 33–44.

Freeman, L.C. (1979). Centrality in Social Networks: I. Conceptual Clarification. *Social Networks, 1,* 215–239.

Graen, G. (1976). Role making processes within complex organizations. In M. D. Dunnette (Ed.), *Handbook of industrial and organizational psychology* (pp. 1201–1245). Chicago: Rand McNally.

Graen, G. B., & Uhl-Bien, M. (1995). Relationship-based approach to leadership: Development of leader–member exchange (LMX) theory over 25 years: Applying a multi-level multi-domain perspective. *Leadership Quarterly, 6,* 219–247.

Heider, F. (1958). *The psychology of interpersonal relations.* New York: Wiley.

Hollander, E. (1978). *Leadership dynamics.* New York: Free Press.

House, R. J. (1971). A path–goal theory of leader effectiveness. *Administrative Science Leadership Review, 16,* 321–339.

House, R. J., Spangler, W. D., & Woycke, J. (1991). Personality and charisma in the US presidency: A psychological theory of leader effectiveness. *Administrative Science Quarterly, 36,* 364–396.

Howell, J., & Shamir, B. (2005). The role of followers in the charismatic leadership process: Relationships and their consequences. *Academy of Management Review, 30,* 96–112.

Ibarra, H., & Andrews, S. B. (1993). Power, social influence, and sense making: Effects of network centrality and proximity on employee perceptions. *Administrative Science Quarterly*, *38*, 277–303.

Kerr, S., & Jermier, J. M. (1978). Substitutes for leadership: Their meaning and measurement. *Organizational Behavior and Human Performance*, *22*(3), 375–403.

Klein, K. J., & House, R. (1995). On fire: Charismatic leadership and levels of analysis. *Leadership Quarterly*, *6*(2), 183–198.

Krackhardt, D. (1988). Predicting with networks: Non-parametric multiple regression analysis of dyadic data. *Social Networks*, *10*, 359–381.

Krackhardt, D. (1990). Assessing the political landscape: Structure, cognition, and power in organizations. *Administrative Science Quarterly*, *35*, 342–369.

Krackhardt, D., Blythe, J., & McGrath, C. (1995). *KrackPlot 3.0: User's manual.* Columbia, SC: Analytic Technologies.

Krackhardt, D., & Porter, L. T. (1985). When friends leave: A structural analysis of the relationship between turnover and stayer's attitudes. *Administrative Science Quarterly*, *30*, 242–261.

Kuhn, T. (1970). *The structure of scientific revolutions.* Chicago: Chicago University Press.

Larsen, R. J., & Diener, E. (1987). Affect intensity as an individual difference characteristic: A review. *Journal of Research in Personality*, *21*, 1–37.

Lewin, K., & Lippit, R. (1938). An experimental approach to the study of autocracy and democracy. *Sociometry*, *1*, 292–300.

Lord, R. G., & Smith, J. E. (1983). Theoretical information processing, and situational factors affecting attribution theory models of organizational behavior. *Academy of Management Review*, *8*, 50–60.

McCrae, R. R., & Costa, P. T. (1991). Validation of the five-factor model of personality across instruments and observers. *Journal of Personality and Social Psychology*, *52*, 81–90.

Meindl, J. R. (1990). On leadership: An alternative to the conventional wisdom. In B. M. Staw & L. L. Cummings (Eds.). *Research in organizational behavior* (Vol. 12, pp. 159–203). Greenwich, CT: JAI Press.

Meindl, J. R. (1993). Reinventing leadership: A radical social psychological approach. In K. Murnighan (Ed.), *Social psychology in organizations: Advances in theory and research* (Vol. 12, pp. 159–203). Englewoods Cliffs, NJ: Prentice Hall.

Meindl, J. R. (1995). The romance of leadership as follower-centric theory: A social constructionist approach. *Leadership Quarterly*, *6*, 329–341.

Meindl, J. R., & Ehrlich, S. (1987). The romance of leadership and the evaluation of organizational performance. *Academy of Management Journal*, *30*, 91–109.

Meindl, J. R., Erlich, S. B., & Dukerich, J. M. (1985). The romance of leadership. *Administrative Science Quarterly*, *30*, 78–102.

Meindl, J. R., Pastor, J. C., & Mayo, M. (2004). The romance of leadership. In J. M. Burns, G. R. Goethals, & G. Sorenson (Eds.), *The encyclopedia of leadership*. Palo Alto, CA: Sage.

Nanus, B. (1992). *Visionary leadership.* San Francisco: Jossey Bass.

Newcomb, T. (1961). *The acquaintance process.* New York: Free Press.

Pastor, J. C., Mayo, M., & Meindl, J. R. (2004). Managing leadership images. In S. Chowdhury (Ed.), *Next generation business handbook* (pp. 142–156). Hoboken, NJ: Wiley.

Pastor, J. C., Mayo, M., & Shamir, B. (2006). *Adding fuel to fire: The impact of followers' arousal on charismatic leadership.* Unpublished manuscript.

Pastor, J. C., Meindl, J. R., & Mayo, M. (2002). Network effects model of attributions of charismatic leadership. *Academy of Management Journal, 45*(2), 410–420.

Pfeffer, J., & Salancik, G. E. (1978). *The external control of organizations: A resource dependence perspective.* New York: Harper & Row.

Pillai, R., & Meindl, J. R. (1991). The impact of a performance crisis on attributions of charismatic leadership: A preliminary study. *Proceedings of the 1991 Eastern Academy of Management Meetings,* Hartford, CT.

Rogers, E. M. (1983). *The diffusion of innovations* (3rd ed.). New York: Free Press.

Rogers, E. M. (1995). *The diffusion of innovations* (4th ed.). New York: Free Press.

Salancik, G., & Pfeffer, J. (1978). A social information processing approach to job attitudes and task design. *Administrative Science Quarterly, 23,* 224–253.

Schacter, S. (1959). *The psychology of affiliation.* Stanford, CA: Stanford University Press.

Shamir, B., & Howell, J. M. (1999). Organizational and contextual influences on the emergence and effectiveness of charismatic leadership. *Leadership Quarterly, 10*(2), 257–284.

Sherif, M. (1936). *The psychology of social norms.* New York: Harper.

Sherif, M. (1965). Formation of social norms: The experimental paradigm. In H. Proshansky & B. Seidenberg (Eds.), *Basic studies in social psychology* (pp. 461–470). New York: Holt, Rinehart, and Winston.

Tannenbaum, R., & Schmidt, W. H. (1958). How to choose a leadership pattern. *Harvard Business Review, 36*(2), 95–101.

Thomas, J. G., & Griffin, R. W. (1983). The social information processing model of task design: A critical review. *Academy of Management Review, 8,* 672–682.

Tichy, N., & Devanna, M. (1986). *Transformational leadership.* New York: Wiley.

Tichy, N., Tushman, M., & Fombrum, C. (1979). Social network analysis for organizations. *Academy of Management Review, 4,* 507–519.

Valente, T. H. (1995). *Network models of the diffusion of innovations.* Cresskill, NJ: Hampton Press.

Weick, K. (1995). *Sensemaking in organizations.* Thousand Oaks, CA: Sage.

Yukl, G. A. (1989). *Leadership in organizations.* Upper Saddle River, NJ: Prentice-Hall.

CHAPTER 6

ORGANIZATIONAL CHANGE, MEMBER EMOTION, AND CONSTRUCTION OF CHARISMATIC LEADERSHIP

A Follower-Centric Contingency Model

Chao C. Chen
Liuba Y. Belkin
Terri R. Kurtzberg
Rutgers Business School

ABSTRACT

Building on the romance of leadership theory and the social construction perspective as proposed by Meindl (1990), we take a follower-centric perspective and develop a theoretical model depicting how organizational members construct charismatic leadership as they experience radical organizational change. We propose that the perception of charismatic leadership is first and foremost affected by the change strategy adopted by the organization: a growth strategy will increase charismatic leadership attribution more than will a retrenchment strategy. Furthermore, we propose that

Follower-Centered Perspectives on Leadership, pages 115–134
Copyright © 2007 by Information Age Publishing
All rights of reproduction in any form reserved.

the impact of a change strategy on charisma attribution is mainly due to different emotions aroused by the change strategy, namely, a growth strategy will arouse optimistic emotions and create emotional convergence among organizational members, whereas a retrenchment strategy will arouse pessimistic emotions and create emotional divergence. Finally, we identify a set of factors that may moderate either the relationship between the change strategy and charisma perception or the relationship between the change strategy and emotions. These moderators range from the individual dispositions of the organizational members, to group network structure, to the symbolic characteristics of the leader.

The role of followers has been recognized by charismatic leadership research, more so than by research on any other types of leadership. Charisma, for example, is defined in terms of the leader's intellectual, sociopsychological, and even behavioral effects on the follower (Fiedler, 1996; George, 2000; House, 1977; House, Spangler, & Woycke, 1991; Willner, 1984) or as reflecting the quality of relationship between the leader and the follower (Howell & Shamir, 2005; Klein & House, 1995). However, such recognition by and large is through the perspective of the leader, known as leader-centric, which has serious limitations as critiqued by Meindl (1990, 1995). First, there is a risk of tautology in the leader-centric perspective of charisma in that a key leadership characteristic is itself defined in terms of effectiveness. If, for example, follower identification with and loyalty to the leader is already an integral part of a leader's charisma, it would be somewhat redundant to focus on how charismatic leaders are more effective than say transactional leaders. Second, the role of the follower is by and large conceived as passive, if not negative. Most past research focused on the leaders' charismatic traits or behaviors, which influence the followers in a unidirectional, "top-down" manner (Fiedler, 1996; House, 1977; Pescosolido, 2002; Sashkin, 1992). In this perspective, followers are treated as passive, often blind, recipients of great charismatic personas or actions. Even in some works that take into account followers' perspectives and follower–leader relationships (e.g., Klein & House, 1995), potential or actual followers are referred to as "flammable material," with the charismatic leader as the spark and the environment as oxygen (Howell & Shamir, 2005). Third, the leader-centric perspective provides limited insight into the process of charisma emergence. If indeed a follower's attribution is part of the charisma phenomenon, as most leader-centric researchers acknowledge, focusing on the leader overlooks how the same leader trait or act may or may not come to be perceived as charismatic depending on members' experiences, cognitions, and affect (Meindl, 1995).

In view of the limitations of the leader-centric perspective on charisma attribution, Meindl (1990) proposed a follower-centric perspective. First, in contrast to the traditional view that leadership resides in or emanates from the leader, who uses leadership as a means to influence organizational members to achieve organizational objectives, the follower-centric perspective and the romance of leadership theory contend that leadership resides in and emanates from organizational *members*, who use leadership as a means to understand and evaluate their organizational experiences. Accordingly, Meindl (1990, 1995) advocated switching research focus away from the leader as the primary determinant of followers' charisma perceptions. Instead, he emphasized follower characteristics and social-organizational contexts as the primary determinants of charisma attribution.

Second, leadership is by and large a given in leader-centric theories and research in that presumed followers are studied to validate the existence of charisma in the leader. From the follower-centric point of view, charismatic leadership is contested, negotiated, and constructed. Accordingly, the primary objective of the traditional leadership research is to uncover the process of the effective exercise of leadership, whereas the primary objective of the follower-centric leadership research is to uncover the process of leadership construction.

Third, due to differences in the conceptions of charisma and in the research objectives, the follower-centric perspective pays greater attention to the underlying cognitive and affective mechanisms by which charismatic leadership is constructed. The emergence of charisma, that is, the construction of charisma in the minds of organizational members, is itself a worthy outcome variable. Additional outcome variables can include the consequences of charisma attribution, such as employee attitudes and behaviors with regard to the leader and the organization.

Finally, it is worth pointing out that the follower-centric view of leadership does not object to nor negate the role of the leader in the followers' construction of leadership in general and charisma in particular. Rather, it holds that the role of the leader has been exaggerated and romanticized so much that it is necessary to pursue a follower-centric perspective to the exclusion of the leadership role until the followers' role is well understood. In this chapter, we build on and extend Meindl's follower-centric perspective of charismatic leadership by exploring the process of charisma attribution during times when organizations experience dramatic transformations. We contribute to the follower-centric perspective in a number of ways. First, we situate our theoretical model in the context of organizational change, when charisma is "up for grabs" with a change of leadership. The backdrop of organizational change and leadership change, in our view, is most conducive to examine the emergence of charismatic leadership. Second, focusing on how charisma becomes perceived and attributed to the change leader by organizational members, we approach all relevant factors purely from the vantage point of the follower, whether the change relates to organizational strategy, network structure, or the symbolic characteristic of the leader.

Third, we place organizational members' emotions at the center of our theoretical model. Specifically, we examine how organizational change strategies arouse different kinds of emotion in organization members and how emotions can mediate between change strategy and the perception of charismatic leadership. Finally, we identify a series of individual, group-, and organizational-level factors that interact with change strategies to influence emotion and charisma attribution.

ORGANIZATIONAL CHANGE AND CHARISMATIC LEADERSHIP ATTRIBUTION

Charismatic Leadership Attribution during Organizational Change

Researchers have defined charismatic leadership in various ways, with many acknowledging the role of subordinates or followers as a critical element. House and colleagues (1991), for example, offered some representative definitions of charisma: "Charisma refers to the ability of a leader to exercise diffuse and intense influence over the beliefs, values, behavior, and performance of others through his or her own behavior, beliefs, and personal example.... We define charisma here as a relationship or bond between a leader and subordinates or other followers" (p. 366). Our follower-centric perspective on charisma is distinct in two major ways. First, while the leader-centric perspective holds that followers' charisma attribution is mainly a reflection of their leader's substantial traits or behaviors, we seek to investigate how charisma attribution is part and parcel of organizational members' cognitive and emotional responses to the unfolding

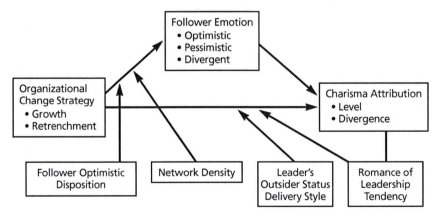

Figure 6.1.   A follower-centric contingency model of charismatic leadership attribution.

organizational change. The second distinction of our follower-centric perspective is that we are as interested in the charisma attribution process as we are in the outcome. This will be reflected in the selection of not only independent variables and moderators but also in the dependent variables in our model. In this chapter, we target two dependent variables. The first is the level of perceived charismatic leadership and the second is the variance of such perception, namely, the degree of divergence of charismatic leadership perception among members of the organization.

Previous researchers have postulated that organizations in crisis provide fertile grounds for the emergence of charismatic leaders (e.g., Ashkanasy, Hartel, & Daus, 2002; Bass, 1985; House, 1977; Klein & House, 1995; Pillai, 1996; Pillai & Meindl, 1998; Weick, 1993; Willner, 1994). Bass (1985), for example, observed that charismatic leadership is more likely to be found in a new and struggling, or in an old and failing, organization, as opposed to a successful and stable one. Pillai (1996) found evidence in a lab experiment that individuals in threatening situations are more likely to make charisma attribution to emergent leaders than those in normal, nonthreatening situations.

Most of the observations about crises indicate the presence of uncertainty and stress in times of crisis. We focus on organizational change instead of crisis as the backdrop for our theoretical dialogue. This we believe is necessary for the process of charismatic leadership emergence and construction. Organizational change may either be triggered by a crisis itself, or may be a proactive response to anticipated crisis. Change resembles crisis in that it is uncertain and stressful, but crisis itself does not create charisma, neither in the leader's persona nor as subjectively constructed in the minds of the followers. The precondition for the emergence of a charismatic leader is that he or she provides a resolution of the crisis or is believed to have the ability to do so. In explaining why "crisis breeds charisma," Klein and House (1995) state: "In crisis individuals are uncertain and stressed and, thus, open to the influence of pervasive leaders who offer a hopeful, inspiring vision of the crisis resolved" (pp. 185–186). Note that to be perceived charismatic by organizational members the leader has to provide "a hopeful, inspiring vision" for resolving the crisis. We further argue that the provision of hope and inspiration is itself amendable by subjective construction because organizational change increasingly carries a mixture of positive and negative consequences and its implications depend on perspectives and interests of different stakeholders (Perrow, 1972; Pfeffer & Salancik, 1978). It is the organizational response to crisis, rather than crisis per se, that provides ideal testing grounds for the construction of charismatic leadership.

Organizational Change Strategy and Attribution of Charismatic Leadership

Organizational change from the evolutionary perspective has been characterized as either minor, incremental change that adjusts and refines operations within the existing system or radical, transformational change that involves core changes of the system in areas such as organizational strategy and structure (Amburgey, Kelly, & Barnett, 1993; Halliday, Powell, & Tinsley, 1994; Tushman & Anderson, 1997). Transformational organizational change can be further distinguished into two types: growth and retrenchment (Tushman & Anderson, 1997). A growth strategy refers to the aggressive expansion of existing business or diversification into new businesses, whereas a retrenchment strategy is a significant downscoping so as to focus on corporate core competences (Koskisson & Hitt, 1994), often involving reduction of the size and diversity of business operations. The two strategies are both radical changes and both carry uncertainty as they bring disruptions of established routines and authority relationships (e.g., mergers and acquisitions in growth strategies and downsizing in retrenchment strategies).

We propose that a growth change strategy is more likely to increase the perception of charismatic leadership by organizational members than a retrenchment change strategy. We are aware that this proposition may run counter to perceptions of charismatic leadership by external parties such as the media and industry analysts, who evaluate the short- or long-term merits of retrenchment versus growth strategies from a somewhat disinterested perspective. For example, to the extent a retrenchment strategy signifies more radical change than does a growth strategy, executives adopting the former strategy, everything else equal, may be portrayed in the media as more charismatic than those adopting the latter strategy. Organizational members, however, may respond differently than the media because they are more likely to assess a change strategy according to its consequences on their own personal career and life. Where consequences have not materialized or are uncertain for ongoing changes, according to prospect theory (Kahneman & Tversky, 1979), people will evaluate a change strategy according to the probability that it will bring about a better or worse future than the status quo of the prechange situation. Members of organizations adopting a growth strategy will see more opportunities for organizational and personal growth, whereas those in organizations adopting a retrenchment strategy will see the restriction of operations and the possibility of layoffs. In the case where organizational change has already borne results, members of expanding organizations are more likely to be retained and be given increasing responsibilities, whereas those in downsizing organizations are likely to see the resources being dwindled and coworkers being laid off. Organization members therefore assess effectiveness of organizational change primarily in terms of its effect on their own life and career, be they anticipated or realized. It should be pointed out that retrenchment change may eventually bring about a future that is drastically better than the prechange status quo but such an eventuality could be too far ahead for the current organizational members to foresee.

The assessment of the impact of the organizational change will be linked to charisma attribution if and when such impact is attributed to the leader in the mind of the organizational members. Such linkage, we believe, is quite strong for two reasons. First, previous theory and research on leadership attribution predict that members construct leadership images according to performance outcomes. Studies on the effects of performance cues found that leadership images are based on the direction of performance outcomes, positive for positive group performance and negative for negative group performance (e.g., Staw, 1975). A similar phenomenon occurs at the organizational level when concepts of leadership are appealed to when the economy or business is doing either very well or very poorly but not moderately (Meindl & Erlich, 1987). Second, in addition to the general tendency to explain organizational outcomes in terms of leadership, organizational change often coincides with the change of a company CEO. Indeed it is often the case that the new executive is hired with great expectation to resolve an existing organizational crisis. The co-occurrence of leadership and organizational change therefore further reinforces the general romance of leadership tendency to attribute anticipated outcomes of organizational change to the leader. In summary, we propose:

Proposition 1:   *A growth change strategy will be more likely to increase the perception of charismatic leadership by organizational members than will a retrenchment change strategy.*

While the above proposition is about the level of charisma attributed to the leader who is supposed to embody the organizational change strategy, the change strategy itself may also affect the consensus or divergence of charisma attribution. To the extent organizational members differ in their assessment of the positive–negative impact of organizational change, there will be greater variation in the construction of charismatic leadership within the organization. In fact, scholars of charisma have remarked how charismatic leaders often create bipolar love–hate relationships with followers and nonfollowers (Dasborough & Ashkanasy, 2002). Of interest to us is whether such a difference exists among organizational members at the very beginning, when charisma is being constructed. We hold that there will be variations among employees in the assessment of change outcomes in both growth and retrenchment organizations. In companies pursuing rapid growth such as aggressive mergers and acquisitions, there will be a reallocation of authorities and resources and some parts of the company may lose while others may gain. Accordingly, assessments of the organization's future as well as assessments of future personal careers may not be monolithically positive among all organizational members. Similarly, in retrenching organizations, assessment of the future will not be monolithically negative among all organizational members because some parts of the company may gain more authority and resources even though most parts are downsizing. In spite of the above argument about variations within either growing or retrenching organizations, we nevertheless contend that the variation of one's future outcome assessment will be greater for the latter than the former. This is because a growth strategy, despite its accompanying uncertainty and stress, is expected by the majority of employees to move the company in a positive direction, whereas members of retrenching companies will be more divided in their assessment of the company's future because the change for them may have a stronger short-term impact, while the long-term change benefits are less certain. Due to the link between organizational performance outcomes and leadership attribution, then, variations in outcome assessment will be related to variation in charisma attribution. We therefore propose:

Proposition 2:   *A growth change strategy will be more likely to be associated with less divergence in the perception of charismatic leadership among organizational members than will a retrenchment change strategy.*

THE MEDIATING ROLE OF EMPLOYEE EMOTIONS

Scholars in the leadership field began focusing on the value of emotions in the charisma attribution process fairly recently, but mostly through a leader-centric perspective, either in the sense that follower-emotion is a response to leader-emotion, or in that effective leadership involves the management of follower-emotions. For instance, Lord, Brown, and Freiberg (1999) proposed that supervisors often unconsciously influence employees with their affective states. Brown and Keeping (2005) showed that affect mediates the relationship between leaders' and followers' performances. Specifically, followers' liking of a leader also leads to higher transformational leadership ratings (Brown & Keeping, 2005). George (2000) stated that emotional intelligence, or the ability to understand and manage moods and emotions in the self and others, contributes to effective leadership in organizations. Even when authors have considered the attribution of charisma as a reciprocal emotional process between the leader and the followers, follower-emotion is not directly linked with organizational change and is conceived of as more responsive to leader-emotion than vice versa (e.g., Lord et al.,

1999; Willner, 1984). In summary, most of the research emphasized the role of leaders' emotions as a primary focus of their research and follower-emotion is merely a byproduct of the leader's emotions, or the target rather than the source of influence in charisma attribution.

In the spirit of the follower-centric perspective, we propose that employee emotions originate from their own perception and assessment of organizational change, which in turn affect their charisma attribution. However, we do not mean that employees' assessment of organizational change and the associated emotions are formed in isolation of any influence from their peers or leaders. While we address those factors later, we here theorize about how employee emotions mediate their assessment of an organization's future and their charisma attributions.

Organizational Change Strategy and Member Emotions

We define emotion as a specific affective occurrence that is identified with or directed toward particular stimuli. Emotions are relatively high in intensity and short in duration, can disrupt ongoing thought processes (Barry, 1999; Forgas, 1992; Frijda, 1993), and are often considered in discrete dimensions, such as happiness, anger, fear, joy, anxiety, elation, guilt, and so on (Brief & Weiss, 2002; van Kleef, De Dreu, & Mainstead, 2004a, 2004b). Previous research in psychology and organization studies has primarily examined mood states and emotions along two dimensions: valence (positive–negative direction of affect) and arousal (high–low intensity of affect) (see Russell, 1979; Watson & Tellegen, 1985). Because organizational change is typically charged with intense emotions (Ashkanasy et al., 2002), in this chapter we focus on the direction of emotions. In addition to the individual level of analysis, we are also interested in the emotional consensus among members of an organization. In particular, relevant to the study of variance in charisma attribution, we are interested in emotional divergence in organizations (high if organizational members experience diametrically opposed emotions and low if they experience similar emotions either in the positive or in the negative direction).

Though organizational change is often surrounded by high levels of uncertainty, which may create a prevailing negative emotion of anxiety, we expect both positive and negative emotions to appear. In the above section, we discussed how different change strategies may affect organizational members' assessment of change outcomes. Here we further argue that such assessment of the change strategy is rarely cool-headed but rather is likely to be emotionally charged, both because the stakes involved are so high and because organizational transformation is often accompanied by organizational politics, characterized by alliances and contestation among different stakeholders (Pfeffer, 1981). To the extent different organization change strategies arouse different attitudes toward the change, employee emotions will be significantly related to the change strategy. As described above, we expect that members of organizations adopting a growth strategy will be more likely to experience optimistic emotions such as hope and excitement about organizational change, whereas those of a retrenchment change strategy will be more likely to experience pessimistic emotions such as fear and insecurity about the change. Furthermore, because there is higher consensus regarding outcome assessment for growth than for retrenchment strategy, we expect more emotional convergence among members of growing companies than among those of retrenching companies. We therefore propose:

Proposition 3a: *Organizational members will experience stronger optimistic emotions under a growth change strategy but stronger pessimistic emotions under a retrenchment change strategy.*

Proposition 3b: *There will be less divergence in emotions among organizational members under a growth change strategy than under a retrenchment change strategy.*

Member Emotion and Charisma Attribution

We propose that charisma attribution will be affected by attributors' emotions in that people with optimistic emotions will make more charisma attributions than will people with pessimistic emotions. It is worth noting that this proposition is different from the general assertion that people in a crisis situation (Pillai, 1996; Tichy & Devanna, 1986), or under high emotional arousal (Mayo, Pastor, & Meindl, 1996), are more likely to perceive charisma than are people in normal conditions. We assert that it is primarily not the high arousal or stress per se but the direction of the emotion that affects charisma attribution.

There is ample research evidence that emotion colors perception in that positive emotions generate more favorable perceptions than do negative emotions (Isen, 1987; Seligman & Csikszentmihalyi, 1991). Applying this emotion-colors-perception principle to the organizational context, it is expected that because charisma is generally viewed as a positive attribute, optimistic emotions should lead to more charisma perceptions while pessimistic emotions to less charisma perceptions. Furthermore, as discussed earlier, according to the romance of leadership perspective, there is a general tendency that organizational members attribute organizational events and experiences to those in leadership positions. This general tendency gets reinforced and intensified during an organizational change that explicitly ties the change to the change agent, namely the new CEO. The same new CEO therefore will be perceived differently depending on how the members feel about the consequences of the organizational change.

In summary, we expect a link between outcome assessment of an organizational change and emotion on one hand, and a link between emotion and charisma attribution on the other hand. Thus, we propose:

Proposition 4a: *Optimistic emotions will have a positive effect on the perception of charismatic leadership, whereas pessimistic emotions will have a negative effect on the perception of charismatic leadership.*

Proposition 4b: *The greater the divergence in emotions among organizational members the greater the divergence in the perception of charismatic leadership.*

MODERATING FACTORS OF CHARISMA ATTRIBUTION

As stated earlier, taking the follower-centric perspective does not preclude consideration of nonfollower factors. Furthermore, the proposed theoretical relationships among organizational change, member emotion, and charisma attribution may or may not hold true depending on multiple factors at the individual, group, or organizational level. In this section, we seek to identify these factors.

Member Dispositions

Optimistic Disposition
Research on positive emotions has demonstrated that some people are able to cultivate positive emotions in times of crises (Folkman & Moscowitz, 2000) and use them strategically by looking for opportunities to achieve their desired outcomes (Folkman, 1997; Tugade & Frederickson, 2002). These individuals are viewed as having a resilient personality. Similarly, research on optimism–pessimism has also identified a stable individual characteristic that orients individuals to approach adverse situations optimistically versus pessimistically (Peterson, Seligman, & Vaillant, 1988; Seligman, 1991). Relating this individual characteristic to the link between organizational change strategy and member emotion, we propose that an optimistic disposition will moderate the effect of an organizational change strategy on emotions such that:

Proposition 5:   *Organizational members with higher as opposed to lower optimistic dispositions will experience stronger optimistic emotions under a growth change strategy but weaker pessimistic emotions under a retrenchment change strategy.*

Romance of Leadership Tendency

The romance of leadership tendency refers to an individual's tendency to attribute organizational events and outcomes to those in leadership positions. Such a tendency is more likely to be aroused when explanations are sought to account for drastic performance fluctuations (Meindl & Ehrlich, 1987). Furthermore, the romance of leadership tendency is also conceived of as a stable individual attribute (Meindl, 1990), which directs some individuals more than others to attribute outcomes to leaders across a variety of situations. Following previous theory and research we propose that the romance of leadership tendency will enhance the link between organizational change strategy and charisma attribution such that:

Proposition 6:   *The positive effects of a growth change strategy and the negative effects of a retrenchment change strategy on the perception of charismatic leadership will be stronger for organizational members with a strong romance of leadership tendency than for those without it.*

Organizational Network Density

One important social mechanism for influencing the convergence versus divergence of emotion is known as social contagion, which Meindl (1990) considered to be key to the construction of leadership among followers. "In its broadest sense, social contagion is defined as the spread of affect, attitude, or behavior from Person A (the "initiator") to Person B (the "recipient"), where the recipient does not perceive an intentional influence attempt on the part of the initiator" (Levy & Nail, 1993, p. 266). In other words, social contagion is a process where individual emotional states and behaviors spread to others through communication or the mere physical presence of initiators.

Leader-centric research has examined how a leader's emotions and moods are contagious to followers and influence their attitudes and performance (e.g., Brown & Keeping, 2005; Cherulnik, Donley, Wiewel, & Miller, 2001; Gaddis, Connelly, & Mumford, 2004; Lewis, 2000; McColl-Kennedy & Anderson, 2002). For example, Cherulnik and colleagues (2001) demonstrate that by exhibiting positive emotions through nonverbal behaviors (such as frequent intense smiles or maintaining close visual contact with the audience) leaders can be perceived by followers as charismatic through the process of social contagion. A follower-centric perspective, however, focuses on social contagion among peers (Meindl, 1990; Pastor, Meindl, & Mayo, 2002). Here, we consider the impact of the employee network structure on emotional contagion. More specifically, we expect network density, which reflects the frequency of contact and communication among network ties, to have an impact. Previous research has shown that individuals' emotions are highly influenced by social contexts (Fiol, 2002; Weick & Roberts, 1993), and group structure can even influence the emotional convergence of group members (Bartel & Saavedra, 2000). Specifically, these authors found that mood convergence was higher based on the degree to which group members worked together closely and saw each other socially. Thus, we would expect network density to have a systematic (main) effect on both emotional valence and on emotional convergence, namely, members of very dense networks are more likely to share similar emotions. However, putting the generation and dispersion of emotion into the context of organizational change, we also propose an interaction effect between the organizational change strategy and the organizational network density. We propose that the organizational network density will enhance the effect of the organizational change strategy on emotion and emotional divergence such that:

Proposition 7a: *The positive emotional effect of a growth change strategy and the negative emotional effect of a retrenchment change strategy will be stronger in high-density organizational networks than in low-density organizational networks.*

Proposition 7b: *The difference in emotional divergence between the two change strategies will be greater for members with high-density organizational networks than for those with low-density organizational networks.*

Symbolic Characteristics of the Leader

Researchers of a strict follower-centric perspective would exclude the consideration of the role of the leader in their theory building (Meindl, 1995). This is partly because the follower-centric perspective is aligned with the romance of leadership perspective, which offers a social construction critique of the excessive fascination and prominence of the leader-centric perspective with the leader's personality. The social constructive perspective of leadership holds that "rather than assuming leaders and followers are linked in a substantially causal way, it assumes that the relationship between leaders and followers is primarily a constructed one" (Meindl, 1995, p. 330). Another reason for excluding the leader is more pragmatic and tactical, as the follower-centric researchers want to reserve their complete devotion to the underdeveloped follower-centric perspective. In the spirit of building a bridge between the leader-centric and follower-centric perspectives and yet staying true to the social constructive perspective, we examine two leader characteristics that are more symbolic than substantial.

Insider and Outsider Status of the Leader

Organizational change could be initiated and implemented by a new leader brought in from the outside or by one who has been chosen from inside the company. There are advantages and disadvantages to each insider and outsider status for the effectiveness of organizational change (Gabarro, 1987; Kotter & Heskett, 1992; Shen & Cannella, 2002). An outsider CEO is generally expected to have a broader perspective, more change experience, and is more detached from the old ways of doing things in the company. Due to these expectations, we contend, the status of the individual, perhaps even more so than their actual capabilities, carries important information for the construction of charismatic leadership by organizational members. Our position is consistent with the argument that new leaders are more likely to be perceived as charismatic when they replace a noncharismatic old leader (Shamir & Howell, 1999). Bligh and colleagues' (Bligh, Kohles, & Meindl, 2004; Bligh, Kohles, & Pillai, 2004) research on political leadership found that new leaders (challengers) received higher charismatic attributions than the previous, established leader in the California recall election. Instead of proposing the main effect of insider–outsider status, we propose an interactive effect between the organizational change strategy and the change of the leader's insider–outsider status. This shift is again primarily due to the salience of the context of organizational change. We propose that the insider–outsider status of the leader will moderate the effect of the organizational change strategy on the perception of charismatic leadership such that:

Proposition 8: *Being an outsider will increase the positive effect of the growth change strategy on the perception of charismatic leadership but decrease the negative effect of the retrenchment strategy.*

Leader's Delivery Style

Existing research already supports the notion that communication style contributes to perceptions of charisma (e.g., Bligh, Kohles, & Meindl, 2004; Bligh, Kohles, & Pillai, 2004; Groves, 2005). Specifically, Bligh and colleagues (2004) investigated how perceptions of leaders change in times of crisis, and have demonstrated that the changes in communication and language (e.g., shift in message delivery, such as articulation of similarity to followers, collective focus, action, adversity, etc.) has been linked to an impression of the leader as charismatic. Moreover, as Bligh and colleagues demonstrated, situational factors coupled with leaders' communication style can influence followers' perceptions of leaders, resulting in higher ratings of charisma. Building on the above evidence, we propose that a leader's "charismatic" delivery style will moderate the effect of the chosen organizational change strategy on the attributions of charisma. Specifically, we propose:

Proposition 9:   *The positive effect of a growth change strategy on charisma attribution will be greater when the leader's delivery style is perceived to be charismatic, whereas the negative effect of a retrenchment change strategy will be reduced by a leader's charismatic delivery style.*

DIRECTIONS FOR FUTURE RESEARCH

Building on the romance of leadership theory and the social construction perspective as proposed by Meindl (1990, 1995), we developed a theoretical model depicting how organizational members construct charismatic leadership as they experience dramatic organizational change. We propose that the perception of charismatic leadership is first and foremost affected by the kind of change strategy adopted by the organization: a growth strategy is more likely to be associated with charismatic leadership attribution than is a retrenchment strategy. Furthermore, we propose that the impact of the change strategy on charisma attribution is mainly due to different emotions aroused by the change strategy, namely, a growth strategy will arouse optimistic emotions and create emotional convergence among organizational members, whereas a retrenchment strategy will arouse pessimistic emotions and create emotional divergence. Finally, we identify a set of factors that may moderate either the relationship between change strategy and charisma perception or the relationship between change strategy and emotions. These moderators range from the individual disposition of the organizational members to group network structure and to the symbolic characteristics of the leader.

The follower-centric contingency model points out new directions for research on charismatic leadership. First, we direct attention to organizational change (as opposed to crisis) as the context in which charismatic leadership is constructed. One advantage of studying organizational change is that as an independent variable it has greater variability. While crisis is typically contrasted with absence of crisis, organizational change can be further differentiated into radical versus evolutionary change, reactive versus proactive change, adaptive versus disruptive change, and growth versus retrenchment change. The more we can segment change into distinct types, the easier it will be for future research to connect these categories with crisis events, and study possible interaction effects of types of organizational change and types of organizational crisis on emotional response and charisma construction. For example, organizational crisis can be of a political as opposed to a financial nature. And a retrenchment strategy following a financial crisis may be more justified, hence more likely to facilitate charisma construction than will a retrenchment strategy following a succession crisis in which the company's financial situation is stable.

The second advantage is, even without operationalizing organizational change as a variable, it can serve as a given context to examine the process of social construction of charismatic leadership. For example, when an organization is experiencing growth or retrenchment, different units of the same organization may be differentially affected. Will those differences of emotions and charisma perceptions between the change strategies hold for different subunits within the same change strategy? For example, an overall retrenchment strategy may not be applied equally across all subunits of the organization, which will result in different emotions in members of between different subunits and affect their perceptions of charisma.

The second research direction is in the focus on the perspectives of organizational members who are experiencing the organizational change, as opposed to those of the leader or those of external observers such as the media. Past research on the media, for example, has made a great contribution to the understanding of charismatic leadership attribution, yet it is not clear if media-constructed charismatic leadership can be generalized to organizational members. Executives of retrenchment change, especially those of companies that brought positive change outcomes to shareholders, may well be hailed as charismatic heroes by the business media. Will they be viewed equally or uniformly as charismatic by employees of those companies? Our theoretical model suggests otherwise. Results of studies investigating employees who are directly affected by organizational change may well challenge some of the assumptions of previous research. For example, the effect of crisis and its associated uncertainty and stress on charisma attribution may not be as straightforward as has been previously thought. That effect may depend very much on organizational members' anticipation of personal outcomes from the organizational change.

Third, our theoretical model seeks to identify underlying mechanisms through which charismatic leadership attribution is made. We posit emotion valence and divergence as important affective mechanisms that mediate the relationship between change strategy and perception of charismatic leadership. Previous literature on crisis and charisma rarely considered emotion divergence among followers and in the case of emotion valence, it is far from specific and explicit as it implies that the prevailing follower emotions are uncertainty and stress. Our conceptions of emotion are more target-specific, namely, we focus on emotions regarding organizational change and we include both positive and negative emotions. Future research may consider the effects of mixed positive and negative emotions and measure leader-specific emotions as well. Besides affective mechanisms, one could also posit cognitive mechanisms. Implicit in our model is the cognitive assessment of costs and benefits regarding the outcomes of organizational change. Researchers can also explore the independent and interactive effects of cognitive and affective mechanisms on charisma attributions in organizations.

Finally, the contingency model points to the importance of identifying factors that moderate either the main effect of the organizational context or the mediating effect of emotion and cognition. Note that although the moderators we selected cut across different levels of analysis, they may not necessarily be the most relevant and are definitely not complete as they only represent our first attempt to move charismatic leadership research in this direction. For example, the reputation of the change leader could also be an important moderator for the effect of change strategy. Depending on the research focus of a particular study, some of these moderators may be included as control variables. For example, the symbolic characteristics of a leader could be control variables in a strictly follower-centric research design.

In summary, through the follower-centric contingency model of charismatic leadership attribution we seek to stimulate and guide research on the process of charismatic leadership construction by organizational members during major organizational change.

ACKNOWLEDGMENT

We thank Wei Shen for his insights on change strategy and the insider–outsider status of the change leader and we also thank Mary Uhl-Bien for her constructive comments on the manuscript.

REFERENCES

Amburgey, T. L., Kelly, D., & Barnett, W. P. (1993). Resetting the clock: The dynamics of organizational change and failure. *Administrative Science Quarterly, 38,* 51–73.

Ashkanasy, N. M., Hartel, C. E. J., & Daus, C. S. (2002). Diversity and emotion: The new frontiers in organizational behavior research. *Journal of Management, 28,* 307–338.

Barry, B. (1999). The tactical use of emotion in negotiation. *Research on Negotiation in Organizations, 7,* 93–121.

Bartel, C. A., & Saavedra, R. (2000). The collective construction of work group moods. *Administrative Science Quarterly, 45,* 197–231.

Bass, B. M. (1985). *Leadership and performance beyond expectations.* New York: Free Press.

Bligh, M. C., Kohles, J. C., & Meindl, J. R. (2004). Charisma under crisis: Presidential leadership, rhetoric, and media responses before and after the September 11 terrorist attacks. *Leadership Quarterly, 15,* 211–239.

Bligh, M. C., Kohles, J. C., & Pillai, R. (2004). Crisis and Charisma in the California recall election. *Leadership, 1,* 323–351.

Brief, A. P., & Weiss, H. M. (2002). Organizational behavior: Affect in the workplace. *Annual Review of Psychology, 53,* 279–307.

Brown, D. J. & Keeping, L. M. (2005). Elaborating the construct of transformational leadership: The role of affect. *Leadership Quarterly, 16,* 245–272.

Cherulnik, P. D., Donley, K. A., Wiewel, T. S. R., & Miller, S.R. (2001). Charisma is contagious: The effect of leaders' charisma on observers' affect. *Journal of Applied Social Psychology, 31,* 2149–2159

Dasborough, M. T., & Ashkanasy, N. M. (2002). Emotion and attribution of intentionality in leader–member relationships. *Leadership Quarterly, 13,* 615–634.

Fiedler, F. E. (1996). Research on leadership selection and training: One view of the future. *Administrative Science Quarterly, 41,* 241–250.

Fiol, M. C. (2002). Intraorganizational cognition and interpretation. In J. A. Baum (Ed.), *Companion to organizations.* Malden, MA: Blackwell Publishers Inc.

Folkman, S. (1997). Positive psychological states and coping with severe stress. *Social Science and Medicine, 45,* 1207–1221.

Folkman. S., & Moskowitz, J. T. (2000). Positive affect and the other side of coping. *American Psychologist, 55,* 647–654.

Forgas, J. P. (1992). Affect in social judgments and decisions: A multiprocess model. In M. P. Zanna (Ed.), *Advances in experimental social psychology* (Vol. 25, pp. 227–275). San Diego, CA: Academic Press.

Frijda, N. H. (1993). The place of appraisal in emotion. *Cognition and Emotion, 7,* 357–87.

Gabarro, J. J. (1987). *The dynamics of taking charge.* Boston: Harvard Business School Press.

Gaddis, B., Connelly, S., & Mumford, M. D. (2004). Failure feedback as an affective event: Influences of leader affect on subordinate attitudes and performance. *Leadership Quarterly, 15,* 663–686.

George, J. M. (2000). Emotions and leadership: The role of emotional intelligence. *Human Relations, 53,* 1027–1055.

Groves, K. (2005). Linking leadership skills, follower attitudes, and contextual variables via an integrated model of charismatic leadership. *Journal of Management, 31,* 255–278.

House, R. J. (1977). A 1976 theory of charismatic leadership. In J. G. Hunt & L. L. Larson (Eds.), *Leadership: The cutting edge* (pp. 188–207). Carbondale: Southern Illinois University Press.

House, R. J., Spangler, W. D., & Woycke, J. (1991). Personality and charisma in the US Presidency: A psychological theory of leader effectiveness. *Administrative Science Quarterly, 36,* 364–396.

Howell, J. M., & Shamir, B. (2005). The role of followers in the charismatic leadership process: Relationships and their consequences. *Academy of Management Review, 30,* 96–112.

Isen, A. M. (1987). Positive affect, cognitive processes, and social behavior. In L. Berkowitz (Ed.), *Advances inexperimental social psychology* (Vol. 20, pp. 203–253). San Diego, CA: Academic Press.

Kahneman, D., & Tversky, A. (1979). Prospect theory: An analysis of decision under risk, *Econometrica, 47,* 263–292.

Klein, K. J., & House, R. J. (1995). On Fire: Charismatic leadership and levels of analysis. *Leadership Quarterly, 6,* 183–198.

Kotter, J. P., & Heskett, J. (1992). *Corporate culture and performance.* New York: Free Press.

Levy, D. A., & Nail, P. R. (1993). Contagion: A theoretical and empirical review and reconceptualization. *Genetic, Social and General Psychology Monographs, 119,* 233–284.

Lewis, K. M. (2000).When leaders display emotion: How followers respond to negative emotional expression of male and female leaders. *Journal of Organizational Behavior, 21,* 221–234.

Lord, R. G., Brown, D. J., & Freiberg, S. J. (1999). Understanding the dynamics of leadership: The role of followers self-concepts in the leader/follower relationship. *Organizational Behavior and Human Decision Processes, 78,* 167–203.

Mayo, M., Pastor, J. C., & Meindl, J. R. (1996). The effect *of* group heterogeneity on the self-perceived efficacy of group leaders. *Leadership Quarterly, 7,* 265–284.

McColl-Kennedy, J. R., & Anderson, R. D. (2002). Impact of leadership style and emotions on subordinate performance. *Leadership Quarterly, 13,* 545–559.

Meindl, J. R. (1990). On leadership: An alternative to the conventional wisdom. *Research in Organizational Behavior, 12, 159–203.*

Meindl, J. R. (1995) The romance of leadership as a follower-centric theory: A social constructionist approach. *Leadership Quarterly, 6,* 329–341.

Meindl, J. R., & Enrlich, S. E. (1987). The Romance of leadership and the evaluation of organizational performance. *Academy of Management Journal, 30,* 91–109.

Pastor, J., Meindl, J. R., & Mayo, M. C. (2002). A Network effects model of charisma attributions. *Academy of Management Journal, 45,* 410–420.

Pescosolido, A. T. (2002). Emergent leaders as managers of group emotion. *Leadership Quarterly, 13,* 583–599.

Perrow, C. (1972). *Complex organizations: A critical essay.* Glenview, IL: Scott Foresman.

Peterson, C., Seligman, M., & Vaillant, G. (1988). Pessimistic explanatory style is a risk factor for physical illness: A thirty-five-year longitudinal study. *Journal of Personality and Social Psychology, 55,* 23–27.

Pfeffer, J. (1981). *Power in organizations.* Marshfield, MA: Pitman.

Pfeffer, J., & Salancik, G. (1978). *The external control of organizations: A resource dependence perspective.* New York: Harper & Row.

Pillai, R. (1996). Crisis and the emergence of charismatic leadership in groups: An experimental investigation. *Journal of Applied Social Psychology, 26,* 543–562.

Pillai, R.,& Meindl, J. R. (1998). Context and charisma: A "meso" level examination of the relationship of organic structure, collectivism, and crisis to charismatic leadership. *Journal of Management, 24,* 643–671.

Russell, J. A. (1979). Affective space is bipolar. *Journal of Personality and Social Psychology, 37,* 345 –356.

Sashkin. M. (1992). Strategic leadership competencies. In R. L. Phillips & J. G. Hunt (Eds.), *Strategic leadership* (pp. 139–160). Westport, CT: Quorum.

Seligman, M. (1991). *Learned optimism.* New York: Knopf.

Seligman, M., & Csikszentmihalyi, M. (2000). Positive psychology: An introduction. *American Psychologist, 55,* 5–14.

Shamir, B., & Howell, J. M. (1999). Organizational and contextual influences on the emergence and effectiveness of charismatic leadership. *Leadership Quarterly, 10*(2), 257–284.

Shen, W., & Cannella, A. A. (2002). Revising the performance consequences of CEO succession: The impacts of successor type, the postsuccession senior executive turnover, and departing CEO tenure. *Academy of Management Review, 45, 712–733.*

Staw, B. M. (1975). Attribution of the "causes" of performance: A general alternative interpretation of cross-sectional research on organizations. *Organizational Behavior and Human Performance, 13,* 414–432.

Tichy, N. M., & Devanna, M. A. (1986). *The transformational leader.* New York: Wiley.

Tushman, M. L., & Anderson, P. (1997). *Managing strategic innovation and change: A collection of readings. New York:* Oxford University Press

Tugade, M. M., & Frederickson, B. L. (2002). Positive emotions and emotional intelligence. In L. Feldman Barrett & P. Salovey (Eds.), *The wisdom of feelings: Psychological processes in emotional intelligence* (pp. 319–340). New York: Guilford Press.

Van Kleef, G. A., De Dreu, C. K. W., & Manstead, A. S. (2004a). The interpersonal effects of anger and happiness in negotiations. *Journal of Personality and Social Psychology, 86,* 57–76.

Van Kleef, G. A., De Dreu, C. K. W., & Manstead, A. S. (2004b). The interpersonal effects of emotions in negotiations: A motivated information processing approach. *Journal of Personality and Social Psychology, 87,* 510–528.

Watson, D., & Tellegen, A. (1985). Toward a consensual structure of mood. *Psychological Bulletin, 98,* 219–235.

Weick, K. E. (1993). The collapse of sensemaking in organizations: The Mann Gulch disaster. *Administrative Science Quarterly, 38,* 628–652.

Weick, K. E., & Roberts, K. H. (1993). Collective mind in organizations: Heedful interrelating on flight decks. *Administrative Science Quarterly, 38,* 357–381.

Willner, A. R. (1984). *The spellbinders: Charismatic political leadership.* New Haven, CT: Yale University Press.

CHAPTER 7

THROUGH THICK AND THIN?

Follower Constructions of Presidential Leadership Amidst Crises, 2001–2005

Rajnandini Pillai
California State University San Marcos

Jeffrey C. Kohles
California State University San Marcos

Michelle C. Bligh
Claremont Graduate University

ABSTRACT

This study examined the impact of followers' perceptions of crises and effectiveness in dealing with crises on their evaluations of President George W. Bush's transformational and charismatic leadership over a period of five critical years of his presidency (2001–2005). James R. Meindl's follower-centered and social constructionist approaches to leadership were used as a framework to explore these relationships. Data were collected over eight time periods from 477 individuals who were asked about their perceptions of the terrorism crisis and economic crisis facing the nation, as well as the effective-

Follower-Centered Perspectives on Leadership, pages 135–165
Copyright © 2007 by Information Age Publishing
All rights of reproduction in any form reserved.

ness of the President and his team in dealing with these crises. Results showed that perceptions of effectiveness in handling both crises strongly predicted ratings of transformational and charismatic leadership of the President. In addition, followers who perceived a terrorism crisis *and* perceived that the President was effective in dealing with this crisis used more transformational and charismatic constructions to evaluate him. This was not the case for perceptions of economic crisis, indicating that different types of crisis may have varying implications for attributions of leadership. In a pattern that was consistent with previous studies, party affiliation also played an important role in these leadership ratings. Implications of these findings for future leadership research and practice are discussed in the context of Meindl's overall body of work and the research tradition he inspired.

"Whatever personal traits and behaviors best distinguish our leaders, it is powerful social processes that are likely to sustain their charismatic effects on us, encouraging our romanticized, iconical images of them."

"Leadership comes and goes and comes around again."

—Jim Meindl

INTRODUCTION

One of Jim Meindl's seminal contributions to scholarship on leadership was his thought-provoking work on the romance of leadership, in which he suggests that leadership is a social construction that is influenced by what goes on in the thoughts of followers and is affected by the contexts in which they are embedded. In certain contexts (e.g., a crisis), charismatic leadership may function as a collective coping mechanism, where followers attribute charismatic qualities to a leader who appears as if he or she has a solution for the crisis (Meindl, 1995). This is particularly true of political leaders who preside over the fates of nations or emerge in opposition as an alternative to the status quo. The changing fortunes of President George W. Bush over the course of his presidency, through the attacks on September 11, 2001, and the Iraq War, provide a rich opportunity to study the relationship between perceptions of crisis and leadership evaluations using the framework suggested by Meindl. In this chapter, we examine the impact of particular contexts on followers' constructions of President George W. Bush's leadership through the turbulent first 5 years of his presidency.

Following Meindl's work on the romance of leadership and his suggestion that attributions of charisma in political contexts are transmitted through social contagion, Jim Meindl inspired many of his students and colleagues to explore the role of charismatic and transformational leadership attributions by followers in U.S. presidential elections (e.g., Pillai &

Williams, 1998; Pillai, Williams, Lowe, & Jung, 2003), and during key events in a presidency such as the crisis of September 11, 2001 (e.g., Bligh, Kohles, & Meindl, 2004a, 2004b). Several studies on the U.S. presidential elections have demonstrated the relationship between charismatic and transformational leadership attributions and perceptions of personality, trust in the leader, and actual voting behavior (Pillai & Williams, 1998; Pillai et al., 2003). These studies have also shown that a leader's charisma (in the eye of the follower/voter) waxes and wanes with the leader's performance in the election. In addition, research in the context of the California crisis of 2003 showed that a belief that California was in a state of crisis decreased the perception of the incumbent governor as a charismatic individual who could solve the state's problems and increased the attractiveness of the challenger (Bligh, Kohles, & Pillai, 2005). Thus, this previous research suggests that perceptions of leader ineffectiveness in handling challenges (e.g., those posed by an economic downturn or a terrorist attack) may broadly influence followers' attributions of leadership on a number of dimensions.

In this chapter, we present an analysis of followers' perceptions of President Bush's charismatic and transformational leadership from November 2001, shortly after the terrorist attacks of September 11 and the major crisis of Bush's first term, through November 2005 at the height of the reported disillusionment with his policies regarding Iraq as expressed through declining poll ratings (e.g., "Bush ratings hit new low," October 6, 2005, *CBS News Poll;* "Bush approval mark at all time low, November 14, 2005, *CNN/USA Today/Gallup Poll;* "Bush's approval rating falls again, polls show," November 17, 2005, *Wall Street Journal).* The popular press tracks the President's leadership ratings and opinions about the President's policies through his administration. These ratings, which are snapshots in time, are widely disseminated and are given a great deal of weight by the public and the members of the two major political parties. A high rating or a series of high ratings can put the proverbial "wind in the sails" of the President, creating perceptions of political momentum and growing influence, while a low rating can embolden the opposition and influence the perceptions of followers that the current leadership is losing political capital. We track these ratings using psychometrically sound leadership questionnaires and examine their relationship to effectiveness during two types of crises. We also examine the role of party affiliation, perceptions of two different types of crises, and leader effectiveness in handling these crises in influencing constructions of charismatic and transformational leadership. Following Jim Meindl's (1995) contention that various individual and situational factors combine to produce a level of arousal in followers that influences leadership constructions, we sought to explore the degree to which party affiliation, perceptions of crisis, and leadership effectiveness impact the President's leadership ratings over time.

THEORETICAL BACKGROUND

Do President Bush's Transformational and Charismatic Leadership Ratings Track the National Polls?

In the past several decades, the focus of leadership research has shifted from traditional or transactional models of leadership to a new genre of leadership theories, which are proposed to have extraordinary effects on individuals and organizations (House & Shamir, 1993; Meindl, 1995). The impact of this shift has rejuvenated the study of leadership (Hunt, 1999) and made theories of charismatic, visionary, and transformational leadership the most studied area of leadership in the last decade (Lowe & Gardner, 2000). However, in the wake of the scandals involving the so-called "curse" of the superstar CEOs (Khurana, 2002) and Collins's (2001) enormously popular work on *Good to Great* companies and their humble yet fiercely determined Level 5 leaders, there has been much hand wringing and debate about the usefulness of the charismatic savior. Research, however, has shown that these leadership behaviors may have a much greater impact on subjective and objective measures of performance than traditional or "transactional" models of leadership (Lowe, Kroeck, & Sivasubramaniam, 1996).

Transformational leaders motivate their followers to higher performance levels by activating followers' higher order needs, fostering a climate of trust, and inducing followers to transcend their self-interest for the sake of the organization. Avolio and Bass's (2002) conceptualization of transformational leadership treats the concept of charisma as a central aspect of transformational leadership, which is also comprised of the dimensions of intellectual stimulation, individualized consideration, and inspirational motivation. Podsakoff, MacKenzie, Moorman, and Fetter (1990) developed their model of transformational leadership and identified intellectual stimulation, individualized support, high performance expectations, fostering the acceptance of group goals, role modeling, and identifying and articulating a vision as the key behaviors of transformational leaders.

Max Weber (1968) first used the term "charismatic" to describe a form of social authority that devolved on an individual believed to be endowed with the gift of divine grace. His conceptualization has remained singularly influential throughout the years, as interest in analyzing social change using cultural frameworks has grown (Jermier, 1993). Some researchers

(Shamir, 1995; Yammarino, 1994) have argued that both transformational and charismatic leadership are operational at both the immediate follower and the distanced follower levels. The series of presidential leadership studies referred to earlier assume that these forms of leadership are particularly susceptible to interpretation by distanced followers (i.e., the electorate) and that follower perceptions of candidates' transformational and charismatic leadership, together with party affiliation, drive voting behavior. This leads to our first hypothesis:

H1:   *President Bush's ratings of transformational and charismatic leadership will vary significantly over the course of his presidency*

Is Crisis a Contextual Factor for Leadership Ratings?

Research on transformational and charismatic leadership in a variety of settings has empirically established the link of such leadership to individual and organizational outcomes such as performance, satisfaction, and commitment (Avolio, Waldman, & Einstein, 1988; Awamleh & Gardner, 1999; Bass, 1988; Lowe et al., 1996). However, the relative lack of attention to structural features and social system characteristics associated with leadership processes has been an important limitation of this body of research (Meindl, 1990; Shamir & Howell, 1999). Following Meindl's (1990, 1995) arguments, the impact of contextual and follower characteristics on these relationships is of critical importance, and is only recently beginning to be explored (e.g., Bligh et al., 2005; Shamir & Howell, 1999).

One such contextual factor impacting the social construction of leadership may very well be the presence of—and perhaps more importantly, perceptions of—crisis. Specifically, crisis has been argued to be one of the most important influences on the charismatic leadership relationship (e.g., Pillai, 1996). Following Weber (1947), times of crisis have been argued to create a social precondition for charismatic leadership to emerge, and a number of studies have examined the effects of crisis on the leadership relationship (e.g., Bligh et al., 2004a, 2004b, 2005; House, Spangler, & Woycke, 1991; Hunt, Boal, & Dodge, 1999; Lord & Maher, 1991; Pillai, 1996; Pillai & Meindl, 1998). Previous theoretical and empirical work thus suggests that the occurrence of a crisis may dramatically alter the relationship between a leader and his or her followers (Bligh et al., 2004a, 2004b, 2005; House et al., 1991; Pillai, 1996; Pillai & Meindl, 1991, 1998). However, as Shamir and Howell (1999, p. 258) point out, "while crisis can facilitate the emergence of charismatic leadership, it is not a necessary condition for its emergence, nor for the success of such leadership."

As Pearson and Clair (1998) argue, crisis situations engender perceptions of uncertainty and ambiguity in followers. Other scholars have suggested that feelings of uncertainty may foster a greater appreciation for strong, decisive leadership often associated with charismatic leaders (Lord & Maher, 1991; Stewart, 1967, 1976; Yukl, 2006). During a crisis, followers may display a propensity for charisma that has been described as a desire, a need, or a state of readiness and/or susceptibility (Beyer, 1999a, 1999b; Madsen & Snow, 1991). According to Shamir and Howell (1999, p. 260), followers in the post-crisis situation "will readily, even eagerly, accept the influence of a leader who seems to have high self-confidence and a vision that provides both meaning to the current situation and promise of salvation from the currently acute distress."

Boal and Dodge (1999) found that "crisis-responsive" and "visionary-under-crisis" leadership produced high levels of charismatic attributions in followers as measured by leader affect, leader-attributed charisma, performance beyond expectations, and confidence in the leader. In the context of presidential elections in the United States, McCann (1997) found that more charismatic presidents are likely to be elected during threatening times, and that more charismatic winners are likely to have much wider victory margins during threatening times (Bligh et al., 2005). As a general rule, attributes typically associated with transformational and charismatic leadership are more affected by contextual cues such as crisis perceptions than those linked with transactional leadership (Meindl, 1995).

Previous studies on crisis have often focused on a specific crisis manipulation or a specific situation facing the organization or political entity. However, Jim Meindl often discussed the importance of studying different types of crisis and their relationship to charismatic leadership. In the current study, we sought to examine how two different types of crises (terrorism and economic) might impact perceptions of charismatic and transformational leadership. Pearson and Mitroff (1993) present a 2 X 2 crisis typology for organizations in which they distinguish among crises based on two independent factors: the origination of the crisis (from normal to severe) and the nature of the crisis (human/social vs. technical/economic). On the first dimension, normal crises originate through relatively mundane, everyday events that represent the escalation of relatively "ordinary" occurrences into major crises (e.g., computer or equipment breakdowns that create massive disruptions). In contrast, severe crises originate from aberrant or deviant causes (e.g., sabotage or kidnapping). On the second dimension, technical/economic crises that occur because of breakdowns in technical procedures or information systems are distinguished from human/social crises that occur due to breakdowns in human behavior or social systems.

In the current study, we included perceptions of crisis as a result of the terrorist threat following the 9/11 attacks on the country and other terrorist activities around the world. We also included perceptions of economic crisis in the wake of rising debt, job losses due to outsourcing, natural disasters, and high oil prices. Based on Pearson and Mitroff's (1993) typology, the terrorism crisis would be classified as a severe human/social crisis, and as such more sudden and unavoidable, while the economic crisis would be classified as a normal technical/economic crisis, and as such more mundane and potentially avoidable. Thus, we posit that followers will distinguish between types of crisis and consider the crisis posed by the terrorist attacks to be much more significant than the one posed by economic issues: the former presents a threat to one's life or personal security, whereas the latter presents a relatively lesser immediate threat to one's livelihood and economic security.

Based on this distinction, we also expect that the relationship between crisis and transformational and charismatic leadership might differ based on the type of crisis. Following previous studies (Bligh et al., 2005; Williams, Pillai, Jung, & Herst, 2005), we expect that there will be a *negative* association between perceptions of an economic crisis and ratings of transformational and charismatic leadership, because the incumbent will be perceived as being the cause of the crisis. This predication is also in line with Meindl, Tsai, and Lee's (1988) exploration of follower attributions in situations of shared responsibility, whereby "blame tends to remain focused on the most salient, main character" identified as the "leader" in situations in which the cause is somewhat ambiguous. In contrast, the negative relationship between crisis and leadership attributions may not hold for perceptions of the terrorism crisis, as George W. Bush is not likely to be perceived as being directly responsible for this crisis.

H2: *Followers will consider the terrorist crisis to be of significantly higher magnitude than the economic crisis.*

H3: *Based on follower attributions of blame, the economic crisis will be significantly and negatively related to perceptions of President Bush's leadership.*

H4: *Based on follower attributions of blame, the terrorist crisis will be unrelated to perceptions of President Bush's leadership.*

How Does Perceived Effectiveness in Dealing with Crisis Influence Perceptions of Leadership?

Lord and Maher (1991) identify an inferential model of the cognitive processes people adopt in forming leadership perceptions, which suggests that knowledge of performance outcomes, rather than actual leader behavior, leads to inferences of leadership. As Awamleh and Gardner (1999, p. 350) explain, "upon securing information on organizational outcomes, observers (including followers) engage in cause and effect analyses, before making attributions about leadership. When the focal actor is deemed to be responsible for a successful outcome, leadership is inferred; conversely, when an actor is judged to be responsible for a negative outcome, inadequate leadership is inferred." In fact, a number of studies have shown that performance outcomes impact perceptions of leader effectiveness (e.g., Meindl, Ehrlich, & Dukerich, 1985; Phillips & Lord, 1981).

Pillai and Meindl (1991) manipulated the information that raters received regarding the performance patterns of a company. They exposed subjects to the same descriptions of the leader and varied the performance patterns associated with him and found that charismatic leadership attributions were significantly higher in the turnaround and high performance conditions as opposed to the low performance condition. In the context of the presidency, Jimmy Carter's performance as President and Ronald Reagan's performance as Governor of California cued voters to rate their leadership (Miller, Wattenberg, & Malanchuk, 1986). Furthermore, Butterfield and Prasad (1990) showed that Bush Sr.'s leadership abilities were linked in voters' minds to perceptions of Ronald Reagan's performance as president. Such perceptions should be particularly enhanced when a leader is associated with a crisis situation.

President Bush—whose leadership poll ratings were quite mediocre in the wake of the controversial 2000 election, and amidst widespread perceptions that he might not be up to the job—suddenly found himself the recipient of unprecedented approval ratings following his speeches at the site of the September 11, 2001, attacks and the Washington Cathedral in the aftermath of the attacks. As Bligh and colleagues (2004a) argue, such high approval ratings are more likely in the wake of a crisis, because crises provide leaders with opportunities to take bold and decisive actions, and when they come through, followers see them as being increasingly transformational and charismatic. During the more recent 2004 presidential elections, the first after the 9/11 terrorist attacks, most of the popular polls indicated that "leadership" ranked very high in the minds of the electorate as they were evaluating their candidates (*Pew Research Center for the People and the Press*, November 11, 2004). In addition, the incumbent George W. Bush consistently received high ratings based on his first-term record following the attacks. In a study of the 2004 elections, Williams and colleagues (2005) found that perceptions of leadership and leader decisiveness influenced voting behavior. Following Meindl's arguments and the subsequent findings of Bligh and colleagues (2004a), we would therefore expect that followers who perceive a crisis *and* perceive that the president is effective in dealing with this crisis will use more transformational or charismatic constructions to evaluate him. Thus,

H5: *The relationship between perceptions of crisis and leadership will be moderated by perceptions of leadership effectiveness.*

Does Party Affiliation Affect Leadership Ratings?

In addition to neglecting contextual influences, traditional approaches to the study of charismatic and transformational leadership frequently focus primarily on leader characteristics, allocating secondary status to follower characteristics. However, there is considerable evidence that follower characteristics, particularly party identification, can dramatically influence perceptions of leadership (see Bligh et al., 2005; Pillai & Williams, 1998; Pillai et al., 2003; Williams et al., 2005). This research consistently demonstrates that during a campaign, Republicans tend to rate their presidential or gubernatorial candidate significantly higher on transformational and charismatic leadership than do Democrats. A similar pattern emerges with Democrats and their candidates, with Independent ratings of leaders somewhere in between the other two parties. Over the course of the 1980 Carter versus Reagan campaign, for instance, Democrats became more convinced that Ronald Reagan could not handle the job, and the decline in the public's assessment of President Carter's leadership was steep among Republicans and negligible among Democrats (Miller & Shanks, 1982). In the 1988 presidential elections, Maurer and colleagues (1993) found that Republicans and Democrats had different prototypes of effective leaders: Republicans described effective leaders as being more patriotic, religious, aggressive, tough, and optimistic than did Democrats, while Democrats described effective leaders as being more humanitarian than did Republicans (Pillai & Williams, 1998). Shamir's (1994) study, set in the context of the 1992 Israeli elections, found that leaders' perceived charisma was strongly related to voters' ideological positions, as voters are more likely to attribute positive leadership qualities to a leader who is perceived as embodying their views. In addition, followers' attitudes and beliefs are often manifested in their evaluations of leader charisma (House, 1977; Shamir, 1994).

Based on this previous research, we used party identification in the current study as a proxy for followers' values. Thus, following the tradition of previous studies, we would expect that Republicans would rate President Bush higher than the Democrats on transformational and charismatic leadership across all 5 years, as they are more likely to believe that he is a strong leader who embodies their values. Furthermore, we think that although there is a general tendency to evaluate leaders using charismatic and transformational criteria during a crisis, this effect may be much less pronounced for followers who possess a different value system from that of the leader. Specifically, there may be a stronger effect of crisis and perceived effectiveness in dealing with the crisis on President Bush's leadership ratings for Republicans than for Democrats.

H6:   *Followers' party affiliation will influence leadership evaluations such that Democrats will rate President Bush as significantly less charismatic and transformational than Republicans.*

METHOD

Sample

Four hundred and seventy-seven college students were recruited from graduate and undergraduate business courses in a large public university in the western United States. All data collection was completed in eight separate waves across a 5-year time period: November 2001, May 2002, August 2002, December 2002, April 2003, September 2003, April 2004, and October 2005. For the purpose of the analyses, the data were aggregated by year with 78 participants in 2001, 89 in 2002, 92 in 2003, 120 in 2004, and 98 in 2005. Participants were between the ages of 19 and 82 ($M = 28.41$, $SD = 8.50$; $Mdn = 26$), and gender was split almost evenly with 47% female. Respondents were primarily white (66%), and political affiliation was divided between Democrat (28%) and Republican (43%), with 23% listing their party affiliation as Independent and 6% as "Other."

Measures

Transformational Leadership
The 23-item measure of transformational leadership (Transformational Leadership Inventory), developed by Podsakoff and colleagues (1990), was employed. The measure includes six transformational leadership behaviors that have been reported to have high reliabilities and a stable factor structure supported by confirmatory factor analyses (see Pillai & Williams, 1998; Schriesheim, Castro, Williams, Cardone, & Medsker, 1997). In the current sample, the alpha reliabilities were .85 for articulating a vision (Sample item: "Is able to get others committed to his dream"), .86 for providing an appropriate role model ("Provides a good model for his followers to follow"), .88 for fostering the acceptance of group goals ("Gets the group to

work together for the same goal"), .81 for high performance expectations ("Insists on only the best performance"), .85 for individualized support ("Shows respect for his followers' personal feelings"), and .86 for intellectual stimulation ("Has stimulated followers to rethink the way they do things"). A 7-point Likert scale ranging from 1 = "strongly disagree" to 7 = "strongly agree" was employed for all items. The overall or global measure of transformational leadership for George W. Bush, used in the analyses, was computed using the above scales. The alpha reliability for this overall measure was .96.

Attributed Charisma

The eight-item scale of attributed charisma from the Multifactor Leadership Questionnaire (Bass & Avolio, 1995) was utilized. A sample item is, "Displays a sense of power and confidence." A 7-point Likert scale ranging from 1 = "strongly disagree" to 7 = "strongly agree" was employed. Although numerous concerns have been raised regarding the factor structure of the MLQ (Antonakis, Avolio, & Sivasubramaniam, 2003; Awamleh & Gardner, 1999; Bycio, Hackett, & Allen, 1995; Tejeda, Scandura, & Pillai, 2001), it has been extensively utilized and validated across a wide variety of contexts (Bass & Avolio, 1993, 1995). An exploratory factor analysis, utilizing principal components analysis with varimax rotation, yielded a single factor for this scale, and the alpha coefficient was .93.

Perceptions of Terrorism Crisis, Economic Crisis, and Crisis Effectiveness

Perceptions of terrorist crisis and economic crisis were both measured by single items ("In your opinion, the U.S. is still facing a crisis after the September 11, 2001, terrorist attacks" and "In your opinion, the country is in an economic crisis"). All items were measured using a 5-point Likert scale ranging from 1 = "strongly disagree" to 5 = "strongly agree." Perceptions of leadership effectiveness in dealing with the crises were measured individually for the terrorist crisis ("In your opinion, Bush is winning the war on terrorism") and economic crisis ("In your opinion, Bush is handling the economic situation effectively") using the same 5-point scale. Following the launch of the Iraq War in 2003, a measure of effectiveness in Iraq was added: "In your opinion, the liberation of Iraq is an example of effective presidential leadership." For the year 2005, a single item measure of effectiveness in dealing with Hurricane Katrina was also included: "In your opinion, the response to Hurricane Katrina is an example of effective presidential leadership."

Background and Control Variables

Party identification is also likely to play an important role in attributions of charisma and expected effectiveness. Shamir's (1994) study of the 1992

Israeli elections demonstrates that a voter's ideological position strongly influences a leader's perceived charisma. In addition, Pillai and colleagues' (2003) findings suggest that voters are more likely to evaluate a leader from their own political party as charismatic or transformational, and party affiliation has an important influence on voting behavior (see also Pillai & Williams, 1998). Respondents indicated their party affiliation as Democratic, Republican, Independent, or other. Finally, participants were asked to respond to standard demographic questions, including age, gender, education, and work experience.

RESULTS

Table 7.1 presents the means, standard deviations, and intercorrelations for the key study variables. Attributed charisma and transformational leadership are positively correlated with all measures of effectiveness and negatively correlated with perceptions of economic crisis. The correlations with terrorism crisis are not significant. Demographic statistics on the equivalency of the samples across the 5 years of data collection are included in Table 7.2.

Table 7.3 shows the mean differences across the key variables by year using a one-way analysis of variance (ANOVA). Overall, the significant ANOVA results (see Table 7.3) suggest that there are significant differences between time periods for all of the variables except for the perceptions of both types of crisis (economic and terrorism). We followed up the significant ANOVA differences with pairwise comparisons, using the Bonferroni correction procedure for multiple comparisons. Regarding Hypothesis 1, results for transformational leadership show that President Bush had the highest ratings ($M = 5.45$) in November 2001 (a couple of months after the September 11 attacks) and the lowest ratings in November 2005 ($M = 4.16$; mean difference $= -1.29$, $p < .001$), which mirrors the average popular poll ratings of job approval. There is a minor spike in 2003 ($M = 5.08$) relative to 2002 ($M = 4.74$, mean difference $= -.34$, ns) and 2004 ($M = 4.68$, mean difference $= -.40$, $p < .10$); this spike may be partially attributed to the fact that 2003 was the year that the Iraq war was declared and the famous "mission accomplished" declaration was issued. The finding parallels the national polling data and provides strong support for the idea that the president's leadership ratings vary with the triumphs and tribulations of his presidency over time, and suggests that these rating variations are very similar to the approval ratings that are obtained in the national polls.

The ratings for attributed charisma follow a similar pattern with an average rating of 5.41 in 2001, 4.18 in 2005 (mean difference $= -1.23$, $p < .001$), and a spike of 5.18 in 2003 (mean difference $= 1.00$, $p < .001$). There is a

Table 7.1. Correlation Matrix for the Study Variables (N = 477)

Variables	Mean	s.d.	1	2	3	4	5	6	7	8	9	10	11	12	13	14
1. Age	28.41	8.50	—													
2. Gender	.53	.50	.01	—												
3. Ethnicity	.67	.47	.06	.16**	—											
4. Party: Democrat	.28	.45	.01	-.09*	-.22**	—										
5. Party: Republican	.43	.50	.05	.06	.31**	-.54**	—									
6. Registered to Vote	.82	.39	.06	.00	.27**	-.02	.15**	—								
7. Economic Crisis	3.38	1.11	.01	-.21**	-.23**	.18**	-.17**	-.05	—							
8. Terrorism Crisis	4.10	.98	.09*	.02	-.00	.06	-.03	.08	.20**	—						
9. Economic Effectiveness	2.83	1.11	.01	.10	.22**	-.34**	.47**	.01	-.40**	-.01	—					
10. Terrorism Effectiveness	3.41	1.25	-.03	.17**	.22**	-.18**	.38**	.15**	-.24**	.10*	.58**	—				
11. Iraq Effectiveness	3.06	1.32	.03	.13*	.15**	-.34**	.49**	.09	-.36**	.06	.60**	.71**	—			
12. Katrina Effectiveness	2.01	1.14	.19	-.04	.16	-.37**	.56**	.18	-.38**	-.08	.60**	.56**	.64**	—		
13. Transformational	4.69	1.01	.05	.07	.25**	-.34**	.49**	.11*	-.33**	.05	.66**	.72**	.72**	.73**	—	
14. Attributed Charisma	4.85	1.39	.02	.07	.22**	-.35**	.50**	.08	-.29**	.01	.64**	.64**	.71**	.72**	.88**	—

Note: Sample sizes are 477 for the intercorrelations of all variables, with the following exceptions: 360 for Variables 7 and 9, 308 for Variable 11 and 98 for Variable 12.

* $p < .05$, ** $p < .01$

147

Table 7.2. Demographic Sample Characteristics by Year of Data Collection

Variables	2001 n = 78	2002 n = 89	2003 n = 92	2004 n = 120	2005 n = 98
Average Age	29	28	30	24	32
% Female	44	42	47	50	50
% Registered Voters	92	80	78	80	80
% Republican	41	43	47	45	39
% Democrat	37	29	25	23	27
% Independent	17	17	22	27	29
% White	78	67	66	62	60
% Hispanic	10	3	9	10	11
% African American	1	2	2	1	2
% Asian	4	12	10	13	10
% Full-time Employed	89	82	83	88	81

steady decline for ratings of effectiveness in handling the Iraq War (from a mean rating of 3.38 in 2003 to 2.79 in 2005, mean difference = –.59, $p < .01$) and similarly for effectiveness in handling the crisis presented by terrorism (from a mean rating of 4.59 in 2001 to 2.67 in 2005, mean difference = –1.92, $p < .001$). As a result, and in relation to Hypothesis 1, we can conclude that both transformational and charismatic leadership ratings for the President do vary significantly over time.

Furthermore, a paired samples t-test indicates that there is a significant difference in the magnitude of perceived crisis: Across years, the terrorism crisis is perceived as being of greater magnitude than the economic crisis (mean difference = –.67; t (359) = –9.29, $p < .001$). This finding supports Hypothesis 2 and our assertion that followers do distinguish between types of crisis, and rated the crisis posed by the terrorist attacks to be significantly more severe than the one posed by economic issues.

To examine our remaining hypotheses regarding how different types of crisis, effectiveness ratings, and party affiliation affect perceptions of President Bush's leadership, we conducted hierarchical regressions comprising four steps for each analysis (see Tables 7.4–7.5). Step 1 examined the effects of the demographic control variables (age, gender, and ethnicity). Step 2 added the effects of party affiliation and whether or not the respondent indicated that they were registered to vote. Step 3 added the main

Table 7.3. Mean Scores and Standard Deviations for Ratings of Crisis and Leadership Perceptions by Year

Variables	2001 n = 78		2002 n = 89		2003 n = 92		2004 n = 120		2005 n = 98		Across Years		Univariate F
	Mean	s.d.	Mean	s.d.	Mean	s.d.	Mean	s.d.	Mean	s.d.	Mean	s.d.	
Economic Crisis	—	—	3.62	1.12	3.35	1.11	3.33	1.06	3.33	1.15	3.38	1.11	.96
Terrorism Crisis	4.33	.77	4.13	.97	4.02	1.06	4.02	1.07	4.05	.96	4.10	.98	1.55
Economic Effectiveness	—	—	2.63	.91	2.96	1.07	2.98	1.12	2.64	1.19	2.83	1.11	2.68*
Terrorism Effectiveness	4.59	.71	3.52	1.16	3.46	1.13	3.12	1.12	2.67	1.21	3.41	1.25	36.15***
Iraq Effectiveness	—	—	—	—	3.38	1.29	3.03	1.22	2.79	1.41	3.06	1.32	4.98**
Katrina Effectiveness	—	—	—	—	—	—	—	—	2.01	1.14	—	—	—
Transformational	5.46	.92	4.74	1.20	5.08	1.00	4.68	1.06	4.16	1.26	4.79	1.17	17.11***
Attributed Charisma	5.41	1.21	4.84	1.46	5.19	1.18	4.77	1.33	4.18	1.44	4.85	1.39	11.17***

Note: Total $N = 477$; sample size is 360 for Economic crisis and Economic effectiveness, 308 for Iraq effectiveness and 98 for Katrina effectiveness.

Table 7.4. Hierarchical Regression Results for Terrorism Crisis and Effectiveness on Leadership Perceptions[a]

Dependent Variable	Independent Variable	Model 1		Model 2		Model 3		Model 4	
		Beta	SE B	Beta	SE B	Beta	SE B	Beta	SE B
Transformational Leadership	Age	.03	.01	.02	.01	$.06^{\dagger}$	.01	$.06^{\dagger}$	.00
	Gender	.02	.11	.01	.10	$-.07^{*}$	.08	$-.08^{*}$	.08
	Ethnicity	$.25^{***}$	.12	$.09^{\dagger}$	.11	.04	.09	.05	.09
	Political affiliation: Rep.			$.41^{***}$	.12	$.20^{***}$	.10	$.21^{***}$	.10
	Political affiliation: Dem.			$-.10^{\dagger}$	.13	$-.14^{***}$	.10	$-.13^{***}$	.10
	Registered to Vote			.02	.13	-.02	.10	-.02	.10
	Terrorism Crisis					.01	.04	.03	.04
	Terrorism Effectiveness					$.57^{***}$	.03	$.56^{***}$	.03
	Terrorism Crisis X Effectiveness							$.06^{*}$	.04
	R^{s}	.06		.26		.52		.53	
	F for change in R^{s}	10.22^{***}		40.53^{***}		124.09^{***}		3.52^{*}	

Dependent Variable	Independent Variable	Model 1 Beta	Model 1 SE B	Model 2 Beta	Model 2 SE B	Model 3 Beta	Model 3 SE B	Model 4 Beta	Model 4 SE B
Attributed Charisma	Age	.09	.01	.07	.01	$.13^\dagger$	.01	$.14^\dagger$	.01
	Gender	-.08	.13	-.06	.11	$-.14^\dagger$	.09	$-.13^\dagger$	.09
	Ethnicity	.12	.14	-.01	.13	.05	.11	.04	.11
	Political affiliation: Rep.			.45***	.14	.10	.12	.13	.12
	Political affiliation: Dem.			-.08	.15	-.10	.12	-.10	.12
	Registered to Vote			.06	.15	-.10	.12	-.10	.12
	Terrorism Crisis					-.09	.05	-.04	.05
	Terrorism Effectiveness					.64***	.04	.59***	.04
	Terrorism Crisis X Effectiveness							.07*	.04
	R^s	.05		.26		.51		.52	
	F for change in R^s	7.41***		44.16***		113.48***		4.13*	

[a]N = 450. Beta coefficients are standardized.
$^\dagger p < .10$; $^* p < .05$; $^{**} p < .01$; $^{***} p < .001$.

Table 7.5. Hierarchical Regression Results for Economic Crisis and Effectiveness on Leadership Perceptions[a]

Dependent Variable	Independent Variable	Model 1 Beta	Model 1 SE B	Model 2 Beta	Model 2 SE B	Model 3 Beta	Model 3 SE B	Model 4 Beta	Model 4 SE B
Transformational	Age	.03	.01	.01	.01	.02	.01	.02	.01
Leadership	Gender	.04	.12	.01	.11	-.01	.09	-.01	.09
	Ethnicity	.24***	.13	.05	.12	.01	.11	.01	.11
	Political affiliation: Rep.			.45***	.13	.27***	.12	.26***	.12
	Political affiliation: Dem			-.15**	.14	-.08†	.12	-.08†	.12
	Registered to Vote			.00	.14	.04	.12	.03	.12
	Economic Crisis					-.07†	.05	-.08†	.05
	Economic Effectiveness					.46***	.05	.46***	.05
	Economic Crisis X Effectiveness							-.01	.04
	R^s	.06		.32		.50		.50	
	F for change in R^s	7.44***		42.64***		61.51***		.05	

Dependent Variable	Independent Variable	Model 1 Beta	Model 1 SE B	Model 2 Beta	Model 2 SE B	Model 3 Beta	Model 3 SE B	Model 4 Beta	Model 4 SE B
Attributed Charisma	Age	.01	.01	-.01	.01	-.00	.01	-.00	.01
	Gender	.04	.15	.01	.13	-.01	.11	-.01	.11
	Ethnicity	.21***	.16	.03	.14	-.01	.13	-.01	.13
	Political affiliation: Rep.			.47***	.15	.28***	.14	.28***	.14
	Political affiliation: Dem.			-.12*	.17	-.06	.15	-.06	.15
	Registered to Vote			-.03	.16	.01	.14	.01	.14
	Economic Crisis					-.04	.06	-.03	.06
	Economic Effectiveness					.48***	.06	.48***	.06
	Economic Crisis X Effectiveness							-.02	.05
	R^s	.05		.31		.49		.49	
	F for change in R^s	5.47***		41.83***		60.25***		.36	

^{a}N = 349. Beta coefficients are standardized.
$^\dagger p < .10$; $^* p < .05$; $^{**} p < .01$; $^{***} p < .001$.

effects of crisis perceptions and perceptions of leadership effectiveness in dealing with the crisis. Finally, Step 4 added the hypothesized moderator effect (Crisis X Effectiveness).

Following the procedure outlined in Villa, Howell, Dorfman, and Daniel (2003), we first standardized each variable and then constructed a cross product that was entered into Step 4 of each regression. Thus, the regression analyses consider the potentially confounding effects of all control variables before assessing main effects and the potential moderating effects of crisis perceptions. Increments in R^s, changes in F, and standardized betas were examined to determine if significant variance is accounted for by the addition of the moderated variables ($R^s2 - R^s1$; Cohen & Cohen, 1983). Tables 7.4 and 7.5 show the results of regressions across all 5 years with the background variables, party affiliation, perceptions of each type of crisis, effectiveness in handling the crisis, and an interaction term of crisis and effectiveness as independent variables predicting attributed charisma and transformational leadership, respectively.

We first examined the direct effects of both types of crisis on ratings of charismatic and transformational leadership. For the economic crisis, we found a marginally significant negative relationship between perceptions of economic crisis and transformational leadership ($b = -.08$, $p < .10$). The relationship between economic crisis and charismatic leadership was also negative, but not significant ($b = -.03$, ns). Thus, Hypothesis 3 is only partially supported. As expected, however, Hypothesis 4 was supported in that there were no significant relationships between perceptions of terrorism crisis and transformational and charismatic leadership ($b = .04$, ns and $b = .05$, ns, respectively.)

Examining the analyses for the terrorism crisis, our results suggest that party affiliation plays an important role in ratings of leadership, with Democrats rating the President more negatively on transformational ($b = -.13$, $p < .001$) and charismatic ($b = -.10$, ns) leadership, and Republicans rating him more positively ($b = .21$, $p < .001$ for transformational; $b = .13$, ns for charismatic, respectively). Thus, Hypothesis 6 is supported with regard to transformational but not charismatic leadership. Whereas the prospect of facing a terrorism crisis by itself does not significantly predict attributed charisma ($b = .03$, ns), the perception that the President is handling it effectively significantly predicts perceptions of transformational leadership ($b = .56$, $p < .001$).

In addition, there is a marginally significant interaction of perceptions of a terrorism crisis and effectiveness on ratings of transformational leadership ($b = .06$, $p < .05$; explaining an additional 1% of the variance). To aid in the interpretation of the interaction term, we used a median split to divide the sample into high and low perceptions of the terrorism crisis. Individuals with high perceptions of the terrorist crisis and the President's effectiveness in overcoming that crisis were more likely to see him as transformational. This relationship disappears, however, for followers who did not perceive the crisis was as serious. Paralleling the findings for transformational leadership, there is also a marginally significant interaction of perceptions of a terrorism crisis and effectiveness on ratings of attributed charisma ($b = .07$, $p < .05$; explaining an additional 1% of the variance). Again, individuals with high perceptions of the terrorist crisis and the President's effectiveness in overcoming that crisis were more likely to see him as charismatic. This relationship disappears, however, for followers who did not perceive the terrorism crisis was as serious. Therefore, in relation to Hypothesis 5, we can tentatively conclude that there is an interaction between crisis and effectiveness in their relationship to transformational leadership: followers who perceive a terrorism crisis, *and* perceive that the President is effective in dealing with this crisis, will use more transformational and charismatic constructions to evaluate him.

Turning to the results for the economic crisis analyses, party affiliation again plays an important role, with Democrats rating the President more negatively on transformational ($b = -.08$, $p < .10$) and charismatic ($b = -.06$, *ns*) leadership, and Republicans rating him more positively ($b = .26$, $p < .001$ for transformational; $b = .28$, $p < .001$ for attributed charisma, respectively). So, Hypothesis 6 is again partially supported. Whereas the prospect of facing an economic crisis by itself is only marginally related to ratings of transformational leadership ($b = -.08$, $p < .10$), it is unrelated to ratings of attributed charisma ($b = -.03$, *ns*). The perception that the President is handling the crisis effectively is again strongly related to ratings of both transformational leadership and attributed charisma ($b = .46$, $p < .001$ for transformational; $b = .48$, $p < .001$ for charismatic, respectively). As distinguished from the results for perceptions of a terrorism crisis, when economic crisis is combined with perceived effectiveness in handling the crisis, there is no significant interaction effect for either transformational leadership or attributed charisma. This finding may suggest that perceptions of a terrorism crisis and the perceived effectiveness of handling it by the President are considered to be more significant in followers' eyes. Thus, the type of crisis does matter with regard to perceptions of effectiveness and the effect on leadership ratings; Hypothesis 5 is supported with regard to the terrorism crisis, but not the economic crisis.

Overall, our results suggest followers' party affiliation plays a significant role in three of the four analyses, with Democrats rating the president negatively on leadership and Republicans rating him more positively. Whereas the prospect of facing a terrorist crisis by itself does not significantly predict transformational leadership or attributed charisma, when it is combined with perceived effectiveness in handling the crisis, there is a significant interaction effect. For the economic crisis, we have a similar pattern of results, except that the interaction of perceptions of crisis and effectiveness is not significant.

DISCUSSION

In his social constructionist follower-centered perspective, Jim Meindl (1995) saw transformational (and transactional) leadership as a rough approximation of a leadership construction used by followers to make sense of various situations and contexts (e.g., crisis, performance). Furthermore, he saw the correlated perceptions between leadership ratings by followers and effectiveness as "data relevant to understanding the process and the contents of construction" (1995, p. 332). Meindl also saw the presidency as providing a rich context to study leadership with a follower-centric perspective, and inspired a series of studies on the U.S. presidency cited earlier. This chapter is a tribute to Meindl's perspective, and incorporates not only elements of the context such as perceived crisis relating to recent key events in President Bush's presidency, but also followers' values as represented by party affiliation and their perceptions of leadership effectiveness. Furthermore, to the best of our knowledge, this is the first study that attempts to explore these relationships over a period of 5 years of the presidency.

We conducted the study from November 2001 through November 2005, and tracked follower perceptions of charismatic and transformational leadership through the various crises faced by the administration; this is a unique aspect of this research. This approach allowed us to determine that, not surprisingly, leadership ratings for President Bush did in fact vary significantly over time. More importantly, our study also showed that the President's transformational and charismatic leadership ratings significantly fluctuated over time in a manner consistent with approval ratings for the President over the same time period. A recent study adopting a follower-centered approach to transformational leadership found that subordinates, peers, and supervisors of target leaders engaged in social information processing when evaluating the leaders and evaluated the leader's behavior high on transformational leadership when they perceived agreement among members of one of the groups (Feinberg, Ostroff, & Burke, 2005). It is quite likely that there is also a social contagion effect when followers rate their Presidents, and they may be strongly influenced by results of popular polls: when the President's approval ratings are low during a particular period (as evidenced by information gathered from a sample of the population and subsequently reported widely in the media), other members of the citizenry also rate him low on leadership.

This social contagion effect may also help to explain how our independently obtained leadership ratings consistently track the approval ratings reported in the news media. In fact, the *Wall Street Journal* on November 17, 2005, compiled ratings of the President and his cabinet from 2001 through 2005 from several sources, and they showed that these ratings were strikingly similar to the findings in our study for ratings of transformational and charismatic leadership over the same period. In 2001, when the citizenry shared the common perception of uncertainty and feelings about the American "way of life" being under attack, they expressed a desire for the strong leadership usually associated with charismatic and transformational leadership (Bligh et al., 2004b) and evaluated him more favorably using these leadership criteria (see also Thompson, Kohles, Otsuki, & Kent, 1997, for a discussion of the effects of ingroup/outgroup homogeneity under threatening conditions). In 2003, his popularity was once again at a high (following a slight dip in 2002) in the wake of the war in Iraq, which was then framed to the American people as the continuation of the war against terrorism in Afghanistan, and an attempt to rid the world of a dictator who was developing weapons of mass destruction. It is conventional wisdom that when a nation is at war, the citizens rally behind their president. Furthermore, the President's performance was also viewed in positive terms because combat operations in Iraq seemed to be so successful in the initial stages of the invasion, particularly in light of iconic images like the fall of Saddam Hussein's statue in Baghdad.

With the war dragging on through 2004, we see a decline in the leadership ratings during that election year, reflecting the public opinion polls. However, this did not seem to affect the outcome of the election, as there was greater confidence regarding national security and leadership devolved onto the incumbent, who was rated higher on transformational and charismatic leadership than his Democratic challenger, and was therefore reelected (Williams et al., 2005). In 2005, with the multiple crises presented by the ongoing terrorist insurgency in Iraq, the devastating failures of the federal administration during Hurricane Katrina, and rising oil prices, we subsequently see a more marked decline in leadership ratings for the President, that again mirror the public opinion polls. However, we ran separate regression analyses for the year 2005 following Hurricane Katrina, and again found that perceived effectiveness in handling the aftermath of the Hurricane, along with perceptions that the country was moving in the right direction, were most strongly related to ratings of transformational and charismatic leadership. Overall, our results suggest that these contextual factors are critical in the social construction of leadership from the followers' perspective over time, through "thick and thin."

Our findings also show that although followers use charismatic criteria to evaluate a president, it is not enough that a president is perceived as charismatic or transformational. He must also be seen to be effective in handling the crisis itself, and this is consistent with Weber's (1947) contention that charisma is validated by repeated successes. Contrary to our predictions, perceptions of either type of crisis (terrorism or economic) did not directly impact perceptions of transformational and charismatic leadership, although there was some evidence to suggest that economic crisis perceptions negatively impacted ratings of the President's leadership. This may be due in part to the fact that economic crises may be more directly attributed to elected leaders than are external attacks committed by terrorists. Future research should examine the extent to which different types of crisis and situational outcomes impact the degree to which followers more or less readily place blame on the current leadership for those crises (Meindl et al., 1988; Meindl & Tsai, 1988).

In addition, our findings regarding the terrorism crisis suggest that in cases of severe, external human/social crises in which the current leadership is not held directly responsible, there may be an interactive effect in that followers who perceive a crisis and the effectiveness of the current leadership may be even more likely to use charismatic and transformational constructions. Interestingly, this is not the case with the economic crisis, which in Pearson and Mitroff's (1993) terms is considered to be a relatively more normal, internal, and technical/economic crisis. Our results also suggest that followers differentiate between types of crises in terms of severity; future research should continue to examine multiple types of crisis and their potential impact on social constructions of leadership.

Not surprisingly, and consistent with previous studies on presidential and gubernatorial leadership, this study shows that followers are not totally objective in their evaluation of leadership, and instead exhibit partisanship: Democrats consistently evaluate President Bush negatively, whereas Republicans evaluate him more positively, using transformational and charismatic criteria. Contrary to our expectations, additional analyses did not uncover a consistently stronger effect of crisis and perceived effectiveness in dealing with the crisis on President Bush's leadership ratings for Republicans versus Democrats or Independents. This may be due to the fact that we considered party affiliation as a proxy for value congruence; future research might also examine the extent to which followers perceive value congruence with candidates from their own and other parties in addition to party identification. We did, however, find marginally significant relationships between gender, age, and ethnicity in many of the analyses, suggesting that follower characteristics and perceptions are important influences on constructions of charismatic and transformational leadership. Future research should supplement these demographic measures as proxies for follower characteristics with additional measures such as an individual's propensity to romanticize leaders (using the Romance of Leadership Scale, or RLS; Meindl & Ehrlich, 1988); perceptions of threat, uncertainty, and fear; perceptions of situations of greater or lesser ambiguity (i.e, Mischel's [1977] distinction between "strong" vs. "weak" situations); perceptions of how others in their social networks perceive leaders; and perceptions of ingroup versus outgroup distinctions (including a common enemy or external threat).

Limitations and Implications for Future Research

The study is not without limitations. All of our measures are self-reported, and several of them are single-item measures. It may also be argued that with the ratings of charisma and transformational leadership so highly correlated, we could have used one of them as a proxy for the other, resulting in a single set of analyses. However, our key dependent variables of attributed charisma and transformational leadership are well established and have been frequently used in previous research, including many of the studies discussed earlier on presidential leadership. We have retained them both in an attempt to be consistent with that body of research, as well as in hopes of fostering future research into the discriminant validity of these measures. According to Meindl's (1995, p. 332) approach, "reports made by followers regarding their leaders are treated as information regarding the constructions of followers, not information about the qualities and activities of the leader as with more leader-centric approaches." The romance of leadership perspective thus treats correlated perceptions as a revelation into the thought systems and ideologies regarding leadership that are espoused by followers (Meindl, 1995). We find that our results showing high correlations between the outcome variables in this study are consistent with this framework. Our findings here, as well as those of Bligh and colleagues (2005) and Awamleh and Gardner (1999), suggest that ratings of attributed charisma, transformational leadership, and perceived effectiveness are very highly correlated; future research might specifically examine the interrelationships among these common dependent variables in leadership research. For example, under what circumstances might leaders be perceived as charismatic and ineffective, charismatic and nontransformational, or highly effective and yet uncharismatic? As Meindl (1995) argues, these ratings of leadership may be extremely subject to halo effects and the romance of leadership, making them highly correlated across a variety of leadership situations.

Furthermore, this is the first study that has attempted to study leadership constructions of followers over the term of a presidency. The multiwave nature of the study, we believe, strengthens our findings, particularly in regard to the socially constructed nature of the leadership process. However, it is important to note that our findings cannot speak to the causality of the relationships among these variables; it is entirely possible, for example, that perceptions of charisma and transformational leadership may lead to higher ratings of effectiveness in dealing with crisis, rather than the other way around.

Bligh and colleagues (2005) argued that future studies should examine different levels and types of crises, and this study attempted to explore this distinction through perceptions of both terrorism and economic crises in light of Pearson and Mitroff's (1993) typology. In general, we found that followers reacted more strongly to a terrorism crisis than an economic crisis. It may well be that there are some crises that are perceived as critical by a greater number of followers because of the threat to life and personal security, while there is a level of consensus that is not the case with other types of crisis (e.g., an economic crisis). For an economic crisis to be perceived as a critical crisis situation, it may necessitate something like the Great Depression and a catastrophic failure of the stock market or other financial institutions. Future research should further examine the effects of different types and levels of crisis on followers' need for, and social construction of, charismatic and transformational forms of leadership.

Our findings that a leader needs to be perceived as effective for charismatic and transformational attributions to take place, even after controlling for major demographic characteristics and party affiliation, suggests that leaders may want to better manage these contexts and constructions themselves rather than solely focusing on leader behaviors. This is exactly what Meindl (1995) suggested. For instance, when the poll ratings are down, we see the President aggressively engaging in active communication through speeches to various follower groups, touting the administration's progress on the terrorism and economic fronts. It remains to be seen whether his approval ratings and perceptions of leadership become stronger after a series of such appearances.

Final Comments on a More Personal Note

We would like to note that all three authors of this chapter were former students of Jim Meindl's at various points in time, and as such our experiences with him span over 15 years. As a result (and it should be clear from reading this chapter), we have tremendous respect for Meindl not only as a scholar, but also as a professor, coauthor, mentor, and friend. In addition to his obvious impact on our lifelong passion for the study of leadership, it is very important to point out that he was also a genuinely nice guy, with a quick wit, great sense of humor, and a real zest for life (and yes, he *was* at Woodstock in 1969).

In the realm of leadership, it is an understatement to point out that Meindl's work was widely known and highly respected. While the volume and quality of Jim Meindl's work speaks for itself, it is also worth noting that his unique approach to the study of leadership continues to influence the field. We have no doubt that forward and progressive thinking in the realms of leadership research and practice will continue to advance the perspectives he originally developed.

Despite his impact on the field, Meindl was a tremendously humble person who never bragged about himself, belittled others, or even mentioned his accomplishments. Those outside of the academic world, including some of his closest family and friends, had absolutely no idea that he was such an influential and innovative scholar until after his death. Ironically, this tribute volume to Jim Meindl is in some ways a social construction of *his leadership*, his lasting impact on us (his followers), and his overall influence on the field. We think he would have appreciated this irony, as well as our humble attempts to ultimately romanticize him and his leadership.

Cheers, Jim!

REFERENCES

Antonakis, J., Avolio, B. A., & Sivasubramaniam, N. (2003). Context and leadership: an examination of the nine-factor full-range leadership theory using the Multifactor Leadership Questionnaire. *Leadership Quarterly, 14*(3), 261–295.

Avolio, B. J., & Bass, B. M. (2002). *Developing potential across a full range of leaderships: cases on transactional and transformational leadership.* Mahwah, NJ: Erlbaum.

Avolio, B. J., Waldman, D. A., & Einstein, W. O. (1988). Transformational leadership in a management game simulation. *Group and Organization Studies, 13,* 59–80.

Awamleh, R., & Gardner, W. L. (1999). Perceptions of leader charisma and effectiveness: The effects of vision content, delivery, and organizational performance. *Leadership Quarterly, 10*(3), 345–73.

Bass, B. M. (1988). Evolving perspectives on charismatic leadership. In J. A. Conger & R. N. Kanungo (Eds.), *Charismatic leadership* (pp. 40–77). San Francisco: Jossey-Bass.

Bass, B. M., & Avolio, B. J. (1993). Transformational leadership: A response to critiques. In M. M. Chemers & R. Ayman (Eds.), *Leadership theory and research: Perspectives and directions* (pp. 49–80). New York: Academic Press.

Bass, B. M., & Avolio, B. J. (1995). *Manual for the multifactor leadership questionnaire: Rater form (5X Short).* Palo Alto, CA: Mind Garden.

Beyer, J. M. (1999a). Taming and promoting charisma to change organizations. *Leadership Quarterly, 10,* 307–330.

Beyer, J. M. (1999b). Two approaches to studying charismatic leadership: Competing or complementary? *Leadership Quarterly, 10,* 575–588.

Boal, K. B., & Dodge, G. E. (1999) The effects of visionary and crisis-responsive charisma on followers: An experimental examination of two kinds of charismatic
leadership. *Leadership Quarterly, 10*(3), 423–448.

Bligh, M. C., Kohles, J. C., & Meindl, J. R. (2004a). Charisma under crisis: Presidential leadership, rhetoric, and media responses before and after the September
11th terrorist attacks. *Leadership Quarterly, 15,* 211–239

Bligh, M. C., Kohles, J. C., & Meindl, J. R. (2004b). Charting the language of leadership: A methodological investigation of President Bush and the crisis of 9/11.
Journal of Applied Psychology, 89(3), 562–574

Bligh, M. C., Kohles, J. C., & Pillai, R. (2005). Crisis and charisma in the California
recall election. *Leadership, 1*(3), 323–352.

Butterfield, A., & Prasad, A. (1990). *Leadership and the 1988 presidential election: A gallup "phrase portrait" view.* Paper presented at the 27th annual meeting of the
Eastern Academy of Management, Buffalo, NY.

Bycio, P., Hackett, R. D., & Allen, J.S. (1995). Further assessments of Bass's (1985)
conceptualization of transactional and transformational leadership. *Journal of
Applied Psychology, 30,* 468–478.

Cohen, J., & Cohen, P. (1983). *Applied multiple regression/correlation analysis for the
behavioral sciences* (2nd ed.). Hillsdale, NJ: Erlbaum.

Collins, J. (2001). *Good to great: Why some companies make the leap...and others don't.*
New York: HarperCollins.

Feinberg, B., Ostroff, C., & Burke, W.W. (2005). The role of within-group agreement in understanding transformational leadership. *Journal of Occupational
and Organizational Psychology, 78,* 471–488.

House, R. J. (1977). A 1976 theory of charismatic leadership. In J. G. Hunt & L. L.
Larson (Eds.), *Leadership: The cutting edge* (pp. 189–207). Carbondale: Southern Illinois University Press.

House, R. J., & Shamir, B. (1993). Toward the integration of transformational, char-
ismatic, and visionary theories. In Martin M. Chemers & Roya Ayman (Eds.),
Leadership theory and research: Perspectives and directions (pp. 81–103). San Diego,
CA: Academic Press.

House, R. J., Spangler, W. D., & Woyke, J. (1991). Personality and charisma in the
U.S. presidency: A psychological theory of leader effectiveness. *Administrative
Science Quarterly, 35,* 317–341.

Hunt, J. G. (1999). Transformational/charismatic leadership's transformation of
the field: An historical essay. *Leadership Quarterly, 10,* 129–144.

Hunt, J. G., Boal, K. B., & Dodge, G. E. (1999). The effects of visionary and crisis-
responsive charisma on followers: An experimental examination of two kinds
of charismatic leadership. *Leadership Quarterly, 10:* 423–448.

Jermier, J. M. (1993). Introduction—Charismatic leadership: Neo-Weberian perspectives. *Leadership Quarterly, 4,* 217–233.

Khurana, R. (2002) *Searching for a corporate savior: the irrational quest for a charismatic
CEO.* Princeton, NJ: Princeton University Press.

Lord, R. G., & Maher, K. J. (1991). *Leadership and informational processing: Linking
perceptions and performance.* Boston: Unwin Hyman.

Lowe, K. B., & Gardner, W. L. (2000). Ten years of *The Leadership Quarterly:* Contributions and challenges for the future. *Leadership Quarterly, 11,* 459–514.

Lowe, J., Kroeck, G., & Sivasubramaniam, N. (1996). Effectiveness correlates of transformational and transactional leadership: A meta-analytic review of the MLQ literature. *Leadership Quarterly, 7,* 385–425.

Madsen, D., & Snow, P. G. (1991). *The charismatic bond: Political behavior in time of crisis.* Cambridge, MA: Harvard University Press.

Maurer, T. J., Maher, K. J., Ashe, D. K., Mitchell, D. R., Hein, M. B., & Van Hein, J. (1993). Leadership perceptions in relation to a presidential vote. *Journal of Applied Social Psychology, 23,* 959–979.

McCann, S. J.H. (1997). Threatening times and the election of charismatic U.S. presidents: With and without FDR. *Journal of Psychology, 131*(4), 393–400.

Meindl, J. R. (1990). On leadership: An alternative to the conventional wisdom. In B. M. Staw & L. L. Cummings (Eds.), *Research in organizational behavior* (Vol. 12, pp. 159–203). Greenwich, CT: JAI Press.

Meindl, J. R. (1995). The romance of leadership as a follower-centric theory: A social constructionist approach. *Leadership Quarterly, 6*(3), 329–341.

Meindl, J. R., & Ehrlich, S. B. (1988). Developing a romance of leadership scale. *Proceedings of the Eastern Academy of Management,* pp. 133–135.

Meindl, J. R., Ehrlich, S. B., & Dukerich, J. M. (1985). The romance of leadership. *Administrative Science Quarterly, 30,* 78–102.

Meindl J. R., & Tsai, C. (1988). *Blaming leaders.* Unpublished manuscript, School of Management, State University of New York at Buffalo.

Meindl, J. R., Tsai, C., & Lee, W. S. (1988). *The leader–manager distinction as a context for blaming.* Unpublished manuscript, School of Management, State University of New York at Buffalo.

Miller, A. H., Wattenberg, M. P., & Malanchuk, O. (1986). Shematic assessments of presidential candidates. *American Political Science Review, 80,* 521–539.

Miller, W. E., & Shanks, D.E. (1982). Policy directions and presidential leadership: Alternative interpretations of the 1980 presidential election. *British Journal of Political Science, 12,* 299–356.

Mischel, W. (1977). The interaction of person and situation. In D. Magnusson & N. S. Endler (Eds.), *Personality at the crossroads: Current issues in interactional psychology* (pp. 333–352). Hillsdale, NJ: Erlbaum.

Pearson, C. M., & Clair, J. A. (1998). Reframing crisis management. *Academy of Management Review, 23*(1), 59–76.

Pearson, C. M., & Mitroff, I. I. (1993). From crisis prone to crisis prepared: A framework for crisis management. *Academy of Management Executive, 7*(1), 48–59.

Phillips, J. S., & Lord, J. R. (1981). Causal attributions and perceptions of leadership. *Organizational Behavior and Human Performance, 28,* 143–163.

Pillai, R. (1996). Crisis and the emergence of charismatic leadership in groups: An experimental investigation. *Journal of Applied Social Psychology, 26*(6), 543–562.

Pillai, R., & Meindl, J. R. (1991). The impact of a performance crisis on attributions of charismatic leadership: A preliminary study. *Proceedings of the 1991 Eastern Academy of Management Meetings,* Hartford, CT.

Pillai, R., & Meindl, J. R. (1998). Context and charisma: A "meso" level examination of the relationship of organic structure, collectivism, and crisis to charismatic leadership. *Journal of Management, 24*(5), 643–664.

Pillai, R., & Williams, E.A. (1998). Does leadership matter in the political arena? Voter perceptions of candidates' transformational and charismatic leadership and the 1996 U.S. presidential vote. *Leadership Quarterly, 9*, 397–416.

Pillai, R., Williams, E. A., Lowe, K. B., & Jung, D. I. (2003). Personality, transformational leadership, trust, and the 2000 U.S. presidential vote. *Leadership Quarterly, 14*(2), 161–192.

Podsakoff, P. M., MacKenzie, S. B., Moorman, R. H., & Fetter, R. (1990). Transformational leader behaviors and their effects on followers' trust in leader, satisfaction, and organizational citizenship behaviors. *Leadership Quarterly, 1*, 107–142.

Poll: Bush approval mark at all-time low. (2005, November 14). *CNN/USA Today/ Gallup Poll*. Retrieved December 3, 2005, from http://www.cnn.com/2005/ POLITICS/11/14/bush.poll/

Poll: Bush ratings hit new low. (2005, October 6). *CBS News Poll*. Retrieved December 3, 2005, from http://www.cbsnews.com/stories/2005/10/06/opinion/ polls/main924485.shtml

Schriesheim, S. L. Castro, E. A. Williams, L. A., Cardone, & Medsker, G. J. (1997). *Validity and reliability of the transformational leadership inventory: Two laboratory experiments and one field study.* Unpublished manuscript, University of Miami.

Shamir, B. M. (1994). Ideological position, leaders' charisma and voting preferences—personal vs. partisan elections. *Political Behavior, 16*, 265–287.

Shamir, B. (1995). Social distance and charisma: Theoretical notes and an exploratory study. *Leadership Quarterly, 6*, 19–47.

Shamir, B., & Howell, J. M. (1999). Organizational and contextual influences on the emergence and effectiveness of charismatic leadership. *Leadership Quarterly, 10*(2), 257–283.

Stewart, R. (1967). *Managers and their jobs: A study of the similarities and differences in the way managers spend their time.* London: MacMillan.

Stewart, R. (1976). *Contrasts in management.* Berkshire, UK: McGraw-Hill.

Tejeda, M. J., Scandura, T. A., & Pillai, R. (2001). The MLQ revisited: Psychometric properties and recommendations. *Leadership Quarterly, 12*(1), 31–52.

Thompson, S. C., Kohles, J. C., Otsuki, T. A., & Kent, D. R. (1997). Perceptions of attitudinal similarity in ethnic groups in the US: Ingroup and outgroup homogeneity effects. *European Journal of Social Psychology, 26*, 815–826.

Villa, J. R., Howell, J. P., Dorfman P. W., & Daniel, D. L. (2003). Problems with detecting moderators in leadership research using moderated multiple regression. *Leadership Quarterly, 14*, 3–23.

Voters Liked Campaign 2004, But Too Much "Mud-Slinging." (2004, November 11). *Pew Research Center for People and the Press.* Retrieved December 7, 2005, from http://people-press.org/reports/display.php3?ReportID=233

Wall Street Journal (2005, November 17). Bush's approval rating falls again, polls show. Retrieved November 29, 2005 from http://www.wsj.com.

Weber, M. (1947). *The theory of social and economic organizations* (A. M. Henderson & T. Parsons, Eds.). New York: Free Press.

Weber, M. (1968). *Economy and society* (Vols. 1–3) (G. Roth & C. Wittich, Eds.) New York: Bedminister.

Williams, E. A., Pillai, R., Jung, D., & Herst, D. (2005). *Crisis, charisma, values, and the 2004 presidential vote.* Paper presented at the 2005 Southern Management Association Meetings, Charleston, SC.

Yammarino, F. J. (1994). Transformational leadership at a distance. In B. M. Bass & B. J. Avolio (Eds.), *Improving organizational effectiveness through transformational leadership* (pp. 26–47). Thousand Oaks, CA: Sage.

Yukl, G. A. (2006). *Leadership in organizations* (6th ed.). Upper Saddle River, NJ: Prentice-Hall.

CHAPTER 8

PUTTING THE VISUAL INTO THE SOCIAL CONSTRUCTION OF LEADERSHIP

Brad Jackson
The University of Auckland Business School

Eric Guthey
The Copenhagen Business School

ABSTRACT

Our interest in visual images of business leadership builds on the solid foundation of research into the social construction of leadership images developed by the late James Meindl and his various research partners. This important research stream analyzes print articles in the popular business media to better understand the constructed nature of the leadership attributes of high-profile CEOs. We propose that analysis of the *visual* construction of such images via photographs and portraits can supplement and enhance Meindl's pioneering work. We pay close attention to those critical points at which leadership figures either become elevated into prominence or torn back down again, because such periods of transition have become increasingly visual. The photographs and portraits that accompany the "CEO

Follower-Centered Perspectives on Leadership, pages 167–186
Copyright © 2007 by Information Age Publishing

celebrity backlash" bring into sharp focus the visually constructed nature of business leadership.

INTRODUCTION

"When Thai protesters recently set alight pictures of Ho Ching, chief executive
of Temasek Holdings, it was further indication that the Singapore state investment
company was confronting growing political problems as it expands in Asia."

—Burton (2006)

We live in an era in which visual images have become paramount, taking center stage in the news, politics, advertising, corporate communication, and media coverage of management concepts and events (Frosh, 2003; Merzoeff, 1999; Schroeder, 2002; Thompson, 2000; Thrift, 2000). In this context photographic images and portraits of top business leaders have become the wallpaper of corporate capitalism, plastered on newspapers, magazines, annual reports, newsletters, airport book jackets, and corporate websites. Many of these images appear so bland and so similar that we barely even notice them. But there must be a reason that they exist in such great numbers, and they don't always appear so innocuous. The recent burning of portraits of Temasek Holdings CEO Ho Ching provides just one example. The shifting fortunes of celebrity CEOs and other business heroes often give rise to intense bouts of what we might call "visual politics," symbolic contests in which photographic portraits of the executives in question play a prominent role.

In this chapter we make the case for the importance of visual images in the study of the social construction of leadership. We begin by reviewing the important contributions made by Jim Meindl and his various writing partners in a series of empirical studies of leadership images in a wide variety of contexts (Bligh, Kohles, & Meindl, 2004; Bligh & Meindl, 2005; Chen & Meindl, 1991; Meindl, Ehrlich, & Dukerich, 1985; Meindl & Thompson, 2005). Meindl's research in this area has provided a theoretical framework for understanding the central aspects of the social construction of leadership, and highlights the media's significance in shaping and influencing ideas and beliefs about leadership in ways that scholars previously had overlooked.

At the center of this research lies the concept of image. Images have been described by Meindl and others as a collective mental impression or set of perceived attributions, and investigated with the use of surveys and analyzing readers' responses to newspaper articles and other texts about leaders (e.g., Bligh et al., 2004; Bligh & Meindl, 2005; Chen & Meindl, 1991; Hayward, Rindova, & Pollock, 2004; Hegele & Kieser, 2001; Meindl et al., 1985; Meindl & Thompson, 2005;). While research in this vein often uses visual metaphors and terminology to explain the concept of image, it has not yet explored its grounding in actual visual images, that is, in photographs and other visual representations of business leaders.

We argue that research into the social construction of leadership can productively expand its focus to include analysis of the *visual* construction of leadership (Guthey & Jackson, 2005). Visual images of CEOs and top executives deserve close scrutiny as an important window into how business celebrity, firm reputation, and corporate legitimacy are constructed and deconstructed in the media. Photographs and portraits of business leaders are not merely window dressings. An appreciation of their function and significance can supplement research that emphasizes abstract and collective aspects of leadership images with a focus on concrete phenomena and embedded social processes. Meindl and others have made it clear that leadership images often reflect the general views of the business community, the commercial and organizational imperatives of the media, or the collective conceptions of organization and leadership dominant in the national culture at large (Bligh et al., 2004; Bligh & Meindl, 2005; Chen & Meindl, 1991). A focus on visual images makes it clear that they also can function very actively as rhetorical tools in ongoing symbolic struggles over the legitimacy of individual business leaders, and over the social legitimacy of corporate organization writ large.

Ventresca (2004) and Galvin, Ventresca, and Hudson (2005) have observed that the concept of legitimacy in organizational research has become reified and static, as if it was some sort of tangible resource that can be quantified and traded by individuals, organizations, and industries. By contrast, these authors argue for a greater understanding of legitimacy as a verb, rather than as a noun. That is, it should be understood as a dynamic process embedded in specific institutional and cultural contexts and characterized by a struggle for predominance between conflicting authority systems and social structures. Such an approach parallels and reinforces our emphasis on the dynamic, embedded, and often contentious nature of leadership images. These parallels become particularly evident with respect to the flurry of images often produced in connection with the changing fortunes of prominent CEO celebrities. For this reason we will illustrate our debt to Meindl's work, and our extension of his ideas, with a discussion of our ongoing research into the visual politics of what we have called the "celebrity CEO backlash." This term refers to the period of widespread media recrimination and criticism directed against former business heroes and celebrity CEOs. This was set in motion with the collapse of the dot.com bubble and the corporate scandals of the late 1990s and currently continues, for example, with the recent ouster of Carly Fiorina as CEO of Hewlett-Packard and the ongoing saga of the Enron trial.

The CEO backlash is a highly visual phenomenon, and therefore provides an important window for examining how visual images can work to *deconstruct* images of business leadership and set in play multiple and even conflicting leadership images at the same time. In this sense it represents the flipside of Meindl and colleagues' scholarly interest in the collective construction of CEO celebrity. Attention to the CEO backlash can help supplement Meindl's work with a fuller picture of the relational and often contentious dynamics of the social construction of leadership images.

MEINDL'S CONTRIBUTIONS: THE SOCIAL CONSTRUCTION OF LEADERSHIP PERSPECTIVE

As the title of this collection of essays attests, Jim Meindl's major contribution was to advance a "follower-centric" approach to leadership studies as a much-needed counterweight to the widespread preoccupation with leader-centric approaches. Consolidating earlier work by Pfeffer (1977), Pfeffer and Salancik (1978), and Calder (1977), he rightly observed that while most leadership scholars recognize that leadership is fundamentally predicated by the relationship between leaders and followers, followers almost invariably take a minor supporting role in the analysis of leadership. Reading Meindl's work, one is struck by the depth of his discomfort with this tendency to place such great stock in the role of leaders, especially those at the apex of the organization. This often misplaced faith remains strong in spite of the overwhelming weight of evidence suggesting that external forces and a myriad of alternative internal factors exert considerably more influence over organizational performance. "The concept of leadership is a permanently entrenched part of the socially constructed reality that we bring to bear in our analysis of organizations," Meindl concluded with more than a hint of resignation. "And there is every sign that the obsessions and celebrations of it will persist" (Meindl et al., 1985, p. 78).

But rather than turning their back on leadership studies, Meindl and his colleagues decided to turn this tendency to overestimate the significance of leaders and leadership into their central research concern. At the heart of their analysis lies the notion of the "romance of leadership," which they suggest "denotes a strong belief—a faith—in the importance of leadership factors to the functioning and dysfunctioning of organized systems" (Meindl & Ehrlich, 1987, p. 91). As summarized by Awamleh and Gardner (1999), "the commonly assumed direction of the leadership–performance relationship is backwards: instead, organizational performance is seen as a cause, rather than a consequence, of charismatic leadership" (p. 346). Meindl observed further that this tendency toward romanticization holds the greatest sway in extreme cases. When organizations fare either extremely well or extremely poorly, observers will tend to understand such developments in terms of leadership (Meindl et al., 1985).

Meindl did not advance the follower-centric approach in an effort to compete or to replace the dominant leader-centric approach. He insisted that the romance of leadership perspective was not "anti-leadership." Rather, it provided "an alternative to theories and perspectives that place great weight on 'leaders' and on the substantive significance to their actions and activities" (Meindl, 1995, p. 330). This alternative concerns itself with how followers construct and represent leaders in their thought systems. Thus, the approach Meindl spearheaded does not merely accept the relationships between leaders and followers as a given, but explores instead how both leaders and followers actively construct their identities and their interrelationships. This approach connects closely with charismatic attribution theory (Conger & Kanungo, 1987) and with self-concept theory (Shamir, House, & Arthur, 1993). Both highlight the reciprocal nature of charismatic leadership, as well as the construction of both leaders and followers, by means of relational dynamics rather than by imposition of predetermined and fixed roles.

The writings in which Meindl developed these perspectives are impressive. The consistently high quality of the work he produced in collaboration with a number of colleagues, as well as the unwavering commitment he demonstrated to critiquing mainstream leadership studies, in his typically gentle and diplomatic manner, from a position that was well within the mainstream is remarkable. He never wavered from the project of asking penetrating questions about the mundane, taken-for-granted aspects of leadership—pressing questions that others rarely took the time to ask, let alone answer in as careful and thoughtful manner as he did.

From our perspective, the pinnacle of Meindl's published work was the article that he coauthored with Chao Chen entitled "The Construction of Leadership Images in the Popular Press" (Chen & Meindl, 1991). We have returned often to this article for insight and inspiration. The authors highlight how the business press, in conjunction with the reading public, constructs a leader's image over time in light of radical changes in the fortunes of a firm. The empirical case in point is the career of People Express founder and chief executive Donald Burr, whose airline enjoyed a brief but highly celebrated heyday before encountering insurmountable financial problems and folding into Texas Air just 5 short years after it made its inaugural flight in 1981. Analyzing the tropes and metaphors used to describe Burr, Chen and Meindl conclude that the press constructed him as an idealized representation of the American entrepreneurial spirit.

On the basis of this case the article makes two very important contributions. First, it persuasively demonstrates the benefits of introducing a social constructionist perspective (Berger & Luckmann, 1966) to leadership studies. While this perspective previously had enjoyed considerable influence in other spheres of organizational research, leadership scholars had not embraced it with any conviction. To correct this oversight Chen and Meindl (1991) argued that "collective conceptions of organization, and of leadership, in particular, are expressions of national culture at large in which both leaders and followers are embedded." Furthermore, they added, these conceptions are heavily influenced by "those institutional forces that create and disseminate 'business' news and information" (p. 521). In this manner Chen and Meindl introduced the notion that leaders do not control their own destiny. The identity and influence of leaders depends to a large extent on the manner in which their followers conceive of them. Both leaders and followers are subject to a range of forces beyond their control, prominent among them is the dynamics of the news industries that disseminate information about leaders to followers, and the wider society. The business media in turn is subject to a variety of internal and external pressures, including the vagaries of the national cultural context; the pronounced bias toward antideterminism evinced by the business press; and the weight of previous attribution histories regarding the leader in question at any given time that constrains the business press from revising the image of a particular leader too far and too fast in order to preserve the appearance of credibility.

These latter comments point toward the second major contribution of the Chen and Meindl (1991) article. They highlighted and specified the role that the media, particularly the business media, play in shaping the attributions that followers might give to a particular leader, and also in shaping their general beliefs about what constitutes effective and ineffective and ethical and unethical leadership. Leadership scholars have been peculiarly uneasy about recognizing the influence that the media exerts. Chen and Meindl note that the media's tendency to personalize news promulgates from the antideterminist belief that individual leaders control the fate of organizations rather than relational or structural forces. They also note that the media tends to take an "outcome-primacy" approach in constructing leader images by matching leader characteristics with performance outcomes. Consequently, the CEO of a successful firm will tend to be depicted with positive personal qualities and vice versa.

Confronted with a decline in organizational performance, Chen and Meindl went on to explain that the media logically could be expected to revise the image of any given leader that it represents. But they also noted that the media can be constrained from changing this image because of the investment it places upon maintaining editorial consistency, and thereby credibility. Chen and Meindl argued that the case of Donald Burr demonstrated the media's commitment to maintaining a consistent image of a business leader over time, because the business press collectively clung to its original, highly positive image of Burr even in the face of the drastic downturn in People Express's performance. For example, the authors' analysis of press coverage of People Express reveals the prevalence and persistence of the metaphorical description of Burr as a preacher. This concept was "elaborated in successive historical periods and served to retain an essential commitment to Burr's leadership as a way to understand both the initial success and the ultimate demise of People Express" (1991, p. 541).

The Burr article echoed important themes that Meindl refined in other contexts with other coauthors. Taken as a whole, his work has done organizational studies a great service by mobilizing the concept of image to highlight the socially constructed nature of leadership, leadership concepts, and individual leaders. In the spirit of constantly questioning basic assumptions in precisely the manner that Meindl himself always championed, we believe that the central notion of image itself deserves an even closer examination. In the following section we make the case for a revisualization of the concept of image, and outline some of the insights to be gained from an investigation of how photographs and portraits can function as significant sites for the social construction of leadership.

REVISUALIZING THE SOCIAL CONSTRUCTION OF LEADERSHIP

Even the brief overview in the previous section makes it clear that Jim Meindl's work challenges scholars to continue to grapple with a very basic and important question, what exactly is an image? As pointed out by picture theorist and art historian W.J.T. Mitchell, the term refers to a variety of phenomena, including "pictures, statues, optical illusions, maps, diagrams, dreams, hallucinations, spectacles, projections, patterns, memories, and even ideas" (Mitchell, 1984, p. 504). At first glance this seemingly disparate grouping may appear to have little in common. But Mitchell argues that the many and diverse approaches to image still constitute a "far-flung family," and he even sketches a family tree in order to explain how they are related. On the far left branch of the tree are graphic images as exemplified by visual pictures, paintings, statues, and photographs. On the far right branch are verbal images such as metaphors, descriptions, and writing. In between are optical images (e.g., mirrors, projections), perceptual images (e.g., sense data, appearances) and mental images (e.g., dreams, memories, ideas).

The concept of image employed in research on the social construction of leadership belongs on the right side of this tree. Organization scholars have favored an abstract understanding of image as a mental construct or projection consisting of a collection of attributes or characteristics attached to an individual (e.g., self-image or persona), a group or class of individuals (e.g., professional image), or an organization (e.g., organizational or corporate image). Although such approaches invoke many concrete, visual metaphors—including *vision, visibility, snapshots, mirrors, eyes, pictures,* and *portraits*—they have not yet explored the centrality of visual images to the construction of "image" in the abstract sense. Meindl himself often interchanged the terms "image" and "portrait." His use of these terms was fundamentally metaphorical, because he did not refer to actual visual images or portraits, but only to mental conceptions held by readers—such as the "image" of Burr as a preacher—based on written accounts.

Chen and Meindl supported this approach to media images with references to the work of such scholars as Walter Lippmann (1921) and Daniel Boorstin (1961). In another paper in progress we explore the intellectual lineage of these thinkers, and make clear the links between Meindl's approach to image and Lippmann's notion of "the pictures in our heads" (Guthey, Jackson, and Clark, 2006). When deploying the term "image" in a metaphorical sense, what we are really doing is referring to images as pictures in our heads. This provides a powerful way of talking about the influence of mental constructs and beliefs. But it is useful to remember that this is in fact a metaphor. We cannot literally "see" pictures in our heads, and certainly not the ones in other people's heads. Research founded on a metaphorical conception of image, therefore, has to take care not to reify an abstract, aggregate, and elusive construct that has to be pieced together from multiple texts or survey questionnaires. On the basis of these considerations, we believe that research on leadership images can benefit from taking a look at the pictures in front of our eyes as well.

In contrast to mental constructs, visual images are material objects—tangible, physically present, and directly accessible to researchers, their audience, and others. Visual images can exert an immediate, direct, and powerful influence on followers in ways that words and texts often cannot. "Readers" of the business press invariably look at the pictures, whether or not they actually take the time to read the articles they function to illustrate. Nowhere is this tendency more evident than in a cursory observation of the reading habits of commuters. First, they scan the newspaper, taking in the headlines, photographs, and accompanying bylines, then perhaps they focus on a particular article and actually read the text. On a personal note, the first author was struck by the thorough and enthusiastic attention readers gave to the portraits that were included, largely as an afterthought, in a book he coauthored on New Zealand chief executives (Jackson & Parry, 2001). Would that they have read the pages of text that had been so painstakingly written with as much care and attention!

Aside from such anecdotal and common-sense reasons for looking more closely at visual images, there are several productive ways in which this shift in focus can refine, supplement, and in certain respects challenge the existing theory on the social construction of leadership. For example, Meindl and other scholars have tended to focus primarily on the convergence of one, homogenized view of a given leader or organization at a given time. Thus the central issue at stake for Chen and Meindl (1991) is the predominant image of Donald Burr generated by the success of People's Express. This image becomes challenged by the subsequent failure of the airline, creating problems primarily for news organizations and their credibility. The logical conclusion of this collective approach to images is that whole national cultures can entertain the same image at the same time, as Chen and Meindl in fact suggest. This may be the case in certain instances, but a focus on visual images makes it clear that the opposite is also just as likely to be true. In the contemporary media environment, where an ever increasing number of business news organizations and a multitude of channels compete for attention, it is often the case that many divergent images of any given business leader coexist at the same time. For example, Guthey (2004) has explored the many different images and portrayals of Microsoft founder Bill Gates. He concludes that Bill Gates is in fact a fiction—not because the "image" of Bill Gates is false, but because there are multiple Bill Gates images that can be deployed in different ways on behalf of different interests in different narrative contexts. Not only can a number of conflicting images of the same leader coexist at any given time, but audiences—and even single individuals—can entertain multiple, conflicting interpretations of a single image of that leader as well.

Our point about the multiple and multivalent nature of visual images and portraits is not just a picky one. In many instances, a focus on visual images can help make researching the social construction of leadership images more descriptively accurate and more reflective of the rich texture of leadership images. It can also help render this research as more truly *social*. In a later work, Meindl and Thompson seek to clarify their approach to images with the notion of "social representation" (Meindl & Thompson, forthcoming). This is a potentially useful term for describing precisely the kind of multivalent and relational approach to images we find most promising. But the term deserves careful examination, because it has been developed within certain circles in social psychology in an almost exclusively collective and abstract sense. In terms familiar to organization scholars, much of the scholarly work on social representations has embraced what Joanne Martin (1992) would call an integration perspective that emphasizes consistency, clarity, and consensus, while shunning difference and ambiguity to the margins.

Meindl and Thompson (forthcoming) introduce this concept of social representations to emphasize the socially constructed nature of the images in question, stating, for example, "the concept of social representation emphasizes the extent to which our understandings of the world are socially conditioned." They explain further:

> These representations provide frameworks for understanding among members of the business community. The portraits of firms and CEOs produced and consumed on the pages of the popular business press, and the reputations they entail, are essentially social representations. They are a system of beliefs, a collectively defined set of social "attitudes" toward or about organizations and the people—that is the CEOs—who presumably control them. (forthcoming, p. 3)

Again, the prominence of the word "collective" is important here. It connotes that which is unitary, consensual, and univocal. In this sense the realm of the social certainly includes collective phenomena, which is why Meindl's observations about collective leadership images remain important. But the notion of collectivity does not encompass the full plenitude of these social phenomena, which would also include dissent, conflict, difference, and alienation from the collective. These are important aspects of the social that the notions of collectivity and social representations tend to smooth over or ignore altogether. On just this basis Ian Parker (1989) delivers a bracing critique of the notion of social representations, in particular taking to task Farr and Moscovici (1984), upon whose work Meindl and Thompson draw to introduce the concept in their research. If we distinguish, as Parker does, between the social and the collective, then there is a potential contradiction in Meindl and Thompson's description of social representations as *"social in origin and collective in nature."* Socially defined images presumably would be the product of a social process—that is, they would be defined by a process of interaction, negotiation, contention, and even political, organizational, or ideological struggle. Moreover, the end result of that process also would be social but not necessarily collective. From this perspective, social representations would carry within them the mark of the relational social processes that produced them—they would be multivalent, contested, and dialogic.

We propose, therefore, to revise Meindl and Thompson's statement to maintain that leadership images are social representations because they are *social in origin and social in nature*—that is, they can function as key instruments in processes of negotiation and conflict over the nature and legitimacy of leadership and leaders. The quotation at the beginning of this chapter regarding the burning of the photographs of the Temasek Holdings' CEO provides just one striking example of how images can play this role. Our research into the visual politics of the celebrity CEO backlash provides a wealth of further examples.

THE VISUAL POLITICS OF THE CELEBRITY CEO BACKLASH

In the article mentioned above, Chen and Meindl described People Express CEO Donald Burr as "one of the most celebrated sagas of business management and entrepreneurial spirit of the last decade" (1991, p. 521). But Burr has since vanished from the recognized pantheon of business heroes, highlighting one of the hazards of this kind of research—namely, that yesterday's business news very quickly becomes tomorrow's "fish and chips" paper. If anything, the shelf life of celebrity CEOs is much shorter than it was during Burr's moment in the limelight. Booz Allen Hamilton's annual study of CEO succession reveals that the tenure of all CEOs continues to get shorter (Lucie, Schuyt, & Tse, 2005). This latter study also reinforces our point about the contentious nature of CEO celebrity by pointing out that *forced* resignations of CEOs in the world's top 2,500 companies increased some 300% between 1995 and 2004. Closely related to the increasingly rapid turnover of even garden-variety CEOs is the phenomenon we have described as the celebrity CEO backlash.

Webster's New World Dictionary of the American Language (1974) defines a backlash as "a quick, sharp recoil" as well as "any sudden or violent reaction [such as a] strong political or social reaction resulting from fear or resentment of a movement, candidate, etc." (p. 102). The CEO backlash represents a strong negative reaction against the period of exuberant CEO hero worship and celebration that coincided with the new economy era and the stock market bubble of the 1990s. The same pundits and media outlets that previously had fueled the engines of CEO hype suddenly seemed to delight in ridiculing CEOs as mendacious and self-serving, if not outright criminal. "Over the past decade we've inflated the myth of the savior CEO, the chest-beating action figure who could single-handedly save or sink billion-dollar organizations," complained *Fortune* magazine. "The notion was mostly a crock—in truth, a company's fate depends on everything from market trends to an organization's history to pure luck" (Useem, 2002). The transformation from the era of CEO celebrity to the current moment of disillusionment and finger-pointing seemed like it had occurred almost overnight—precipitated by the bursting of the dot.com bubble and the continuing cascade of revelations about corporate scandal, insider trading, and executive wrongdoing. The shifting press coverage of Jack Welch, former chair and chief executive of General Electric and one-time *Fortune* magazine "Manager of the Century," exemplifies this transition. "Rogues at companies like WorldCom and Enron were bad enough," declared *The New York Times*, "but even superstar executives like Jack Welch contributed to the staining of corporate America" (O'Neal, 2002).

By the fall of 2002, the backlash against formerly deified CEOs and top executives had become more than an institutionalized feature of the business media landscape. It also had become a source of Halloween costume inspiration. "This Halloween, Dracula and Frankenstein's monster seem positively cuddly," declared *Forbes* magazine. "To inspire some real fear, try dressing up as one of these current or former chief executives." In an astonishing display of disrespect for its own target audience, the online version of the self-proclaimed "magazine for the world's business leaders" instructed readers to click on images of several previously venerated celebrity CEOs to access "full-size, printer-friendly masks" they could wear around the office or to a Halloween party. The choice of CEOs—united by their involvement in corporate scandals—included Worldcom's Bernie Ebbers, Enron's Kenneth Lay, Tyco's Dennis Kozlowski, and the eponymous Martha Stewart. The accompanying text concluded, "Now that's scary!" (Herper, 2002).

Before the onset of the backlash, such a feature in a business magazine like *Forbes* would have been almost inconceivable. The *Forbes* Halloween masks highlight the intensely visual nature of the CEO media backlash. We argue that photographs and other illustrations play an indispensable role in these developments for three important reasons:

1. Institutional and competitive pressures force media outlets to illustrate their news stories with arresting visuals. But it is impossible to "see" a corporation, much less take its picture. For this reason CEOs often come to symbolize and embody their companies as part of the continuous project of bolstering individual firm reputation and maintaining the authenticity and legitimacy of corporate capitalism as an institution (Guthey & Jackson, 2005). They do so not only in a representative and figurative sense, but in a visual sense—which helps explain the proliferation of CEO and top executive portraits in the media (Guthey & Jackson, 2004).

2. Scandals are as old as human society itself. But as Thompson (2000) demonstrates, the economic, social, and technological changes that gave rise to new media technologies and industries in the 18th and 19th centuries created the modern phenomenon of *mediated scandals*. As a mediated response to such scandals, the CEO celebrity backlash is not simply a phenomenon that happens to get reported by the media. Rather, the dynamics of media representation and organization are central to the form and content of the backlash. One important dynamic Thompson highlights is that people tune into mediated scandals intermittently and with varying levels of attentiveness, "paying more attention to the headlines... that to the fine detail" (p. 89).

3. In this context the power of visual imagery and the representational dynamics of the medium of photography can play a much more cen-

tral role than written accounts in the creation and reporting of scandals. Several commentators have made this point in relation to the horrific images of the U.S. military abusing Iraqi prisoners. "Photographs have an insuperable power to determine what we recall of events," said the late Susan Sontag in her essay on the Abu Ghraib photographs. "Apparently it took the photographs to get their attention, when it became clear they could not be suppressed, it was the photographs that made all this 'real' to Bush and his associates" (Sontag, 2004).

Backlash photographs have the power to make corporate scandals "real" by deconstructing business celebrity rather than building them up. They do so by exposing the seams with which images of celebrity CEOs get stitched together in the first place. For this reason backlash photos employ visual conventions that foreground the constructed nature of CEO images. Three different examples of such conventions will serve to illustrate this point.

1. One important visual dynamic of CEO backlash involves the juxtaposition of negative images of "fallen" CEOs with previously celebratory images of the same individual in their heyday, as exemplified by a CNN web feature entitled "Martha Then and Now" (see Figure 8.1). This particular feature illustrates the power of visual framing actively constructing opposing CEO identities—because the supposed "before" picture also was taken during Stewart's trial, not before her downfall. The photograph may appear to portray Stewart in a happier, more carefree time because of the visual convention whereby we expect a "before" picture in this context. The simultaneous display of such (supposedly) conflicting images of the same celebrity CEO—as a business icon *and* as a shameless or even criminal profiteer—further suggests that both images are socially determined constructions (Chen & Meindl, 1991; Guthey & Jackson, 2004). The rest of the CNN feature hammered this point home with a string of such

Figure 8.1.   "Martha Then and Now." (CNN, 2004)

conflicting images (a luxury condo and a jail, fashion apparel and a prison jumpsuit). In fact, all backlash images implicitly exhibit this "then and now" dynamic, since they all gain their shock value by contrast with the previously lofty image of the now degraded subject. As the *Forbes* Halloween feature jokes, "[Bernie] Ebbers' visage, which was worshipped during the boom, is now enough to chill investors to their very souls" (Herper, 2002).

2. Backlash photographs also highlight their constructed nature through overt and even ritualized staging and choreography. This dynamic is best illustrated by the ubiquitous images of the CEO "perp walk," in which indicted executives are taken into custody and paraded into the courthouse, often in handcuffs (refer to Figures 8.2, 8.3, and 8.4). As newsworthy events, perp walks are pure theater (*as if* Martha Stewart or Ken Lay actually would wrestle the federal marshals to the ground and make a getaway). Nonetheless they have become an essential visual element of the backlash ritual. As a *Washington Post* business columnist declared after the arrest of Ken Lay, "We finally got the photo op that so many people have wanted to see for so long: Ken Lay doing the perp walk, almost three years after Enron's collapse touched off the current corporate scandal fest" (Sloan, 2004).

Figure 8.2.
Kenneth Lay, Enron
(Stravato, 2004)

Figure 8.3.
Jeffrey Skilling, Enron
(Coomer, 2004)

Figure 8.4.
Martha Stewart
(Reuters, 2004)

3. Finally, backlash photos foreground their fundamentally constructed nature through the digital alteration and enhancement of the image itself, as exemplified by the *Forbes* Halloween masks, and by the *BusinessWeek* cover illustration titled "Downsizing the CEO" (see Figure 8.5). Barely concealed behind the CEO masks lurks the implication

Figure 8.5.   "Downsizing the CEO," (*BusinessWeek*, 2005.

that all CEO images are masks, elaborate constructions intended to align the public's perceptions with corporate interests. As if to reiterate this point, *Forbes*'s 2003 collection of Halloween masks featured CEOs who have not even been charged with crimes, implying that they are just as "scary." This time around the magazine employed even more digital alteration, rendering Larry Ellison as a werewolf, Steve Jobs as a pirate, and Bill Gates as Frankenstein's monster (see Figure 8.6). The extensive use of digital manipulation in backlash photos again highlights the constructed nature of CEO images—when the proper image cannot be simply snapped with a camera, it can be constructed in Adobe Photoshop.

Consistent with the antideterminist manner in which celebratory CEO narratives attribute firm success to the individuals so celebrated (Guthey, 1997; Hayward, Rindova, & Pollock, 2004; Meindl & Thompson, forthcoming), backlash narratives and photographs attribute corporate wrongdoing and firm failure to the individual "bad apples" singled out for humiliation. They often attribute the construction of the previously celebratory images to the deceptive practices of the individual CEOs as well. They imply that the CEO scourges were hiding behind a mask of their own devising before, and that now their true selves have been "unmasked." But while celebrity CEOs may exert a (somewhat) stronger influence on the celebratory photographs, they do not appear to influence the negative ones at all. Indeed, they would rather that such photos of them (in handcuffs, for example)

Figure 8.6.   Bill Gates mask (Herper, 2003).

didn't exist at all, although they no longer have the power or influence to put a stop to them.

By means of these and other conventionalized representational practices, CEO backlash images wear their constructedness on their sleeves, thereby bolstering Meindl and Thompson's point that CEO celebrities should be understood as elaborate media constructions. Backlash photos are constructed and staged by a variety of other actors besides the CEO—among them photographers, photo editors, digital artists, and even law enforcement officials. For this reason they exemplify Meindl and Thompson's point that CEO images are "social in origin." The content of backlash photographs is also social—while ostensibly intended to discredit individual CEO celebrities as criminals or reprobates, they simultaneously, and often very self-consciously, call into question the whole institution of CEO celebrity as an artificial construction. As *social representations,* backlash photographs reflect and reproduce what Meindl and Thompson called a "collectively defined set of social 'attitudes' toward or about organizations and the people—that is, the CEOs—who presumably control them" (forthcoming, p. 4). But they also fill out our picture of social representations by highlighting the way that they can also function as sites of interaction, conflict, and struggle over the legitimacy, indeed, even the criminality, of prominent business leaders and leadership in general.

CONCLUSION

We are indebted to Jim Meindl and his various writing partners for building a theoretical framework to help us better understand some of the most important processes associated with the social construction of leadership. We believe that the next phase of this work could profitably expand its vista to encompass images in the form of photographs and other visual representations of business leaders. For this reason we have argued in this chapter for the importance of photographic and pictorial evidence to the study of the social construction of leadership. CEO and top executive photographs deserve close scrutiny as an important window into how business celebrity, firm reputation, and corporate legitimacy are constructed and deconstructed in the media precisely because they are a primary means by which followers encounter and make sense of leaders. In this case we mean "primary" first, because a photograph is often the first piece of data that a follower will be exposed to about a potential or new leader; and second, because individuals derive more information about a leader than they may either be conscious of, or even comfortable with. As the old adage states, when it comes to the social construction (or deconstruction) of a leader, a picture really is "worth a thousand words."

To summarize our argument, the strength of an emphasis on actual visual images is that it introduces plurality, production, and the possibility for multiple interpretations into the analysis of the social construction of leadership. That is to say, a focus on leadership images as social representations creates an incomplete picture of those representations as the collective (read consensual) product of a society that shares the same views on any given phenomenon. Because a focus on visual images must take into account many such images, it inherently highlights the plurality, and perhaps the divisive contradictions, between multiple salient images.

The next phase of our research focuses on how individual followers make sense of executive portraits. In designing early exploratory studies we have been inspired and guided by Meindl's empirical studies exploring the way audiences construct leadership images on the basis of narrative texts (Meindl & Ehrlich, 1987; Meindl, Ehrlich, & Dukerich, 1985). But in order to investigate the visual construction of leadership in depth, we believe that leadership scholars will have to loosen their dependence on well-established quantitative and social science methodologies, and to draw upon interpretative methodologies and aesthetic insights from the humanities, from art history, and from photography theory and criticism. Recalling Daft's (1980) continuum of language variety in organizational research, we need to learn to incorporate into leadership research the interpretation of "higher variety" and nonverbal languages, the sort employed in photographs and other visual images. This is not to suggest in any romanticized way that visual representations are "better" than lower variety languages such as analytical mathematics, linear statistics, categorization, or even general verbal expression. But we may have to trade off some of the greater precision that these latter quantitative languages provide, if we wish to grasp some of the more complex interpretive dimensions of organizational life and leadership dynamics.

In one of Meindl's last published pieces, he observed that, "despite all of the scientific ambiguities and uncertainties of such work, one thing is clear to us: As industries and organizations are constructed, leaders are also constructed, and in the process, celebrities are produced" (Meindl & Thompson, forthcoming). We are grateful that he took on the task of exploring these issues despite the ambiguities and uncertainties, thereby breaking the trail and pointing the way forward for others. In common with every author in this collection, we hope that we can honor his legacy and create fresh and innovative insights into the social dynamics of leadership.

REFERENCES

Awamleh, R., & Gardner, W. L. (1999). Perceptions of leaders charisma and effectiveness: The effects of vision content, delivery, and organizational performance. *Leadership Quarterly, 10*(3), 345–373.

Berger, P. L., & Luckmann, T. (1966). *The social construction of reality.* Garden City, NY: Doubleday.

Bligh, M. C., Kohles, J. C., & Meindl, J. R. (2004). Charisma under crisis: Presidential leadership, rhetoric, and media responses before and after the September 11th terrorist attacks. *Leadership Quarterly, 15*(2), 211–239.

Bligh, M. C., & Meindl, J. R. (2005). The cultural ecology of leadership: An analysis of popular leadership books. In D. M. Messick & R. M. Kramer (Eds.), *The psychology of leadership: Some new approaches* (pp. 11–52). Mahwah, NJ: Erlbaum.

Boorstin, D. J. (1961). *The image.* New York: Atheneum.

Burton, J. (2006, March 24) Backlash for Temasek over "Singapore imperialism." *Financial Times,* p. 7.

BusinessWeek (2005, April 25) Downsizing the CEO. Retrieved April 29, 2006 from http://www.businessweek.com.

Calder, B. J. (1977). An attribution theory of leadership. In B. M. Staw & G. R. Salancik (Eds.), *New directions in organizational behavior* (pp. 179–204). Chicago: St. Clair.

Chen, C. C, & Meindl, J. R. (1991). The construction of leadership images in the popular press: The case of Donald Burr and People Express. *Administrative Science Quarterly, 36*(4), 521–551.

CNN (2004, July 21). Martha Then and Now. Retrieved July 28, 2004 from http://money.cnn.com.

Conger, J., & Kanungo, R. (1987). Toward a behavioral theory of charismatic leadership in organizational settings. *Academy of Management Review, 12*(4), 637–647.

Coomer, B. (Getty Images Photo). (2004, February 20). Former Enron CEO Jeff Skilling is escorted into the Houston federal courthouse… *Seattle Times.* Retrieved February 24, 2004 from http://seattletimes.nwsources.com.

Daft, R. (1980). The evolution of organizational analysis in *ASQ,* 1959–1979. *Administrative Science Quarterly, 25,* 623–636.

Farr, R., & Moscovici, S. (1984). *Social representations.* Cambridge, UK: Cambridge University Press.

Frosh, P. (2003). *Image factory: Consumer culture, photography and the visual content industry.* Oxford, UK: Berg.

Galvin, T., Ventresca, M., & Hudson, B. (2005). Contested industry dynamics: New directions in the study of legitimacy. *International Studies of Management and Organization, 34*(4), 57–84.

Guthey, E. (2004). New economy romanticism, narratives of corporate personhood, and the antimanagerial impulse. In K. Lipartito & D. S. Sicilia (Eds.), *Crossing corporate boundaries: History, politics, culture* (pp. 321–342). New York: Oxford University Press.

Guthey, E., & Jackson, B. (2004). *The CEO celebrity backlash and the visual politics of corporate leadership.* Paper presented at the British Academy of Management annual meeting, St. Andrews, Scotland.

Guthey, E., & Jackson, B. (2005). CEO portraits and the authenticity paradox. *Journal of Management Studies, 42*(5), 1057–1082.

Guthey, E., Jackson, B., & Clark, T. (2006). *Pictures in our heads?: Reframing image in leadership and organization studies.* Working paper in progress.

Hayward, M. L. A., Rindova, V. P., & Pollock, T. G. (2004). Believing one's own press: The causes and consequences of CEO celebrity. *Strategic Management Journal, 25*(7), 637–653.

Hegele, C., & Kieser, A. (2001). Control the construction of your legend or some one else will: An analysis of texts on Jack Welch. *Journal of Management Inquiry, 10*(4), 298–309.

Herper, M. (2002, October 28). CEO halloween masks. *Forbes.* Retrieved October 29, 2002, from http://www.forbes.com/2002/10/28/cx_mh_1028halloween.html

Herper, M. (2003, October 29). CEO halloween masks. *Forbes.* Retrieved October 29, 2003, from http://www.forbes.com/2003/10/28/cx_mh_1028ceomasks.html

Jackson, B., & Parry, K. (2001). *The hero manager: Learning from New Zealand's top executives.* Auckland: Penguin.

Khurana, R. (2002). *Searching for a corporate savior: The irrational quest for charismatic CEOs.* Princeton, NJ: Princeton University Press.

Lippmann, W. (1921). The world outside and the pictures in our heads. In W. Schramm & D. Roberts (Eds.), *The process and effects of mass communication* (2nd ed., pp. 265–286). Urbana: University of Illinois Press.

Lucier, C., Schuyt, R., & Tse, E. (2005). CEO succession 2004: The world's most prominent temp workers. *strategy + business, 39*, 1–16. Retrieved March 31, 2006, from www.boozallen.com

Martin, J. (1992). *Cultures in organizations: Three perspectives.* Oxford, UK: Oxford University Press.

Meindl. J. R. (1995). The romance of leadership as follower-centric theory: A social constructionist approach. *Leadership Quarterly, 6*(3), 329–341.

Meindl, J. R., & Ehrlich, S. B. (1987). The romance of leadership and the evaluation of organisational performance. *Academy of Management Journal, 30*(1), 91–109.

Meindl, J. R., Ehrlich, S. B., & Dukerich, J. M. (1985). The romance of leadership. *Administrative Science Quarterly, 30*(1), 78–102.

Meindl, J. R., & Thompson, K. J. (forthcoming). The celebrated CEO: Notes on the dynamic ecology of charisma constructions. In M. Ventresca & J. Porac (Eds.), *Constructing identities and markets.* New York: Elsevier.

Merzoef, N. (1999). *An introduction to visual culture.* London: Routledge.

O'Neal, M. (2002 December 29). Coming up roses in a downcast year. *New York Times,* Section 3, p. 1.

Parker, I. (1989). *The crisis in modern social psychology, and how to end it.* London: Routledge.

Pfeffer, J. (1977). The ambiguity of leadership. *Academy of Management Review, 2*(1), 104–112.

Pfeffer, J., & Salancik, G. R. (1978). *The external control of organizations: A resource dependency perspective.* New York: Harper & Row.

Reuters. (2004, March 6). Martha Stewart Leaves Federal Court in New York. *Houston Chronicle.* p. 1. Retrieved March 6, 2004 from www.chron.com.

Schroeder, J. E. (2002). *Visual consumption.* London: Routledge.

Shamir, B., House, R. J., & Arthur, M. B. (1993). The motivational effects of charismatic leadership: A self-concept based theory. *Organization Science, 4*(4), 1–17.

Sontag, S. (2004, May 23). Regarding the torture of others. *New York Times Magazine.* Retrieved May 23, 2004, from www.nytimes.com

Stravato, M. Associated Press. (2004). A handcuffed Ken Lay is led into federal court in Houston. *San Francisco Chronicle.* July 7. p. A1.

The 10 greatest CEOs of all time. (2003, July 21). *Fortune,* p. 54.

Thompson, J. B. (2000). *Political scandal: Power and visibility in the media age.* London: Polity Press.

Thrift, N. (2000). Performing cultures in the new economy. *Annals of the association of American Geographers, 90*(4), 674–692.

Useem, J. (2002, November 18). Special issue: The CEO under fire: From heroes to goats...and back again? *Fortune,* p. 41.

Ventresca, M. J. (2004). *Rethinking legitimacy for institutional theories of organization: political phenomenology and pragmatism in action.* Working paper, Said Business School, University of Oxford.

Webster's new world dictionary of the American language. (1974). New York: William Collins and World Publishing.

CHAPTER 9

THE ROMANCE
OF LEADERSHIP AND THE
SOCIAL CONSTRUCTION
OF *FOLLOWERSHIP*

Mary Uhl-Bien
University of Central Florida

Rajnandini Pillai
California State University San Marcos

ABSTRACT

Over the years, leadership studies have tended to emphasize the thoughts, actions, and personas of leaders over those of followers; in addition, leadership situations have tended to be defined from the perspectives of leaders and not of followers (Meindl, 1995). As described by Meindl (1990, 1993), this preoccupation with leaders represents a "romance of leadership"—an infatuation with what leaders do, what they are able to accomplish, and the effects they have on our lives. In this chapter we suggest that a corollary to the romance of leadership may be the "subordination of followership," and that this subordination occurs in the social construction of followership. We propose that just as leadership is in the eye of the beholder, so is follower-

Follower-Centered Perspectives on Leadership, pages 187–209
Copyright © 2007 by Information Age Publishing
All rights of reproduction in any form reserved.

ship. We explore the meaning of the social construction of followership relative to followership concepts, implicit theories of followership, and group-level social construction, including social contagion and emergent norms. We also discuss different types of constructions of followership and why they have particular relevance in today's work context.

INTRODUCTION

Perhaps the most well known of Jim Meindl's many contributions to leadership is the concept of "romance of leadership," which describes leadership as a social construction process among followers (Meindl, Ehrlich, & Dukerich, 1985). The romance of leadership focuses on how views of leaders are constructed and represented in the thought systems of followers and the images of leaders that followers construct for one another (Meindl, 1990, 1993, 1995). Prominent in this approach is the idea that leadership is an emergent phenomenon—leadership is considered to have emerged when followers construct their experiences in terms of leadership concepts, that is, "when they interpret their relationship as having a leadership–followership dimension" (Meindl, 1995, p. 332). In other words, leadership is very much in the eyes of the beholder; followers, and not the leader, define it (Meindl, 1995).

While the romance of leadership represents a follower-centered approach to leadership (Meindl, 1995), an area that has not been explored relative to this approach is the social construction of *followership*. Research has examined how images and social contagion contribute to social constructions that followers make of *leaders* and their relationship to leaders; however, this is still somewhat leader-centric in its focus on the leader. It does not consider socially constructed views that may be created of followers and followership. For example, the images we create of leaders not only influence attributions about leadership but also attributions followers make about *themselves* and their own roles and participation in the leadership process. As noted by Meindl (1995), followers' orientation to the leader and the self-perception of followers are precursors to overt acts of followership. As such, considering how individuals make social constructions of followership may help us to understand not only the romance of leadership, but also the enactment of followership.

Therefore, the purpose of this chapter is to explore the social construction of followership: how views of followership are constructed and represented in the thought systems and meanings that followers construct for themselves and one another. We explore how implicit theories about followership are formed by the image that is held of what leadership and followership are, as interpreted and constructed by followers. We also address how social contagion and emergent norms among followers influence these constructions at the group level. We consider that just as the romance of leadership suggests that leaders and leadership issues often become the favored explanations for various events in and around organizations, perhaps followers and followership are conferred a more *subordinate* role in explanations of organizational events and outcomes. If this proposition is accepted, it could help explain many detrimental behaviors that occur among followers in the leadership process, such as filtering of communication, lack of initiative, denial of responsibility, overreliance on the leader for one's motivation, and so on. By addressing the romance of leadership relative to the social construction of followership, we hope to present romance of leadership as a more complete follower-centric perspective of leadership.

THE ROMANCE OF LEADERSIHP AND THE "SUBORDINATION" OF FOLLOWERSHIP

"Romance of leadership" refers to the tendency for actors and observers of events to attribute organizational outcomes to the acts of leaders. It reflects a potential bias, or false assumption making, about the importance of leadership in the functioning of groups and organizations (Meindl, 1995). "The romance of leadership notion asserts that people have a biased preference to explain the performance of groups and organizations—both good and bad—in terms of leadership" (Meindl, 2004, p. 464). This bias displays itself in highly romanticized, heroic views about leadership—what leaders do, what they are able to accomplish, and the general effects they have on our lives (Meindl et al., 1985).

One of the principal elements of this romanticized conception is that leadership is a central organizational process, the "premier force" in the scheme of organizational events and activities (Meindl et al., 1985, p. 79). It amounts to what might be considered "a faith in the potential if not in the actual efficacy" of leaders who hold positions of formal authority (p. 79). Meindl and colleagues (1985) describe it as a way people attempt to make sense out of organizationally relevant phenomena (cf., Weick, 1995). An important part of this sense making is a desire to generate causal attributions for organizational events and occurrences. For example, Meindl and colleagues found that interest in leadership in the popular business press and scholarly publications alike became more intense as "organized systems swung towards the extremes of their performance curves in either a positive or negative direction. It was as if people were using leadership as a way to explain performances that were extreme departures from more typical performance levels" (Meindl, 1990, p. 164).

Bluedorn (2002) notes that the desire to attribute causes for events to such things as the ability to rationally plan and to have plans carried out by implementers (i.e., managers, "leaders") represents a mindset that has permeated our thinking for so long it has become a basic underlying assumption in the general culture of management, and one of which we are largely unaware. This mindset can be traced back to worldviews that began their ascendancy in the 14th century (e.g., Newtonian logic) when new perspectives on order and causality began to emerge. This new scientific worldview was grounded in assumptions that events can be linearly attributed to simple causes (e.g., A causes event B; event B is proportionally related to A) and any event can be attributed to *something* (Marion, 1999).

In management, this worldview plays out in a mindset focused on planning, directing, and controlling, and an epistemology based on acts of leaders (Marion, in press). It sees organizations as intended to enable workers to efficiently produce useful outcomes on a large scale, which is accomplished when leaders focus on rational analysis, forecasting, and the installation of negative feedback processes aimed at the removal of uncertainty and conflict to sustain equilibrium adaptation (Streatfield, 2001). Management's job is to control the movement of the organizational system. They do this by monitoring and managing the system, from the present to the future, to realize their chosen goals or visions through paths that are intended, selected, and planned by the hierarchically most powerful. The assumption is that the goal and the path are largely known and they are formulated by management intention so that the organization progresses in a way that is stable, regular, predictable, and, in principle, certain (Streatfield, 2001).

Contrary to this view are perspectives that question the ability of management to exert control over the activities and outcomes of their organizations (Lieberson & O'Connor, 1972; Marion & Uhl-Bien, 2001; Salancik & Meindl, 1984). These perspectives recognize that powerful environmental and nonlinear forces, combined with a large number of constituencies and interacting agents, affect an organization's functioning in ways that are often unpredictable and uncontrollable (Finkelstein, 2002). They see organizations as interconnected patterns of action in time and geographic space characterized by continuity and transformation at the same time (Streatfield, 2001). From this perspective, managers cannot control the paradoxical movement of continuity and transformation, because it is impossible to be in control of it. Rather, managerial action forms the movement of the organization, while at the same time being formed by it (Streatfield, 2001). As Vecchio (1997) argues, a strong case may be made for the fact that when we commonly speak of effective leadership, we are really speaking of effective followership. This is because we measure a manager's effectiveness by examining the performance of his or her unit. The performance of a unit, however, has more to do with the skills and contributions of the followers than the leader. Subordinate talent and motivation, according to Vecchio, can have far more to do with the unit's performance than the leader's efforts.

Although management is likely aware of these limitations on their ability to be "in control" (Streatfield, 2001), they must still deal with stakeholders, who are often, and likely unknowingly (Bluedorn, 2002), mired in the traditional worldview that maintains assumptions of control. As noted by Salancik and Meindl (1984), these stakeholders hold management accountable for organizational outcomes and will withdraw support if their interests go unsatisfied (even though management may not be able to control the factors that determine these outcomes). Therefore, instead of acknowledging the complex and uncontrollable reality of their situations, managers engage in strategic attempts to maintain an illusion of control (Salancik & Meindl, 1984)—a "public face," even though the private face inside the organization may be quite different (Jermier, Slocum, Fry, Gaines, 1991). For example, they promote the belief among constituencies that they direct organizational activities and outcomes by providing attributions that give "the appearance of efficacy in a world in which control is often elusive" (Salancik & Meindl, 1984). They use language that conveys the sense that they are actively taking steps to "wrestle their unruly environment" (Salancik & Meindl, 1984) in strategic attempts to communicate to constituents that the firm's outcomes are intentional and planned (Eccles, Nohria, & Berkley, 1992). This can be taken to extremes, as in the last days of the life of Enron in 2001 when CEO Kenneth Lay suggested that the balance sheet was strong and that the company would make the numbers, shortly before it filed for bankruptcy protection (http://money.cnn.com/2006/01/11/news/companies/enron_fortune/index.htm).

For followers, maintenance of this illusion could reinforce a belief in human agency and control that provides security and comfort, particularly in the face of uncertainty. Ken Lay's pronouncements were designed to serve this very purpose and reassure not only followers but also other stakeholders of Enron. Streatfield (2001) described a situation in which people who displayed self-confidence were deemed powerful because they conveyed the illusion that they knew more than others. This illusion acted to alleviate the anxieties of others around them:

> In the merger situation, people seen as powerful because of the self-confidence they displayed and the connections they were known to have, were able to exert some kind of controlling influence over others. It seemed that their self-confidence provided a solid sense of presence, allowing the others to feel that this person had a way of handling the anxiety of the uncertain situation.... In a sense, these powerful people might become containers for other's

anxieties about the future. Somehow we vest capabilities in these people to control the uncertainties that cause us to feel concern in our lives. (p. 87)

Perhaps for reasons such as these, the romance of leadership is a powerful and deeply embedded phenomenon (Meindl, 1990, 1993, 1995), one that may serve many purposes in organizational life. A consequence of the romanticized notion, however, and one that has not been fully explored, is the effect it may have on followership. For example, when the image is condoned that performance is due to *leaders*, the contribution of followers is diminished. To the extent that followers' contributions are acknowledged, they would likely be seen as due to the outstanding behaviors and skills of the *leader* who was able to motivate and inspire followers, as in the transformational and charismatic leadership perspectives. This, in essence, has a demeaning effect on the role of followership and relegates followers to bit players in the performance. Therefore, it is possible that a corollary to the "romance of leadership" may well be the "subordination of followership."

The subordination of followership can be seen in the images that are conveyed of leadership. In these images, followers are often portrayed as sheep, unquestioningly and blindly obeying management's command (Dixon & Westbrook, 2003). They subordinate their interests for the good of the organization. As described by Howell and Shamir (2005), followers in charismatic relationships are willing to transcend their self-interests for the sake of the collective, engage in self-sacrifice for the mission, identify with the vision of the leader and show strong emotional attachment to him or her, internalize the leader's values and goals, and demonstrate strong commitment to the leader's values and goals. It is especially in the context of charismatic leadership that followers are given the least weight and the focus is almost entirely on the leader (Meindl, 1990). This is because charismatic leaders are often associated with a crisis and the feelings of uncertainty engendered by a crisis call for leadership that is bold, decisive, and visionary (Bligh, Kohles, & Pillai, 2005; Pillai & Meindl, 1998). Other images often convey the idea that good followers show passive, blind, unreflective, and committed obedience to the leader (Frisina, 2005).

Perhaps these images and this mindset are also so prevalent because they serve management's need to maintain effective coordination and control structures in the organization. "It may be that the romance and mystery surrounding leadership concepts are critical for sustaining followership and that they contribute significantly to the responsiveness to the needs and goals of the collective organization" (Meindl et al., 1985, p. 100). It may also be that they serve to clarify expectations of followers; followers may welcome the responsibility for outcomes being ascribed to the leader because it diffuses their own responsibility and reduces the pressure on them to be accountable. This may of course depend on factors such as followers' personality characteristics. For instance, followers with an external locus of control are much more likely to avoid taking responsibility for poor performance and welcome the opportunity to blame the leader.

An alternative perspective, however, may lie in the social construction of leadership and followership. It may be that the subordination of followership is inherent in the utmost core of how individuals see leadership, and that the "enactment" of followership is viewed as taking a lower position to another. It is possible that this interpretation emerges through a process of socialization from a very early age through exposure to heroic tales of leaders, comic books with superhero themes, movies, and, of course, the playground where roles are clearly defined. The very construction of leadership and followership may create inherent status differentials that individuals, singularly and collectively (i.e., groups), interpret to mean showing deference to another. This deference can be interpreted and enacted in multiple forms, but by far the most predominant appears to be subordination.

THE SOCIAL CONSTRUCTION OF FOLLOWERSHIP

As described by Chen and Meindl (1991), a social constructionist view suggests that much about the way we understand organizations lies in the way we construct meaning regarding events. These constructions are based on implicit theories we hold and social interactions we have with others who affect the availability, salience, vividness, and value of the information we receive. This process occurs at two levels, an individual level and a group level (Meindl, 1995). At the individual level, situational and individual difference variables influence the construction of leadership within individual actors. At the group level, the constructions of individual members combine to become a collaborative, negotiated, intersubjectively shared system of leadership concepts that link and unify followers within the group (Meindl, 1995). Through these processes, followers understand themselves and one another relative to the leader and the task. The outcome of social construction is commitment to the leader and self-defined followership, both of which serve as precursors to overt acts of followership (Meindl, 1995).

According to a social construction approach, "leadership is considered to have emerged when followers construct their experience in terms of leadership concepts" (Meindl, 1995, p. 332). An issue that has not been explicitly addressed, however, is how followers construct their experience in terms of *followership* concepts. This view presents an interesting twist on prior leadership perspectives. Rather than focusing on leaders and their roles and behaviors, the focus becomes the followers and their roles and behavior; that is, *leadership is enacted when followers begin seeing themselves (and acting) as followers.* But what does this mean? How do followers begin seeing themselves as followers (i.e., How is followership socially constructed and enacted)?

While an immense amount of work has focused on leadership, we know surprisingly little about followership. Leadership has traditionally been considered in isolation, as if the behavior of followers were irrelevant (*The Economist,* 2004). As noted in *The Economist* (2004), "As a concept, 'followership' scarcely exists" (p. 78). Berg (1998) worries that the increasing preoccupation with leadership runs the risk of relegating followership to the dim, gray, and often shameful back alleys of organizational life. Howell and Shamir (2005) concur: "Beyond paying lip service to the importance of followers, few scholars have attempted to theoretically specify and empirically assess the role of followers in the leadership process" (p. 96). Therefore, we attempt here to identify what consideration of *followership concepts* in the social construction of leadership may entail.

Followership

As mentioned above, from a social construction perspective, followership occurs when individuals begin to see themselves as followers—when followers construct their experiences in terms of followership concepts. A simple way of defining someone as a follower is by viewing him/her as a "subordinate" in a hierarchical structure. This is the traditional view of organizational leadership study and the basis for the vast majority of leadership research (Bedeian & Hunt, 2006). From this perspective, subordinates are followers of managerial leaders, with leaders responsible for defining direction, establishing rules and regulations for how to behave, and using authority to enforce expected behaviors of followers.

However, as Meindl (1995) points out, leadership is not limited to formal, hierarchical relationships—it lies in the figures identified as leaders by followers. Vecchio (1997) states that being a follower and being a subordinate are not equivalent notions, as being a leader and being a supervisor are also not equivalent terms. Therefore, we must distinguish between being a follower and a subordinate. For the purpose of discussion below, we define the former as someone who socially constructs leadership and identifies him/herself as a follower in that construction; we define the latter as a person holding and acting in a formal role in an organization, that of being a "subordinate" or "direct report" to a manager. They are different in that the former is an individual's construction of leadership, whereas the latter is a formally defined role. As we will see in the discussion below, much of the social construction of leadership and followership will likely

involve being subordinate, but when we use that term we will not be referring to the formal role but rather the *enacted* role that individuals take on
in the social construction of followership.

Social Construction: Individual Level

How, then, do we know when followership has been socially constructed—what does it mean to say that followers construct their experience in terms of followership concepts?

According to Frisina (2005), "Followership is the art or condition of following a leader. To be a follower is to *subordinate* one's self to another" (p.
12, emphasis added). By definition, subordinating one's self means putting
oneself in a lower or inferior rank or class, making oneself subservient, or
subduing (*dictionary.com*).

While it may seem odd that individuals would want to subordinate
themselves to another, Kets de Vries (1993) describes it as a fundamental
human need:

> All community-dwelling creatures need leaders; there is a leader in every
> pack, both of wolves and wolf cubs.... When people are deprived of leaders,
> whether nominal or actual, they will search for them, particularly in times of
> crisis and rapid change. This fundamental need operates on a huge sliding
> scale...ranging from the harmless to the devastating. An obvious implication
> of this need for leaders is a predisposition to follow; indeed it might be said
> that humans must do one or the other—lead or follow—in whatever social
> context we find ourselves. (pp. 1–2)

Our need for leaders may also be due to our demands for certainty and
orderliness in an unorderly world, our search for meaning in an existential
world, and our desire for importance and achievement in demanding societal contexts (Lipman-Blumen, 2005).

These psychological needs send us in search of authority figures
(Sankowsky, 1995) who can offer us comfort and promise to satisfy our
longings:

> The most relevant psychological needs are those for authority figures to
> replace our parents and other early caretakers; for membership in the
> human community; for a conception of ourselves as significant beings
> engaged daily in noble endeavours in a meaningful world; for the hope that
> we can live at the centre of action; where powerful leaders congregate to
> make important decisions. Our fears that we are personally powerless to chal-
> lenge bad leaders also contribute to our reluctance to confront them. (Lip-
> man-Blumen, 2005, p. 2)

Follower needs may operate in combination with implicit theories to form followers' social constructions. For followers, implicit theories represent cognitive categories, or schemas, that provide them with an underlying structure of meaning regarding what followership is; these theories persist over time, shaping followers' perceptions, interpretations, and behaviors (cf., Epitropaki & Martin, 2004; Jelinek, Smircich, & Hirsch, 1983). Followership schemas are developed through socialization and past experiences with leaders and other followers, stored in memory, and activated when followers interact with a person in a leadership position and/or with other followers (cf., Lord & Maher, 1993). Followers categorize themselves as followers based on the perceived match between their behavior or character and the prototypical attributes of a preexisting followership category (cf., Epitropaki & Martin, 2004; Rush & Russell, 1988).

Follower schemas would be invoked when followers recognize the presence of a leader. This recognition would occur when followers begin to see another as more competent or capable than oneself such that the "follower" allows the other (the "leader") to make decisions and influence him or her. At its core, followership involves deferring to the directives, decisions, or desires of another, thereby giving another higher status and legitimacy in determining the course of events (cf., Hogg, 2001). As described by Meindl (1995), in the instances when leadership is constructed, followers perceive "that they are indeed followers, who are committed to the causes, missions, goals, and aspirations that the leader presumably embodies, exemplifies, and symbolizes" (p. 333). Followers self-define their role and their commitments to "the personification of causes, as embodied in the figure of the leader" (p. 333).

In accordance with such implicit theories, prototypical followership behaviors would likely involve some form of deference to the leader. Once deference is gone, so is leadership (if leadership involves actively influencing others, then followership involves allowing oneself to be influenced). There are many forms of deference subordinates can display, and these can vary in strength. Followers can agree with the leader and go along with the group; they can comply with requests, suggestions, and orders (Hogg, 2001); they can show commitment and loyalty to the leader's cause; or they can internalize the leader's vision and actively work to support and promote it. As long as the follower continues to comply, the leader has legitimacy and status. If a follower begins resisting, they only continue to be a follower to the extent that they allow the leader some form of influence over their behavior (since we are not talking about a formal role, once a follower resists completely, he/she would no longer be a follower).

Proposition 1:   *Prototypical followership behaviors involve some form of deference to the leader; once deference is completely gone, so is leadership (and followership).*

While leadership can be constructed in many ways, so can followership. In the context of manager–subordinate leadership relationships, the construction of followership would be grounded in hierarchy and authority. In hierarchy, perceptions of leadership and power are often linked to perceptions of responsibility—those in higher positions have responsibility for and authority over those below them (Vanderslice, 1988). In such cases, followers, who recognize another as a leader, will likely see that individual as having greater responsibility and accountability for outcomes. This diffuses the follower's own sense of responsibility-taking.

This reduced responsibility-taking may have implications for motivation, initiative, and performance (Vanderslice, 1988). Because in managerial contexts "leaders" (i.e., managers) are often assigned the responsibility for increasing the motivation and performance of subordinates, "followers" (i.e., subordinates) in this context would be expected to develop constructions of followership where the leader, rather than the follower, is responsible for motivation and performance. Furthermore, in this construction of followership, if motivation is not occurring, the followers would see a "leadership" problem rather their own problem, and the less motivated they become the more they construct a leadership (rather than a followership) problem. As described by Vanderslice (1988), there is substantial research evidence that when labels are introduced (e.g., leader and follower), individuals adjust their beliefs about themselves, and consequently their performance, to the expectations provoked by those labels. When the labels of leader and follower are introduced, therefore, followers lower their expectations and their own behavior to meet the label (e.g., offering less initiative and less creative input to processes that they perceive are the ultimate responsibility of the leader). "Subordinate labels create negative self-expectations that lead to decreased task persistence, poorer performance, and consequently lowered self-esteem, decreased self-expectations, etc....[as such] the dynamics created by role-related status differences may be working counter to their purposes" (Vanderslice, 1988, p. 680).

In this way, the social construction of followership may differentiate leaders and followers on a dimension associated with power, thereby creating a status difference between the leader and follower. As noted by Frost (1987), "relationship power" is a function of the meaning introduced into exchanges between actors. When another individual is given higher status, such as perceived expertise, the status becomes a resource, and enhances the value attributed to those with the status in exchanges with other members. Frost also notes that attributions such as these can be intentionally managed by actors to maintain as well as alter the balance of power in the dependency relationship. Therefore, status-based structural differentiation carries implications for follower constructions of behavior. For example, referring to Mulder's (1971) findings, Vanderslice (1988) reported that the greater the discrepancy in perceived expertise, the more those low in expertise withdrew from the decision-making process and believed themselves to be unqualified to participate.

Hierarchical constructions of followership may also influence how followers perceive they should communicate with leaders. Followers may be hesitant to speak up or make suggestions to the leader for fear of being seen as criticizing or attempting to usurp the leader's power (Vanderslice, 1988). Consistent with research that shows that individuals in lower hierarchical rank demonstrate strong propensity to distort messages to those in higher positions (Dansereau & Markham, 1987), they may filter or frame their communications in the presence of the leader to make it more positive in content (Back et al., 1950). This is aimed perhaps at positively reinforcing the leader's self-concept (Vanderslice, 1988) or appearing in conformance with the leader's perspective.

Contrary to these constructions would be views of followership as "dynamic" (Latour & Rast, 2004) or "courageous" (Chaleff, 1995). From this perspective, followers would see themselves more as partners, participants, co-leaders, and co-followers (Dixon & Westbrook, 2003). As opposed to hierarchical constructions of followership, these perceptions of followers could be seen as collaborative constructions, somewhat akin to the third stage in leader–member–exchange theory (Graen & Uhl-Bien, 1995) where followers and leaders partner effectively for the benefit of the group. Followers have a relationship that goes beyond the traditional hierarchically defined work relationship with the leader. According to Chaleff (1995), the concept behind his theory of followership is not synonymous with subordinate:

> Followers engage body, mind, soul, and spirit in the commonly held purpose and vision of the organization. Being a subordinate is mechanical or physical; it is being under the control of superiors as if in some hypnotic trance. Being a follower is a condition, not a position. (Dixon & Westbrook, 2003, p. 20)

Consistent with this view, followership behaviors would involve such things as the courage to assume responsibility (e.g., demonstrate ownership, generate new ideas, initiate actions), the courage to serve (e.g., unburden the leader, act as a team player), the courage to challenge (e.g., initiate confrontation when appropriate, open, honest), the courage to participate in transformation (e.g., champion change), and the courage to take moral action (e.g., "our duty to obey, our duty to disobey, and our duty to take positive action"; Kelley, 1991) (Chaleff, 1995; Dixon & Westbrook, 2003). According to Kelley (1991), such followership would be based on critical thinking and participation. Critical thinking involves an active mental debate with things or events that we could otherwise process at face value (Latour & Rast, 2004); follower behaviors based on critical thinking would involve using an active, independent mind to confront and scrutinize situations to consider all implications and possibilities. Participation involves behaviors in which the follower anticipates requirements and plans accordingly (vs. passive followership behaviors, which remain trapped in a perpetually reactive mode) (Latour & Rast, 2004). Thus, in this view, it would be possible for followers to see themselves as a bulwark against a leader's excesses because their constructions of followership would include critically and collaboratively assessing a leader's values and directives.

Proposition 2:   *Follower deference to the leader may be constructed in different ways; followers may construct their roles based on strong status differentials or followers may construct their role as partners, participants, co-leaders, and/or co-followers.*

Proposition 3:   *In manager–subordinate contexts, followers are more likely to construct their roles based on status differentials than as partners, participants, co-leaders, and/or co-followers, due to the hierarchical nature of manager–subordinate relationships.*

Proposition 4:   *Followers who construct their roles based on status differentials will exhibit greater reduced responsibility-taking (i.e., less initiative, more denial or responsibility, overreliance on the leader for one's motivation) and greater filtering of communication than followers who construct their role as partners, participants, co-leaders, and/or co-followers.*

Social Construction: Group Level

At the group level, the constructions of individual members combine to become a collaborative, negotiated, intersubjectively shared (Meindl, 1995) system of understanding about followership and what it means in the group. This shared system is a result of lateral social influence processes, or "social contagion" among followers (Meindl, 1990, 1993). Social contagion occurs when people change their behavior as a result of interaction with others (Brett & Stroh, 2003; Grosser, Polansky, & Lippitt, 1951). The social comparisons that occur in this process contribute not just to the transmission of norms but also to their escalation (Latane, Ilgen, & Hulin, 2000).

From a follower-centered perspective of leadership, social contagion changes the focus from behaviors of the leader to contagious expressions of followers (Meindl, 1995). Followers will make attributions based on the actions of peers and coworkers who display certain orientations and motivations and will be mobilized into action (Meindl, 1990). Followers will also react to influence the leader as members of a group, not only as individuals, and their level of support may increase or reduce the leader's self-confidence and their readiness to continue to invest in the group's collective mission (Howell & Shamir, 2005). This perspective suggests that the interacting individual constructions of followers, in reaction to the leader and the overall context, determine how followership is constructed and enacted. But what factors would influence this "contagious" expression of followership? Below we describe multiple views of social construction that have been presented in the social psychology literature: social contagion, emergent norm theory, and social identity theory.

Social Contagion

As described in Levy and Nail (1993), contagion is the spread of behavior from one person to another or to a whole group (Redl, 1949). Factors that determine contagion may include the status of the initiator, the "value ratings" (i.e., relative importance) of the behavior in the "group code" (i.e., prevailing norms), and the extent to which the behavior "gives vent" to the suppressed needs of the largest number of group members with high status (Redl, 1949, as reported in Levy & Nail, 1993). In a test of the relationship among contagion and status in the group, Polansky, Lippitt and Redl (1950) showed that among the children in the study, those higher in prestige were more frequently the initiators of behavioral contagion and direct influence attempts (Levy & Nail, 1993). Furthermore, although the higher prestige children were more susceptible to influence through contagion, they were also better able to resist direct influence. As described by Hogg (2001), within a group, people who are perceived to occupy the most prototypical position are believed to best embody the behaviors to which other, less prototypical members, conform.

Another perspective of contagion is offered by Turner and Killian (1957), who propose that "milling" is the basis of social contagion and represents the fundamental process through which a common mood is developed in a collectivity. Milling is a search for socially sanctioned meaning in a relatively unstructured situation (Levy & Nail, 1993). When an individual is placed in an ambiguous situation, he or she seeks social cues in the reactions of others to help define the situation (Levy & Nail, 1993). This search for social cues leads to milling, which then results in the sensitization of individuals to each other, the development of a common mood, and a collective definition of the situation. For instance, during a crisis, group members may look to one another and decide that the situation calls for intervention by someone who is seen to possess extraordinary qualities and the only unique solution to the crisis (i.e., a charismatic leader). Followers may recognize their own helplessness in the situation after taking their cues from one another. Immunity to social contagion, according to Turner and Killian (1957), is a function of the extent to which the situation is subjectively well defined and the rigidity of attitudes, as well as the intensity of motivation of those individuals who do not succumb (Levy & Nail, 1993). This may explain why charismatic leaders may be unsuccessful in stable situations: Followers may have a shared understanding that they do not need them in such situations.

Taken in combination, this line of reasoning suggests that social construction of followership through contagion might be influenced by: (1) the status of followers, (2) the salience of the behavior to group members, (3) the ambiguity of the situation (and the extent to which a member is new to the group), and (4) the consequences for actions. Specifically, high-status members may be more influential in determining the emergent norms for behavior among followers, and may be more resistant to change regarding what the norm should be (cf., Polansky et al., 1950). Moreover, the influence of high-status members in the construction process may be stronger when situations arise in which followers are unsure how to act (e.g., in situations of change, when the follower or leader is new to a group), and when the actions carry potentially important consequences.

Emergent Norm Theory

In contrast to contagion, a perspective that may be more appropriate to group construction is emergent norm theory (Turner, 1964). Though contagion and emergent norm theories both developed as explanations of crowd behavior, they have implications for other collective behavior, such as followership in groups. Emergent norm theory views collective behavior as regulated by a social norm that arises in ambiguous situations when individuals turn to others for cues as to the appropriate course of action (e.g., milling; Turner & Killian, 1957) (Levy & Nail, 1993). It is a view of intragroup, rather than between-group, processes (Turner, 1964), and has several important differences from contagion (described as follows by Levy & Nail, 1993): (1) contagion views participant behavior as unanimous, whereas emergent norm theory asserts a differential member expression; (2) contagion views behavior as arising spontaneously, whereas emergent norm theory sees it as a consequence of the imposition of conformity under the impact of a norm; (3) contagion is limited to arousing situations, whereas emergent norm theory is equally applicable to subdued and excited states; (4) contagion focuses primarily on the transmission of the dominant emotion in a crowd (e.g., collective), whereas emergent norm theory emphasizes the transmission of norms; and (5) contagion stresses the importance of anonymity as an antecedent to crowd (e.g., collective) behavior, while emergent norm theory maintains that crowd behavior is a function of a member's recognizable identity.

Turner and Killian (1957) noted that whereas contagion (and convergence) theories explain collective behavior as arising from the individual and then spreading to the group, emergent norms reflect the imposition of new group norms on the individual (Levy & Nail, 1993). Turner (1964) did not deny the existence of contagion and convergence; however, his central proposition was that the origin of all collective behavior arises from emergent norms (Levy & Nail, 1993). Thus, emergent norm theory describes a group process of developing and applying agreed-upon norms for behavior in the group. It suggests that social construction of followership in groups may be influenced by individuals who show differential expressions of behavior, may be based on recognizable identities of individual members of the group, and may be fundamentally a process of imposing group norms on individual members of the group.

Social Identity Theory

In addition to contagion and emergent norm theory, social identity and self-categorization theory may also be informative regarding construction in groups. Hogg (2001) describes a social identity theory of leadership, which views leadership as a group process that arises from the social categorization and depersonalization associated with social identity. From this perspective, prototype-based depersonalization and the behavior of followers play a critical role. Followers empower individuals as leaders—they create a status differential between the leader and the rest of the group and set up conditions conducive to the use (and abuse) of power (Hogg, 2001). Leadership, then, is about how some individuals or cliques have disproportionate power and influence to set the agenda, define identity, and mobilize people to achieve collective goals. Leadership is very much a group process, with leaders having disproportionate influence, which is given to them by followers through consensual prestige or the granting of power.

Hogg (2001) further suggests that the self-concept of followers may influence how strongly entrenched leadership becomes. When followers are self-conceptually uncertain about things that matter, they are more inclined to identify with groups, particularly with groups that have clearly focused and consensual prototypes (these groups can often be extreme). In these conditions of high self-conceptual uncertainty, a group dynamic can emerge where members, in search of simple and distinct prototypes, identify highly with a strong leader and vision and work to purify the group of deviants (Hogg, 2001). However, as Howell and Shamir (2005) argue, followers with high self-conceptual clarity may choose a leader and decide to follow him or her based on the extent to which the leader embodies the followers' values and identities.

Thus, a clear theme emerges from this literature that could inform us regarding intragroup social construction of followership. First, the development of group norms is a process that likely becomes more salient in situations of ambiguity and high importance behavioral outcomes (Redl, 1949). It is also likely to be influenced by status, with high-status members having more influence on, and being more resistant to, the development of norms (Polansky et al., 1950). Newer members will engage in greater search for group norms, though some newer members may quickly become influential in the process of norm development if they are believed to represent highly prototypical behavior (Hogg, 2001). Moreover, the followers in the group will demonstrate differential expressions and have recognizable identities in this process (Turner, 1964), with a probable hierarchical status order emerging among followers. Once a norm is constructed, imposition of conformity will introduce standards to act in accordance with the norm (Turner, 1964), and deviance from the norm will generate strong pressure or action from other group members (Hogg, 2001).

Proposition 5:   *At the group level, social constructions of followership (e.g., based on strong status differentials or as partners, participants, co-leaders, co-followers) will be positively associated with the individual constructions of high-status and/or "highly prototypical" (Hogg, 2001) group members.*

Proposition 6:   *The influence of high-status group members in the social construction of followership will be stronger in situations in which followers are unsure how to act (e.g., in situations of change, when the follower or leader is new to a group, etc.), and when the actions carry potentially important consequences.*

Proposition 7:   *Individuals who try to construct followership roles contrary to the socially constructed group norms will be pressured by other group members to act in conformance with the group construction.*

CONCLUSION

In this chapter we explore the social construction of followership, at both the individual and group levels. We suggest that just as individuals socially construct leadership, they socially construct followership, and this construction is a process of collective emergent norm development and enforcement. Therefore, both leadership *and* followership are "in the eyes of the beholders."

Consideration of followership is becoming increasingly important as we move further into the 21st century knowledge era. This era requires full deployment of the workforce to ensure competitiveness and survival in a rapidly changing world. This means that both leaders and followers must be fully engaged and committed to the collective mission. Sometimes, this process might best be led by leaders, but at other times or in specific contexts this process can be initiated by followers who empower the leader to achieve the organization's collective mission. Unfortunately, in the formal study of leadership, the word "follower" has a pejorative connotation (Frisina, 2005). It connotes a central leader who serves as the source of guidance, motivation, and authority; followers are labeled as "passive or lacking the right stuff, or worse, as inferior and lacking drive and ambition" (Frisina, 2005, p. 12). As noted by Howell and Shamir (2005), followers in charismatic relationships have been described in the literature as flammable material (with oxygen a conducive environment): "by viewing followers as 'flammable material' waiting to be ignited by the leader, these scholars portray followers in a limited and passive role" (p. 99). While the traditional constructions of leadership may be intended to enhance the organization by creating alignment, coordination, and efficiency, as discussed by Vanderslice (1988), they may be working counter to the very purposes they intend to serve.

We suggest that the negative connotation of followership is not necessarily the creation of leaders but, rather, may be something followers create themselves:

> Followers provide their leader with power by following his or her lead. To take away this power, they need only to exercise their right to disobey their leader. Although disobedience is often met with ruthless force, eventually, like water wearing down a stone, it will prevail and then the leader who was unreachable will shrink down to nothing.... Followers can evaporate a leader's mask of power merely by dis-believing in it. Authority does not reside in those who issue orders; rather, authority lies with*in* the *responses* of persons to whom those orders are addressed.... Even in totalitarian states, followers hold significant power, but only if they are ready to *act* on it. Holocaust and genocide continue to this day despite hand wringing because some of us are unwilling to make the sacrifice to confront it. We turn our eyes away because in some ghastly way it benefits us perhaps by merely creating a distraction for those who would challenge us. (Ba Banutu-Gomez, 2004, p. 147)

Because it is socially constructed by followers, however, it may also be socially *re*constructed by followers:

> We do not have to wait for valid leaders to appear to tell us it is time to offer the gift of our own exemplary followership to each other. There is no need for us to be hypnotized by the myth of leadership created by those who would have us remain passive instead of active. We only have our own selfishness to blame for our powerlessness. We willingly gave up our power to buy freedom from risk, responsibility and accountability. (Ba Banutu-Gomez, 2004, p. 147)

Such *re*construction may be difficult given that views of followership may be deeply imbedded both in the culture and meaning surrounding leadership and followership. Based on long-standing mindsets regarding the nature of order and control (Bluedorn, 2002), the "romanticization of leadership" and "subordination of followership" are powerful concepts that align with our needs and desires to generate causal attributions for events around us. From very young ages, we are socialized into this order and the value systems that accompany it (e.g., that leadership has higher value than followership). This need for leaders and willingness to become passive in their presence may also have a basis in deep psychological needs (Kets de Vries, 1993; Lipman-Blumen, 2005).

Therefore, for understandable reasons, people tend to exaggerate the importance of leaders and downplay their own role in the continuities or changes of society (Rosenau, 2004). They fail to appreciate that the course of events is sustained by the interactions that endlessly unfold between leaders' conduct and followers' attitudes and actions (Rosenau, 2004). However, this view may be misleading, as the value of leaders is really determined by the social constructions of followers. We can hope that the spate of scandals involving "larger than life" leaders such as Bernie Ebbers of Worldcom and Jeff Skilling and Kenneth Lay of Enron and the popularity of the Level 5 leadership paradigm (Collins, 2001), in which humble leaders give all the credit for their success to their teams, will spur interest in follower-centered approaches to leadership. Leadership has its limits; perhaps it is time to focus on the other side of the equation.

Given the dearth of understanding about how followers construct these attitudes and actions, we need to better examine and explore the social construction and enactment of followership. We need to generate theories and empirical investigations of followership (Dixon and Westbrook, 2003), develop follower-competency-based approaches in practice (Latour & Rast, 2004), and better theoretically specify and empirically assess the role of followers in the leadership process (Howell & Shamir, 2005).

For example, future research could examine the ways in which individuals and groups enact followership. Such work could explore the role of power distance in the social construction of followership. At the group level, one scenario could involve followers developing norms of conformity and compliance with the leader with high power distance and strong pressure to not speak up about issues. Another scenario could involve intragroup power distance, in which the distance occurs among followers rather than the leader and follower. This construction would be one that is based on fear, subordination, strong conceptions of hierarchy, and pressure to not take initiative or outstep the bounds of "followership." This effect could be amplified in cultures that are traditionally characterized as having high power distance.

Alternatively, constructions could occur in which high-status members see followership as a "partnership" or a "collaborative" effort in which it is their responsibility to demonstrate initiative, communicate openly with the leader, maintain balances of power, and work together to further collective norms. In such cases, high-status individuals could pressure other members to demonstrate this behavior, establishing a construction of "dynamic" or "courageous" followership (Chaleff, 1995). The implication for the leader would be to engage the high-status individuals in the group in order to successfully influence other members of the group. High-status members could "infect" all group members with the desire to trust in the leader and demonstrate commitment and citizenship.

In sum, though Meindl (1995) offers a follower-centered perspective of leadership, this perspective still focused on the constructions of leadership rather than followership. In this chapter, we suggested that Meindl's view can be further augmented through a discussion of how followers construct "followership." We believe this chapter offers ideas to help start this process, but future research is needed to more fully delineate a social construction model of followership.

REFERENCES

Ba Banutu-Gomez, M. (2004). Great leaders teach exemplary followership and serve as servant leaders. *Journal of American Academy of Business, Cambridge*, pp. 143–151.

Back, K. W., Festinger, L., Hymovitch, V., Kelley, H. H., Schachter, S., & Thibaut, J. W. (1950). The methodology of rumor transmission. *Human Relations, 3*, 307–312.

Bedeian, A., & Hunt, J.G. (2006). Academic amnesia and vestigial assumptions of our forefathers. *The Leadership Quarterly, 17*(2), 190–205.

Berg, D. N. (1998). Resurrecting the muse: Followership in organizations. In E. B. Klein, G. Faith, & P. Herr (Eds.) *The psychodynamics of leadership* (pp. 27–52). Madison, CT: Psychosocial Press.

Bligh, M. C., Kohles, J. C., & Pillai, R. (2005). Crisis and charisma in the California recall election. *Leadership, 1*(3), 323–352.

Bluedorn, A. (2002). Images of planning, performance, and other theory. In F. Yammarino & F. Dansereau (Eds.), *The many faces of multi-level issues* (Vol. 1, pp. 67–72). New York: Elsevier Science/JAI Press.

Brett, J. M., & Stroh, L. K. (2003). Working 61 plus hours a week: Why do managers do it? *Journal of Applied Psychology, 88*(1), 67.

Chaleff, I. (1995). *The courageous follower: Standing up to and for our leaders*. San Francisco: Berrett-Koehler.

Chen, C. C., & Meindl, J. R. (1991). The construction of leadership images in the popular press: The case of donald burr and people express. *Administrative Science Quarterly, 36*(4), 521.

Collins, J. (2001). *Good to great.* New York: HarperCollins.

Dansereau, F., & Markham, S. E. (1987). Superior–subordinate communication: Multiple levels of analysis. In F. M. Jablin, L. L. Putnam, K. H. Roberts, & L. W. Porter (Eds.), *Handbook of organizational communication: An interdisciplinary perspective* (pp. 343–388). Newbury Park, CA: Sage.

Dixon, G., & Westbrook, J. (2003). Followers revealed. *Engineering Management Journal, 15*(1), 19–25.

Eccles, R. G., Nohria, N., & Berkley, J. D. (1992). *Beyond the hype: Rediscovering the essence of management.* Boston: Harvard Business School Press.

Epitropaki, O., & Martin, R. (2004). Implicit leadership theories in applied settings: Factor structure, generalizability, and stability over time. *Journal of Applied Psychology* (Vol. 89, pp. 293–310). Washington, DC: American Psychological Association.

Finkelstein, S. (2002). Planning in organizations: One vote for complexity. In F. Yammarino & F. Dansereau (Eds.), *The many faces of multi-level issues* (Vol. 1, pp. 73–80). New York: Elsevier Science/JAI Press.

Frisina, M. E. (2005, March). Learn to lead by following. *Nursing Management,* p. 12.

Frost, P. (1987). Power, politics, and influence. In F. M. Jablin, L. L. Putnam, K. H. Roberts, & L. W. Porter (Eds.), *Handbook of organizational communication: An interdisciplinary perspective* (pp. 503–548). Newbury Park: Sage.

Graen, G. B., & Uhl-Bien, M. (1995). Relationship based approach to leadership: Development of leader–member exchange theory over 25 years: Applying a multi-level, multi-domain perspective. *The Leadership Quarterly, 6,* 219–247

Grosser, D., Polansky, N., & Lippitt, R. (1951). A laboratory study of behavioral contagion. *Human Relations, 4,* 115.

Hogg, M. A. (2001). A social identity theory of leadership. *Personality and social psychology review, 5*(3), 184–200.

Howell, J. M., & Shamir, B. (2005). The role of followers in the charismatic leadership process: Relationships and their consequences. *Academy of Management Review, 30*(1), 96–112.

Jelinek, M., Smircich, L., & Hirsch, P. (1983). Introduction: A code of many colors. *Administrative Science Quarterly, 28*(3), 331–338.

Jermier, J. M., Slocum, J. W., Fry, L. W., & Gaines, J. (1991). Organizational subcultures in a soft bureaucracy: Resistance behind the myth and facade of an official culture. *Organization Science, 2*(2), 170.

Kelley, R. E. (1991). Combining followership and leadership into partnership. In R. Kilmann & I. Kilmann (Eds.), *Making organizations competitive: Enhancing networks and relationships across traditional boundaries* (pp. 195–220). San Francisco: Jossey-Bass.

Kets de Vries, M. F. R. (1993). *Leaders, fools, and impostors: Essays on the psychology of leadership.* San Francisco: Jossey-Bass.

Latane, B., Ilgen, D. R., & Hulin, C. L. (check this2000). Pressures to uniformity and the evolution of cultural norms: Modeling dynamic social impact. In *Computational modeling of behavior in organizations: The third scientific discipline* (pp. 189). Washington, DC: American Psychological Association.

Latour, S. M., & Rast, V. J. (2004). Dynamic followership. *Air and Space Power Journal, 18*(4), 102–110.

Levy, D. A., & Nail, P. R. (1993). Contagion: A theoretical and empirical review and reconceptualization. *Genetic, Social, and General Psychology Monographs, 119*(2), 233–284.

Lieberson, S., & O'Connor, J. F. (1972). Leadership and organizational performance: A study of large corporations. *American Sociological Review, 37*(2), 117.

Lipman-Blumen, J. (2005). The allure of toxic leaders: Why followers rarely escape their clutches. *Ivey Business Journal, 69*(3), 1–8.

Lord, R. G., & Maher, K. J. (1993). *Leadership and information processing: Linking perceptions and performance.* London: Routledge.

Marion, R. (1999). *The edge of organization: Chaos and complexity theories of formal social organization.* Newbury Park, CA: Sage.

Marion, R. (in press). Complexity in organizations: A paradigm shift. In A. Sangupta & M. Nashed (Eds.), *Proceedings of the international workshop: Math and physics of complex and nonlinear systems.* Berlin: Springer-Verlag.

Marion, R., & Uhl-Bien, M. (2001). Leadership in complex organizations. *The Leadership Quarterly, 12,* 389–418.

Meindl, J. R. (1985). Spinning on symbolism: The liberating potential of symbolism. *Journal of Management, 11*(2), 99.

Meindl, J. (1990). On leadership: An alternative to the conventional wisdom. In B. M. Staw & L. L. Cummings (Eds.), *Research in organizational behavior* (Vol. 12, pp. 158–203). Greenwich, CT: JAI Press.

Meindl, J. (1993). Reinventing leadership: A radical social psychological approach. In J. K. Murnighan (Ed.), *Social psychology in organizations* (pp. 89–118). Englewood Cliffs, NJ: Prentice-Hall.

Meindl, J. R. (1995). The romance of leadership as a follower-centric theory: A social constructionist approach. *The Leadership Quarterly, 6*(3), 329.

Meindl, J. R. (2004). The romance of teams: Is the honeymoon over? Comment. *Journal of Occupational and Organizational Psychology, 77*(4), 463.

Meindl, J. R., Ehrlich, S. B., & Dukerich, J. M. (1985). The romance of leadership. *Administrative Science Quarterly, 30*(1), 78–102.

Mulder, M. (1971). Power equalization through participation? *Administrative Science Quarterly, 16,* 31–39.

The neglected art of followership. (2004, September, 4). *The Economist, 372,* 78–79.

Pillai, R., & Meindl, J. R. (1998). Context and charisma: A "meso" level examination of the relationship of organic structure, collectivism, and crisis to charismatic leadership. *Journal of Management, 24*(5), 643–664.

Polansky, N., Lippitt, R., & Redl, E. (1950). An investigation of behavioral contagion in groups. *Human Relations, 3,* 319–348.

Redl, E. (1949). The phenomenon of contagion and "shock effect" in group therapy. In K. R. Eissler (Ed.), *Searchlights on delinquency* (pp. 315–328). New York: International Universities Press.

Rosenau, J. (2004). Followership and discretion: Assessing the dynamics of modern leadership. *Harvard International Review,* pp. 14–17.

Rush, M. C., & Russell, J. E. (1988). Leader prototypes and prototype-contingent consensus in leader behavior descriptions. *Journal of Experimental Social Psychology, 24,* 88–104.

Salancik, G. R., & Meindl, J. R. (1984). Corporate attributions as strategic illusions of management control. *Administrative Science Quarterly, 29*(2), 238.

Sankowsky, D. (1995). The charismatic leader as narcissist: Understanding the abuse of power. *Organization Dynamics*, pp. 57–71.

Streatfield, P. J. (2001). *The paradox of control in organizations.* London: Routledge.

Turner, R. H. (1964). Collective behavior. In R. E. L. Faris (Ed.), *Handbook of modern sociology* (pp. 382–425). Chicago: Rand McNally.

Turner, R. H., & Killian, L. M. (1957). *Collective behavior.* Englewood Cliffs, NJ: Prentice-Hall.

Vanderslice, V. J. (1988). Separating leadership from leaders: An assessment of the effect of leadership and follower roles in organizations. *Human Relations, 41*(9), 677–696.

Vecchio, R. P. (1997). Effective followership: Leadership turned upside down. In R. P. Vecchio (Ed.), *Leadership: Understanding the dynamics of power and influence in organizations* (pp. 114–123). Notre Dame, IN: University of Notre Dame Press.

Weick, K. (1995). *Sense-making in organizations.* Thousand Oaks, CA: Sage.

CHAPTER 10

HERE TODAY, GONE TOMORROW

Follower Perceptions of a Departing Leader and a Lingering Vision

Melissa K. Carsten
Claremont Graduate University

Michelle C. Bligh
Claremont Graduate University

ABSTRACT

The dominant leader-centric theories suggest that implementing a vision requires an existing leader who not only develops a vision, but also actively supports followers as they modify their work roles to align with it (e.g., Bass, 1985; Conger & Kanungo, 1987, 1998; Kirkpatrick, Locke, & Latham, 1996). However, fewer studies have investigated follower perceptions of vision and the processes followers use to "buy in" to the vision. Using Meindl's (1995; Meindl, Ehrlich, & Dukerich, 1985) romance of leadership theory as a guide, this study examines follower perceptions of vision and the ramifications of a leader's departure during the height of vision implementation. Through

Follower-Centered Perspectives on Leadership, pages 211–241
211

qualitative analysis of 19 interviews, we explore followers' identification, internalization, and commitment to a vision before and after a leader's exit. Findings from this study suggest that internalization of the vision may lead to perceptions of misalignment between followers' socially constructed understanding of the vision and the leader's strategy for implementation. Results further indicate that post-departure followers are likely to perceive the vision as strongly intertwined with the departed leader and less directly relevant to their work.

INTRODUCTION

Although the "dot com exodus" in the year 2000 represented a new zenith in levels of executive turnover, there are growing indications that high turnover at the uppermost echelons of today's organizations is a trend that is here to stay. Experts say that 2005 set a record for the most CEO departures in history (Taub, 2005), leaving researchers and practitioners alike struggling to explain both the antecedents and consequences of this growing phenomenon. While some have suggested that higher rates of executive turnover are a result of the extremely high standards that CEOs are expected to meet (i.e., Drake, Beam, & Morin, Inc.), a survey by Booz Allen Hamilton suggests that more CEOs are leaving voluntarily rather than being forced out or dismissed against their will (Jusko, 2004). Regardless of the underlying reasons for CEO turnover, the ramifications of a CEO's departure can catch many organizations off guard despite the best laid succession plans (Fiegener, Brown, Prince, & File, 1996), and few researchers have explored the ramifications of a leader's departure for employees at all levels of the organization.

While there is evidence to suggest that organizations and their members experience some degree of post-departure turbulence during executive turnover (Gilmore, 1998; Heller, 1989), much of the succession research has focused on predicting productivity losses, the subsequent departure of top management, and how a successor is chosen and transitioned into the organization (e.g., Garman & Glawe, 2004; Helmich, 1978; Lauterbach, Vu, & Weisberg, 1999; Pitcher, Chreim, & Kisfalvi, 2000; Shen & Cannella, 2002). This dominant emphasis on leader-centered perspectives of executive turnover has produced only minimal knowledge concerning followers' responses to a leader's departure. Given that many leadership theories highlight the importance of executive leaders in building follower commitment, reverence, motivation, and effectiveness (i.e., Bass, 1985, 1990; Conger & Kanungo, 1987; Conger, Kanungo, & Mennon, 2000; Levin, 2000; Posner & Kouzes, 1988), it is somewhat surprising that few researchers have chosen to investigate executive turnover from the perspective of followers. More specifically, few studies have focused on followers' reactions to a leader's departure, and many have overlooked the potential effects that a leader's departure can have on the followers who have invested themselves in the leader's strategic initiatives.

By definition, executive leaders are responsible for creating strategic direction, overarching goals, and a vision for the future of their company (Hart & Quinn, 1993; Westley & Mintzberg, 1989; Zaccaro, 2001; Zaccaro & Banks, 2004). Moreover, the leader must also garner enthusiasm for the vision by working with organizational members to ensure that the vision is understood and accepted (Conger & Kanungo, 1987; Gardner, 1990; Kirkpatrick, Locke, & Latham, 1996). The rise of interest in charismatic and transformational leadership has contributed to the notion that effective leaders raise followers' levels of consciousness about the importance and value of obtaining the leader's vision, encourage followers to transcend their own self-interest for the sake of vision attainment, and activate followers' higher-order needs (Bass, 1985, 1990; Bass & Avolio, 1990, 1993). However, given the strong evidence that many leaders turnover prior to the 5–10 years that are often required to meet strategic initiatives or fully realize a vision, one must ask: How do followers' perceptions of the leader's vision and strategic initiatives change when the leader suddenly departs? And once identified with the value and importance of the vision, after sacrifices have been made, and in the wake of newly realized needs that have been fully activated, how do followers respond to the sudden absence of an influential leader?

Using Meindl's (1995; Meindl, Ehrlich, & Dukerich, 1985) romance of leadership theory as a guide, this study highlights one important aspect of leadership that is theorized to create reverence among followers and engender follower enthusiasm and energy around a common organizational direction: organizational vision. Given that a leader's vision has been found to have a direct impact on follower commitment and performance (i.e., Baum, Locke, & Kirkpatrick, 1997; Kirkpatrick & Locke, 1996; Shamir, House, & Arthur, 1993; Testa, 1999; Zacarro, 2001), this study examines followers' perceptions of the leader's overarching vision, as well as perceptions of vision implementation, both prior to and after the announcement of a leader's departure. In order to highlight the importance of investigating executive turnover from followers' perspectives, we first review existing literature on executive turnover from both the leader's and the follower's perspective. Next, we turn to a discussion of follower-centric approaches to leadership and vision. Finally, in an effort to integrate a more follower-centric approach to leadership with the literature on executive turnover, we explore pre- and post-departure interview data collected from followers who were directly influenced by a leader, his vision, and his strategy for vision implementation. We conclude with implications of our findings for researchers, employees, and organizations faced suddenly with a departed leader and his or her lingering vision for the future of the organization.

Literature on Executive Turnover

Despite the fact that turnover in the upper echelons is eventually inevitable, it is nonetheless a difficult event that organizations continue to grapple with. Companies that lose their CEO or president are at risk for losses in productivity, strategy, and subsequent turnover within top management teams (Clayton, Hartzell, & Rosenberg, 2005; Gifford, 1997; Grusky, 1963). Furthermore, in cases where the announcement of the CEO's departure is not anticipated, Beatty and Zajac (1987) suggest that companies are more likely to see a decrease in stock price, which can have subsequent implications for the overall stability of the company. Regarding company performance, there are three competing theories that have been argued to account for a company's subsequent increased performance (Guest, 1962), decreased performance (Grusky, 1963), or unchanged performance (Gamson & Scotch, 1964) after the announcement of a CEO's departure. The lack of conclusive evidence regarding predictable company performance in the midst of executive turnover has lead some to conclude that post-departure performance is contextually dependent (White, Smith, & Barnett, 1997). In addition, some researchers have suggested that a company's performance after the departure of an incumbent CEO will depend on whether the successor is chosen from the outside or brought up from within the organization's ranks (Shen & Cannella, 2002; Zajac, 1990).

Similar to the inconclusive evidence on executive turnover and company performance, research on employee responses to a departing leader has produced no conclusive evidence regarding a prototypical reaction that can be expected among followers. Whereas some studies have found evidence for follower distress and mourning (e.g., Helmich & Brown, 1972), other studies have found that followers express a renewed sense of purpose and identity in the wake of executive turnover (e.g., Allen, Panian, & Lotz, 1979). Although the body of literature on employee reactions to a leader's departure is relatively small compared to the literature on firm performance or succession processes, some have suggested that a leader's departure can negatively affect follower morale and productivity (Gilmore, 1988).

Heller (1989) describes executive turnover as a large-scale change initiative that requires the organization to deal with loss, substitution, and renewal. In some cases, organizations may even be forced to redefine themselves in the wake of a leader's departure. The process of equating executive succession with organizational change is not new to the leadership succession literature (Tichy, 1996). Many researches have noted that executive turnover often elicits the type of emotional reactions that would be expected among employees during a large organizational change initiative (Magee, Beach, & Mitchell, 1991; Miller, 1998; Tichy, 1996; White, Smith, & Barnett, 1997). It appears that the common denominator between executive succession and organizational change is that both tend to disrupt the status quo and create concern and ambiguity about the future of the company (Heller, 1989).

Gifford (1997) states that the departure of an incumbent CEO and the subsequent selection of a successor send a "symbolic" message to employees about the company's reformed vision and strategy. Employees will shift their perceptions of the company's stability as well as their interpretation of company values based on this symbolic message. Employees may perceive the CEO's departure as having either a positive or negative impact on the company's future, depending largely on the circumstances surrounding the leader's exit (Lin & Li, 2004). More specifically, when the old leader is perceived as being responsible for organizational losses or reduced market share, many employees may see the leader's departure as a form of renewal and an impetus for the organization's advancement (Gifford, 1997). On the other hand, when an incumbent leader is revered as the instigator of organizational success, his or her sudden departure can leave many employees feeling somber and void of direction (Gilmore, 1988). Farquhar (1991) suggests that each case of executive turnover will trigger different reactions among followers because "circumstances surrounding the incumbent's departure determine employee emotion" (p. 203).

In an effort to better understand followers' emotional reactions to a departing leader, Kotin and Sharaf (1967) present a theory on the "polarization of affect" wherein followers either romanticize or degrade the departing leader (Farquhar, 1991; Heller, 1989). At the moment the leader turns over, followers experience anxiety over the loss of guidance and direction. Followers will either become angry and blame the departing leader for abandoning them, or cling tightly to the leader's memory, believing that they will never find a replacement. In the findings of her case study, Heller (1989) reports that followers may spare themselves from disheartenment by degrading the former "leadership regime" and glorifying the new order. Other researchers suggest that followers can become so distraught over the loss of a leader that they become "immobile" and unable to move on from the memory of the old order (Gilmore, 1988).

The research presented above suggests that followers may experience emotional turbulence after the departure of an incumbent leader; however, there is no consensus on the type of emotional reaction that can be expected or the circumstances that may fuel affective responses. Whereas some researchers suggest that negative emotional reactions are to be expected given that leadership succession is synonymous with organizational change (Heller, 1989; Tichy, 1996), there is still a great deal to be learned about how followers cope with the loss of their leader.

In particular, given that leaders are responsible for influencing the vision, values, and goals of the organization, it is possible that followers may experience post-departure confusion about the organization's strategic objectives. Friegener and colleagues (1996) state, "Organizations are especially susceptible to loss of vision and purpose during periods of CEO transition, as the leaders who helped shape the vision are replaced by others who may not share the same values and abilities" (p. 15). Thus, followers may perceive a loss of purpose as they question the importance of attaining a vision articulated and supported by a leader that is no longer a part of the organization. While the notion of lost vision, and subsequent lost direction, are discussed throughout the succession literature, there is no empirical evidence that directly examines how this potential loss of vision may affect followers' dedication to organizational initiatives that are aligned with the vision, or their own perceived roles in achieving the vision.

The leadership literature might suggest that follower reactions are dependent on whether or not they have "bought in" or identified with the departing leader's vision. Many leadership theorists suggest that a leader's vision can engender an emotional response among followers and help to foster commitment to organizational goals and objectives (Conger & Kanungo, 1987; Conger et al., 2000; Gardner, 1990). If followers have invested in, or identified with, their leader's vision, they may be disheartened and disillusioned at the announcement of the leader's departure. However, it is difficult to predict how followers will react to the vision of a departing leader given that few leadership researchers have investigated vision from the follower's perspective.

Leadership and Vision: From Articulation to Implementation

Leadership theorists rarely separate the concept of vision from the leaders who create and communicate it, suggesting implicitly or explicitly that leaders play a critical role in vision development and implementation. While vision can be created at any organizational level and often takes shape through a participatory process, some theorists argue that it is the leader who is ultimately responsible for the quality of the organization's vision. For example, Gardner (1990) suggests that a leader must both envision the idealized future and communicate its greatness to followers. Conger (1989) defines vision as a mental image that a leader evokes to portray an idealized state for the organization. Levin (2000) states that the "vision should be future oriented, compelling, bold, aspiring, and inspiring, yet believable and achievable" (p. 92). As a result, vision has been frequently defined and operationalized as a primary instrument of effective leadership (i.e., Bass, 1985; Conger & Kanungo, 1989; Kirkpatrick et al., 1996).

Empirical research on vision and leadership has reinforced the important role that *leaders* play in creating a vision that is effective in inspiring, motivating, and directing follower performance. For example, there is a great deal of evidence to suggest that vision positively affects follower performance (Baum et al., 1998; Kirkpatrick & Locke, 1996), job satisfaction (Testa, 1999), inspiration (Conger et al., 2000; Posner & Kouzes, 1988) and helps to build collective identity among organizational members (Shamir, Arthur, & House, 1994; Shamir, House, & Arthur, 1993). However, many researchers argue that merely espousing an inspiring vision is not enough to foster the positive follower effects that are reported above (Gill, 2003; Hopper & Potter, 2000). Leadership theorists including Bass (1985), Conger and Kanungo (1987), and Gardner (1990) have noted that vision will only engender desired follower responses if the leader takes an active role in reinforcing the vision and role-modeling behaviors that are aligned with the vision. In other words, these authors suggest that vision cannot merely be cast as a rhetorical slogan, but rather behavioral efforts must be directed at implementing the vision at all organizational levels as well.

While there is no universal definition of vision implementation, it is defined here as the efforts taken by the leader or organization to align employee motivation, goals, and work behaviors around a common overarching objective (Kirkpatrick et al., 1996; Locke et al., 1991). Many times, vision implementation takes the form of a strategic initiative or action plan that is put in place to ensure that the organization is working toward the visionary state (Hopper & Potter, 2000; Kotter, 1996; Zaccaro, 2001). The initiative or action plan could be as simple as a plan for vision diffusion or as complex as a plan for people, process, or technology improvement. Regardless of the method of implementation, Gill (2003) and Hopper and Potter (2000) suggest that the leader is responsible for ensuring that followers are behind the implementation effort. Follower alignment, or "emotional alignment" as Hopper and Potter (2000) have labeled it, is marked by a shared interpretation of the company's direction and a unified sense of urgency around arriving at the desired future state (Gill, 2003). In other words, followers must understand the vision and wholeheartedly accept and engage in the method of implementation. In the case where vision implementation requires a change in employee behavior or work roles, this approach suggests that leaders may need to be extra vigilant and proactive in order to ensure buy-in and combat resistance.

Zaccaro (2001) argues that one of the primary characteristics of visions "is that they become symbols of change used by executive leaders to re-orient the collective behavior of organizational members" (p. 235). As symbols of change, successful visions frequently manifest themselves in smaller organizational subgoals or short-term strategies that are implemented by changing employee work behaviors and priorities. Leaders play a critical role in communicating, rewarding, and role-modeling commitment to the vision and guiding employees through the change process (see Kotter, 1996; Schein, 1983, 1992). Thus it is imperative that organizations undergoing the changes inherent in vision implementation have the kind of leadership that inspires, supports, and unites followers under a common organizational goal (Gill, 2003).

Taken together, the aforementioned theory and research demonstrates that the leader is a crucial component in the vision creation and implementation process; however, few researchers have chosen to study vision interpretation, acceptance, or implementation from the perspective of followers. Whereas many authors have suggested that the follower perspective is an important ingredient in gaining a holistic understanding of vision (Collins & Porras, 1991; Sashkin, 1986), few researchers have promoted a more follower-centric theory of vision. The application of follower-centric theories of leadership, such as the romance of leadership perspective proposed by Meindl and colleagues (1985), can thus aid in our effort to understand how followers socially construct a shared understanding of vision and what vision implementation entails. Specifically, the application of more follower-centric approaches to vision research may offer additional insight into the processes that followers use to interpret, understand, and enact their leader's vision.

Toward a More Follower-Centric Approach to Vision Implementation

Previous research and theory have defined vision implementation in a variety of ways, and have noted that vision is not always a top-down process (Ibarra & Sackley, 1995; Westly & Mintzberg, 1988). For example, Westly and Mintzberg (1989) note that leaders and followers work together in translating and disseminating the vision. More specifically, the authors note that the vision may originate as an idea of the leader, but that followers are often solicited to assist with the vision implementation process. Some authors have also suggested that structured participation in the vision implementation process will foster shared understandings of the vision and increase follower buy-in (Collins & Porras, 1991). However, under circumstances where the leader plays a directive role in vision creation and implementation, followers may be left to derive their own meaning of the vision, as well as strategies for vision implementation, through the process of social construction.

In their classic theory on the romance of leadership, Meindl and colleagues (1985) propose a social constructionist theory to describe the relationship between leadership and followership. The theory outlines the follower processes involved in socially constructing an understanding of the leader's personality, behaviors, and effectiveness. Within this model, leadership is literally understood "through the eyes of the follower." As proposed by Meindl (1995, p. 330), "followers react to, and are more influenced by, their constructions of the leader's personality than they are by the 'true' personality of the leader."

Meindl suggests that followers construct an image of their leader, and subsequently deem him or her responsible for organizational events and outcomes. This leadership construction is built on social processes and situational factors rather than objective leader behaviors. Social constructions, according to Meindl, are a product of individual and group consensus on events, as well as an interpretation of the significance of events to the organization. Through the process of constructing a social relationship with the leader, followers begin to better understand their relationship to the organization and their specific duties within it.

From this perspective, it is important to remember that survey responses primarily provide insights to followers' socially constructed understanding of the leader, and as such should not be regarded as objective truth (Meindl, 1995). In a series of studies conducted by Meindl and colleagues (1985), the authors found evidence that followers create a perception of leadership that they use to make sense out of organizationally relevant phenomena. When business students were presented with performance data and information on a leader, they consistently cited the leader rather than alternative sources as the primary cause of firm performance.

Subsequent research found that when participants were presented with information about the success of a company, evaluations of outcomes attributed to leadership were significantly higher than evaluations of outcomes attributed to other internal and external organizational factors (Meindl & Ehrlich, 1987). More specifically, students who read excerpts on leader behaviors judged the firm's performance to be more satisfactory than students who read excerpts on company accounting. A follow-up study by Shamir (1992) found that followers who perceive the leader as energetic, dynamic, and self-confident have a greater tendency to label their leader as "charismatic" than followers who perceived their leader as lacking such qualities. This study also found that followers with strong beliefs regarding the influence that leadership has on organizational outcomes reported stronger attributions of general charismatic qualities to a leader. As Meindl and Ehrlich (1987) note, "These results suggest that something akin to a powerful halo characterizes leadership as an explanatory concept, so that anything connected to or associated with the concept tends to take on similar value and significance" (p. 105).

Other follower-centric theories may offer additional explanations for how followers interpret and understand their leader's vision. However, empirical research on the follower-side of vision has primarily chosen to focus on the direct relationship between the leader's vision and followers' productivity or satisfaction (Lord & Brown, 2001), neglecting followers' social constructions of their leader's vision. While the vision literature frequently references the *identification* and *internalization* processes that occur as a follower accepts and applies the vision to their daily tasks (i.e., Conger & Kanungo, 1987; Gardner, 1990; Kirkpatrick et al., 1996; Westley & Mintzberg, 1989), no empirical research has been devoted to investigating these processes and how they are socially constructed.

Existing theoretical work, however, does explore the identification and internalization processes that followers use to interpret and enact their leader's vision. According to Hirschhorn (1998), identification occurs when a follower recognizes that the leader's vision is securely grounded in the *shared values* of the organization and its members (Kirkpatrick et al., 1996), a process likely grounded in both social construction and social contagion processes. The leader's vision is argued to provide followers with a standard of performance by clarifying the organization's purpose and objectives. When followers understand and identify with this standard, they are more likely to intensify their work behaviors in order to work toward or meet the specified standard. Similarly, follower internalization or individualization (Kirkpatrick et al., 1996) involves a personalization process wherein the follower redefines the leader's broad message to be more specifically related to their role and work behaviors (Hirschhorn, 1998). Specifically, the follower begins to "make the vision their own so that they can begin the process of shaping, refining, and applying the vision to everyday reality" (Hirschhorn, 1998, p. 115). Similar to Meindl's theory on social construction, Hirschhorn (1998) posits that followers will invest cognitive energy in socially constructing an understanding of the leader's vision and, from this understanding, infer its relevance to their position or role in the organization. Since every organizational member has different roles and responsibilities, it may be possible that followers construct different interpretations of the vision depending on their hierarchical level, functional orientation, or work group membership.

If these follower-centric approaches to vision acceptance are correct, we can conclude that followers devote a certain degree of cognitive energy toward interpreting and deriving meaning from their leader's vision, as well as potentially mocking and or undermining the vision. In cases where the organization has taken efforts to implement the vision, it is possible that followers are also asked to redefine work activities or goals to be aligned with the vision. Taken together, the literature presented above suggests that followers play an important role in enacting (or resisting) the leader's vision. Likewise, the leadership literature suggests that leaders must also play an active role in communicating the vision and helping followers to understand the organization's desired direction. In essence, this literature does suggest that ultimately realizing a vision requires a joint partnership between the leader who creates and articulates the vision, and the followers who modify work behaviors and goals to actualize it, possibly modifying the content or focus of the vision itself in the process.

Given the strong evidence to suggest that a leader will turn over prior to these two parties making significant progress toward meeting their ultimate objective (i.e., the realization of the vision under circumstances where followers have begun to identify with or "buy in" to the leader's vision), what are the ramifications of a leader's departure during the height of vision implementation? The literature on executive turnover presented above would suggest that the vision and strategic initiatives set forth by the departing leader are often abandoned altogether. Given the loss of vision and purpose hypothesized in the succession literature, what happens to followers who have internalized the departing leader's vision and redefined their work roles to align with its core elements as the leadership literature might suggest? The study presented in this chapter set out to explore this question.

The purpose of this exploratory study was to investigate followers' processes of identification, internalization, and commitment to a vision both before and after a leader's exit, in hope of adding to our knowledge of followers' perspectives of leadership, vision, and executive turnover. Using qualitative data collected before and after a leader's departure, this study will determine whether there are pre- and post-departure differences in: (1) the degree to which followers *identify* with the leader's vision and perceive that it is aligned with the organization's goals and guiding philosophy; (2) the degree to which followers invest cognitive energy in vision *internalization* or personalization processes; and (3) followers' perceptions of the leader's action plan for vision implementation. Given that Hirschhorn's model has not been empirically tested, this study hopes to offer insight on vision identification and internalization processes by investigating follower perceptions both before and after a leader's exit.

METHOD

Research Site: Selection and Background

Participants in this study were selected from a small university on the West Coast that was undergoing the intermediate stages of vision implementation at the time of data collection. Since assuming office 6 years prior to data collection, the president of the university had been developing and articulating a vision of transdisciplinarity. The president defined transdisciplinarity as a form of scholarship that "forces us to think across, beyond, and through academic disciplines represented at the university to encompass all types of learning and knowledge about an idea, issue, or subject" (Presidential Address, 2000). For two years prior to the president's departure, university administration worked to devise a plan to implement this vision. In the meantime, the president continued to articulate his vision in a way that painted an idealized future state for the university, stating "through transdisciplinary scholarship, whole new fields of knowledge are created" (President's Keynote Address, 2001).

As the university's administration debated plans to implement the vision, faculty, staff, and students became increasingly involved in both the vision and its translation from an abstract concept to a more concrete idea. Based on previous literature (see Bass, 1985; Conger & Kanungo, 1987; Kirkpatrick et al., 1996; Levin, 2000), vision implementation is defined in the current study as the university's efforts to (1) create subgoals that transform the vision from an abstract to a concrete form, and (2) devise an action plan to achieve those subgoals. In the current study, the subgoal of introducing transdisciplinarity to first-year doctoral students was enacted by mandating a "core course" that would enable students from different disciplinary backgrounds to assemble and discuss a single problem or topic.

Midway through data collection, the president suddenly disseminated an email that announced his departure from the university. The email outlined his plan to leave and his appreciation for the time he had spent at the university. No specific information regarding the reasons behind his departure was released to the university's constituents.

Sample

A purposeful sampling method was used to ensure that respondents accurately represented the seven schools that comprised the larger university. The university has an average of nine faculty members and three staff per department, thus limiting the total number of respondents that could be selected from any one school. In an effort to represent the entire population of faculty and staff, two to four members from each school were chosen to participate in this study. The total sample consisted of six faculty and three staff members who were interviewed prior to the announcement of the president's departure, and eight faculty and two staff members interviewed after the announcement (N = 19). Given our qualitative approach and the fact that the interview protocol did not change from pre- to post-departure interviews, a new sample of respondents was chosen for post-departure interviews. All post-departure interviews were conducted in the immediate wake of the president's announcement and before a successor had been selected.

Procedure

Participants were contacted via email and asked to participate in a short interview regarding their knowledge of transdisciplinarity. Interviews ranged from 25 minutes to 1½ hours in length, and were based on a 10-question interview protocol (see Appendix). All interviews were tape recorded and transcribed.

Analysis Strategy

Following the recommendations of Miles and Huberman (1994), a provisional coding scheme was created based on the findings of previous research as well as follower-centric theories of vision (see Hirschhorn, 1998). According to Miles and Huberman, provisional coding categories are derived "from the conceptual framework, list of research questions, hypotheses, and/or key variables that the researcher brings to the study" (p. 58). In the present study, the initial coding categories were developed to investigate Hirschhorn's theory of vision identification and vision internalization as social construction processes that followers used to understand their leader's vision. To this end, vision identification and vision internalization were treated as superordinate or pattern-level themes comprised of multiple subordinate codes. The subordinate coding categories that were used to further define vision identification and vision internalization were also derived from Hirschhorn's theory and included elements of personal and institutional compatibility, as well as the degree to which followers had redefined the vision to be compatible with their job or role (see coding definitions in Table 10.1).

In addition to the themes derived from Hirschhorn's model, three more superordinate coding categories were created based on other follower-centric theories of vision implementation (Dvir, Kass, & Shamir, 2004; Testa, 1999; Zacarro, 2001). For example, themes associated with vision implementation were adapted from Gill (2003) and Hopper and Potter (2000) to assess perceived alignment between the vision and the strategy for implementation, as well as followers' affective responses to the implementation effort. The final superordinate category was derived from previous empirical findings (see Dvir et al., 2004; Testa, 1999) and assessed followers' commitment to both the vision as well as the organization.

Table 10.1.   Coding Frequencies and Descriptions

Code	Definition	Pre-Departure N	Post-Departure N	Total
Vision Identification Elements				
Personal Compatibility	The degree to which the follower sees the vision as compatible with his or her role in the university.	18	20	38
Institutional Compatibility	The degree to which the follower sees the vision as compatible with the organization's purpose and guiding philosophy.	22	29	51
Inspiring	The degree to which the follower sees the vision as inspirational, exciting, or motivating.	8	4	12
Leader Association	The degree to which the follower sees the vision as inseparable and indistinguishable from the leader.	3	24	27
Vision Internalization Elements				
Redefinition	The degree to which the follower socially constructs a personalized definition of the vision to fit his/her specialization or area of expertise.	7	17	24
Application to Work Behaviors	The degree to which the follower applies the redefined vision to specific work behaviors.	5	3	8
Responses to Implementation Strategy				
Alignment	The degree to which followers believe that the action plan is aligned with their socially constructed definition of the leader's vision.	16	18	34
Action	The degree to which the follower was involved in or took personal action in defining the action plan for vision implementation (i.e., serving on committees, panels, advocating privately or publicly for the action plan, etc.).	5	6	11
Affective Responses to Implementation				
Positive Affective Response	Feelings that the action plan will achieve positive results in the university.	2	3	5
Negative Affective Response	Feelings that the action will achieve negative results in the university.	14	27	41

Table 10.1   Coding Frequencies and Descriptions (Continued)

Code	Definition	Pre-Departure N	Post-Departure N	Total
	Commitment			
Vision Commitment	The degree to which the follower is committed to realizing the vision.	6	7	13
Organizational Commitment	The degree to which the follower is committed to the organization as a whole and making the organization successful in its endeavors.	2	7	9

Subordinate codes were assigned to statements or sentences within the respondent's interview transcript. To ensure that the coding frequencies were not overinflated, a particular code was applied only once per question, regardless of the number of times the respondent expressed that theme in the same answer. In an effort to understand the variables that are hypothesized to influence vision identification and vision internalization, only subordinate codes were applied to interview text.

In the final stage of analysis, Atlas/ti, a code-and-retrieve software program, was used to attach codes to data and display the frequencies of major themes. One author and one independent coder coded documents separately and met twice to resolve discrepancies. Interrater reliability was calculated after all documents had been coded and resulted in a high agreement rating of .92. Descriptive codes that occurred with a frequency greater than six were retained for further analysis. In an effort to address the research questions outlined above, descriptively coding frequencies from pre- and post-departure interviews were examined for similarities and differences.

RESULTS

In order to understand the full ramifications of a leader's departure in the height of vision implementation, it is first necessary to assess the degree to which followers have identified with and internalized the departing leader's vision. Hirschhorn's (1998) model of vision identification and internalization was used to examine pre- and post-departure differences for each of the superordinate coding categories (vision identification, internalization, implementation, and commitment). As mentioned previously, Hirschhorn's model outlines the process by which followers come to identify with and internalize a leader's vision. To *identify* with the vision,

Hirschhorn suggests that followers must first perceive the vision as being grounded in the organization's guiding purpose and relevant to their organizational role. Subsequently, followers may begin to internalize the vision by redefining the broad concept to be more directly related to their particular role and work behaviors. Thus, Hirschhorn's theory specifically defines the type of cognitive energy that followers are likely to invest in socially constructing an understanding of the leader's vision, and presents a framework for investigating how these processes may change or be disrupted when the leader turns over. Table 10.2 provides sample quotations for each of the subordinate vision elements coded in the data.

Followers' Cognitive Investment in the Vision: Identification and Internalization Elements

Themes associated with the superordinate category of *vision identification* were mentioned most frequently across all interview responses. Specifically, respondents placed heavy emphasis on the *institutional compatibility* (n = 51) and the *personal compatibility* (n = 38) of the leader's vision. Followers also spoke about the vision as a source of *inspiration* (n = 12) and placed particular emphasis on the *association* (n = 27) between the president and his vision.

Institutional Compatibility

With regard to institutional compatibility, pre-departure respondents spoke frequently about the added value that the transdisciplinarity vision would bring to the university, as well as the alignment between the vision and the university's philosophy (n = 22). For example, one respondent mentioned that the transdisciplinarity vision "gives us more of a general academic common mission." Another respondent put it this way: "I think it is a way to get students in a small university to have some common ground." Some respondents believed that the vision would set the university apart and bring a unique brand to the institution. For example, one respondent stated, "It would help to put you on the map because it would be so unique; and if it's done right, it would help enhance the productivity of faculty and students."

While there were no significant post-departure differences in the frequency with which respondents mentioned the institutional compatibility of the leader's vision (n = 29), there were noticeable differences in their willingness to speak out against the vision after the leader had announced his departure. For example, post-departure respondents placed greater emphasis on the misalignment between the vision and the organization's philosophy or mission, stating "I don't know that I would do this as an insti-

Table 10.2.   Sample Quotations for Open Coding of Vision Elements

Vision Identification Elements	
Personal Compatibility	"I'm already in a sense reaping the benefits of transdisciplinarity because I am working in mathematics and biology. I also teach a sort of transdisciplinary course that straddles math and biology."
Institutional Compatibility	"There are definite advantages for T-University to be known as being at the forefront of this, and T-University is the natural place to do it in the sense that it's not going against the grain."
Leader Association	"I think you've got to have a leader behind that idea, and if the new president comes in with a different take on it, I would say that it would change. And I would bet that any new president is going to have some difference there."
Inspiring	"I want to pursue an idea wherever it takes me, across disciplines, and I want to be thinking in terms of the big picture, the biggest possible picture."
Vision Internalization Elements	
Redefinition	"In my world, it might be why a software solution might be adopted or not: It might have economic issues, it might have social issues. Having a background in all those areas will make you a better researcher."
Application to work behaviors	"I think it has really helped me in problem solving, and helping students do research, and all those kinds of activities I do in my job. I can view problems from any perspective, and I don't always have to have this narrow feeling about it."
Response to Implementation Strategy	
Alignment	"Again it comes back to implementation. Having a core course just doesn't do it because it doesn't make sense to me to have an interdisciplinary course between the sciences and the humanities."
Action	"I am one of the faculty who is involved in trying to think about T-courses for the spring."
Affective Response to Implementation	
Positive Affective Response	"I love the theme. I think studying poverty, justice, and capitalism is just a smart way to do it."
Negative Affective Response	"I think it will turn out to be a big waste of time and money."
Commitment	
Vision Commitment	"I am really committed to the idea of community, intellectual community, and the ways in which we foster more intellectual community at T-University. I really would work hard to try and do that."
Organizational Commitment	"I mean it's a special place, and I have devoted my whole career to it, so I have liked the people and their workings."

tutional focus." Another respondent mentioned his unhappiness with the movement toward transdisciplinarity as a shared organizational goal. According to this respondent, "There are botanists who are very happy just doing botany, they do not want to work on poverty, capital, and ethics, they want to work on plants and agriculture. And if that's what they want to work on, who's to say that it's our responsibility to require them to do something different."

Personal Compatibility

Similar to the findings on institutional compatibility, there were no major differences between the pre- and post-departure coding frequencies for personal compatibility (pre-departure, n = 18 vs. post-departure, n = 20). Across all interviews, followers consistently stated that the vision was compatible with their roles in the university. As one respondent noted, "I'm in a field that is very interdisciplinary, and at T-University we emphasize the interdisciplinary nature of it." Another echoed this sentiment, stating, "I have always worked in a transdisciplinary way." Many of the respondents noted that they valued interdisciplinary work and practiced an interdisciplinary philosophy long before the president created the vision. Specifically, one respondent stated, "Well, my field is so broad in a sense that you really can't be very narrow and do well because there is always so many other forces operating, so you have to be transdisciplinary."

Inspiration

Themes related to the vision's ability to *inspire* followers were not as heavily emphasized (n = 12); however, followers tended to place more salience on the inspirational value of the vision before the leader's departure (pre-departure, n = 8 vs. post-departure, n = 4). Prior to the leader's exit, one respondent mentioned that the transdisciplinarity vision allows for "a sort of intimate setting where intelligent people can sit down and work on a problem together, and I think that is sort of exciting." Another described the transdisciplinarity vision as "a bold venture, it's something new, something different, it's very stimulating." Many of the respondents noted that academia was very discipline specific and the transdisciplinarity vision presented an opportunity to break out of the routine. One respondent stated, "It gives you the opportunity to explore, to try new things, and be much more creative in your research." Followers who were interviewed after the leader's departure also mentioned that they were inspired by the transdisciplinarity vision, albeit less frequently than those interviewed before the leader's exit. For example, one post-departure respondent stated, "I have a million ideas for projects that I want to work on with students and many of them are interdisciplinary. I love the idea of collaborative research. I love the idea of team projects."

Leader Association

An analysis of the pre- and post-departure interviews provide evidence that followers perceived the vision as being more closely linked to the president *after* his departure. While the president's association with the vision was only mentioned 27 times across all interviews, it was much more prevalent in the post-departure interviews (n = 24) than the pre-departure interviews (n = 3). Prior to the leader's departure, one respondent referred to the vision as a product of the president by stating, "He's the one who is trying to move this along." Another respondent described the president's reasoning behind the transdisciplinarity vision as "A branding, a brand unique to T-University. 'Oh yes, they do transdisciplinary stuff there.' I think that is closer to the vision of the president."

On the other hand, follower responses revealed a more salient link between the president and the vision after the president's departure. For example, when post-departure respondents were asked about the president's plan for vision implementation, one respondent stated, "The president was behind it 100% and he had the moral authority to push it. A new president may have the moral authority to push it away." In the immediate wake of the president's announcement, one respondent could not engage in a discussion about the core course, simply stating, "Ah, I am heartbroken. I don't even want to talk about it. I am in mourning."

These reactions to the president's departure suggest that respondents had difficulty separating the vision from the leader who articulated it. Even the core course was seen as a product of the president rather than a plan to be enacted or owned by followers. One respondent who had volunteered to teach the inaugural core course stated: "I am one of the faculty who is involved in trying to think about the t-courses for the spring, and we haven't met this summer, and we're going to have a meeting, and I'm actually going to go into the meeting saying I think that it's a bad idea this year with the president gone. We're really just on hold." Another respondent spoke fervently about the instability of the core course without the president's support and direction: "I think the president's not being here, at a minimum makes this a much shakier proposition because you don't know what's going to happen."

An analysis of the *vision internalization* elements revealed that followers placed greater emphasis on their socially constructed definition of the vision than their efforts to modify existing work behaviors. Followers spoke of socially constructed definitions that were relevant to their area of specialization (n = 24), highlighting the importance or meaning of the vision not as the leader had explicitly defined it, but in terms of their own personal *redefinition.* Surprisingly, followers placed a stronger emphasis on their socially constructed definition of the vision after the president's departure (pre-departure, n = 7 vs. post-departure, n = 17). Prior to the leader's exit, a professor of humanities presented the salience of transdisci-plinarity by describing an ongoing debate around the study of rhetoric: "Rhetoric is another one where people in my area disagree. Plato thought in contrast that rhetoric wasn't a discipline at all." Another respondent put it this way: "One of my favorite things is taking people who are just into straight economics and explaining to them that if they are going to be use-ful, they need to learn something about political economy." Even after the president's departure, followers continued to speak about their individual-ized definition of the vision. For example, when describing the transdisci-plinarity vision, one respondent stated, "In my world, it might be why a certain software solution is adopted or not, it might have economic issues, it might have social psychology issues, it certainly has software technology issues." Taken together, these quotes provide some evidence that respon-dents had begun to redefine the vision to be compatible with their area of specialization, and that followers' socially constructed definitions were more salient after the announcement of the president's departure.

Application

Respondents in this study did not, however, speak readily about chang-ing their work behaviors to align with the vision (n = 8), although there were some minor differences across pre- and post-departure interviews. More specifically, followers spoke slightly more frequently about applying the vision to their work behaviors before the announcement of the leader's departure (pre-departure, n = 5 vs. post-departure, n = 3). Prior to the president's departure, one respondent stated, "Now, I am meeting with people that I haven't had a reason to meet with before, in different disci-plines that I would often not have much contact with." However, when one post-departure respondent was asked if he had modified any work behav-iors to align with the vision, he simply stated, "I haven't been asked to and I really don't want to."

Follower Responses to Implementation Strategy: Vision versus Core Course

In addition to the analysis of identification and internalization ele-ments, we also examined the degree to which followers perceived align-ment between the broad vision and the president's implementation strategy. Overall, followers spoke about perceptions of *misalignment* between the vision and the core course and showed markedly negative *affect* when discussing the implementation strategy. Furthermore, followers revealed that they had taken minimal *action* in helping to define the core course or socialize the new program among the university's constituents.

Alignment

Followers' responses to the implementation of the core course were highly prevalent across all of the interviews, with issues of *alignment* being the most salient (n = 34). Almost unanimously, followers stated that they did not agree with the action plan being implemented by the president, and this theme was similarly emphasized by both pre- and post-departure respondents (pre-departure, n = 16 vs. post-departure, n = 18). Prior to the president's exit, one respondent voiced concern over her perceived discrepancy between her understanding of the broad vision and the way that it was being implemented: "The other thing is that I think it is being implemented through the notion of a core course, and I just don't see that fitting my definition of transdisciplinarity." Another respondent put it this way: "Having a core course just doesn't do it because it doesn't make sense to have a course between the sciences and humanities." Some respondents even offered suggestions for how they might modify the action plan in an effort to garner enthusiasm for implementation. One stated, "I would be much more interested in encouraging [students] to take a transdisciplinary course than a transdisciplin*arity* course."

After the announcement of the leader's departure, respondents spoke more candidly about their dissatisfaction with the action plan. Some respondents were even angry at the attempt to bring transdisciplinarity to the university through implementing a core course: "Just creating a core course is sort of the lowest common denominator, the least we could do to foster [transdisciplinarity], and that's what we've done." Another echoed this sentiment, stating that the idea of transdisciplinarity is important, "but just creating a core course is kind of trivial."

Action

Very few followers mentioned that they had been *actively* involved in the creation of the implementation strategy or development of the core course (n = 11). In addition, there were no noticeable differences in the coding frequencies of pre- and post-departure interviews (pre-departure, n = 5 vs. post-departure, n = 6). While respondents seemed to only minimally involve themselves with the core course, one respondent took action in trying to understand how transdisciplinarity could be achieved at the university: "I tried to lead a discussion about transdisciplinarity, and I found that it can't just be the humanities that do this, but it has to be everyone."

Affective Responses to Vision Implementation

Respondents in this study placed heavy emphasis on their feelings toward the implementation strategy, and overall the affective responses were quite negative. Across all interviews, followers spoke more frequently about their negative feelings toward the core course (n = 41), with very few followers expressing positive affective reactions (n = 5). In addition, followers placed a heavier emphasis on their negative feelings toward the action plan after the leader's departure (pre-departure, n = 14 vs. post-departure, n = 27), while the number of positive responses did not change from pre- to post-departure interviews (pre-departure, n = 2 vs. post-departure, n = 3). Prior to the president's exit, some respondents praised the president for taking a big step in a new direction, stating, "It's kind of exciting to be at a place where something new is happening." However, the majority of the pre-departure respondents felt that the implementation of the transdisciplinarity vision could have negative consequences for the university. One respondent put it this way: "If you are asking was it the right thing to do for us, it was exactly the wrong thing in my opinion." In addition, some pre-departure affective responses were more ambivalent. This was the case for one respondent who stated, "I think [transdisciplinarity] could be great fun. But I also think that spending a semester in Paris would be great fun too, but it wouldn't do the students a hell of a lot of good."

On the other hand, responses from post-departure interviewees were more negative overall. For example, one respondent stated, "I am actually skeptical that it will do anything for T-University in terms of our reputation." Another respondent spoke fervently about the core course as a distraction that could hurt the university: "I think it's imprudent and I think it will turn out to be a big waste of time and money."

Follower Commitment to the Vision and the University

Commitment was assessed both quantitatively and qualitatively. First, respondents were asked to rate their commitment to the broad *vision* on a scale from 1 (not at all committed) to 5 (highly committed). Additionally, respondents were asked to discuss their rating. Overall, the mean for vision commitment was moderately high (*Mean* = 4.00) and there were no pre- or post-departure differences in the number of times that followers mentioned their commitment to the vision (pre-departure, n = 6 vs. post-departure, n = 7; total, N = 13). As one respondent stated, "I think I am highly committed, as an experiment. If it fails, I know how to do the other stuff." When asked about his commitment to the vision, another respondent made an effort to distinguish between the vision and the implementation strategy, stating, "I am very committed to the concept, if you can distinguish between that and the way that it is being implemented. I am not very committed at all to the way that it is being done."

When asked about their commitment to the *university*, followers reported a higher level of commitment overall (*mean* = 4.75), and placed more emphasis on their organizational commitment after the leader's departure (pre-departure, n = 2 vs. post-departure, n = 7; total, N = 9). For example, after the announcement of the president's departure, one respondent stated, "I am very committed to T-University. I would like to see it be the best university in the world." Another respondent echoed this statement in the immediate wake of the president's departure, simply stating, "This is a difficult time, but my loyalty, I don't think anyone could question my commitment or loyalty to this school overall."

CONCLUSIONS AND IMPLICATIONS

The dominant leader-centric theories suggest that implementing a vision requires an existing leader who not only develops a vision but also actively supports followers as they modify their work roles to align with it. However, as the number of CEO departures continues to rise, it is increasingly important that organizations understand the widespread implications that a leader's departure has on follower perceptions of the leader's strategic initiatives. The findings of this exploratory study provide some evidence that a leader's vision can have a lasting impact on follower role definitions, and that followers can simultaneously demonstrate commitment to the abstract vision and cynicism for the method of implementation. Given that this study offers preliminary support for Hirschhorn's (1998) identification and internalization processes, organizations may need to devote continued attention to the departing leader's initiatives even as they prepare for the successor's arrival. Most notably, the finding that a leader's departure can disrupt follower perceptions of the leader, the vision, and the implementation strategy may require that organizations continue to address concerns about the vision even after the leader who created it turns over.

The results of this study offer preliminary support for the vision identification and internalization processes hypothesized by Hirschhorn (1998). Followers spoke enthusiastically about their perceived alignment between the vision and the university's overarching purpose or guiding philosophy. Respondents also revealed that they had invested cognitive energy in socially construing an understanding of the leader's vision, providing further evidence for the theoretical importance that Meindl (1985) places on follower interpretations of a leader's actions, behaviors, and values. According to Hirschhorn, followers will redefine the leader's broad vision in an effort to extract its meaning or relevance to their particular organizational role. In this specific sample, followers tended to redefine the vision as it related to their area of specialization in research and teaching, or the unique expertise that they brought to the university. Furthermore, the finding that followers placed a stronger emphasis on internalization after the leader's departure has implications for organizations that are coping with the loss of a leader. Followers who have been active in defining the vision's relevance to their particular role may continue to embrace the vision even after the leader's exit. Whereas this may be desirable in cases where the organization intends to uphold the vision and strategic objectives of the departing leader, it could conversely create problems for the acceptance of a new leader and a new vision. According to Gabarro (1998), a successor may be inclined to stamp the organization with his or her footprint by changing the strategy or direction of the organization soon after taking office. Successors should be cautious about creating and disseminating a new vision in the event that followers have invested cognitive energy in personalizing the departing leader's vision. It may be necessary for the organization to assess the degree to which followers continue to embrace the vision prior to designating a new direction or set of strategic objectives.

The findings of this study also suggest that a leader's departure could adversely affect vision implementation efforts. Despite the strong theme of misalignment between followers' socially constructed interpretation of the vision and the president's implementation strategy, followers seemed more committed to the vision and more willing to accept implementation efforts prior to the president's departure. Under these circumstances, the process of vision internalization may have negatively impacted the implementation process, as no one implementation plan or strategy could have adequately captured the extreme variation in followers' socially constructed definitions of transdisciplinarity. These findings are consistent with Gill's (2003) proposition that without alignment, followers will resist the changes required in implementing a new program. Commitment to the implementation effort may have been higher had the organization taken more time to align the action plan with follower interpretations of the vision or involve followers in the development of the action plan.

Results also show that after the president's departure, followers placed more emphasis on their affective reactions to the implementation effort. While we obviously cannot conclude whether the president's departure created dissension toward the core course or merely created a forum for uncensored comments, it is clear that followers placed greater emphasis on their disapproval of the core course after the leader's exit. The finding that followers had a greater tendency to degrade the president's implementation strategy after his departure is consistent with Heller's (1989) finding regarding the polarization of affect. According to this theory, followers who feel disillusioned by the leader's departure may degrade the former leadership regime and the strategic initiatives of their departed leader (Kotin & Sharaf, 1967). Whereas followers in this study reported positive feelings about the broad vision overall, post-departure responses revealed a more pronounced aversion for the leader's vision implementation strategy. This finding has strong implications for organizations that choose to continue striving for vision implementation even after the leader has departed. Given that vision implementation requires that the leader reward and reinforce followers through the change process (Kotter, 1996; Schein, 1983, 1992), organizations should be extra vigilant to ensure that commitment toward vision implementation does not flounder in the wake of the leader's departure. Due to the similarity between vision implementation and organizational change (Zaccaro, 2001), a leader's departure might create the opportunity for vocalized dissension and an excuse to return to the status quo. Organizations may need to find an alternative sponsor of the implementation effort to maintain movement toward the vision and combat confusion and resistance.

Along similar lines, the finding that post-departure respondents placed less emphasis on advancing the action plan or applying the vision to work behaviors shows that respondents were not as concerned with achieving the vision after the president's departure. Whereas this may be due to the ambiguity that surrounded the vision in the immediate wake of the president's announcement, followers were less likely to take initiative and move the vision forward on their own. In fact, some respondents suggested forfeiting the core course plan altogether. Although these findings were not particularly pronounced in the present study, they reinforce the argument by Friegener and colleagues (1996) that organizations are vulnerable to loss of purpose and direction during executive transitions. This absence of direction could potentially be averted if organizations immediately communicate their plans for continuing or discontinuing vision implementation following the departure of their executive leader. It is possible that followers who are "caught in limbo" find it easier to dismiss the departing leader's initiatives than hang on to an unknown future. If the organization plans to maintain its course toward vision implementation, it is essential that communication regarding the vision, strategic objectives, and implementation strategy be disseminated.

The finding that followers were disinclined to move the vision forward without the president can be explained by follower perceptions that the leader and the vision were inseparable. In accordance with Meindl's (1985) romance of leadership theory, post-departure respondents placed heavy emphasis on the leader as the creator, instigator, and champion of the vision. Followers also noted that the vision would be difficult to maintain and actualize without the president's sponsorship. As a result of this perception, some respondents suggested postponing the core course due to the uncertainty surrounding the initiatives that would be pursued by a new leader. Others automatically assumed that the vision would be discarded, and subsequently became very emotional over the loss of a vision that they believed would benefit the university. More specifically, those followers who most closely identified with the vision and took action to achieve it were disheartened and mournful over the loss of their leader and his vision. These responses suggest that even though followers socially constructed a personalized definition of the vision, they continued to perceive the vision as an artifact of the departed president. It is possible that followers engage in internalization processes in an attempt to derive meaning out of a broad and sometimes vague vision statement, but contrary to Hirschhorn's (1998) assertions, never fully assume ownership of the leader's vision. However, given the circumstances surrounding this particular case, it is more likely that followers failed to assume ownership of the vision because they were not asked to participate in creating the vision or the strategy for implementation. Nonetheless, these findings have strong implications for both the maintenance of the departing leader's vision as well as the creation of a new one. Followers who are disheartened by the loss of a leader and his or her vision may be reluctant to accept the vision of a successor. As others have suggested (e.g., Gabarro, 1998), it may be in the organization's immediate best interest to merely revise the vision of a departed leader to reflect the successor's "new order." This can be accomplished by simply modifying the verbiage of the vision rather than the core message and focus it communicates.

The findings regarding respondents' emotional reactions after the loss of their president offer further evidence for the notion that leader departure can cause followers to feel disheartened and disillusioned (see Gilmore, 1988; Helmich & Brown, 1972). However, we cannot draw any conclusions regarding the contextual dependency of follower reactions given that we examined reactions to voluntary turnover rather than leader dismissal. It is likely that follower reactions may be different under circumstances of executive discharge due to poor performance or company losses. In addition, this study did not examine follower perceptions of the reasons behind the president's departure or speculation about who would replace the departing leader. It is possible that follower anticipation of an internal successor buffers the negative emotions associated with the loss of vision and strategic direction. Those anticipating an external successor might have expected major changes to be initiated by an outsider, thus creating a greater sense of loss and mourning. In the future, researchers should consider addressing the emotional reactions of followers in a variety of contexts and under multiple circumstances of executive departure.

Given our case study approach and small sample size, the findings of this study should be interpreted with caution until they have been replicated in a variety of different settings. Due to the relatively small sample size and the fact that pre- and post-departure interviews were conducted with different respondents, it is possible that differences between pre- and post-departure coding frequencies are more suggestive than conclusive.

In addition, this study was conducted in a short time frame and does not allow us to draw conclusions regarding the progression of identification or internalization processes or the time that should be allowed for followers to fully integrate a vision into their work roles. Future research on these processes will benefit from a more longitudinal approach in order to examine how followers begin to identify with and internalize a leader's vision. In addition, longitudinal research in a variety of industries will allow researchers to assess the potentially far-reaching impact that a leader's departure can have on follower perceptions of the vision and the implementation strategy.

It is also important to note that interview data are a subjective reflection of respondents' perspectives, rather than objective accounts of reality. Although this methodology was appropriate for understanding followers' perceptions of vision in the wake of a leader's departure, future research will benefit from multimethod approaches to data collection that incorporate the perspectives of employees at multiple levels of the organization. Other potentially interesting avenues may include follower perceptions of the differential methods of vision implementation and how various methods of implementation foster more or less commitment toward the vision.

Despite the limitations discussed above, this study provides some preliminary evidence to suggest that followers invest cognitive energy in understanding and interpreting a leader's vision, and that these processes may be disrupted when a leader turns over. The finding that organization members have a tendency to degrade the departing leader and his initiatives has important implications for how organizations communicate their direction and strategic objectives to followers in the immediate wake of a leader's departure. It is important for organizations to understand how they can help followers to best cope with the loss of a leader whose vision has a lasting impact on followers' perceptions and roles, and how to facilitate the continual process of vision implementation throughout the transition from old leader to new.

REFERENCES

Allen, M. P., Panian, S. K., & Lortz, R. E. (1979). Managerial succession and organizational performance: A recalcitrant problem revisited. *Administrative Science Quarterly, 27,* 538–547.

Bass, B. M. (1985). *Leadership and performance beyond expectations.* New York: Free Press.

Bass, B. M. (1990). *Bass & Stogdill's handbook of leadership: Theory, research, and managerial applications* (3rd ed.). New York: Free Press.

Bass, B. M., & Avolio, B. J. (1990). The implications of transactional and transformational leadership for individual, team, and organizational development. *Research in Organizational Change and Development, 4,* 231–272.

Bass, B. M., & Avolio, B. J. (1993). Transformational leadership: A response to critiques. In M. Chemers & R. Ayman (Eds.), *Leadership theory and research: Perspectives and directions* (pp. 49–80). San Diego, CA: Academic Press.

Baum, J. R., Locke, E. A., & Kirkpatrick, S. A. (1998). A longitudinal study of the relation of vision and vision communication to venture growth in entrepreneurial firms. *Journal of Applied Psychology, 83*(1), 43–54.

Beatty, R. P., & Zajac, E. J. (1987). CEO change and firm performance in large corporations: Succession effects and manager effects. *Strategic Management Journal, 8,* 305–317.

Clayton, M. C., Hartzell, J. C., & Rosenberg, J. (2005). The impact of CEO turnover and equity volatility. *Journal of Business, 78*(5), 1779–1809.

Collins, J. C., & Porras, J. I. (1991). Organizational vision and visionary organizations. *California Management Review, 34*(1), 30.

Conger, J. A. (1989). *The charismatic leader: Behind the mystique of exceptional leadership.* San Francisco: Jossey Bass.

Conger, J. A., & Kanungo, R. N. (1987). Toward a behavioral theory of charismatic leadership in organizational settings. *Academy of Management Review, 12,* 637–647.

Conger, J. A., & Kanungo, R. N. (1998). *Charismatic Leadership in Organizations.* Thousand Oaks, CA: Sage.

Conger, J. A., Kanungo, R. N., & Menon, S. T. (2000). Charismatic leadership and follower effects. *Journal of Organizational Behavior, 21*(7), 747–762.

Drake, Beam, & Morin, Inc. (2000). *CEO turnover and job security: Research highlights from a worldwide study.* Retrieved November 23, 2005, from www.dbm.com

Dvir, T., Kass, N., & Shamir, B. (2004). The emotional bond: Vision and organizational commitment among high-tech employees. *Journal of Organizational Change Management, 17*(2), 126–143.

Farquhar, K. (1991). Leadership in limbo: Organization dynamics during interim administrations. *Public Administration Review, 51*(3), 202–211.

Fiegener, M. K., Brown, B. M., Prince, R. A., & File, K. M. (1996). Passing on strategic vision. *Journal of Small Business Management, 34*(3), 15–27.

Gabarro, J. J. (1988). Executive leadership and succession: The process of taking charge. In H. Thomas & D. E. Schendel (Eds.), *The executive effect: Concepts and methods for studying top managers* (pp. 237–268). Greenwich, CT: JAI Press.

Gamson, W., & Scotch, N. (1964). Scapegoating in baseball. *American Journal of Sociology, 70,* 69–72.

Gardner, J. W. (1990). *On leadership.* New York: Free Press.

Garman, A. N., & Glawe, J. (2004). Succession planning. *Consulting Psychology Journal, 56*(2), 119–128.

Gifford, D. (1997). CEO Turnover: The importance of symbolism. *Harvard Business Review, 75*(1), 9–12.

Gill, R. (2003). Change management—or change leadership? *Journal of Change Management, 3*(4), 307–407.

Gilmore, T. N. (1988). *Making a leadership change: How organizations and leaders can handle leadership transitions successfully*. San Francisco: Jossey-Bass.

Grusky, O. (1963). Managerial succession and organizational effectiveness. *American Journal of Sociology, 69,* 21–31.

Guest, R. (1962). Managerial succession in complex organizations. *American Journal of Sociology, 68,* 47–64.

Hart, S. L., & Quinn, R. E. (1993). Roles executives play: CEO's, behavioral complexity, and firm performance. *Human Relations 46*(5), 543–574.

Heller, T. (1989). Conversion processes in leadership succession: A case study. *Journal of Applied Behavioral Science, 25*(1), 65–77.

Helmich, D. L., & Brown, W. B. (1972). Successor type and organizational change in corporate enterprise. *Administrative Science Quarterly, 17,* 371–381.

Hirschhorn, L. (1998). The psychology of vision. In E. B. Klein, F. Gabelnick, & P. Herr (Eds.) *The psychodynamics of leadership* (pp. 109–125). Madison, CT: Psychological Press.

Hopper, A., & Potter, J. (2000). *Intelligent Leadership*. London: Random House.

Ibarra, H., & Sackley, N. (1995, January 26). Charlotte Beers at Ogilvy & Mather Worldwide. *Harvard Business School Cases.*

Jusko, J. (2004). CEO turnover slows in 2003. *Industry Week, 253*(7), 20.

Kirkpatrick, S. A., & Locke, E. A. (1996). Direct and indirect effects of three core charismatic leadership components on performance and attitudes. *Journal of Applied Psychology, 81*(1), 36–51.

Kirkpatrick, S. A., Locke, E. A., & Latham, G. P. (1996). Implementing the vision: How is it done? *Polish Psychological Bulletin, 27*(2), 93–106.

Kotin, J., & Sharaf, M. R. (1967). Intrastaff controversy at a state mental hospital: An analysis of ideological issues. *Journal of the Study of Interpersonal Processes, 30*(1), 16–29.

Kotter, J. P. (1996). *Leading change*. Boston: Harvard Business School Press.

Lauterbach, B., Vu, J., & Weisberg, J. (1999). Internal vs. external successions and their effect on firm performance. *Human Relations, 52*(12), 1485–1505.

Levin, I. M. (2000). Vision revisited: Telling the story of the future. *Journal of Applied Behavioral Science, 36*(1), 91–107.

Lin, Z., & Li, D. (2004). The performance consequences of top management succession. *Group and Organization Management, 29*(1), 32–66.

Locke, E. A., Kirkpatrick, S. A., Wheeler, J., Schneider, J., Niles, K., Goldstein, H., et al. (1991). *The essence of leadership*. New York: Lexington Books.

Magee, R. R., Beach, L. R, & Mitchell, T. R. (1991). Leadership succession: Tactics for change. *Group and Organization Studies, 16*(2), 125–142.

Meindl, J. R. (1995). The romance of leadership as a follower-centric theory: A social constructionist approach. *Leadership Quarterly, 6*(3), 329–341.

Meindl, J. R., & Ehrlich, S. B. (1987). The romance of leadership and the evaluation of organizational performance. *Academy of Management Journal, 30*(1), 91–109.

Meindl, J. R., Ehrlich, S. B., & Dukerich, J. M. (1985). The romance of leadership. *Administrative Science Quarterly, 30*(1), 78–102.

Miles, M. B., & Huberman, A. M. (1994). *Qualitative data analysis: An expanded sourcebook*. Thousand Oaks, CA: Sage.

Miller, E. J. (1998). The leader with the vision: Is time running out? In E. B. Klein, F. Gabelnick, & P. Herr (Eds.), *The psychodynamics of leadership* (pp. 3–24). Madison, CT: Psychological Press.

Pitcher, P., Chreim, S., & Kisfalvi, V. (2000). CEO succession: Methodological bridges over troubled waters. *Strategic Management Journal, 21*(6), 625–646.

Posner, B. Z., & Kouzes, J. M. (1988). Rating leadership and credibility. *Psychological Reports, 62,* 527–530.

Sashkin, M. (1986). True vision in leadership. *Training and Development Journal, 40*(5), 58–61.

Schein, E. H. (1983, Summer). The role of the founder in creating organizational culture. *Organizational Dynamics,* pp. 13–28.

Schein, E. H. 1992. *Organizational culture and leadership* (2nd ed.). San Francisco: Jossey-Bass.

Shamir, B. (1992). Attribution of influence and charisma to the leader: The romance of leadership revisited. *Journal of Applied Social Psychology, 22*(5), 386–407.

Shamir, B., Arthur, M. B., & House, R. J. (1994). The rhetoric of charismatic leadership: A theoretical extension, a case study, and implications for research. *Leadership Quarterly, 5*(1), 25–42.

Shamir, B., House, R. J, & Arthur, M. B. (1993). The motivational effects of charismatic leadership: A self-concept based theory. *Organization Science, 4*(4), 577–594.

Shen, W., & Cannella, A.A. (2002). Revisiting the performance consequences of CEO succession: The impacts of successor type, postsuccession senior executive turnover, and departing CEO tenure. *Academy of Management Journal, 45*(4), pg. 717.

Taub, S. (2005, November 9). *Record for CEO turnover in 2005.* Retrieved November 13, 2005, from http://www.cfo.com

Testa, M. R. (1999). Satisfaction with organizational vision, job satisfaction and service efforts: An empirical investigation. *Leadership and Organizational Development Journal, 20*(3), 154–161.

Tichy, N. (1996). Simultaneous transformation and CEO succession: Key to global competitiveness. *Organizational Dynamics, 25*(1), 45–59.

Westley, F. R, & Mintzberg, H. (1988). Profiles of strategic vision: Levesque and Iacocca. In J.A. Conger & R.N. Kanungo (Eds.), *Charismatic leadership: The elusive factor in organizational effectiveness.* San Francisco: Jossey-Bass.

Westley, F., & Mintzberg, H. (1989). Visionary leadership and strategic management. *Strategic Management Journal, 10,* 17–32.

White, M. C., Smith, M., & Barnett, T. (1997). CEO succession: Overcoming forces of inertia. *Human Relations, 50*(7), 805–839.

Zaccaro, S. J. (2001). *The nature of executive leadership: A conceptual and empirical analysis of success.* Washington, DC: American Psychological Association

Zaccaro, S. J., & Banks, D. (2004). Leader visioning and adaptability: Bridging the gap between research and practice on developing the ability to manage change. *Human Resource Management, 43*(4), 367–380.

Zajac, E. J. (1990). CEO selection, succession, compensation, and firm performance: A theoretical and empirical analysis. *Strategic Management Journal, 11,* 217–230.

APPENDIX

Interview Protocol

Introduction: Thank you for taking the time to talk to me about your knowledge of transdisciplinarity at this university. The purpose of this study is to better understand how people come to know about organizational vision. I will be asking you some questions about your current knowledge of transdisciplinarity and how it has affected you in your position at this university. Your responses to these questions will be held strictly confidential and none of the information you share with me will be disclosed to the university. Be assured that there are no right or wrong answers to these questions so please try to be as honest and forthright as possible. For accuracy reasons, I would like to ask you permission to tape record today's interview. Would you be willing to have the interview tape recorded?

1. What does transdisciplinarity mean to you? What does it mean to this university?
2. Based on your knowledge of transdisciplinarity, how do you feel about the way the vision has been implemented?
3. What might be the advantages of transdisciplinarity for this university? What might be the disadvantages?
4. What might be the advantages of transdisciplinarity for you personally? What might be the disadvantages?
5. How committed are you to transdisciplinarity at this university on a scale from 1 (not at all committed) to 5 (highly committed)? Tell me more about your commitment rating?
6. Do you think that the vision is compatible with what you do in your particular job? If so, how? If not, why?
7. Have you modified any work-related activities because of this university's vision?
8. Would you be willing to teach a transdisciplinarity course at this university?
9. Overall, how committed are you to this university on a scale from 1 (not at all committed) to 5 (highly committed)?
10. Is there anything else you would like to add?

CHAPTER 11

NOT LEADERS, NOT FOLLOWERS

A Postmodern Discourse of Leadership Processes

Dian Marie Hosking
University of Utrecht

ABSTRACT

This chapter begins by noting calls for paradigm diversity in the leadership field and proposes a *postmodern discourse of leadership as process.* The second section outlines a view of local–cultural–historical processes as processes in which relational realities are constructed—including the (local) realities of leadership. The third and last section puts this postmodern, constructionist discourse to work in relation to practices of leadership training and development. Attention is directed to training and development possibilities that go beyond overly simple "outsider" assumptions about who are leaders and who are followers; embrace the possibility of distributed—and not just focused— leadership; take seriously the involvement of (what some might call) "followers" in leadership processes, and; give space to developing "followers" into leaders. Useful practices are suggested to include ways that (1) work with *local* leadership constructions; (2) *involve all participants*—not just formally

Follower-Centered Perspectives on Leadership, pages 243–263
Copyright © 2007 by Information Age Publishing

appointed leaders; (3) generate and support *multiple* local constructions, and so; (4) construct and legitimate the principle of open, multilogical, collaborative ways of relating.

TRANSITIONAL SPACES, NEW QUESTIONS, NEW POSSIBILITIES

Talk about leaders and followers and leadership processes necessarily implicates many assumptions. Just what is assumed and what is offered for discussion depends on the particularities of local–cultural discourses. Taken-for-granted knowledge and assumptions recently became the focus of many methodologies of change, development, and learning. For example, attempts at organizational change often work with clients to surface fundamental assumptions and to explore particular practices, identities, and relations (e.g., Argyris & Schön, 1978; Isaacs, 1993). A central approach in this and related methodologies is to open up new possibilities and to reconstruct meanings and related practices so that the locals find them more helpful and supportive of their identities and relations (e.g., Barrett, Thomas, & Hocevar, 1995).

The above approach suggests some interesting ways to work with leadership constructions—both in academic theories—and in other local leadership practices. Analysis of this sort could identify some implicit assumptions and pragmatic implications that, in turn, could create a transitional space in which to explore other possible realities and relationships (see, e.g., Bouwen & Hosking, 2000). In principle, this "space" could include diverse and perhaps radically different "paradigms" (Kuhn, 1970), "discourses" (Deetz, 2000), or "intelligibility nuclei" (Gergen, 1994). Indeed, contributions of this sort have been called for by a number of leadership researchers (Bryman, 1996; Dachler & Hosking, 1995; Morley & Hosking, 2003). Bryman (1996), using the duality of modern/postmodern, called for more work that problematizes the nature of leadership, that views leadership settings or cultures as fragmented and ambiguous, and that departs from "modernist" assumptions about the rationality of such settings. Many modernist assumptions have been identified, including the assumption of (1) individual rationality, (2) empirical knowledge of an independently existing world, and (3) language as a means to represent the world as it really is (Gergen & Thatchenkerry, 1996).

Leadership researchers, suggested Bryman, should engage with ideas and standpoints from different inquiry paradigms characterized by different assumptions about actors and relations (Bryman, 1986, 1996). Openness to multiple paradigms and to dialogue between paradigms remains relatively undeveloped in the field of management and organization studies

(Bouwen & Hosking, 2000; Weick, 1999), particularly in the subfield of leadership. Achieving such openness and dialogue constitutes a major challenge in that communication between paradigms—like any other intercultural communication—is not easy. For example, it is hard to avoid imposing one local–cultural set of assumptions upon another, particularly when assumptions are implicit and unavailable for critical reflection. As a result, other offerings are likely to be read as (poorer) constructions of one's own worldview and therefore as already (and better) said. Accusations of ignorance, irrationality, and unnecessary obfuscation also are common.

Perhaps a new sort of "voyage of discovery" (Harding, 1998) will allow that there are different discourses characterized by different resources, different limitations, and different standards for evaluation. Perhaps it is possible to construct what Sandra Harding (a philosopher of science) called a "thinking space" in which "new kinds of questions can be asked" and "new kinds of possible futures... articulated and debated" (Harding, 1998, p. 17). The purpose of this chapter is to introduce *postmodern* arguments about social construction to the field of leadership. This postmodern discourse can help with the (modernist) issues identified by Bryman. First, it problematizes leadership by theorizing "empty" processes(i.e., the "how" of leadership). In this way, abstract theory leaves the "what" of leadership more open to local–emergent (rather than elite/a priori) construction (see Alvesson & Deetz, 2000) and side-steps the discourse of leaders and followers. Second, and relatedly, emphasis is given to multiple local–relational realities and relations as they are (re)constructed in ongoing processes. In this way, the postmodern discourse avoids the discourse of objective and subjective knowledge and "external" reality. Third, rationality—including scientific rationality—is discoursed as an emergent local–historical, local–cultural affair rather than universal and transhistorical or predictably contingent—as in contextualism.

THEORIZING SOCIAL CONSTRUCTION

Modernist Tales

Talk of social construction has come to mean many things. Precisely what it means depends on the wider discourse of which it is a part. And many aspects of the wider discourse are implicit, leaving plenty of space for others to mobilize their own assumptions and interests as they listen and read. This said a "modernist" discourse is by far the most common. It embraces what Guba and Lincoln (1994) referred to as "positivist" and "post-positivist" "paradigms." The central discursive themes of these paradigms will be outlined in order to help clarify the changed themes that will later be presented in a postmodern discourse of social construction.

Guba and Lincoln described *"positivism"* in terms of an ontology of "naive realism," a "dualist" and "objectivist epistemology," and a methodology that is "experimental" and "manipulative" and centers the "verification" of hypotheses. On the first, this is the assumption that "'real' reality" exists "out there" and is fully "apprehendable" (Guba & Lincoln, 1994, p. 109). The "dualism" of which they speak assumes that the knower and the object he or she seeks to know are independent "things" existing in subject–object relation such that the former can produce objective knowledge (free from idiosyncratic bias) or subjective knowledge about the latter. This introduces the related "objectivist" assumption that language maps concepts "onto objects, properties and relations in a literal, unequivocal, context-independent fashion" (Hermans, Kempen, & van Loon, 1992, p. 26) such that it can provide a "naive reflection" of the world. Positivist methodological assumptions center observation, induction, and hypothesis generation (the hypothetico-deductive method) and hypothesis testing (i.e., a version of empiricism) (see, e.g., Gergen, 1994). In this discourse the scientist is assumed to be capable of correct reasoning. The discourse of science is (implicitly) given a special status such that the "context of justification" (i.e., the "meta-theoretical" assumptions about ontology, epistemology, and methodology traditionally viewed as the province of philosophy) is treated as if it were separate from the "context of discovery" (traditionally viewed as the domain of social science).

Guba and Lincoln (1994) described *postpositivism* as a different paradigm—one in which ontological realism became "critical" rather than "naive"; one in which the epistemological and methodological assumptions of positivism are "modified" (p. 109). In this context, the term "critical" is intended to suggest that claims about reality cannot be certain and must be carefully examined (Cook & Campbell, 1979). The modified version of epistemological dualism recognizes that self and Other cannot entirely be separated such that objectivity, although strived for, is imperfectly achieved. Methodology shifts from proof to falsification combined with a widened definition of what can be included within the empiricist remit. In sum, the shift is largely epistemological, accepting that we cannot know that we know the world as it really is, accepting a revised view of truth, and shifting to talk of probabilities. "It is in *this* sense that all modern (some would say modernist) western psychology has long viewed its knowledge as constructed rather than straightforwardly representative" (Hosking, 2005).

Modernist studies of leadership, leaders, and followers privilege the discourse of science, mobilizing it as a tacit and undiscussable context of justification. Empirical work is written up as if the scientist and his discourse of science—whether positivist or post-positivist—were "outside" their discourse of leadership. Furthermore, the scientist populates his or her discourse with (1) leaders and followers who have personal characteristics, who (2) act in relation to one another and in relation to other "objects" in the world, and who (3) build and mobilize knowledge and power in their (modified) dualist relations. Leadership studies of this sort include work that is presented as "social constructi*vist*" or "social constructio*nist*." These modernist tales discourse Other as a sense-maker using, for example, individual-cognitive constructs such as perception, "informal implicitly held models" mind maps, and individual interpretation (e.g., Meindl, Erlich, & Dukerich, 1985). They talk of information-processing biases and "false assumption making" (Meindl, 1995, p. 330). Leaders and/or followers are discoursed as having personal qualities such as needs, minds, and personality. Mind is the locus of social construction. Constructionism of this kind continues to reproduce a modernist scientific interest in how things really are and continues to assume that the language of science may do the (more or less imperfect) job of representing some nondiscursive world. Objectivism remains "a regulatory ideal" (Guba & Lincoln, 1994, p. 110; see also Gergen, 1994) to be pursued via an empirical (but not hard-line empiricist) methodology.

The assumptions of the present discourse are neither positivist nor post-positivist, not modernist but postmodern. The present view does *not* discourse epistemology in terms of objective–subjective knowledge and does *not* discourse ontology as either realist or relativist. Methodology is regarded as a theory-laden process of construction rather than a means to generate data for hypothesis testing. The present view provides another map about another territory (Korzybski, 1933). This "map" includes science in its discourse of social construction. In this sense science is positioned alongside (in equal/symmetric relation with) other local practices or "forms of life" (Wittgenstein, 1963). Social construction is also repositioned. Social construction is not presented as an individual act. Rather, our stories of individuals (and their qualities, minds, behaviors, sense making, etc.) are regarded as social constructions. My present concern is with ongoing (re)constructions of what I shall call relational realities—including constructions of science, of leadership, of leaders and followers. In other words, the present discourse "starts" with processes and not persons, and views persons, leadership, and other relational realities as made in processes. This means that our present tale is very different from other (modernist) tales of social construction, leaders and followers (cf. Bligh, Kohles, & Meindl, 2004; Meindl, 1995; Meindl et al., 1985).

Of course the above requires a rather special discourse of processes—one that does not view them as "intra-" and "interpersonal" or as individual cognitions and acts. The present discourse talks about local–cultural–historical processes as moving constructions of what is "real and good" (Gergen, 1994), so collapsing the modernist distinction between fact and value. Social construction is *not* discoursed as a social epistemology in the context of some independently existing and objectively knowable reality. Rather, our postmodern discourse makes no distinction between ontology and epistemology and construction becomes a matter of how we do our lives. This gives a new role to language—no longer the means for representing reality—but a (perhaps *the*) key process in which relating "goes on" and in so doing, constructs people–world realities and relations. Reality is no longer discoursed as objectively or subjectively known by the mind but as an ongoing construction made in language-based processes. Relations are no longer reduced to an enforced and more or less sharp subject–object dualism. Instead, the modernist separation of the knowing subject (e.g., leader, scientist) and knowable object (e.g., follower, leadership situation) is itself regarded as a construction that could be otherwise. Attention now shifts to processes of construction including, for example, constructions of leaders and nonleaders and their relations, of leadership as focused or dis-tributed—and many other possibilities yet to be *made real.*

A postmodern discourse of construction processes has yet to receive much attention in the literatures of management, organization, and lead-ership (but see, e.g., Chia, 1995; Gergen & Thatchenkerry, 1996; Hosking, Dachler & Gergen, 1995; see also Thompson & McHugh, 1995). Fortu-nately, there is a wealth of resources that can be drawn upon, for example, in the literatures of philosophy of inquiry, feminisms, critical and discur-sive psychology, and cognitive sociology (e.g., Arbib & Hesse, 1986; Edwards & Potter, 1992; Flax, 1987; Gergen, 1994; Harding, 1986; Samp-son, 1993). I will continue by drawing upon these literatures to set out some central premises about relational construction processes. However, I should emphasize that these are not offered as substantive theory that could therefore be empirically tested. Rather, these premises concern "the trans-historical *potentials* of the phenomena that constitute the domain of inquiry"—potentials that may be very differently realized in the varying "empirical flux of events" (Cohen, 1989, p. 17, original emphasis). They are "put to work" in a generative way in the last part of this chapter.

A Postmodern Discourse of Relational Processes

Social constructionist approaches share an emphasis on communication and on language as a means of communication. Sometimes the term *rela-tional* is used in order to stress that communications in some way connect, coordinate, or relate constructed realities (e.g., Hosking et al., 1995). The current view brings relational processes to the foreground. Persons and contexts (self and Other, scientist and research object, leader and follower) are viewed as social constructions constructed "inside" these processes. It then becomes sensible to reflect on the ways in which researcher, leader(s) and nonleaders (followers?) construct their relations and how particular constructions gain authority while other possibilities are unrealized or suppressed.

In the present view, reference to "relational" includes the relating of written and spoken language, as well as the relating of nonverbal actions, things, and events. In this view, processes of relating (words, things, events, etc.) make leaders, organizations, competition real and make these realities heroes and villains, good and bad, right and wrong. You could say that relational processes construct "thingness" and "goodness." Every word, act, and object is a potential contributor to communications and therefore to processes of reality construction.

In other words, the present reference to "relating" should *not* be understood as a reference to one person communicating in face-to-face relations with (an)other(s); we are not speaking of inter-personal (or intrapersonal) processes between already known actors.[1] This means that it becomes necessary to find some other way to speak of what is related with what. The terms "act and supplement" (Gergen, 1994) and/or "text and context" (Dachler & Hosking, 1995) have been used for this purpose. All acts are regarded as *potential* texts in the sense that they *may* be supplemented (context), so contributing to an ongoing process of constructing realities. All acts may be thought of *both* as con-texts that supplement some previous act *and* as texts available for a subsequent co-ordination.

Possible Supplements and Multiple Realities

These tools of text and context, act and supplement are helpful for making several points about construction. The first is that how a process "goes on" depends on if and how an act is supplemented. An act may be supplemented in many ways. For example, suppose that new posters about the latest change initiative are posted around a factory. The poster might, for example, be studiously ignored, covered in graffiti, or referenced in a team meeting. All potential texts are open to being *made* (e.g., relevant or irrelevant, evidence of leadership, a sign of incompetence, good or bad, etc.) according to whether or not they are supplemented and how (Gergen, 1995).

Constructing a particular act, for example, as an act of leadership may implicate multiple simultaneous references to hierarchy, identity (e.g., as a manager, individual, or shared responsibility), or organizational mission, along with perhaps national–cultural discourses of relations, business, and the like. Any reality construction—including those that seem so very natural, so obvious, so self-evident—relies on *multiple text–context (act–supplement) relations*. Furthermore, many of these relatings will be tacit. Linking back to our earlier discussion, development work that uses the methodology of "assumption surfacing" can never make everything explicit. Trying to make explicit what previously was implicit necessarily adds new implicits—adds more equivocality—in a neverending process (Garfinkle, 1967). Finally, while a text may be supplemented in an infinite number of possible ways, very often only a limited range of supplements is probable. Indeed, processes can become "ongoing" precisely because some degree of taken-for-grantedness develops and feeds back into the process. This is what is meant by talk about culture, local realities, or local rationalities. Processes vary in the extent to which they are open to realizing previously unrealized possibilities. Relating can get stuck in "games without end" (Watzlawick, Weakland, & Fisch, 1974) where coordinations become almost canonical in their predictability.

Processes Are Local–Cultural and Local–Historical

The present account of social construction requires no assumption of natural and timeless laws concerning what is real. These propositions are about what works in some "here and now" performance. They are offered as a pragmatic framework for reflecting on how realities are constructed, maintained, and changed. Practitioners show themselves to be knowing (locals) by coordinating in ways that are warranted appropriate and natural *in particular* local–cultural processes. Returning to our earlier example of the difficulties of paradigm diversity and inter-paradigm communication, would-be contributors to the leadership literatures must find ways to coordinate with the texts "already in place" (i.e., with existing constructions). Should their attempts be too different, then communications may break down. Of course, similar issues arise in other leadership relations where what counts as a leadership contribution, and who/what are constructed as leaders, also are a *local* affair. The present discourse presents reality: as multiple and local rather than singular and transcendental; as contesting or suppressing other realities; and as (in principle) always contestable. One implication is that researchers, consultants, and trainers might do well to let go of the assumption that a particular organization has or should have only one organization-wide culture, rationality, and leadership reality.

The present reference to *local* contrasts with general/universal presumptions about reality and the modernist assumption that the knower exists in an independent and separate relationship to "it." Here, the knower is viewed as part of what is known, and what is known is made and remade in relational processes. This is "inside" knowledge—this is knowing from within—remembering that knowledge and action are now joined. Local also means local in a historical sense (i.e., "here and now," "in the moment"—rather than timeless). However, this is not a notion of the "present" in relation to a modernist construction of past, present, and future. Rather, the present view is that relating always supplements coordinations "already in place" (the past is reconstructed in the present) and invites and constrains probable supplements (the future is in the present). This concept of process makes no sense (nonsense) of origins and endings, inputs and outcomes.

Finally, it is important to connect with a frequently mobilized critique of social constructionism, namely that it assumes a relativist ontology and therefore allows that "anything goes" (see, e.g., Burr, 1995). This may mean many things. In the present context, it is useful to remember what these propositions are intended to do. The present turning away from how things "really are" makes prominent the limits constructed and reconstructed in relational processes (i.e., *how things really are made*). As has been seen, limits to what might "go" (e.g., what might be counted as a leadership contribution) here are viewed as local–conventional—but nonetheless limiting. Furthermore, this charge of relativism relies upon modernist assumptions and therefore seeks to impose local–cultural assumptions (in this case, a particular "paradigm") that differ from those presently intended.

Processes Make People and Worlds

The processes of which we have spoken make and remake everything we know including what we know as "self," what and who we know as "other," and self–other relations. The way someone can be and can be known is relational—constructed in particular text–context (act–supplement) relations. A common construction of self and other and relation is the *subject–object construction*. For example, leaders and scientists are often constructed as subjects in the sense of being active in knowing and influencing "Other" ("followers," organizations, the research design and methodology, etc.). Leaders, as subjects, are seen as the architects of organization design and strategy, have vision, diagnose local contingencies, carry responsibility for success and (perhaps) failure. This means that "Other" (persons, followers, organization, environment, etc.) is known from the subject's (singular) point of view and is discoursed (by S) as available to be influenced, motivated, led, studied and manipulated (Dachler, 1991; Dachler & Hosking, 1995; Hosking, 1988).

While self–other relations may be constructed as subject–object, *they do not have to be.* Furthermore, any *singular* claim that leadership *is* a subject–object relation—that this *is* how the world *is*—suppresses other possible realities. This, in turn, suggests the value of theorizing construction processes (including those of leadership) in relatively content-free ways ("empty processes")—in ways that are open to multiple local leadership realities. Perhaps certain leadership constructions cannot be "heard" while subject–object assumptions are in place. Perhaps development work might usefully be directed to realizing other non-subject–object constructions (e.g., of leadership, leaders, and followers).

How, then, might subject–object constructions be changed? Certainly not by some change agent (trainer, consultant, leader, etc.) acting as a knowing subject in relation to some not knowing and formable other—this would simply be "more of the same" (Bateson, 1972; Watzlawick et al., 1974) and would be rather like ordering someone to volunteer. Attempts at radical change (e.g., in substantive theories of leadership or in the content of leadership training) may fail for just this reason. A postmodern discourse allows and invites alternatives to "power over"—tied as it is to subject–object relations. Possibilities include "power to" as it might be constructed in, for example, different but equal relations (see, e.g., Gergen, 1995) or "power with"—as in a participative ontology (e.g., Hosking, 2000; Reason, 1994). But the power to reconstruct self and other now is clearly seen as co-constructed in relational processes and not as an individual act.

Summary of Relational Propositions

- We know only relational realities and these are everything we know including ourselves, other people, "the facts of the market," and leadership.
- Relational realities are constructed in processes of relating text and context, act and supplement, including written and spoken language, nondiscursive actions, objects, and events.
- Multiple text–context coordinations, including many that are tacit, "go together" to construct multiple realities of "self" and "other" in relation. These realities, including the realities of leadership, often are constructed as subject–object relations.
- Realities are local–cultural constructions. They are more or less contested and, in principle, always are contestable.
- Contesting subject–object constructions will reproduce them if the would-be change agent acts to know and influence "other", and if "other" does not have a voice.

LEADERSHIP TRAINING AND DEVELOPMENT

In the preceding discussion the most general theme concerned the identities and relations constructed between self and Other. Positivist and post-positivist paradigms were suggested to construct self and Other as separate identities in subject–object relations. In the subject position, some person(s) (e.g., a leader, trainer, or consultant) is discoursed as knowing and influencing Other—constructing Other only as knowable and formable by self as subject. Given our present postmodern discourse, relations and identities of this sort can be constructed in all social practices *but so too could other identities and relations.* The present discussion focuses on three aspects of leadership training and development: who participates, who defines program content, and the "content" itself. Possible subject–object constructions are suggested to include: (1) training only appointed leaders; (2) predefining program content, and (3) training in individualized skills and attributes, rationality, and "power over." Other (non-subject–object) possibilities are suggested to be: (1) inclusive participation, and (2) generating locally grown "content" in (3) multilogical processes. Such practices (remembering that theory and methodology are now seen as joined) seem to meet Bryman's call to problematize the nature of leadership, to treat leadership settings as fragmented, and to leave aside "modernist" assumptions.

Who Participates

Leadership training has become big business (see Rifkin, 1996a; Sorohan, 1995). In 1995, over 70% of American companies with more than 100 employees sent managers on leadership training courses and leadership courses for senior management and chief executives have expanded enormously (e.g., Fulmer & Vicere, 1996; Rifkin, 1996a). The practice of training/developing only managers seems implicitly to separate and oppose the categories of manager/leader and nonmanager/nonleader or follower. For example, it makes sense to give leadership training only to managers if *only* managers are leaders, if *only* leaders need know, if leaders can and must speak for "followers" and act to structure some common reality.

Of course, there are many pragmatic reasons why managers might be the only ones to attend leadership courses. However, an obvious potential limitation—one that is especially acute given the present discourse—is the absence of "followers" and the absence of leadership relations as an ongoing context of training. Furthermore, leadership is not necessarily something that appointed leaders have and/or do with others who are not leaders; other relations are possible and may be desirable (see Barker, 1997). Indeed, there are formal theories that deal with a variety of possibilities. For example, leadership may be theorized as distributed rather than focused (e.g., Brown & Hosking, 1986; Gibb, 1969; Gron, 2003; Parry & Meindl, 2002), and theories may decenter leaders and followers as separate identities and instead theorize leadership as a collective activity or process (e.g., Grob, 1984; Hosking & Morley, 1991; see also Bryman, 1996). Returning to leadership training and development, a few programs work with intact work teams or with "a majority of managers and employees" (see, e.g., Conger, 1992, p. 199). Such practices have the potential, for example, to blur leader–nonleader divides depending on other aspects of the training. Other relational possibilities arise when development work is conducted with all participants. "All" includes not just managers and employees, but also community groups, suppliers, consumers—all who are in some way implicated in and affected by the organization's activities (e.g., Janov, 1995; Weisbord, 1992; see also Conger, 1992). "All" also includes the trainers/consultants as, in some sense, having equal voice with others; we will return to these possibilities later.

Who Defines Program Content

Training often delivers predefined content that concerns the "what" of leadership. Predefined packages may be more or less driven by academic research and theory (see, e.g., Blanchard & Hersey, 1996; Fiedler, 1996) and/or by corporate policies (see, e.g., Rifkin, 1996b). The predefinition of course content may be something with which some trainees coordinate by supposing that they are being "othered" as not-knowing objects by senior management and/or trainers acting as subjects—by seeming to believe that there is some (one) thing that *is* leadership; that they (trainers, senior management, etc.) know what this is, and that they are ready to impose their definitions on local practices. In other words, trainees may construct the relationship message as subject–object (e.g., Bateson, 1972; Watzlawick, 1990). This can constrain (rather than resource) the training content if the latter is intended, for example, to *enable* participants. Again, this would be the equivalent of ordering someone to volunteer. Of course, it is possible to "customize programs" to fit local needs. Some companies indeed try to do this, and there are many reasons why such an approach might be desirable (see Conger, 1992, Chap. 9). Customized programs can vary in the range of participants they include, and may be more or less open to the notion that leadership may not be a singular affair. Conger describes General Electric's (GE) curriculum as involving action learning in teams working with local business problems. Furthermore, GE's approach apparently embraces the notion that different leadership skills are required at different levels of the organization—at different stages in a manager's career.

However, yet greater departures from subject–object relations can be imagined. Possibilities include shifting further from predefined notions of a singular (managerial) hierarchy of authority, individual identities, and individual action. So, for example, the scope of leadership relations and relational processes could be expanded to include those who are not employees but who have other sorts of relations with the company (supplier, consumer, environmental activist, etc.). In addition, program content could be minimally predefined and multiple voices could generate their own local and multiple constructions of leadership. Identities may be given space to be more open and fluid through practices that position (e.g., corporate officials and trainers/consultants) as "not knowing" and as having no greater authority to "form"/influence content than any other. Everyone and no one could define program content in multilogical relational processes and this could be the point, so to speak. I will return to these possibilities later.

The Content of Training

Leadership training has been said to aim to "grow individuals" who have "experience, wisdom, and insight" (Fulmer & Vicere, 1996, p. 35), to focus on "soft" (people?!) issues, and on "touchy-feely concepts such as self awareness" (Rifkin, 1996b, p. 110). In his discussion of "learning to lead," Conger (1992) identified four areas of training and development: personal growth, skill building, conceptual development, and feedback. Courses very often combine these elements in varying degrees of emphasis. Those aimed at personal growth may include development of leaders in the areas of trust, respect, problem solving, self-confidence, listening skills, and the like.

Leaders' (especially senior executives) conceptual and analytical skills may be developed in the area of strategic visioning and, for example, to diagnose and learn (through feedback) the strengths and weaknesses of their leadership style. However, these skills of "knowing" are of little value unless the results can be "put to work." This means developing leaders' ability to achieve influence over other people and events (i.e., to do some "world making"). So leaders must learn how to form and mobilize others, how to negotiate and inspire, how to gain commitment to their own vision and projects (see, e.g., Conger, 1992; Rifkin, 1996a).

Given our present discourse, training of the sort outlined may too much remove trainees from the relational processes in which their identities—as leaders and acts—as leadership contributions are made sensible. Such approaches may do much to (re)construct the modernist discourse of the "self-contained" individual who "possesses" a certain identity and relatively stable characteristics (see Dachler & Hosking, 1995; Sampson, 1993) and who may develop self-knowledge. Rather than firmly locating skills and attributes in their relational (act-supplement) settings, skills are individualized and attributes are seen to be under individual control. Modernist assumptions are further referenced in the assumption of individual rationality—together with the emphasis on empirical knowledge about self and the world—viewed as singular and as objectively (though imperfectly) knowable realities. Modernist assumptions are further reflected in the discourse of influence skills as individual skills of "power over" where one rationality (the subject's e.g., the leader's) defines how things are and should be—in implicit subject–object relation with "followers" and other Others.

The point is not that these assumptions and practices are wrong. Rather, the point is to consider what other possibilities are made available by a postmodern discourse that opens up alternatives to subject–object constructions. The present discourse warns against decontextualized notions of personal characteristics and, more generally, of knowledge (e.g., Burr, 1995). A more "dialogical" approach (Sampson, 1993) is invited—one that attends to the relational processes in which leadership (or indeed any reality) is constructed. Training and development then may shift from a monological construction of what "leadership *is*" to multilogical processes, to processes that construct "power to" support multiple realities in different but equal relation.

Inclusive, Locally Grown, Multilogical Processes

Additional possibilities for leadership have been identified as arising in practices that break away from subject–object identities and relations. These practices embrace inclusive relations and locally generated realities (rather than outsider expertise); leave aside practices that rely on the notion of a singular "real" reality (e.g., rational analysis and influence to create consensus); enable multiple rationalities (as local cultures and not individual subjectivities), and construct "power to" in the context of multiple local interdependent realities (rather than "power over" in relations of control). These are not offered as *replacements* for existing practices. This said, many contemporary societal, organizational, and technological developments seem as though they might be well served by practices of this sort. These include, for example, moves toward widened participation in decision making, attempts to empower and facilitate local initiatives, the development of internal markets and trading relationships, practices of supply chain management, teamwork, flatter hierarchies, diversity programs, truly worldwide organizations, and global communication technologies.

Many of these developments seem intended more evenly to distribute responsibilities and power and to ease collaborative processes in the context of differing local logics or rationalities. Put slightly differently, these ways of (re)organizing involve relational processes amongst participants whose constructions (e.g., of what is and what is good) are very varied. In a "postcolonial" era (Harding, 1998) very different peoples and worlds—very different local rationalities—are interdependent and wish to coordinate without having one voice or rationality subjugate others (see, e.g., Barker, 1997; Dachler, 1999; Weisbord, 1992). The time has come to look in a little more detail at practices that have the potential to facilitate inclusive, locally grown, multilogical ways of relating.

Consultants as Not Knowing

Moving away from subject–object relations means shifting from practices in which change agents act as knowing about leadership and act to form what trainees need to know. This means that consultants act as part of, rather than apart from, development processes. Some consultants work this way, although, as yet, mostly outside the leadership area. Such practices often are spoken of as "collaborative" or "dialogical." For example, Harlene Anderson (1997), and those involved in the "Public Conversations Project" (e.g., Chasin et al., 1996) have developed collaborative approaches to family therapy and have moved these practices into other consulting arenas.

In collaborative approaches, consultants act from a stance of *not knowing*. This means many things. It is partly a reference to what here has been called content or "product" knowledge (see, e.g., Pearce, 1992). Consultants are freed from having to be an expert, for example, about particular local constructions (Anderson, 1997), about diagnostic tools and categories, or "strategies for fixing this or that situation" (Weisbord & Janov, 1995, p. 7); they resist importing nonlocal theories about content (e.g., leadership is K, problems are X, etc.). Just as importantly, "not knowing" means resisting invitations to facilitate interpersonal dynamics—"not knowing" includes process knowledge. Instead, consultants act to invite a certain sort of "container" as a context for collaborative working—joining with others to expand their ways of "going on" in relationship (e.g., Anderson, 1997; Bass & Hosking, 1998; Farrelly & Brandsma, 1974; Hosking, 2004). As Weisbord and Janov (1995) have said, "We set up conditions under which people can choose new ways of relating" (p. 8) and take responsibility for how they will "go on" together.

Change work includes direct "face-to-face" conversations between consultant and client (e.g., in therapy) along with multiple, crosscutting, and often indirect coordinations with large numbers of participants. Speaking of the former, Anderson (1997) tells how therapists may ask questions and coordinate with texts in ways that reflect a "being-informed" rather than a knowing stance. When many participants and relations are involved, consultants may act to facilitate "a setting conducive to dialogue" (Weisbord, 1992, p. 7) where the emphasis shifts to *multilogical ways of relating between clients*. Such settings could include something like[2] Future Search (Weisbord, 1992), "leadership summits" (Janov, 1995), the Public Conversations Project (Chasin et al., 1996), and the MIT Dialogue Project (Isaacs, 1993).

Multiloging and Constructing "Power To"

In methodologies such as Future Search, multiple and changing group-ings work on a variety of tasks to generate their own content. Such prac-tices have the *possibility* to construct nonhierarchical, multilogical processes in which multiple local rationalities are voiced and locally warranted. This could be one way to implement a "fragmentation" perspective of cultural change (Bryman, 1996, p. 285; Martin, 1992), including change in what some might call leadership realities. In work of this kind participants can learn new, non-subject–object ways of relating (i.e., can construct "power to" go on together in new ways). Of course, they also can continue to reproduce relations of "power over," right–wrong competition for whose reality constructions will prevail!

Multilogical methodologies work with whole systems where possible, not just appointed leaders or even employees. The reference to "whole sys-tems" is, of course, a metaphor—one intended to suggest an attempt to work with all those whose actions are interconnected (Weisbord, 1992). In Future Searches, hundreds may participate at once or in successions of meetings. It is not just the presupposition of leaders and followers that is set aside, but also the presupposition of leadership as a relevant and useful language tool for reality construction. So multilogical methodologies—in so far as this is possible—work with initially "empty processes," so to speak. The process does not "start" with leadership, participants are not related to as "passive receptacles" or as "imaginative consumers" (see Bryman, 1996, p. 286), and all participants are potentially active contributors to local real-ities. Such processes can leave space for participants to generate multiple local cultural realities.

Multilogical development work generates different perspectives that are "allowed to be different" rather than dominated or worked into a consen-sus position. This is very different from practices that aim to diagnose the past, to analyze problems in self–other relations, and then to change these known realities. For a start, relational premises provide no basis for declar-ing some acts to be acts of analysis (diagnosis) and others as intervention. Indeed, in a relational perspective, acts of diagnosis (e.g., asking ques-tions) are also acts of influence over how the process goes on. In addition, rather than, for example, try to unblock "old" identity constructions, multi-logical methodologies may be directed toward enabling new possibilities in the present. Development practices may work with ever moving and multi-ple realities; from the present point of view, this is the point, so to speak (see, e.g. Hosking, 2004).

CONCLUSION

This chapter began by noting calls for greater paradigm diversity and for sensitive dialogues between paradigms. Some of the difficulties in communicating between paradigms also were noted—it is hard to avoid imposing one's own taken-for-granted's and standards. In this context, certain social constructionist themes were introduced and developed in ways that departed from "positivist" and "postpositivist" paradigms and therefore from the "modernist" discourse. These themes dealt with the *potentials* of construction processes—potentials that might be very differently realized depending on the particularities of text–context relations. Central to this enterprise was the focus on relational realities (leaving aside questions of what is "really" real); the treatment of these as ongoing constructions and the treatment of these constructions as necessarily embracing the knowing/acting participant—including the researcher/theorist and her discourse of science.

These themes were applied to leader–followership to suggest that new development possibilities can be imagined and can seem sensible in the context of this postmodern discourse. The discourse is crucial. Practices such as teaching influence skills or listening do not make sense in their own right and do not have just one meaning. Rather, they mean very different things depending on the wider context of assumptions to which they are related in *particular* text–context relations. Certain practices were outlined that might seem nonsensical, crazy, or commonplace, depending on the paradigm context. For example, for consultants to act from a "being informed" rather than knowing stance could seem absurd from a certain point of view. Similarly, finding ways to "make space" for multiple leadership realities can seem frivolous (to say the least) if one supposes that knowledge is objective or subjective, right or wrong.

That different cultures have different ways of knowing—offering different resources and constraints, that none is "perfect," and that there is no single, sufficient standard by which all could be judged now is widely accepted—at least in some literatures (see, e.g., Gergen, 1994; Harding, 1998). Once positivism ceases to be "the only game in town," "new thinking spaces" are "opened up" (Harding, 1998; see also Manicas & Secord, 1983). The present chapter has begun to explore a postmodern discourse of leadership as a process of social construction. In so doing, the three themes identified by Bryman (1996) in his handbook review were addressed: by treating "leadership" as problematic, cultures (leadership settings) as fragmented, and by departing from "modernist" assumptions about rationality.

Finally, and as we noted earlier, the purpose was *not* to offer a substantive theory for subsequent empirical testing. Our premises concerned *abstract* ways of thinking and *potentials* that can be differently realized in different local–cultural–historical processes. In this view, empirical testing is viewed as a process of social construction—one in which theory and findings are inextricably interwoven. This means that empirical work no longer has the central and definitive role given to it by positivism and postpositivism. As stated at the start, our purpose *was* to offer a changed "thinking space," which might invite "new kinds of questions" and might open up "new kinds of possible futures" (Harding, 1998). This brings us back to Bryman's call for work that problematizes leadership, assumes multiple realities, and departs from modernist assumptions. So, our present focus on *processes* rather than constructions (as content) made it possible to show how leadership (and all relational) realities may be variously constructed in different local–cultural–historical processes. Furthermore, by emphasizing language as "world making" and "worlds" (realities, facts) as theory-laden constructions, modernist assumptions about rationality (and empiricism) lost their foundations. This was a different sort of "voyage of discovery" intended to open up new worlds—new questions, new possibilities, and new standards for evaluation.

NOTES

1. In other words, we are not "starting with" a priori constructions of what it is to be a person, or of particular individuals (e.g., as leaders or followers) but giving more space for locally emergent constructions.
2. I say "something like" for the reason given earlier—in the present discourse, methodologies are neither independent of theory nor singular "things."

REFERENCES

Alvesson, M., & Deetz, S. (2000). *Doing critical management research.* London: Sage.

Anderson, H. (1997). *Conversation, language, and possibilities: A postmodern approach to therapy.* New York: HarperCollins.

Arbib, M., & Hesse, M. (1986). *The construction of reality.* Cambridge, UK: Cambridge University Press.

Argyris, C., & Schön, D. A. (1978). *Organizational learning: A theory of action perspective.* Reading, MA: Addison-Wesley.

Barrett, F. J., Thomas, G. F., & Hocevar, S. P. (1995). The central role of discourse in large scale change. *Journal of Applied Behavioural Science, 31*(3), 352–372.

Barker, R. A. (1997). How can we train leaders if we do not know what leadership is? *Human Relations, 50*(4), 343–362.

Bass, A., & Hosking, D. M. (1998). A changed approach to change. *Aston Business School Research Paper Series, RP 9808.*

Bateson, G. (1972). *Steps to an ecology of mind.* San Francisco: Chandler.

Blanchard, K., & Hersey, P. (1996). Great ideas. *Training and Development, 50*(1), 42–47.

Bligh, M., Kohles, J. C., & Meindl, J. R. (2004). Charisma under crisis: Presidential leadership, rhetoric, and media responses before and after the September 11th terrorist attacks. *Leadership Quarterly, 15*, 211–239.

Bouwen, R., & Hosking, D. M. (2000). Reflections on relational readings of organizational learning. *European Journal of Work and Organizational Psychology, 9*(2), 267–274.

Bryman, A. (1996). Leadership in organizations. In S. R. Clegg, C. Hardy, & W. R. Nord (Eds.), *Handbook of organization studies* (pp. 276–293). London: Sage.

Bryman, A. (1986). *Leadership and organizations.* London: Routledge Kegan Paul.

Brown, H., & Hosking, D. M. (1986). Distributed leadership and skilled performance as successful organization in social movements. *Human Relations, 39*(1), 65–79.

Burr, V. (1995). *An introduction to social constructionism.* London: Routledge.

Chasin, R., Herzig, M., Roth, S., Chasin, L., Becker, C., & Stains, R. (1996). From diatribe to dialogue on divisive public issues: Approaches drawn from family therapy. *Mediation Quarterly, 13*(4), 323–344.

Chia, R. (1995). From modern to postmodern organizational analysis. *Organization Studies, 16*(4), 579–604.

Cohen, I. J. (1989). *Structuration theory: Anthony Giddens and the constitution of social life.* New York: St. Martin's Press.

Conger, J. (1992). *Learning to lead: The art of transforming managers into leaders.* San Francisco: Jossey-Bass.

Cook, T., & Campbell, D. T. (1979). *Quasi-experimentation: Design and analysis issues for field settings.* Chicago: Rand McNally.

Dachler, H. P. (1991). Management and leadership as relational phenomena. In M. V. Cranach, W. Doise, & Mugny, G. (Eds.), *Social representations and the social bases of knowledge* (pp. 169–178). Bern, Germany: Hogrefe & Huber.

Dachler, H. P. (1999). Threats to the potential of global leadership. In W. H. Mobley (Ed.), *Alternatives of individual conceptions of global leadership: Dealing with multiple persepectives* (pp. 75–98). Stamford, CT: JAI Press.

Dachler, H. P., & Hosking, D. M. (1995). The primacy of relations in socially constructing organizational realities. In D. M. Hosking, H. P. Dachler, & K. J. Gergen (Eds.), *Management and organization: Relational alternatives to individualism* (pp.1–29). Aldershot, UK: Avebury.

Deetz, S. (2000). Describing differences in approaches to organisation science. In P. Frost, R. Lewin, & D. Daft (Eds.), *Talking about organisation science.* Thousand Oaks, CA: Sage.

Edwards, D., & Potter, J. (1992). *Discursive psychology.* London: Sage.

Farrelly, F., & Brandsma, J. M. (1974). *Provocative therapy.* Cupertino, CA: Meta Publications.

Fiedler, F. E. (1996). Research on leadership selection and training: One view of the future. *Administrative Science Quarterly, 41*, 241–250.

Flax, J. (1987). Postmodernism and gender relations in feminist theory. *Signs: Journal of Women in Culture and Society, 12*(4), 621–643.

Fulmer, R. M., & Vicere, A. A. (1996, January/February). An analysis of competitive forces. *Forbes*, pp. 31–36.

Garfinkle, H. (1967). *Studies in ethnomethodology*. Englewood Cliffs, NJ: Prentice Hall.

Gergen, K. J. (1994). *Realities and relationships*. Cambridge, MA: Harvard University Press.

Gergen, K. J. (1995). Relational theory and the discourses of power. In D. M. Hosking, H. P. Dachler, & K. J. Gergen (Eds.), *Management and organization: Relational alternatives to individualism* (pp. 29–51). Aldershot, UK: Avebury.

Gergen, K. J., & Thatchenkerry, T. (1996). Organization science as social construction: Postmodern potentials. *Journal of Applied Behavioural Science, 32*(4), 356–377.

Gibb, C. A. (1969). Leadership. In G. Lindzey & E. Aronson (Eds.), *Handbook of social psychology* (pp. 205–282). Reading, MA: Addison-Wesley.

Grob, L. (1984). Leadership: The Socratic model. In B. Kellerman (Ed.), *Leadership: Multidisciplinary perspectives* (pp. 263–280). Englewood Cliffs, NJ: Prentice-Hall.

Gron, P. C. (Ed.). (2003). *Distributed organizational leadership*. Greenwich, CT: Information Age.

Guba, E., & Lincoln, Y. S. (1994). Competing paradigms in qualitative research. In N. K. Denzin & Y. S. Lincoln (Eds.), *Handbook of qualitative research* (pp. 105–117). London: Sage.

Harding, S. (1986). *The science question in feminism*. Milton Keynes, UK: Open University Press.

Harding, S. (1998). *Is science multicultural?* Bloomington: Indiana University Press.

Hermans, H., Kempen, H., & van Loon, R. (1992). The dialogical self: Beyond individualism and rationalism. *American Psychologist, 47*(1), 23–33.

Hosking, D. M. (1988). Organizing, leadership and skilful process. *Journal of Management Studies, 25*(2), 147–166.

Hosking, D. M. (2000). Ecology in mind, mindful practices. *European Journal for Work and Organizational Psychology, 9*(2), 147–158.

Hosking, D. M. (2004). Changeworks: A critical construction. In J. Boonstra (Ed.), *Dynamics of organizational change and learning* (pp. 259–279). Chichester, UK: Wiley.

Hosking, D. M. (2005). Bounded entities, constructivist revisions and radical reconstructions. *Cognitie, Creier, Comportament/ Cognition, Brain, Behavior, 9*(4), 609–622.

Hosking, D. M., & Morley, I. E. (1991). *A Social Psychology of Organising*. Chichester, UK: Harvester Wheatsheaf.

Hosking. D. M., Dachler, H. P., & Gergen, K. J. (Eds.). (1995). *Management and organization: Relational alternatives to individualism*. Aldershot, UK: Avebury.

Isaacs, W. N. (1993). Taking flight: dialogue, collective thinking, and organizational learning. *Organization Dynamics, 22*(2), 24–39.

Janov, J. (1995). Creating meaning: The heart of learning communities. *Training and Development, 49*(5), 53–58.

Korzybski, A. (1933). *Science and sanity: An introduction to non-Aristotelian systems and general semantics*. Englewood, NJ: Institute of General Semantics.

Kuhn, T. (1970). *The structure of scientific revolutions.* Chicago: University of Chicago Press.

Manicas, P., & Secord, P. (1983). Implications for psychology of the new philosophy of science. *American Psychologist, 38,* 399–413.

Martin, J. (1992). *Cultures in organizations: Three perspectives.* New York: Oxford University Press.

Meindl, J. R. (1995). The romance of leadership as a follower-centric theory: A social constructionist approach. *Leadership Quarterly, 6*(3), 329–341.

Meindl, J. R., Erlich, S. B., & Dukerich, J. M. (1985). The romance of leadership. *Administrative Science Quarterly, 30*(1), 78–102.

Morley, I. E., & Hosking, D. M. (2003). Leadership, learning and negotiation in a social psychology of organising. In N. Bennett & L. Anderson (Eds.), *Re-thinking educational leadership* (pp. 43–60). London: Sage.

Parry, K., & Meindl, J. (Eds.). (2002). *Grounding theory and leadership research: Issues and perspectives.* Greenwich, CT: Information Age.

Pearce, W. B. (1992). A "camper's guide" to constructionisms. *Human Systems: The Journal of Systemic Consultation and Management, 3,* 139–161.

Reason, P. (Ed.). (1994). *Participation in human inquiry.* London: Sage.

Rifkin, G. (1996a, April). Green buttermilk and some real leadership: Can it be learned? *Forbes,* pp. 100–108.

Rifkin, G. (1996b, April). One man's search for leadership. *Forbes,* p. 110.

Sampson, E. E. (1993). *Celebrating the other.* Hemel Hempstead, UK: Harvester Wheatsheaf.

Sorohan, E. (1995, August). Developing leaders. *Training and Development, 49,* 13.

Thompson, P. R., & McHugh, D. (1995). *Work organisations: A critical introduction.* Basingstoke, UK: Macmillan Business.

Watzlawick, P. (1990). *Munchausen's pigtail.* New York: Norton.

Watzlawick, P., Weakland, J., & Fisch, R. (1974). *Change: Principles of problem formation and problem resolution.* New York: Norton.

Weick, K. (1999). Theory construction as disciplined reflexivity: Tradeoffs in the '90s. *Academy of Management Review, 24*(4), 797–807.

Weisbord, M. (Ed.). (1992). *Discovering common ground: How future search conferences bring people together to achieve breakthrough innovation, empowerment, shared vision, and collaborative action.* San Francisco: Barrett-Koehler.

Weisbord, M., & Janoff, S. (1995). *Future search—An action guide to finding common ground in organizations and communities.* San Francisco: Barrett-Koehler.

Wittgenstein, L. (1963). *Philosophical investigations.* New York: MacMillan.

CHAPTER 12

THE SOCIAL CONSTRUCTION OF A LEGACY

Summarizing and Extending Follower-Centered Perspectives on Leadership

Michelle C. Bligh
Claremont Graduate University

Rajnandini Pillai
California State University San Marcos

Mary Uhl-Bien
University of Central Florida

"The concept of leadership remains largely elusive and enigmatic."
—Meindl, Ehrlich, & Dukerich (1985, p. 78)

"The 'romance of leadership' notion was meant to call attention to the fact that whatever the realities regarding the 'true' impact of leaders and leadership processes, such concepts have become extremely popular in our analyses of organizations."

Follower-Centered Perspectives on Leadership, pages 265–277
Copyright © 2007 by Information Age Publishing

> *"Consider the implications of relaxing the typical assumption that leadership*
> *is important in its own right..."*
>
> —Meindl (1990, p. 161)

A tribute volume is, by nature, a collective endeavor. In addition, it is in itself a process of social construction. In this chapter, we attempt to summarize what we might take away from the various follower-centered perspectives on leadership included in this volume, drawing parallels between similar ideas and pointing out areas of overlap, contradiction, and directions for future research. Consistent with the goals of the volume to look back and honor the work of a remarkable scholar, as well as to look ahead and spur new thinking and active discussion in the arena of follower-centered perspectives on leadership, in this chapter we attempt to tie together the multitude of ways in which Jim Meindl's scholarship and mentorship have impacted the field of leadership. We also highlight the various streams of research in the volume that have been inspired by his work. In this process, we "socially construct" a legacy of Jim Meindl's work.

If the chapters in this volume are any indication, a key element of Jim's legacy is that he drew attention to followers' perceptions of leadership. This emphasis on followers and followers' perceptions has been extrapolated and enacted in a multitude of ways throughout this volume. For example, authors describe the strong needs of followers to have leaders who can keep them safe in uncertain situations (Lipman-Blumen) and provide vision (Carsten & Bligh) and direction (Uhl-Bien & Pillai), particularly in times of crisis (Pillai, Kohles, & Bligh). Probably because of these needs, followers socially construct leadership (and followership, Uhl-Bien & Pillai) through their interactions with one another (Chen, Belkin, & Kurtzberg), in groups (van Knippenberg, van Knippenberg, & Giessner), or in social networks (Mayo & Pastor). Followers construct these views through cognitive inference processes by which they infer that leadership has occurred (Lord & Medvedeff) and by looking to reference points that exist in their social groups, which become a critical source of information about leadership and social reality (van Knippenberg et al.). Consistent with these ideas, leadership research can be broadened by considering organizational change strategies from the perspectives of followers (Chen et al.), follower-centered perspectives of vision implementation (Carsten & Bligh), how visual images of leadership introduce plurality and the possibility for multiple follower interpretations in the social construction of leadership (Jackson & Guthey), and how emotional reactions of followers play into attributions and the subsequent constructions of leaders (Chen et al.). More radically, follower-centered perspectives move away from traditional conceptualizations of leaders and followers (Hosking) to describe leadership as distributed (Hosking) or shared (Offermann & Scuderi), involving the recognition that followers have long shared leadership with those who have led them (Offermann & Scuderi). As these chapters collectively illustrate, the growing recognition of the importance of followers' perceptions of leaders and leadership processes is an important trend in the field, and Meindl's work can be credited with inspiring at least some of this increasing attention to the follower side of the leadership equation.

Ironically, Jim himself would likely have pointed to this increased attention as a trend or fad in itself, and might have challenged his colleagues and students to examine some of the underlying reasons driving this trend. In this tradition, we hope the present volume will likewise encourage its readers to consider some of the larger societal and cultural values or needs that underlie this growing emphasis on followership. Is it the dissatisfaction with some of our most venerated and respected leaders that have publicly and shamefully fallen from their pedestals (e.g., the scandals of the Clinton presidency, Enron, WorldCom, and the United Nations)? Or is it the emergence of new organizational structures, globalization, and the deconstruction of knowledge brought about by the World Wide Web that is driving our increased focus on how followers shape and inform leadership? If this is the case, is the renewed emphasis on followership restricted to the North American continent or is it much more widely dissipated? While we sadly miss Jim's thoughts on these and other issues, we hope this volume, which includes contributions from scholars around the world, will help to continue to spark scholarship and debate within the field of leadership on the functions leadership serves within society, and the broader trends and values that inform the controversies, trends, and dialogues that surround it.

In the remainder of this chapter, we focus on several overarching themes and ideas that seem to weave across and through the various contributions to this tribute volume. In particular, we focus on how different chapters enact the theme of follower perceptions of leadership, and attempt to illustrate how each one focuses on various aspects of this theme. Next, we turn to ramifications of Jim's work for the construction of charismatic leadership and subsequently the importance of context in the leadership process, as well as considering the parallel ideas of social constructionism and social identification as they relate to leadership and followership. We then conclude with some interesting directions for future research that we hope will continue to inspire others in these various traditions to carry on Jim's legacy.

A MYRIAD OF FOLLOWER PERCEPTIONS OF LEADERSHIP

All of the chapters in this volume deal with follower perceptions of leadership, and the chapters are consistent in enacting Meindl's shift in focus from leader-centric approaches to more explicitly considering the role of the followers in the "construction" of leadership. However, each chapter approaches this overarching theme from a different aspect. Offermann and Scuderi view leadership as a communal process of influence toward the accomplishment of objectives, and focus on how leadership is shared across group members, ranging from *co*-leadership, which is the most restricted form of shared leadership, to *collective* leadership, which is the most complete or evolved form of shared leadership. Lipman-Blumen focuses on why followers are drawn to toxic leaders using Meindl's romance of leadership framework, and suggests ways in which followers can individually and collectively counter the effects of such leaders. Pillai and colleagues focus on variations in follower evaluations of President George W. Bush's leadership during different types of crises, and the roles that party identification and perceptions of leader effectiveness play in these assessments using charismatic criteria. Across these chapters, followers' attributional processes, implicit theories, and psychological needs and schemas play a critical role in the leadership process.

Several of the chapters explore and even problematize the meaning of followership itself, and what using the labels of "leader" and "follower" might signify. Using a postmodern perspective, Hosking focuses on relational realities involving constructions of the self in relation to others, and explores how someone is constructed as a leader or follower and how these realities are created and changed. Uhl-Bien and Pillai argue that while the romance of leadership takes a follower-centered approach, there are socially constructed views of followership as well, which in turn may influence both attributions of leadership and attributions by followers about themselves and their own roles and participation in the leadership process. For instance, prototypical followership behavioral interpretations might involve some form of deference to the leader, particularly when there are hierarchical constructions of leadership and followership. Across these chapters, the emphasis on follower perceptions and followership as a powerful aspect of what constitutes the leadership process is a consistent theme.

A key point emphasized throughout the volume is the idea that followers are not just connected to their leaders; they are also connected to other followers. This idea is reflected in Mayo and Pastor's argument that followers' perceptions of their leaders are embedded in social networks, and their contention that researchers need to look at *inter*follower processes to get a better understanding of leadership. They call attention to leadership as an emergent phenomenon in which followers play an active role. An important emphasis here is that sense making is integral to the process of leadership, and individuals learn the meaning of leadership behaviors through their interactions with one another. Again and again throughout the volume, we see the idea that these social interactions are absolutely critical to the construction of leadership: Followers' attributions of leadership are, to a great extent, the result of individuals interacting with one another, sharing information about the leader, and comparing one another's views. For example, Offermann and Scuderi point out the interconnectedness of followers through the phenomenon of shared leadership and co-leadership, again suggesting that the interaction of followers themselves is an integral and often overlooked aspect of leadership. These ideas build upon Meindl's views on social contagion among followers, and further describe how followers relate to one another in reacting to and forming attributions about their leaders.

Another important theme throughout the volume is that followers are not hapless beings that exist at the mercy of their leaders. Instead, contributors to this volume emphasize that followers are active, powerful players in the leadership process. For example, in Offermann and Scuderi's view, leadership roles can be shared by several members of the team or group, thus empowering them to achieve common goals together as a collective. This is a very different approach from the traditional view of leaders and followers that emphasize their relative positions in the hierarchy, with followers frequently taking on a passive, understated, or even invisible role. Similarly, in Lipman-Blumen's view, followers can actively counteract the effect of toxic leaders by holding leaders accountable, creating term limits and departure options, and even calling upon their own enduring ambivalence about leaders to drive themselves to action. Implicit in the Pillai and colleagues chapter is the idea that while followers may look for a charismatic leader to lead them out of crisis, ineffective leadership is poorly tolerated (particularly at the presidential level), and followers can and do exercise their rights to vote ineffective leaders out of office. Carsten and Bligh's study illustrates that followers are not just passive recipients of a leader's vision: followers are actively involved in constructing the meaning of the vision to their own work roles, its implementation, and potentially develop both emotional investment as well as skepticism in a leader's vision and his or her plans for implementation. Taken together, the contributions to this volume share a consistent emphasis on followers as both active and interconnected players in the leadership process.

FOLLOWER PROCESSES IN CHARISMATIC LEADERSHIP

Following Meindl's belief that charismatic leadership is a socially constructed phenomenon that says just as much about followers as it does about leaders, several of the chapters in this volume address the follower processes involved in the charismatic leadership phenomenon. For example, Mayo and Pastor argue that rather than being dependent on their interactions with the leader, followers' charismatic experiences are affected, to a great extent, by the experiences of *other followers.* Thus, attributions of charisma to a leader are not solely grounded in the individual interactions between followers and leaders, but rather, they are, to a great degree, the result of followers' lateral interactions with their peers. From this perspective, the focus shifts from the actions of the leader to the contagious expressions and displays of the followers. Thus, the charismatic appeal of the leader is socially constructed, a matter of intersubjectively shared sense making among a group of followers.

Importantly, the chapters in this volume also suggest that the dispersion or degree of consensus among followers regarding the charismatic appeal of their leadership becomes relevant. These individual differences regarding the leader may be interpreted not just as random variance, but *the result of group members defining their own organizational reality,* and developing different constructions of leadership that can *only be understood when we examine the pattern of social ties that link group members to one another.* This is a very different approach to the study of charismatic leadership, and suggests that there is as much interest in the disparities between follower ratings of a charismatic leader as in the level of consensus about his or her charismatic appeal.

This theme is also prevalent in the Jackson and Guthey chapter, which builds on Meindl and colleagues' research into the social construction of business leadership images in order to better understand the construction of the charismatic appeal and other leadership attributes of high-profile CEOs. Their research supplements Meindl's pioneering work on the social construction of leadership images with the analysis of the visual construction of such images through photographic media. In their examination of the "celebrity CEO backlash," or the period of widespread media recrimination and criticism directed against former business heroes and celebrity CEOs, Jackson and Guthey argue that popular business images provide an important window for examining how visual images can work to *deconstruct* images of business leadership and set in play multiple and even conflicting leadership images at the same time. In this sense it represents the flipside of Meindl and colleagues' work concerning the collective construction of CEO celebrity. In other words, attention to the "CEO backlash" augments Meindl and colleagues' original work with an illustration of the contentious dynamics of the social construction of leadership images, and again highlights the importance of the dispersion or degree of consensus among followers regarding the charismatic appeal of their leaders.

In yet another chapter concerning charismatic leadership in this volume, Chen and colleagues investigate how charisma attributions are part and parcel of organizational members' cognitive and emotional responses to the unfolding organizational change. The authors call for additional research into the underlying mechanisms through which charismatic leadership attributions are made, and posit emotion valence and divergence as important affective mechanisms that mediate the relationship between change strategy and perceptions of charismatic leadership. These authors are as interested in the charisma attribution process as they are in the outcome, and target two dependent variables: the level of perceived charismatic leadership and the variance of such perceptions (e.g., the degree of divergence of charismatic leadership perceptions among members of the organization). Again, we see how the role of variance in charismatic perceptions and the distinctive patterns of charismatic attributions across followers thus become critical aspects of the charismatic leadership phenomenon.

Finally, Mayo and Pastor suggest a number of implications for studying charismatic leadership from this perspective. For example, followers vary in their susceptibility to a charismatic leader: the first followers to succumb to the charisma "virus" are likely to be those high in both agreeableness and affect intensity. Yet an understanding of charismatic attributions outcomes is no more complete through an understanding of these follower characteristics as it is through an understanding of the leader's characteristics; we must also examine the interindividual processes involved. From a social network perspective, Mayo and Pastor point out that the individuals most likely to spread charismatic attributions are those who are high in closeness centrality and high in betweenness centrality within a given network.

Together, these chapters illustrate nicely Meindl's (1990, p. 198) comments that "existing leader-centered approaches need to be complemented with follower-centered approaches when it comes to understanding the more transformational aspects of leadership...this alternative should focus on the social psychological process that take place among followers, independent of, or controlling for the actions and traits of the leader." The chapters in this volume have made a great deal of headway toward enacting this alternative.

CONTEXTUAL INFLUENCES: ORGANIZATIONAL CHANGE, CRISIS, AND AMBIGUITY IN SHAPING FOLLOWERS' PERCEPTIONS

Another important theme throughout the volume is that people rely on others to make sense of novel or ambiguous situations and events, and the role of context is critical in understanding processes of social construction, contagion, and identity. Groups with which people identify are a key source of information about social reality, and an important contextual influence for individuals' positions on issues where no objective reference point exists (such as norms and values) (Offermann & Scuderi). Thus, the sociocultural environment surrounding the leadership process becomes critical, and this topic is enacted in various ways throughout the volume. For example, this theme is illustrated in Lipman-Blumen's chapter on toxic leadership, in which she points out that followers' levels of internal needs and anxieties are triggered by the external social context. She explores how this impacts followers' attraction to and potential seduction by toxic leaders.

In a related vein, both Meindl's social constructionist perspective and social identity analyses point specifically to the contextual role of crisis and uncertainty in determining responses to leadership. Meindl inspired many of his students to study the sociopolitical context of leadership, especially the importance of crisis in the emergence of charismatic leadership. Furthermore, he and his students studied the U.S. Presidential elections (Pillai & Williams, 1998; Pillai, Williams, Lowe, & Jung, 2003), the impact of seminal events such as the terrorist attacks of September 11, 2001, on the rhetoric adopted by the President (Bligh, Kohles, & Meindl, 2004a, 2004b), and the influence of the California Recall Election on perceptions of incumbent governor Gray Davis and charismatic challenger Arnold Schwarzenegger (Bligh, Kohles, & Pillai, 2005). The Pillai and colleagues chapter continues this tradition by examining follower attributions of charisma and transformational leadership to President Bush across the major contextual events of his presidency such as the war on terror following the September 11, 2001, attacks and the ongoing war in Iraq. In addition, both the Lipman-Blumen and the Pillai and colleagues chapters specifically discuss the role of crisis in followers' perceptions. In the former case, followers are drawn to toxic leaders after a crisis because they hold the promise of keeping them safe in an uncertain world. In the latter case, involving the relationship between voting citizens and the American President, it is argued that followers look to the President during the threatening times after a crisis to provide a sanctuary from the threats of terrorism, economic downturns, and natural disasters. A few studies have examined the role of crisis in leadership attributions, but the Pillai and colleagues study examines different types of crises on follower attributions of charisma, a line of enquiry that was actively encouraged by Meindl.

In addition to crisis, several of the chapters in this volume examine followers' perceptions of leadership in other important organizational contexts. Carsten and Bligh draw attention to the increasingly common situation in which organizational restructuring leads to leadership turnover, whether internally or externally motivated. Similarly, Chen and colleagues argue that social-organizational contexts are the primary determinants of charismatic attributions, and direct attention to organizational change (as opposed to crisis) as an important context in which charismatic leadership is constructed. As they point out, future research should attempt to identify the factors that moderate the main effect of the organizational or societal context, whether it be a context of change, crisis, or organizational restructuring.

In a related vein, both social construction and social identification analyses point to the role of crisis and uncertainty in determining responses to leadership, and there is a great deal of overlap between the core arguments of these two theories throughout the volume. In the Mayo and Pastor chapter, the authors emphasize the importance of social networks, and argue that contagion evidenced by relative change in the attributions of charisma follows the pattern of communication exchange among individuals. In the van Knippenberg and colleagues chapter, the authors emphasize social identity rather than social contagion. It is interesting to note, however, that while Mayo and Pastor's social network perspective is derived directly from Meindl's work on the social construction of leadership and van Knippenberg and colleagues' social identity perspective was developed separately in social psychology, the latter is very consistent with Meindl's approach. The two vary only slightly in terms of the way each describes the processes by which leadership is constructed.

Thus, although the social construction perspective and the social identity analysis do not necessarily pinpoint the same determinants of leadership perceptions, they seem to be in agreement over the process through which leadership perceptions become socially shared. This is also evident in the similarity between, on the one hand, the moderators of group members' tendency to rely on group memberships and group prototypicality identified in the social identity analysis, and on the other hand, the factors that are proposed to be conducive to perceptions of charisma in the social construction perspective. Whereas the social identity analysis points to identification and social identity salience as the key moderator of the influence of leader group prototypicality, Pillai and Meindl (1998) proposed that collectivistic orientations (i.e., emphasizing the collective identity) are conducive to perceptions of charismatic leadership. As van Knippenberg and colleagues point out in this volume, the social identity analysis thus complements and extends the social contagion analysis proposed by Meindl and colleagues, and both theoretical perspectives point to the critical importance of the situation in shaping followers' perceptions.

DIRECTIONS FOR FUTURE RESEARCH

The various chapters and perspectives in this volume bring to mind a wide-ranging agenda for future research in the traditions of follower perceptions of leadership, interfollower processes, the role of context in understanding leadership processes and outcomes, and the role of follower cognitions and emotions in understanding the leadership process. Below we highlight some specific future directions that were salient as we attempted to summarize the various contributions in this volume and highlight the similar themes suggested. Specifically, future research might explore the following:

- How may leaders play an important and active role in modeling the social context and managing their own leadership images? For example, with the current trends toward portraying a servant leader image in the wake of the corporate scandals involving larger-than-life business leaders, what are the respective roles of leaders and followers in disseminating this image?
- Who are the first followers to succumb to the charisma "virus" in specific contexts (e.g., situations of crisis, organizational change or restructuring)?
- Who are the individuals most likely to spread charismatic attributions and through what behaviors?
- Under what circumstances is there wide dispersion in the degree of charismatic consensus among followers? What role does the business press play in this dispersion? Is it different for cult leaders?
- What contexts (e.g., organizational change, restructuring, leadership turnover) are particularly ripe for charismatic leadership constructions?
- What can be learned through exploring the perspectives of organizational members who are experiencing organizational change (as opposed to those of leaders or external audiences)?
- What are some of the key underlying mechanisms through which charismatic leadership attributions are made?
- What are the key affective (emotional) and cognitive mechanisms that influence leadership constructions? For example, Chen and colleagues posit emotion valence and divergence as important affective mechanisms that mediate the relationship between change strategy and perceptions of charismatic leadership. What other mechanisms may be identified?
- What is the role of different types of crises on leadership attributions? Is a personal crisis more likely to trigger attributions of cha-

risma to a leader than a societal crisis? What about the degree of control that a leader has on the crisis?

- Is shared leadership possible during a crisis? Some studies indicate that during a crisis, leadership often tends to be concentrated in the hands of a single leader or very few and tends to become authoritarian.
- What kinds of crisis situations would call for shared leadership? For instance, a life-threatening crisis facing a medical emergency team would probably call for shared leadership but a crisis engendered by a natural disaster (e.g., Hurricane Katrina) would probably lend itself to more concentrated forms of leadership with a unity of command.
- Is shared leadership by its very nature an antidote to toxic leaders? Or is it possible for several like-minded toxic leaders who share the same corrosive values to get together and lead their followers down the wrong path under the illusion of empowerment?
- What role does social contagion play in the spread of shared leadership? Alternatively, can it resist the spread of toxic leadership? In other words, can followers empower one another to step up and take leadership responsibility, and when necessary, can they infect each other with the ambivalence toward a toxic leader that is collectively more powerful than individual dissent?
- What is the process by which "followership" is socially constructed, and what factors cause it to be constructed in different ways?

CONCLUSION

All of the chapters in this volume draw on Meindl's landmark work on the romance of leadership and expand his follower-centered approach to leadership. These chapters have presented both empirical findings and suggested new theoretical frameworks for continuing Meindl's work and contributing to his legacy. Part of this legacy is the establishment of an ongoing research tradition that approaches leadership as a complex and socially constructed phenomenon involving not only leaders, but also followers and the contexts in which leaders and followers interact.

In closing, another key theme throughout this volume is that leaders can and do play an important role in modeling the social context and managing their own leadership images. While many of the contributors talked about what leaders can do, the chapters by van Knippenberg and colleagues and Chen and colleagues perhaps articulated the strongest perspectives regarding the active role that leaders can play in influencing followers' constructions of their leadership. Mayo and Pastor also point out that leaders can play an important role in modeling the social context and managing their own leadership images. These arguments are consistent with Meindl's own beliefs that social constructionist processes do not negate the role of leaders. As Jackson and Guthey point out, Meindl did not advance the follower-centric approach in an effort to compete with or to replace the dominant leader-centric approach. To those who criticized the romance of leadership perspective as overly one-sided, preferring to focus on more traditional leader-centric approaches, Jim's response was "go for it... *Wunderbar!*" (1998, pp. 322–323). However, despite efforts to characterize it as such, Jim continually pointed out that the romance of leadership perspective was not "anti-leadership"; rather, it represented "an alternative to theories and perspectives that place great weight on 'leaders' and on the substantive significance to their actions and activities" (Meindl, 1995, p. 330). Thus, Jim did not reject or minimize the importance of leadership, but pointed out that "it is easier to believe in leadership than to prove it" (Meindl, 1990, p. 161). Furthermore, he argued for the need to continually question and problematize the prevailing emphasis on leaders to the detriment of followers. In moving toward achieving this goal, we think Jim would have been pleased with the ideas the contributors present here. We hope that this volume not only provides a fitting social construction of his ongoing legacy, but also provokes scholars and practitioners to continue to build on it in the years to come.

REFERENCES

Bligh, M. C., Kohles, J. C., & Meindl, J. R. (2004a). Charisma under crisis: Presidential leadership, rhetoric, and media responses before and after the September 11th terrorist attacks. *Leadership Quarterly, 15,* 211–239.

Bligh, M. C., Kohles, J. C., & Meindl, J. R. (2004b). Charting the language of leadership: A methodological investigation of President Bush and the crisis of 9/11. *Journal of Applied Psychology, 89*(3), 562–574.

Bligh, M. C., Kohles, J. C., & Pillai, R. (2005). Crisis and charisma in the California recall election. *Leadership, 1*(3), 323, 352.

Meindl, J. R. (1998). Thanks—And let me try again. In F. Dansereau & F. J. Yammarino (Eds.), *Leadership: The multiple-level approaches, Part B. Contemporary and Alternative* (pp. 321–326). Stamford, CT: JAI Press.

Meindl, J. R. (1995). The romance of leadership as a follower-centric theory: A social constructionist approach. *Leadership Quarterly, 6*(3), 329–341.

Meindl, J. R. (1990). On leadership: An alternative to the conventional wisdom. In B. M. Staw & L. L. Cummings (Eds.), *Research in organizational behavior* (Vol. 12, pp. 159–203). Greenwich, CT: JAI Press.

Meindl, J. R., Ehrlich, S. B., & Dukerich, J. M. (1985). The romance of leadership. *Administrative Science Quarterly, 30,* 78–102.

Pillai, R., & Meindl, J. R. (1998). Context and charisma: A "meso" level examination of the relationship of organic structure, collectivism, and crisis to charismatic leadership. *Journal of Management, 24*(5), 643–664.

Pillai, R., & Williams, E.A. (1998). Does leadership matter in the political arena?: Voter perceptions of candidates' transformational and charismatic leadership and the 1996 U.S. presidential vote. *Leadership Quarterly, 9,* 397–416.

Pillai, R., Williams, E. A., Lowe, K. B., & Jung, D. I. (2003). Personality, transformational leadership, trust, and the 2000 U.S. presidential vote. *Leadership Quarterly, 14*(2),161–192.

CHAPTER 13

ROMANCING, FOLLOWING, AND SENSEMAKING

James Meindl's Legacy

Karl E. Weick
University of Michigan

"Let no one say that he is a follower of Gandhi. It is enough that I should be my own follower. I know what an inadequate follower I am of myself, for I cannot live up to the convictions I stand for. You are not followers but fellow students, fellow pilgrims, fellow seekers, fellow workers."

—Mahatma Gandhi (1940)

If, at 5:24 A.M., on Saturday, May 6, 2006, you had typed the word "leader" into the Google search engine, you would have been greeted with 852 *million* different items about leaders. If you had then googled the word "follower" you would have found a 'mere' 15 million items. That's 57 items about leaders for every one item about followers. Talk about romance! That imbalance bothered James Meindl and he sought to correct it. His efforts, and those of his associates, represent a determined, remarkably generative set of ideas that continue to help all of us escape the thrall of leadership, decouple leaders from leadership phenomena ("leaders are not necessarily significant for leadership phenomena" [Meindl, 1995, p.

Follower-Centered Perspectives on Leadership, pages 279–291
Copyright © 2007 by Information Age Publishing
All rights of reproduction in any form reserved.

330]), and redirect our attention to earlier, less obvious moments of social construction when people try to make sense of their organizational experience. This chapter is a brief chronicle of just such a reconsideration of leading in light of Meindl's ideas.

When attention is redirected in ways suggested by Meindl, we see leadership differently. A good example of this difference is Dee Hock's (1999) commentary on the partitioning of organizational experience into leader–follower segments. Hock, founder of VISA, said, "true leading and following presumes choice, liberty to sever the relationship and pursue another path.... Followers lead by choosing where to be led." Hock goes on to say, "In the deepest sense, distinction between leaders and followers is meaningless. In every moment of life, we are simultaneously leading and following. There is never a time when our knowledge, judgment, and wisdom are not more useful and applicable than that of another. There is never a time when the knowledge, judgment, and wisdom of another are not more useful and applicable than ours. At any time that 'other' may be superior, subordinate, or peer" (pp. 72–73).

Notice some of the nuances that are suggested, nuances that are already evident in Meindl's thinking. Hock questions the separation of leader–follower as did Meindl. Such questions of separation are found with other dualities in organizational thinking such as the recent reanalysis of Simon's distinctions between fact and value and means and ends (Cohen, in press). The inspiration for such reexamination comes in part from John Dewey's (1896/1998) influential recasting of the elemental distinction between stimulus and response. He argued that psychologists made a big mistake when they said that all action involves a reflex arc consisting of three parts: (1) sensation or stimulus, (2) idea or central activity, (3) reaction or response. Dewey argued that researchers had the sequence backwards. They mistook shifting functions for discrete, sequential parts and they ignored unified acts that were cycles rather than arcs. The sequence was backwards because the so-called originating "sensations" did not become clear until the outcome was known, which meant that "stimuli" could hardly have controlled the unfolding act. In Dewey's words, "the reflex arc idea, as commonly employed, is defective in that it assumes sensory stimulus and motor response as distinct psychical existences, while in reality they are always inside a co-ordination and have their significance purely from the part played in maintaining or reconstituting the coordination.... This circuit is more truly organic than reflex, because response determines the stimulus, just as truly as sensory stimulus determines movement. Indeed, the movement is only for the sake of determining the stimulus, of fixing what kind of a stimulus it is, of interpreting it" (pp. 5, 6). I mention Dewey's analysis because Meindl's conceptualizations of leadership reflect the spirit of Dewey. Meindl's work too incorporates shifting functions, unified acts and cycles, and outcomes that retrospectively define what must have been inputs.

Part of what it means to blur the bright line between leader and follower is also reflected in Hock's image of people who simultaneously know more than others and less than others, a simultaneity that was part of Meindl's worldview. This combination of knowing more and knowing less is the hallmark of wisdom, as defined by Meacham (1990). He argued that "the essence of wisdom...lies not in what is known but rather in the manner in which that knowledge is held and in how that knowledge is put to use. To be wise is not to know particular facts but to know without excessive confidence or excessive cautiousness.... [T]o both accumulate knowledge while remaining suspicious of it, and recognizing that much remains unknown, is to be wise" (pp. 185, 187). Thus, "the essence of wisdom is in knowing that one does not know, in the appreciation that knowledge is fallible, in the balance between knowing and doubting" (p. 210). To treat leading and following as simultaneous is to redistribute knowing and doubting more widely, to expect ignorance and fallibility to be similarly distributed, and to expect that knowledge is what happens between heads rather than inside a single leader's head.

Hock also suggests that choice is a precondition for following, a point to be developed later. Choice as it unfolds in leader–follower relations has a dark side. For example, the wildland firefighting crew at Mann Gulch (Maclean, 1992; Weick, 1993) tragically chose not to comply with their "leader" Wagner Dodge's last-second life-saving invention of an escape fire. Instead, they chose to comply with the shouted appraisal of the second in command, "to hell with that, I'm getting out of here" (Maclean, 1992, p. 99) and tried to outrun the advancing wall of fire. None of them made it.

CHAPTER OVERVIEW

The following brief commentary is a gloss on Meindl's discussions of the romance of leadership, followers, and sense making. The comments are intended to illustrate how Meindl's ideas have a remarkable ability to restir presumably settled analyses. It is a testimonial to Meindl's legacy that when one reexamines one's thinking through Meindl's eyes, the result is an enriched understanding of organizational complexities. This reexamination is even more meaningful for me since I was the *ASQ* editor who accepted and published his romance of leadership article in 1985 (Meindl, Ehrlich, & Dukerich, 1985). It is a pleasure 21 years later to don an editor-like mantle, study Meindl's writing, and scribble an ongoing commentary in the margins of his manuscripts.

ROMANCING LEADERSHIP

The "romance of leadership" is a collective commitment, "manifested as a causal attribution, entailing a strong inclination to reference leaders and leadership when accounting for the fates and fortunes of groups and organizations" (Meindl, 2004, p. 463). To romance something is to "glorify it beyond reality" (p. 464). That gets sticky if we ask, beyond whose reality? If leaders are socially constructed, why should construction stop once it reaches leaders? Isn't the context itself fair game? Richard Rorty (1989) is mindful of the problem here when he talks about self-referential inconsistency (p. 123, note 2). The term describes analysts who claim to know things that they claim cannot be known. An example would be people who claim that what we call "real" is not really real. If that claim is true, how could they know it's true? In my own case I sometimes act as if I have an accurate view of a world in which only plausibility is possible, a world in which all is in flux and prophecies fulfill themselves. I claim to *know* how others make sense, forgetting that my efforts are nothing more than that same sense making. Meindl is similarly tempted to fall into this trap, but generally he maintains his balance by means of an insistence on evidence, by modesty as to how much a follower-centric orientation recasts leadership, by treating reality as the follower perception of what leader behaviors mean, and by attributing a solidity to social reality (e.g., contagion, inter-follower relations, networks) that puts it on a par with physical reality.

To see more of the nuance in Meindl's use of "romance," compare it with the formal description of the word "romantic" as crafted by experts who study synonyms. "Romance" is in the family of words that includes sentimental, maudlin, sappy, and mawkish, all of which mean "unduly or affectedly emotional" (*Merriam-Webster*, 1984, p. 739). When the word "romantic" is used in this context it implies "emotion that has little relation to things as they actually are, but is derived more from one's imagination of what they should be ideally or from one's conceptions of them as formed by literature, art, one's dreams, or the like" (p. 739).

Several features of Meindl's version of romance now stand out. "Things as they actually are" probably is not the standard against which romanticized images of leaders are compared in a socially constructed world. Nor is emotion, in acts of romanticized leadership, necessarily the primary determinant that it is in the formal definition. Instead, emotion-driven romancing gains some of its force because it tends to be backed up with thoughts, justifications, judgments, and images (e.g. Meindl, 1995, p. 332). However, it gains additional force since the consolidation of follower views often occurs under conditions of arousal (e.g., Meindl, 1993, p. 102; Meindl, 1995, p. 335). Meindl suggests that high arousal encourages the emergence of charismatic leadership as a way of thinking. This line of argument has several interesting implications. Organizational failures heighten arousal. And organizational failures often occur because people misspecify, misestimate, or misunderstand what is unfolding (Schulman, 2004). In the face of these misperceptions people may be hard-pressed to imagine that charisma is the answer or that anyone associated with the failures has it. To make things more complicated, failures tend to be known after the fact. As Marianne Paget (1988) put it, actions become mistaken only after they are finished and it's too late to redirect them. People act their way into meaning. This means that in their early stages, and for some stretch of time, actions are becoming meaningful rather than unfolding with clear-cut meaning. And in those moments of uncertainty about what the acting will have become, there is the potential for more or less positive outcomes. This open-ended quality of action is at the heart of Paget's analysis of medical mistakes. "Mistakes are known only after they are made; that is to say, they are known now rather than then.... 'Then' is a fulcrum of meaning....(as in the phrase) 'I didn't think it was a mistake then'.... A mistake follows an act. It identifies an act in its completion. It names it. An act, however, is not a mistake; it becomes mistaken.... As it is unfolding, it is not becoming a mistake at all. It is moving and evolving in time. We take the wrong path as a cognition only after already having taken the wrong path in fact. Reflection returns to the act of becoming mistaken and embraces it with hindsight" (pp. 44–45). If Paget is right, then followers should value leader behaviors associated with containment, recovery, resilience, bricolage, and improvisation.

The formal definition of romance is surprisingly individual and fails to mention interactions, conversations, social influence, networks, and other interfollower relations that are key sources of conceptions. There is the intriguing "opening" supplied by the phrase "derived more from one's imagination of what should ideally be," in the definition. Imagination plays a more central role in social life than even Meindl addressed, and this is evident, for example, in the growing fascination with abduction as a third form of logic added to the conventional ones of induction and deduction (e.g., Eco & Sebeok, 1988; Patriotta, 2004). And imagination is also center stage in discussions of leadership, having been fingered as a significant failure in the run-up to the destruction of the Twin Towers on September 11. As the 9/11 commission said, "Imagination is not a gift usually associated with bureaucracies" (Weick, 2005, p. 425). "Dreams" as the source of leader attributions may draw attention away from the more durable mechanism of self-fulfilling prophecies as the vehicle for romance. If followers treat certain traits as signs of leadership, look for the instances of those signs, enact expectations that draw forth those behaviors from potential leaders, then it will have been the case that followers enact the guidance that leads them.

To romance leadership is to form a bias that exaggerates the relative importance of leadership to the functioning of a group or system. What is interesting here is the possibility that as system awareness increases, romancing decreases. To be system-aware means to appreciate the density of interdependence, the abundance of heedful interrelating (Weick & Roberts, 1993), and the covariation of most elements, all of which mean that when *any* element changes, others change as well. Any node could be causal, not just leadership nodes.

Meindl also makes it clear that romance persists because it can be functional (1993, p. 106) for followers. For example, a leader whose reputation is romanced upward is seen as someone who can impose order on confusion ("I don't have a clue what is happening but she seems to know better"); justify compliance ("She is so smart you'd be nuts not to comply with her suggestions"); improve identification and internalization ("I now know who I want to be, namely, just like her"); structure perception ("I was overwhelmed with data until I saw how few cues she used to guide us back on course"); provide security ("She won't let anything happen to us"); provide a sense of human agency and control ("She has clout and credibility with her boss and can get the resources we need"); and, aid in the reduction of cognitive dissonance ("Her actions and words add consonant elements and importance to my chosen alternatives and highlight the negative qualities of the options that I rejected"). Notice that most of these functions turn on the success with which followers can idealize the leader, which would suggest that attributions of charisma and vision are much more than mere embellishments. If one burrows into these functions one by one, there are straightforward predictions. For example, followers high in self-efficacy should feel less compelled to comply or to justify compliance, which should lead them to use criteria other than charisma to evaluate leaders, and to be wary of those who dwell on this criterion.

Conjectures about romance could move in quite a different direction. It may be functional for me to muddy my thoughts about the characteristics of leaders because, in doing so, I then never have to assume the unequivocal identity of a "follower." If it's hazy just what it means to be a leader in this situation, then what it means to be a follower is just as hazy. Regardless of whether one adopts a leader-centric or follower-centric perspective, there it is assumed that people prefer clarity about leaders and leadership. Maybe not. It's possible that ambiguity concerning leadership can be functional and people strive to maintain that ambiguity. Blurred leadership may forestall identities such as that of follower, which status-conscious people may resist.

FOLLOWING

The basic premise in Meindl's work is that "the behavior of followers is assumed to be much less under the control and influence of the leader, and more under the control and influence of forces that govern the social construction process itself" (1995, p. 330). "Leadership is considered to have emerged when followers construct their experiences in terms of leadership concepts—that is, when they interpret their relationship as having a leadership–followership dimension" (p. 332).

When Meindl describes the relationship of follower, it is clear that he introduces a more complex social world than romancing would suggest. Just consider the word "follow" itself. To follow can mean two different things: (1) to come later in time or sequence or logic or understanding (e.g., to succeed or ensue); and (2) to go after someone (e.g., to chase or to trail). To come after or to go after, which is more characteristic of the follower? It gets even more complicated when you add in the two meanings of follower. A follower is someone who attaches herself to the person or opinions of another, either (1) by choice (e.g., disciple, adherent) or (2) by "personal devotion [which] overshadows or eclipses the critical faculty" (e.g., partisan, satellite) (*Merriam-Webster*, 1984, p. 353).

Thus, we find ourselves with a complex though tidy 2 x 2 matrix that differentiates forms of following. Follower actions can consist of coming after or going after and follower ideologies can be those of a disciple or a partisan. Words like "partisans" and "disciples" suggest higher stakes and stronger emotions than does the more neutral word "follower." Furthermore, words like "disciples" and "partisans" may reinstate a leader-centric view, making it that much harder to grasp follower phenomenology.

Setting aside both of those reservations, if we use the matrix momentarily to impose some order on our thinking, Meindl's work seems best suited to explicate the cell in which the actors are "disciples," and their actions are "pursuit." Disciples are salient because social construction involves efforts to generate images of leaders and to move toward consensus with peers by *choosing* a smaller set of preferred images. Once followers have a smaller set of images in hand, they then search for people who are a good match with preferred images. These acts of search are closer to *pursuit* than to coming after. It may be, however, that the most effective follower actions entail *both* coming after and pursuit. Followers pursue the more fitting candidate and then, having confirmed a reasonable fit between their image and the impression fostered by the candidate leader, followers follow the guidance that flows from their chosen candidate. Compliance confirms the validity of the choice.

If the problem of following and followers is set up this way, then there remain three follower variants that are still neglected: disciple–come after, partisan–pursue, partisan–come after. One obvious move now is to suggest that all four combinations occur some time during the natural history of a follower. For example, it could be argued that a newcomer who joins an intact group "comes after" and joins either as a converted partisan or a tentative adherent. With experience and continued social influence, newcomers may gradually be socialized into a view leadership that either solidifies the position of the current leader or drifts away from what the current leader seems to enact. In the latter case there is a gradual shift toward pursuit and the recovery of a "critical faculty" associated with adherents. Thus, as followers become seasoned and update their views of appropriate leadership, they shift from coming after to pursuit and from partisans to adherents, with the common goal being to reshape leadership into guidance that can then be followed after in the role of partisans.

SENSE MAKING

Organizations are often worlds that are unknowable and unpredictable. Organized life, despite the adjective, remains a "buzzing, pulsating, formless mass of signals, out of which people try to make sense, into which they attempt to introduce order, and from which they construct against a background that remains undifferentiated" (cited in Patriotta, 2003). Reuben McDaniel made a similar point this way: "Because the nature of the world is unknowable (chaos theory and quantum theory) we are left with only sense making. Even if we had the capacity to do more, doing more would not help. Quantum theory helps us to understand that the present state of the world is, at best, a probability distribution. As we learn from chaos theory, the next state of the world is unknowable. And so we must pay attention to the world as it unfolds. Therefore, it is a good thing that we can't do more than sense making...because then we would only be frustrated by our inability to know. But believing enables actions, which leads to more sense (sometimes) and taking action leads to more sense (sometimes) and sense making connects actions to beliefs (sometimes)" (R. McDaniel, Jr., personal communication). It is the combination of thrownness, unknowability, and unpredictability that makes having some direction, any direction, the central issue for human beings, and by implication, the central issue for leadership phenomena. Meindl understands this world when he describes the many options for construction of organizational experience that are available.

Meindl treats acts of romancing and following as efforts to make sense of organizational experience. Referring to the 1985 *ASQ* article, Meindl notes that "we argued that conceptions of leadership were deeply seated cultural expressions of a collective commitment toward understanding organizational performance in terms of leaders." In this sense, leadership "is a simplified, biased, and attractive way to understand organizational performance" (Meindl, 1993, p. 94). He says of his ideas, "more emphasis is placed on discovering when and under what conditions alternative forms of leadership emerge, as the way that followers make sense of and evaluate their organizational experiences" (1995, p. 332). There are two components of this sense making (Meindl, 1995, p. 333): (1) leadership itself is invoked as a way to understand organizational phenomena; and (2) definitions and criteria are selected and constructed in order to evaluate leaders. "The construction process produces leadership concepts and ideologies, judgments, and evaluations" (p. 333)

Meindl's concepts align quite neatly with general properties of sense making (e.g., Weick, 1995, Weick, Sutcliffe, & Obstfeld, 2005). It has been argued that there are at least seven resources that influence the content and guidance associated with sense making. These include social relationships, identity, retrospect, cues, ongoing updating, plausibility, and enactment (summarized by the acronym SIR COPE; Weick, 1999, p. 461). Meindl's view of the construction process used by followers makes contact with all seven. Social resources for sensemaking take the form of social influence and contagion in Meindl's work (e.g., 1995, p. 330); identity is the product of enacting what it means to have a relationship of leader–follower (e.g., 1995, p. 330); retrospect drives social construction since elapsed network experience is a crucial source of definitions and evaluations of leaders (e.g., Meindl & Ehrlich, 1987); cues are present in the leader behaviors that followers single out for interpretation and labeling (e.g., 1995, p. 331); ongoing updating is acknowledged in the increasingly successful efforts to chronicle the development and alteration of leader views over time (e.g., Pillai, Kohles, & Bligh, this volume; Bligh, Kohles, & Meindl, 2004); plausibility rather than accuracy is the criterion for a sensible leader construction since there are so many different cues and explanations that can be gathered into such a construction (e.g., see discussion of Donald Burr as "preacher" in Chen & Meindl, 1991); and enactment is present in the sense that followers "create the possibility for the emergence of leaders and ultimately surrender themselves to their creations" (Meindl, 1993, p. 107).

One means to anchor discussions of sense making in leader–follower relationships is to track those issues in the disaster at Mann Gulch, as portrayed in Norman Maclean's *Young Men and Fire* (1992; see also Weick, 1993). Mann Gulch is the story of 15 wildland firefighters, led by foreman Wagner Dodge, who parachute onto a small fire that is burning near the top of the southeastern slope of Mann Gulch and are joined by the fire guard who first reported the fire. The crew expect to suppress the fire by 10:00 the next morning. But the fire becomes more active as temperatures rise and winds increase until it explodes and sweeps toward the crew. Attempts to escape the exploding fire progress from running uphill away from it, to dropping heavy tools to gain speed, to foreman Dodge burning out an area so the fire will go around the crew, to the rejection of Dodge's escape fire, and a final futile attempt by the crew members to outrun the fire. Thirteen died. Three, including Dodge, survived.

If we analyze the crew chief at Mann Gulch from a romancing perspective, we run into some interesting complications. Dodge made a series of decisions intended to save his crew from a sudden explosive wall of fire that ran toward them. But his final and most creative life-saving act, burning out of an area that would provide a safety zone, was rejected. The rejection of the safety zone is intriguing because followers could make no sense of it, which may reflect the fact that they also had trouble making sense of foreman Dodge. Dodge was a person of few words. He did not explain himself or his decisions and largely gave clipped orders. When Dodge yelled, at the very last moment, "This way, this way!" to direct the crew into the area he had burned out, one member was heard to say, "To hell with that, I'm getting out of here" (Maclean, 1992, p. 99). As survivor Bob Sallee said of Dodge's escape fire, "What the hell is the boss doing lighting another one.... We thought he must have gone nuts" (Maclean, 1992, pp. 74–75). The romancing of Wagner Dodge illustrates *negative* romancing. Followers feel that Dodge had gone nuts, forgetting (?) that he wasn't nuts when he told them to parachute toward a safe spot near the fire, scouted the fire while they ate supper, hiked them toward the river so they could retreat into water if all hell broke loose, turned them around and moved the crew uphill when their path to the river was blocked by fire, and told them to drop their tools so that they could move faster and outrun the fire. Having made good decisions only to have his last decision rejected raises the specter that there can be abrupt reversals in the direction in which romancing moves. In Dodge's case, there was a dramatic shift from high credibility to low credibility in a matter of seconds.

Mann Gulch also highlights the likelihood that concepts of leadership are less salient and less likely to be shared as sense-making tools when you have "a team only in the loosest sense" (Useem, 1998, p. 48). Smoke-jumper teams of varying sizes were assembled in 1949 from a roster on which the people at the top of the list who were most rested from their previous fire. While there may have been some sharing of leader images while jumpers waited to be deployed, the variable number of those actually then deployed in crews would weaken whatever contagion might have developed back at the base. Meindl was concerned with group composition as a key driver of leader attributions. Transient crews should find it hard to consolidate a shared set of leadership criteria and might not even see themselves as having interfollower relations.

When limited contagion occurs in conjunction with a crew chief whose style is one of few words, what does happen to thoughts of leadership? Do people project their ideal picture of a leader onto what is essentially a blank screen? Do they look more eagerly for informal leaders, discount the importance of leaders, or fixate instead on substitutes for leadership? Consider the last possibility. There are clear substitutes for leadership in Mann Gulch since the task of cutting fireline itself is straightforward and clear; the technology of saws, shovels, and Pulaski's is simple; the crew structure involves a foreman, assistant foreman, and workers; the goal is clear, "suppress the fire"; and, once they're on the ground the tough part—the jump down toward fire and tall trees in gusty winds—is over since the fire is usually small. Given also that up to this point in 1949 there had been no casualties despite changes in leaders, followers, and assignments, thoughts of leadership may have been underdeveloped. Meindl is especially insightful on this point when he talks about leadership as the "enrichment" of an appointed leader who assumes a formal superior–subordinate relationship (1993, p. 98). Meindl seeks "a theory about whether or not leadership emerges as an 'overlay' to whatever other formal or informal dimensions individuals use to think about their relationships to other group members and to the tasks at hand" (1995, p. 332). Therefore, an appointment such as a person defined as a supervisor who is higher in a hierarchy than a subordinate simply creates "a context from which leadership may or may not emerge" (1993, p. 96). If it does emerge it tends to move from relationships of compliance to relationships of identification (transactional leader) to relationships of internalization (transformational) (see Kelman, 2006).

CONCLUSION

In my experience, Meindl's thinking deepens almost any leader-centric analysis. For example, while rereading Meindl's writing, I thumbed back through what many regard as one of the best leadership books ever published, McCall and Lombardo's *Leadership: Where Else Can We Go?* (1978). The most-cited piece in that volume is Pfeffer's (pp. 13–34) stirring review of evidence suggesting that leaders make less of a difference than romantics claim. My own chapter in that volume (pp. 37–61) represents a longstanding interest in perception and attention. I focused on the difficult tradeoff in which leaders have to be both impressionable to register what is happening and forceful to provide clear guidance for others. That leader-centric argument can just as well apply to followers, although I didn't see that at the time. Morgan McCall, however, did see that possibility. "Note also that Pfeffer's discussion of attributions to leaders fits into Weick's perspective. The way researchers, subordinates, and organizational members interpret leader behavior depends on their own media qualities. Poor media [i.e., crude sensors that miss most details] would erroneously attribute outcomes to a leader by overlooking other explanations.... Subordinates, for example, may be poor media vis-à-vis leaders; this may be one explanation (there are others!) of why there is little agreement between subordinate- and self-perceptions of a leader's style" (pp. 62–63).

If we shift questions of perception and attention from leaders to followers, then new issues arise. Followers see firsthand where important ambiguities lie, which should influence their collective ideas about what they need by way of guidance, which may or may not be transmitted to the leader, who may or may not be able to supply that guidance. It is followers' ability to be rich media that is crucial to effective performance. Meindl helped me see something in McCall's critique that I had missed for 28 years. So now will I romance followers? Probably. But if I do so I will now do it more mindfully, thanks to Meindl. Meindl models a reluctance to simplify. As organizational scholars we will talk more intelligently about leadership if we follow Meindl's lead.

REFERENCES

Chen, C. C., & Meindl, J. R. (1991). The construction of leadership images in the popular press: The case of Donald Burr and People Express. *Administrative Science Quarterly, 36*, 521–551.

Cohen, M. D. (in press). "Administrative behavior": Laying the foundations for Cyert and March. *Organization Science.*

Dewey, J. (1998). The reflex arc concept in psychology. In L. A. Hickman & T. M. Alexander (Eds.), *The essential Dewey: Ethics, logic, psychology* (Vol. 2, pp. 3–10). Bloomington: Indiana University Press. (Original work published 1896)

Eco, U., & Sebeok, T. (Eds.). (1988). *The sign of three: Dupin, Holmes, Peirce.* Bloomington: Indiana University Press.

Gandhi, M. (1999). Comment in 1940. In L. R. Frank (Ed.), *Quotationary* (p. 444). New York: Random House.

Hock, D. (1999). *Birth of the chaordic age.* San Francisco: Berrett-Koehler.

Kelman, H. C. (2006). Interests, relationships, identities: Three central issues for individuals and groups in negotiating their social environment. *Annual Review of Psychology, 57*, 1–26.

Maclean, N. (1992). *Young men and fire.* Chicago: University of Chicago.

McCall, M. W., & Lombardo, M. M. (Eds.). (1978). *Leadership: Where else can we go?* Durham, NC: Duke University Press.

Meacham, J. A. (1990). The loss of wisdom. In R. J. Sternberg (Ed.), *Wisdom* (pp. 181–211). New York: Cambridge University Press.

Meindl, J. R. (1993). Reinventing leadership: A radical, social psychological approach . In J. K. Murnighan (Ed.), *Social psychology in organizations: Advances in theory and research* (pp. 89–118). New York: Prentice-Hall.

Meindl, J. R. (1995). The romance of leadership as a follower-centric theory: A social constructionist approach. *Leadership Quarterly, 6*(3), 329–341.

Meindl, J. R. (2004). The romance of teams: Is the honeymoon over? *Journal of Occupational and Organizational Psychology, 77*, 463–466.

Meindl, J. R., & Ehrlich, S. B. (1987). The romance of leadership and the wvaluation of organizational performance. *Academy of Management Journal, 30*(1), 91–109.

Meindl, J. R., Ehrlich, S. B., & Dukerich, J. M. (1985). The romance of leadership. *Administrative Science Quarterly, 30*(1), 78–102.

Merriam Webster's Dictionary of Synonyms: A Dictionary of Discriminated Synonyms with Antonyms and Analogous and Contrasted Words. (1984). New York: Merriam-Webster.

Paget, M. (1988). *The unity of mistakes: A phenomenological interpretation of medical work.* Philadelphia: Temple University.

Patriotta, G. (2003). Sensemaking on the shop floor: Narratives of knowledge in organizations. *Journal of Management Studies, 40*(2), 349–376.

Patriotta, G. (2004). *Organizational knowledge in the making: How firms create, use and institutionalize knowledge.* Oxford, UK: Oxford University Press.

Rorty, R. (1989). *Contingency, irony, and solidarity.* Cambridge, UK: Cambridge University Press.

Schulman, P. R. (2004). General attributes of safe organizations. *Quality and Safety in Health Care, 13*(Suppl. II), ii39–ii44.

Useem, M. (1998). *The leadership moment.* New York: Random.

Weick, K. E. (1993). The collapse of sensemaking in organizations: The Mann Gulch disaster. *Administrative Science Quarterly, 38*, 628–652.

Weick, K. E. (1999). Sensemaking as an organizational dimension of global change. In J. Dutton & D. Cooperrider (Eds.), *The human dimension of global change* (pp. 39–56). Thousand Oaks, CA: Sage.

Weick, K. E. (1995). *Sensemaking in organizations.* Thousand Oaks, CA: Sage.

Weick, K. E. (2005). Organizing and failures of imagination. *International Public Management Journal, 8*(3), 425–438.

Weick, K. E., & Roberts, K. H. (1993). Collective mind in organizations: Heedful interrelating on flight decks. *Administrative Science Quarterly, 38*, 357–381.

Weick, K. E., Sutcliffe, K. M., & Obstfeld, D. (2005). Organizing and the process of sensemaking. *Organization Science, 16*(4), 409–421.

JAMES R. MEINDL

James R. Meindl was the Donald S. Carmichael Professor of Organization and Human Resources in the School of Management at the State University of New York at Buffalo from 1982 to 2004. He also served as the Director of the Center for International Leadership, funded by an endowment from HSBC. A social psychologist by training (BA, University of Rochester; MA and PhD, University of Waterloo; Postdoctoral Fellow, University of Illinois at Champaign-Urbana), Professor Meindl was the author and editor of numerous articles, chapters, and books on the behavioral aspects of organizing and leading. He

is best known for his work on the "romance of leadership," a unique perspective emphasizing the follower processes involved in the social construction of leadership. He sat on the editorial boards of leading journals in the field, including: *Academy of Management Journal, Academy of Management Review, Administrative Science Quarterly, Organization Science,* and *The Leadership Quarterly.* He also formerly edited the annual book series titled *Leadership Horizons.* Professor Meindl was an active member of the Academy of Management, a leading professional organization for management scholars and practitioners. He served as the Chair of the Organizational Behavior Division of the Academy, and he was a founding and executive member of the International Association of Chinese Management Research (IACMR) and co-founded the First Conference on Cross Cultural Leadership and Management Studies in Seoul, Korea. Professor Meindl traveled widely to lecture and conduct management development

Follower-Centered Perspectives on Leadership, pages 293–294
Copyright © 2007 by Information Age Publishing
All rights of reproduction in any form reserved.

seminars on leadership, motivation and related topics in North America, Europe, and Asia, and consulted extensively in the areas of organizational change and development. He regularly taught courses on organizational behavior and leadership for executives and MBA students around the globe, and received the prestigious SUNY Chancellor's Award for teaching excellence. Professor Meindl was a devoted scholar, mentor, teacher, husband, and father, and his work continues to influence academics and practitioners of leadership around the world.

LaVergne, TN USA
28 July 2010
191105LV00002B/17/A